Post-Chineseness

SUNY series, James N. Rosenau series in Global Politics
———————
David C. Earnest, editor

Post-Chineseness

Cultural Politics and International Relations

CHIH-YU SHIH

Published by State University of New York Press, Albany

© 2022 State University of New York

All rights reserved

Printed in the United States of America

No part of this book may be used or reproduced in any manner whatsoever without written permission. No part of this book may be stored in a retrieval system or transmitted in any form or by any means including electronic, electrostatic, magnetic tape, mechanical, photocopying, recording, or otherwise without the prior permission in writing of the publisher.

For information, contact State University of New York Press, Albany, NY
www.sunypress.edu

Library of Congress Cataloging-in-Publication Data

Name: Shih, Chih-Yu, author.
Title: Post-Chineseness : cultural politics and international relations / Chih-Yu Shih, author.
Description: Albany : State University of New York Press, [2021] | Series: SUNY series, James N. Rosenau series in Global Politics | Includes bibliographical references and index.
Identifiers: ISBN 9781438487717 (hardcover : alk. paper) | ISBN 9781438487724 (ebook) | ISBN 9781438487700 (pbk. : alk. paper)
Further information is available at the Library of Congress.

10 9 8 7 6 5 4 3 2 1

Contents

List of Illustrations   vii

Acknowledgments   ix

Introduction: An Inescapable Agenda of Post-Chineseness   1

PART 1
DECENTRALIZING CHINESENESS: RELATIONS FROM THE INSIDE OUT

1. Away from China-centrism: Balance of Relationships   19

2. Into the Iron Brotherhood: Relational Epistemology   39

3. Up from Subaltern Identities: Strategic Nonessentialism   63

4. Beyond Fundamentalist Faith: Cultural Nationalism   83

PART 2
STRATEGIZING CHINESENESS: RELATIONS FROM THE OUTSIDE IN

5. Cultural Self Rebalanced: The Vietnamese Practices of Sinology   103

6. Colonial Cleavages: Japanese Legacies in Taiwan's Views on China   127

7 Ethnic Role-Making: China Watchers in the Philippines   145

8 Geopolitical Distancing: Think Tanks in Southern Neighborhood   169

PART 3
BELONGING TO CHINESENESS:
RELATIONS FROM THE IN-BETWEEN

9 Me Inside and Outside: Performing for Hong Kong
   and Singapore   193

10 Sticking My Head Out under the Sky: A Presbyterian for
    Taiwan Independence   211

11 China Watch for No One: Relating Taiwan and China
    in Hong Kong?   227

12 Post-Western Politics and Mainlandization: Between
    Colonialism and Liberalism   247

In Lieu of a Conclusion: Noninternational Relations, Nonidentities   269

Appendix. Post-Asia and IR Research: A Pervasive Agenda   273

Notes   283

References   291

Index   339

Illustrations

Figures

7.1	Two dimensions of post-Chineseness	149
7.2	Post-Chinese evolution in the long run	153

Tables

1.1	Post-Chinese BoR	30
2.1	China as the Imagined Object of an Incurred Relationship	53
2.2	China as the Imagined Subject of an Incurred Relationship	54
4.1	The Cultural Nationalism of Post-Chineseness	85
4.2	Buddhist Mechanisms of Post-Chineseness	90
4.3	Christian Mechanisms of Post-Chineseness	84
4.4	Confucian Mechanisms of Post-Chineseness	97
5.1	Post-Chineseness in the External Perspectives	112
8.1	Role-Playing of a Bridge State	174
11.1	Positioning China-Watch	230

Acknowledgments

An earlier version of chapter 2 was originally published in *The Chinese Journal of International Politics*, Oxford University Press, 11:2 (2018): 131–152, 10.1093/cjip/poy005

An earlier version of chapter 3 was originally published in *Asian Perspective*, Johns Hopkins University Press, 44:2 (2020): 279–302, 10.1353/apr.2020.0008

An earlier version of chapter 8 was originally published in *Third World Quarterly*, Taylor & Francis 40:12 (2019): 2170–2189, 10.1080/01436597.2019.1636642

An earlier version of chapter 11 was originally published in *China Report*, Sage Publications, 54:1 (2018): 118–136, 10.1177/2455632717744405

Introduction

An Inescapable Agenda of Post-Chineseness

Background

While Chineseness, or China for that matter, has always meant different and even incompatible things on the occasions when politicians, marketing staff, journalists, and scholars evoke it in reference to their own distinctive purposes, the intention has been to convey something substantive, affirmative, and discernable. Two developments in 2020 intensified the discursive need to essentialize China, as a one-of-a-kind category and bounded. One is the determination of Washington's national security circles to cope with a perceived China threat (Zuo 2021; Falin Zhang 2021; Scobell 2020; Pilsbury 2016). This leads to a series of confrontational platforms targeting a variety of areas, including investment, social media, artificial intelligence, maritime security, human rights, diplomacy, science and education, public health, and so on, as long as they involve the category/label/name of China. At times, China is, in itself, problematized and interrogated as regards how much control and influence the Beijing authorities are allowed within their Hong Kong, Xinjiang, and Taiwan policies. Even so, the policy discourse seriously diverges in terms of what China represents—the whole of the nation, the Chinese Communist Party (CCP), Chinese civilization, the Beijing authorities, or simply all of the unruly behavior conducted in the name of China.

The other development is that the outbreak of the Covid-19 pandemic has compelled almost every national government to resort to the imposition of quarantine measures, virtually reproducing the territoriality of the nation, with China most obviously included due to being the first territorial jurisdiction that suffered the outbreak, which prompted its authorities to control the border, release nationalism to preempt blame for initial unpreparedness, and celebrate the efficient recovery as a national achievement (Kuik 2021; Q. Huang 2021; Pichamon and Shih 2021). Since the public health authorities lie within the sovereign jurisdiction, a comparison of performance in the months subsequent to the outbreak of the pandemic necessarily reinforces the territorial binaries between different nations. Nevertheless, public health solidarity is apparent at both the governmental and societal levels, with all kinds of mutual support cutting across borders. That said, the blame game continues, based on the ambiguity regarding which China was responsible—the Chinese Communist Party, Chinese culture, the Chinese race, or the entire nation.

The year 2020 has a prior trajectory in the background, against which essentializing discourses had been simultaneously contested and reinforced for some time. On the one hand, indeed, there has been a trend to unlearn the binaries (Babones 2017; Khong 2013). With the governing capacity of the Beijing authorities having risen to become second in the world, a tendency among Chinese scholars to convince the world to appreciate Chinese ways of governance is emerging (Teets 2016; Ambrosio 2012; W. Zhang 2011; Wang 2016). Chinese manners and customs are being introduced to the rest of the world, especially among the former colonies of the Western countries and Japan. At the same time, the seeming readiness of the Chinese populace to learn and embrace life practices elsewhere is likewise evident. Non-Chinese manners and customs are becoming easier for the Chinese to adopt. Both the Chinese and their partners are becoming differently Chinese, in one way or another (Chu 2021; Kavalski 2018; Pan and Kavalski 2018; Hwang, Bunskoek, and Shih 2021). Embedded Chineseness constitutes and revises the identities of different people to different extents. Enabling multiple directions of influences and changes, Sinicization of this sort complicates as well as deconstructs the binaries (Katzenstein 2012a). Chineseness evolves through the agency of businesspeople, priests, migrants, NGO activists, politicians, netizens, journalists, academics, performers, diplomats, and so on. The people in all of these various capacities will be discussed in the following chapters. This changing, diverging Chineseness reflects enthusiasm and yet simultaneously provokes anxiety.

On the other hand, there has arisen another trend of estrangement, resentment, and even resistance or containment, registered in the responses of various significant actors, to the co-constituted Sinicization. One apparent actor is Washington. Together with its strategic allies, each espousing a reason for alarm (McCourt 2021; Hass 2021; Smith and Bolt 2021; Gewirtz

2020), Washington perceives a strategic competitor, ideological revisionist, and even existential threat. For another example, the postcolonial pro-Taiwan independence forces or Hong Kong's prodemocracy forces are constantly alerted by the totalizing mainlandization implied by the pursuit of China's reunification (Y. J. Cheng 2017). Chinese Southeast Asians in, for example, the Philippines, Malaysia, Indonesia, or even Singapore, battling for equal citizenship in their respective nation, constitute yet a third ambivalent and hybrid group (Aryodiguno 2020; Ngeow, Ling, and Fan 2014; Hau 2014). Some may develop a sense of self-esteem through an imagined network of re-Sinicization, but such self-esteem can reproduce ethnic otherness in an indigenous society. It can actually undermine the self-esteem of those Chinese Southeast Asians in their earnest quest for equal citizenship. This latter group wishes to dispense with exotic Chineseness in the eyes of the indigenous society. Finally, in a fourth example, neighboring Vietnam or Mongolia could find the lack of social sensitivity, familiar in their historical relationships with China, an annoying characteristic of the rising nation (Nguyen 2021; Chiung-chiu Huang 2020a, 2020b; Thrift 2014). The ensuing chapters will discuss these actors. They practice exteriority to China in their coping with a China that is imagined to be "out there."

From Chineseness to Post-Chineseness

When seeking to understand the contemporary world, which is informed by certain kinds of Chineseness, it no longer suffices simply to refer to the category "China," which everyone has contributed to making complicated, obscured, and sometimes transcended. Nevertheless, in practice, China continues to be a predominant category, as witnessed in 2020, despite the incompatibility between the narratives. Differently essentialized notions of China undergird the imagination of identities of all kinds. Under this ironic circumstance, in which the category "China" is both indispensable and unstable, China scholars can neither resort to total deconstruction nor adhere to any universal definition. A comparative agenda that allows empirical research on the decentralized uses of China is clearly required (Bunskoek and Shih 2021).

Such an agenda must recognize the mutual constitution of China/Chineseness and the identities of its partners everywhere at their own levels—geocultural, national, ethnic, kin, personal, egoistic, and so on. Its analytical frame must enable an array of perspectives to coexist and communicate intellectually as well as practically. Further, it must acknowledge the unstable characteristics of these perspectives themselves, too. This is tantamount to a quantum theory in the social sciences and humanities, not only because China is ontologically unfixed but also because its partners and researchers are internal to its ontological condition (C. Pan 2020; Cho and Hwang 2020). China/Chineseness can and must adapt and transform, contingent upon the practices and the views of those who employ or study China/Chineseness as a category.

Post-Chineseness is the name that this book gives to the needed agenda and the ontology. Broadly, post-Chineseness is no more than a case of post-identities, which presumably lie everywhere. Specifically, I refer to Chineseness as the *conditions of being Chinese*, while post-Chineseness is the *on-going processes of becoming differently Chinese* through self as well as mutual de/recognition. Recognizing is inevitably mutual and relational. That means people feel related to each other in terms of their respective positions on Chineseness. Each claim to post-Chinese identity necessarily occurs within a prior relationship, in which Chineseness has a trajectory of evolving characteristics shared by the relevant actors, for example, tributary, colonial, war, Confucian, familial, migrant, revolutionary, culinary, religious, alliance, patron-client, hometown relations, and so on. Relational Chineseness is certainly dynamic in nature. This is why and how, historically, all claims to Chineseness are, at the same time, post-Chineseness; hence there is a lacuna of any unified meaning. In a nutshell, studying and using China is about defining Chineseness. Defining Chineseness involves a relationship that produces identities of both China in context and the interacting alter-selves.

The process of recognizing Chineseness affects the approach to China policy and China scholarship. These processes, likewise, shape the self-identities of China scholars and China policy-makers. Understanding, confronting, and promoting China is all about practicing Chineseness alongside the other constituents of self-identities, for example, Christian, capitalist, exceptionalist, patriotic, and colonial, so Chineseness, intertwined with other constituents, does not stand alone. That is why all Chineseness must be, simultaneously, post-Chineseness.

This book seeks to analyze the international and national relationships involving China and Chineseness. It will study how different types of Chineseness constitute corporate as well as individual actors. I hope to explain their behavior by interrogating who they are as regards their relationships to China and Chineseness. Given that these relationships are contingent on the context of the interaction and the choice of actors, they evolve over time and in different places. One can understand how a particular type of relational Chineseness (i.e., post-Chineseness in process and practice) orients the actors toward a particular tendency, but cannot universally explain how the actors adopt or reject a particular type of Chineseness. In other words, actors cannot avoid making decisions on the post-identities of the other parties as well as their own, because this is relationally necessary, but are not structurally determined to make particular decisions. One can explain their behavior only after one gets to know who they are, and the records of their decisions are usually cyclical and inconsistent, with a track record of turns and vicissitudes that is worthy of analysis (Kosuke and Noro 2021; Chen and Kosuke 2019).

Traces of Post-Chineseness in the Literature

Due to their interdisciplinary nature, the studies of cultural politics in this book contribute to a mix of literature that comes from three different areas—international relations theory (primarily part 1), China studies (primarily part 2), and ethnic identity (primarily part 3). All of these areas witness the China question as actors practically encountering the expansion of influence expediently understood as the rise of China. International relations (IR) theory is clearly premised upon the exclusionary ontology of an autonomous nation. It embraces the binary view of the nation versus anarchy (or inside versus outside) that the analysis of this book sets out to deconstruct. In the twenty-first century, IR theory, under the banner of the "Chinese school," is actually emerging to reinforce the binary (Y. Hwang 2021; Wang 2020). Ethnic studies represent Chineseness as ethnicity. The literature records the discrimination that the ethnic Chinese suffer, each residential community differently in their own location. Alternatively, Chineseness can similarly be the cause of suppression when the context shifts to the multiethnic conditions within the People's Republic of China's claimed borders, where national unity is the priority. However, these three areas remain separate, although IR theory and China studies' treatment of China as a distinct entity and ethnic studies' treatment of China and Chineseness as constructed are epistemologically well-aligned.

Specifically, there is a common bias toward binary thinking in all three of these areas. This is a deep bias, though. The three areas support each other in reproducing China as a separate category that can be singled before a universal eye—studied, divided, conquered, contained, Orientalized, developed, romanticized, or baptized. Such a common, prior bias is largely concealed. Even though some scholars of ethnic studies are alert to this, they do not appear to have an alternative discourse to prevent their post-structuralist ideas from being reduced to simply another imagined feature/component of authentic China (J. Pan 2016).

Post-Chinese International Relations

The Chinese School of International Relations

The IR literature provides three points of connection to post-Chineseness. The most obviously relevant literature concerns the Chinese school of IR (Ren 2020; Qin 2018; Zhang and Chang 2016; H. Wang 2013). This literature ponders how China can be a useful resource to IR theorization, especially attending to either a China-unique theory or a China-inspired universal theory. Both take for granted the idea that China is a distinctive category. As a noticeable example, the Chinese IR brings forth the classic notion of Tianxia (or all-under-heaven) (Feng Zhang 2015; Ban Wang 2017; T. Zhao 2019). The literature treats Tianxia as either a culturally bound theory that exclusively explains Chinese foreign policy or as a universally prescriptive theory, especially designed to rescue the West from self-help anarchy. Whichever formulation is adopted, the alleged school reproduces the imagined uniqueness of China and the binary that plagues a sophisticated understanding of the world. Post-Chineseness is a de-national remedy because it studies how to recognize or refuse Chineseness in China as well as in the West. Thus, a seemingly distinctive Chineseness is practically accessible to all and revisable. While China can be conceptualized as a stable characteristic or a way of life, persons or nations cannot be made to be exclusively Chinese or non-Chinese as such. China and the West are not identical, but are not simply different, either. The two cosmological views co-constitute the actors as having unlimited possibilities.

Relational School of International Relations

The second point of connection is relational IR, which traces the norms and values of contemporary IR to a historically developed, shared past that is embedded in modern European political thought, diplomatic practices, and Christian traditions (Jackson and Nexon 2019, 1999; Neumann 2011;

Hafner-Burton, Kahler, and Montgomery 2009). Indicating the limitation of the relational literature on the relationality that constitutes China, China is almost an unrelated alien in this literature (Ling 2014a; Kavalski 2018; Qin and Nordin 2019; Nordin and Smith 2019). Post-Chineseness links the relational literature to China and demonstrates how Chinese norms and values, omitted from European political thought, have already emerged to relate all actors (Y. Zhang 2017), usually each differently, in those processes.

The Post-Western Agenda

The third point is the literature on post-Western IR that endeavors to represent the geocultural sensibilities of all sites that potentially supply resources to retheorize the currently mainly Western IR. The post-Western IR is particularly keen on the mutual constitution of the West and the rest, including China (Ling 2019; Shih et al. 2019; Shih and Yu 2015; C. Chen 2011). However, the post-Western literature rarely deals with China, apart from a few especially commissioned reports (Yiwei Wang 2009; Yongtao Liu 2012). Post-Chineseness fills the lacuna because it is an intuitive extension of the post-Western agenda. In addition, a major caveat of the post-Western studies is the stress on sited difference, which may become another source of binary (Murray 2020). By contrast, post-Chineseness is a deliberate deconstruction of sited difference. It exemplifies post-identities and thus produces a solution for the unintentionally contrived, albeit transitory, binaries existing in the post-Western literature.

Post-Chinese Ethnicity

Chineseness is a major dimension of the ethnic issue in Southeast Asia (Chong 2020; Choiruzzad 2020; Shih et al. 2020; Shih 2017a). The literature reflects more than scholarship; it also records a strategy of survival (Ngeow 2020; G. Wang 2018; Suryadinata 2017, 3–22). The thrust of the research in general, as well as the research of Chinese Southeast Asian scholars in particular, points to a single strategically significant message; namely, there is no such definition of Chineseness that can sufficiently portray Chinese Southeast Asians. In this sense, Chineseness is inevitably post-Chineseness, and post-Chineseness prevents any solidarity from arising among these mutually estranged Chinese populations. Therefore, no claimed threat to the indigenous regimes is plausible. However, this is not the usual lens that indigenous China experts adopt when approaching China (C. C. Huang

2020a, 2020b; Shih 2015). An epistemological search continues for a way to identify and represent China/Chineseness (Ngeow 2019a; Clemente and Shih 2019). In addition, these lenses are often partly acquired from their former colonizers' intellectual legacies (Seo 2020; Chin 2020; S. Lin 2018).

The challenge is everywhere. While the Western China scholarship can be relatively easily accessed, a less frequently tackled agenda is how, for example, Taiwan and Hong Kong painstakingly adjust the lens to understand China in the twenty-first century (H. Chan 2018; Au 2018; Ching-chang Chen 2015; Y. Hwang 2014). Having struggled with their own Chineseness, the studies of Hong Kong and Taiwan sit between the national and ethnic agendas, each with its own combination and fluctuation, while certain features span both communities (Ngeow 2019b; Shih 2018c). With an analytical frame of post-Chineseness proposing behavioral tendencies in association with the post-Chinese types, the adaptation of Hong Kong and Taiwan can be compared with the identity strategies practiced in Southeast Asia. As it currently stands, Chineseness simply connotes that we are all different. Post-Chineseness also responds to the need to study how people are practically related through pacing of post-Chinese cycles that enable acknowledgment, development, refusal, or destruction of their resemblance.

Ethnicity is a critical component of the China studies community but is seldom realized by the China scholars. In Indonesia, for example, China studies and Chinese Indonesian studies are almost identical (Aryodiguno 2020), while in Mongolia, as another example, the term "Chinese migrants" refers primarily to Chinese Inner Mongolians (Thrift 2014). Chinese American scholars on China are usually divided by the same political/ideological alignments that exist within the People's Republic of China rather than those in the United States. Tibetan studies are extremely sensitive precisely because they challenge the sense of the boundary of the Chinese nation (J. Chen 2016). Pakistan achieves the status of being an iron brother to China partly because its leaders consider the Uygur issues a domestic, ethnic issue rather than a religious one. The purpose of the post-Chinese agenda is to trace and record all of these inconsistencies and peculiarities. To that extent, China is constituted by the China studies community, while China studies is an identity strategy of China scholars.

Post-Chinese China Studies

While China studies is arguably not exactly a social science discipline, "China" is included in the name of many research institutes worldwide. These institutes are either centers and societies affiliated with universities and academia to a varying degree, or think tanks. In the absence of a consensual definition of China, the scope of the college textbooks on China is highly territorially overlapping in practice (e.g., Brown 2019; Gamer and Toops 2017). Namely, China is represented by phenomena inside the sovereign borders of the People's Republic of China. In terms of history, whatever is considered Chinese history by PRC academics can fall within the scope of China studies. The popular agenda of China's state-and-society reinforces such a territorially demarcated scope of research. From this agenda arise the studies of reform, democratization, the party-state, civil society, and so on. These topics have remained popular for three decades (see, for example, Shue 1988; Oi 1989; Goodman and Hooper 1994; Solinger 1999; Goldman and Perry 2002; Perry 2007; Wright 2010; Fewsmith 2010; You 2013; Saich 2016; Teets 2016; Economy 2018). Scholars do not need to define China before claiming to make a contribution to China studies. Such a territorial preference is chronic (Duara 2004).

However, for example, the critical self-reflection on Chineseness by Chinese Southeast Asian intellectuals easily challenges the territorially bound scope of China, to the extent that the level of their identification with the motherland obscures the arbitrariness of the PRC borders. The Chinese Civil War legacies in Taiwan, as another example, unexpectedly continue to become the politically incorrect, that is, ironically intimate, link with China. Transnational religious movements, likewise, engender dual identities in their disciples, who may find religious beliefs far more relevant than political loyalty in their daily life (Chen and Chen 2021). Post-Chinese agendas contribute to the China studies literature indirectly but significantly, since territoriality constrains the current research design that the state-and-society sensibilities disproportionately comprise. In contrast, the post-Chinese agendas are consciously neither statist nor state-centrist.

Unconventional and Composite Methodology

This book is only partially compatible with social science methodology. It is compatible to the extent that post-Chinese identities are empirical issues, and also in the sense that the correlations between post-Chinese identities and the behavior of the actors constitute important research topics. However, the research design of the book is not typical social science as regards the relationships between researchers and the actors studied by researchers. In this book, researchers need to know who those actors are that they seek to study. Unless researchers know who they are, these actors' behavior cannot be adequately explained. This is very different from the social science that stresses objectivity and discourages researchers from gathering the subjective views of the actors. According to the philosophy of social science, researchers need not, and indeed should not, know the actors.

On the contrary, this book argues that researchers and policy-makers always analyze, explain, and predict the actors' behavior according to their prior knowledge about the actors in question. This argument involves two stages. The first stage entails studying the *prior knowledge* of the researchers, while the second stage entails gathering and appreciating the *specific perspectives* of the researchers and policy-makers, whose judgment is essential for recognizing the identity choices and strategies of the actors to be explained. The first stage demands the adoption of a certain critical theory (e.g., Marxism, feminism, postcolonialism, constructivism, deconstruction, etc.) that can place the researchers in their historical trajectories. The second stage calls for an intellectual history that recognizes the identity practices of the researchers that enable them to make judgments about the actors.

Post-Western Approach

The book will not discuss methodology except here in the introduction. The particular critical theory that informs the methodology of this book is the post-Western approach. The main thrust of the post-Western agenda is to trace and discover the genealogical trajectory of an institution, value, discourse, identity, or social force that has an imagined origin in the geo-cultural tradition of the population at an inhabited site but the population has experienced assimilation through the colonial and capitalist influences. Post-Western research emphasizes the agency of the colonially constituted population regarding reworlding, *a practice that revises and appropriates the colonial impacts according to the local conditions and purposes*. Post-Western sensibilities are registered in recognizing differences—all are differently different (Trownsell et al. 2021; Bilgin 2012). This is not a romanticizing agenda, though (Shih 2021), as the danger of discrimination and annihilation continues to seek various kinds of reversion of the post-Western order and even the restoration of a certain political correctness (Shih and Ikeda 2016). Therefore, transcending wishes to reestablish the binaries, the post-Western agendas require relational thinking (Pan and Kavalski 2018; Kavalski 2017a, 2017b). Post-Western critics who neglect the relational sensibilities may reinstall the fallacy of the West versus the non-West.

Given that post-Chineseness is both a matter of position and the resources that the actors choose to rely on, it is methodologically by all means exchangeable with other post-identities, contingent upon the resources invoked to undergird an identity. In fact, contemporary post-Chinese identities are almost always "Anglo-Chinese" due to direct as well as indirect Westernization (Katzenstein 2012a). As already discussed, post-Chineseness is post-Western, but more than post-Western. To the extent that the Western identities evolve against the background of Sinicization (Zhang, Suzuki, and Quirk 2016), all of the Western identities will have a post-Chinese component in their reconstruction, be it embracing or denying Chineseness. Once practicing Western identities evokes Chinese references, Western identities will receive different assessments in accordance with Chinese values. This would be "para-Western," a practice that raises coextensive, that is, Chinese, views of relations and identities that have their own cosmology. In short, the Western and Chinese lenses do not share the same universe, but they are not entirely different, either. Post-identities, including post-Western and post-Chinese identities, allow them to communicate, exchange, and coexist.

For yet another alternative lens, there are "non-Western" resources. This is where the Western relations and identities are of little relevance, when retrieving historical or indigenous identities before encountering the Western influence (Y. Zhang 2017). In this situation, indigenous identities will create a non-Western agenda. This agenda contributes to the understanding of different worldviews that enable the acquisition of the Western culture in their own different ways (Acharya 2014a, 2014b).

Relational Lenses

Post-Western perspectives allude to a pessimistic assessment of resistance, which is unlikely, with all being irrevocably intertwined in the colonial and capitalist order in one way or another. However, it likewise reveals the implausibility of dominance, since the Western powers are likewise reconstituted. Philosophically, all dominance and suppression will circularly result in self-suppression. Given the relational necessity, the post-Chinese agenda must recognize not only the assimilation within the Western influence, but as many other strings of resemblance that encompass all as possible. All of the actors are related to the extent that they are co-constituted by these strings of prior resemblance. For the purpose of studying post-Chineseness, these strings can include, at least, (1) the old colonial network and colonialism (colonial relations), (2) the recent Cold War alliance and ideology of anti-communism (Cold War relations), and (3) the consensually perceived rise of China as well as the common quest for global governance that promotes rule-binding coordination (global governance relations). In the historical experience, there are also relational strings in the region whereby certain actors are co-constituted; for example, the legacies of the tributary system, Confucian cultural values, Buddhism, Japanese colonialism, and Chinese migration. Further to the lower levels of gathering, recognizing Chineseness is increasingly contextual and role-making, and hence more improvised compared with the aforementioned prior or imposed relations.

Intellectual History

To understand the behavioral and emotional orientation toward a post-Chinese target, intellectual history is required. An intellectual history agenda examines individualized intellectual growth, on the one hand, and the mutual influences between people from the same communities that constitute a collective tendency, on the other; for example, Chinese-Singaporean scholars on China must face a prior relation that constitutes Singapore and its Malaysian and Indonesian neighbors, and they also each possess a migrant history that has brought them to a Singaporean institution. Intellectual history examines both the prior orientations that constitute the self-identities of all of the actors at a given time and their agency in selecting lenses for recognizing Chineseness both in the self and others. Presumably, intellectual history allows the induction of the entire repertoire of different post-Chinese identities. Through this, it is possible to judge the possibility of shifting from one post-Chinese identity to another and trace the conceptual and practical routes that facilitate such shifts. This is apparent in the case of Hong Kong, where the meanings of the institution of the one-country-two-systems are intensively disputed by scholars, diplomats, activists, and government officials. The other side of the coin is the possibility of referring the evolving (e.g., certain British) self-identities to the strategic recognition of imagined (HK) Chineseness in others. This last agenda shows how the Self and the Other are co-constituted by post-Chineseness.

Structure of the Arguments and Cases

Formatting the Narratives

I will first present how post-Chineseness is both similar to and different from international relations in Western relational thinking. Theoretically, post-Chineseness IR restores bilateralism to relational analysis and transcends concerns with the ontology of the autonomous state or their shared international system. I begin with a theoretical discussion of the Chinese style of relationality in terms of what constitutes relations for those who subscribe to Chinese identities and how they establish and adapt relationships. I proceed to interrogate how post-Chineseness is both the result of practicing Chinese relationality and the method for cutting across the Chinese and Western relations. I cite Sino-Pakistani relations to demonstrate the importance of these sensibilities regarding *bilateral relation*, Sun Yatsen's use of "Yadong" (Asiatic East) to illustrate the plausibility as well as the predicament of a *multilateral relation*, exempt from the self-other binary, and the Chinese religious pluralism that supports a kind of *self-relation* whereby believers strategize the supernatural worlds in such ways so that their self-identities can remain differently related as well as adaptive in a nationalist context.

Then part 2 shows how international relations are equally de/re/constructive from the imagined external perspectives. I rely on Vietnamese sinologists to teach the maneuvering of *cultural* relations informed by a shared Confucian legacy, Taiwanese China scholars to reveal the epistemological cleavages implanted by the Japanese *colonial* relations, Filipino China scholars to sensitize the ethnic relations embedded in the Chinese *migrant* history, and South and Southeast Asian think tank analysts to attest to the irony of knowing their subject exclusively in *geostrategic* relations.

Finally, part 3 evokes the politicized agenda of Hong Kong and Taiwan, where epistemological positioning vis-á-vis either "China" or the West is always ambiguous. I invited two directors of experimental drama and a postcolonial Presbyterian priest to give their testimony regarding the ordeal of being caught between China, the indigenous society, and the migrant China watchers as well as politicians and journalists in Hong Kong and Taiwan to further complicate the undecidability with additional competition for cultural loyalty from the former colonial powers and the West.

The division of the book into three parts flows simultaneously in three different orders. The first order concerns the international *relationalities*. The international relationalities of post-Chineseness are presented in the order of international identification in part 1, international sinology in part 2, and international ethnicity in part 3. It is at the same time in the second order of *self-identities*—the book looks successively ostensibly from inside (part 1), from outside (part 2), and from in-between (part 3), correspondingly. Last but not least, it is in the third order of *worlding strategies*. The three parts adopt the para-Western (part 1), the non-Western (part 2), and the post-Western (part 3) purposes, respectively. The last order is worthy of further comment.

The "para-Western purpose" exists in the nonbinary, fluidity, inconsistency, and multiplicity that are believed to characterize all of the actors, including the West. On the para-Western agenda, post-Chineseness and the West make a composite of universality, or "biversality," which can certainly allude to "pluriversality" (Hutchings 2019). Indicating the *simultaneity of indigenous and Western relations*, this is one universe that contains many universes. The "non-Western" purpose is linked with the indigenous identity strategies that make little sense to those not in the indigenous conditions but greatly influence the lens of assessment of the relationships with the West. The non-Western agenda attends to the deliberate use of *Chinese resources* to suit the purposes of the actors. The "post-Western" purpose is to accept the Western or colonial influences already existing within Chineseness, and yet it will continue to evolve and adapt in the future. The post-Western agenda attends to the deliberate use of *Western/colonial resources* to suit the purposes of the actors.

Snapshots of the Chapters

Essentializing and binaries are what harm the understandings of practices and identities in general, and Chinese identities in particular. The book will begin with a discussion of how, theoretically and practically, decentralism as well as de-essentialism become possible through actors exerting agency to improvise relational identities. Part 1 includes four chapters that aim to "look out" from the positions of imagined China and Chineseness. The purpose of chapter 1 is to theorize and categorize post-Chineseness as imagined relational resemblance; that of chapter 2, to engage in the empirical processes of post-Chineseness in bilateral relations; that of chapter 3, to present a failed case of de-essentializing in multilateral relations; and that of chapter 4, to present a successful case of de-essentializing in self-relations. Part 2 includes discussions of how Chineseness is constructed for the purpose of stabilizing the observers' own identities. In part 2, the four chapters aim to "look in" at an imagined China by painstakingly crafting a self-position outside. The purpose of chapter 5 is to present the knowledge about China informed by prior cultural relations; that of chapter 6, the knowledge informed by colonial relations; that of chapter 7, the knowledge informed by ethnic relations; and that of chapter 8, the knowledge informed by geo-strategic relations. In part 3, the four chapters reveal the undecidability of China scholarship in Taiwan and Hong Kong as well as Singapore in terms of their multiple relationalities and self-identities. Chapter 9 compares a Hong Kong-based cultural strategy of portraying Chineseness and a Singapore-based one. Chapter 10 traces the inspiration of the Presbyterian identity in postcolonial Taiwan's approach to China. Chapter 11 sources the Hong Kong-based China watching from its rich migrant academia. Finally, Chapter 12 interrogates the unstable identities of Taiwan and Hong Kong between the West, the colonial, and Chinese relations.

PART 1

DECENTRALIZING CHINESENESS

Relations from the Inside Out

Part 1 studies how nations practice international identities in relations. It argues that nations discover or improvise their resemblance by reading their self-understanding into others or, reversely, imagining their self-understanding according to selected alter-understanding. In practice, nations only find themselves in different relational settings, bilateral as well as multilateral. Even self-imagination in an ostensibly domestic context must be relational, rendering any claim to national identity a relational statement. Such impossibility of merely being only autonomous and self-centric is exemplified through the substitution of post-identity for identity and, in part 1, post-Chineseness for Chineseness.

Succinctly, part 1 contains a chapter on theorizing relations through the theme of post-Chineseness and, further, three chapters, respectively, on a case of the "bilateral" relations of Chineseness via Pakistan, a case of the "multilateral" relations of Chineseness via East Asia, and a case of the "self"-relations of Chinese cultural nationalism.

Chapter 1 provides the theoretical rationale and an analytical frame regarding why and how actors are obliged to improvise a relationship by constructing or reconstructing their resemblance or lack of it, in context, for each other to acquire a certain post-identity; in our case, post-Chineseness. Epistemologically, it tackles China-centrism and argues why it inevitably results in decentralism. Chapter 2 shows how initially seemingly unrelated corporate actors, that is, Pakistan and China, have discovered their relationships through experiencing each other's concerns. The chapter contends that self-centrism, based upon essentialized national interests, is pseudo-epistemology. In addition, it shows how post-Chineseness is dynamic and improvisational rather than fixed. Chapter 3 contrarily offers a pessimistic assessment of nonessential solidarity that does not rely on a self/other binary. On the one hand, it testifies to the discursive plausibility of nonessential regional identity. On the other hand, it alludes to the tenacity of the hegemonic Cold War relations that insist on a securitizing binary embedded in anti-communism. Opposed to the abortion of nonessentialism during the Cold War, chapter 4 instead gathers from religious practices informed by Chinese nationalism various styles of cultural nationalism to the disadvantage of political nationalism. The variety of individual believers preempts political mobilization through religion.

Chapter 1

Away from China-centrism
Balance of Relationships

Self-centrism and Chineseness of Strangers

Attempting to overcome Eurocentrism in both the intellectual and practical worlds, on the one hand, and avoid committing self-centrism, in our case China-centrism, while engaging in self-empowerment to resist Eurocentrism, on the other hand, poses somewhat of a dilemma (Chu 2020). This dilemma has puzzled modern and contemporary Asiatic thinkers in Japan (e.g., Takeuchi Yoshimi), Korea (e.g., Baik Young-seo), and Taiwan (e.g., Chen Kuang-hsing) as well as in China (e.g., Sun Ge) for over a century (Calichman 2010; Sun, Baik, and Chen 2006). They are fully aware that self-centric thinking is destined to destroy solidarity among the world's subaltern populations, who suffer due to imperialism. This book will rely instead on "post-Chineseness" as an epistemological wedge to open all varieties of self-centrism. Post-Chineseness, alongside other post-identities, can launch a trajectory of practical analysis and theoretical reflection that is premised not upon binaries, but upon relationality. Its geocultural scope of inquiry can be as broad as East Asia, Asia, and the globe and yet reversely dissolved wherever one selects an alternative post-identity, such as post-Asianness, post-Vietnameseness, post-Tibetanness, and so on.

This chapter explores how, theoretically at the international level, post-Chineseness is the natural consequence of a self-regarded Chinese state either preempting a familiar state from becoming estranged or reaching out to a perceived stranger or potential stranger state and making a role for the latter in the hope of neutralizing mutual strangeness in their subsequent relationships. However, the attempt in the literature to bring forth relationality as a constituent of Chinese international relations (IR) tends to look at Chineseness as composed of absolute otherness to the West (Qin 2018; Jacques 2009).

Chinese IR has emerged in recent years to counter Euro- or Western-centrism. Qin Yaqing (Qin 2016a), the leading scholar of Chinese relationality, specifically advocates such a relativist quest for a Sinocentric reinterpretation of Chinese uniqueness. Sinocentrism has received strong support in the studies of Chinese modern history but is more about discovering neglected history than sheerly relativist in nature (P. Cohen 2010; Mizoguchi 1989; P. C. C. Huang 1991, 2016; R. Huang 1999). This relativist challenge to the allegedly universal knowledge arising from the European intellectual traditions has most noticeably emerged in the field of indigenous psychology (Yang 1993; K. Hwang 2001), which made an original inspiration for Qin's relational theory. However, this relativist string of Sinocentrism becomes deeply problematic when applied to relational studies, because the relational agenda substitutes processual practices for substantivism (K. Hwang 2009). Without an ontologically substantive China, any relativist claim on behalf of China is groundless. In this chapter, therefore, I will tackle this ironic synthesis in Chinese IR and restore its processual sensibilities through the approach of post-Chineseness without completely jettisoning Qin's quest for Chinese distinction.

As mentioned above, Sinocentrism refers to understanding the world through a Chinese lens. This book narrows this down to mean *understanding other people through a Chinese lens*. It thus refers to the practice of determining the kind and level of Chineseness in another person as well as in one's self by those acting from an allegedly Chinese identity. In international relations, it is about the Beijing authorities improvising a resemblance to the other national actors by discovering their Chineseness or the potential to have it. These perceived and yet unstable strings of resemblance complicate China as a category. Consequently, Chineseness can only exist in "post-Chineseness" due to its negotiable nature as well as its context- and actor-driven peculiarities. Given that Chineseness is highly uncertain, contextualized, and agentially based, even Beijing, on behalf of the entire country, cannot enforce a coherent resemblance between those considered Chinese.

The chapter will discuss how post-Chineseness supports a system of "balance of relationships" (BoR). This is a system that obliges nations to practice self-restraint and reciprocate benevolence to enable other nations' interests. The stronger the perceived resemblance between nations, the more obliged they are to engage each other using self-restraint, and the more secure they all are. The BoR agenda differs from the current relational IR to the extent that, whereas the former obliges actors to reciprocate benevolence and improvises resemblance between each other in context, the latter imagines a prior string of resemblance that already constitutes all actors, who are able to expect the behavior of one another and even feel a certain level of solidarity.

The balance of relationships joins the relational turn in IR and treats it as an agenda that traces the evolution and practice of the imagined prior resemblances of the actors in terms of genes, geoculture, language, history, values, norms, customs, memories, works, institutions, residence, memberships, threats, interests, and so forth. In a nutshell, no relation exists without some imagined resemblance. These imagined as well as constructed strings of resemblance commonly constitute the identities of the actors and allow the actors to build networks to address collective concerns, recruit and train new members, watch those lacking such resemblance, and, most importantly, gain confidence in the goodwill of the resembled others.

In the situation where there is only thin prior resemblance or where the imagined prior resemblance breaks down, improvised resemblance is the solution. The balance of relationships introduced later reveals these practically (post-)Chinese styles of improvising resemblance. Readiness to improvise resemblance in context and adapt to new circumstances appears to be a short-term orientation, but actually it has a long-term rationale. This has to do with the prior relations being not always reliable where vital interests, for example, a high-staked electoral campaign, or a perceived urgency in context, for example, the 9/11-kind of terrorist attack, can prompt a survival instinct or resort to exceptionalism to abort self-restraint. Then, all would be pushed back to mutual strangeness as if previous solidarity hardly relates them anymore. That is why, for the sake of remaining related and thus secured, the readiness to improvise resemblance between strangers can, even in the long run, be more fundamental to security and welfare than the reliance on prior resemblance. Thus, adjustable Chineseness in others is practically bound to diverge.

In this light, the task of Chinese IR becomes to discover the processes through which a shared sense of Chineseness emerges and adapts in different contexts, in order to appreciate how relational concerns constrain power or interest (Dessein 2016; S. Zhao 2015; Fingar 2012). The main challenge the BoR poses to mainstream IR is that engendering and reproducing Chineseness in others ontologically equalizes the parties of the BoR so that their interaction does not proceed in accordance with the relative level of power (P. C. C. Huang 2016; Noesselt 2015). In fact, both parties contribute to the crafting of Chineseness intersubjectively. Hence, in an asymmetrical power relationship, the weaker party may act strongly, and the stronger party compliantly (Womack 2012; Huang and Shih 2014). An additional challenge lies in the fact that nations do not always pursue apparent national interests (Qin 2016a, 2009; Kalvaski 2016; Shih and Chang 2017).

Sacrificing interests to restore the relational balance embedded in imagined resemblance is common everywhere in the world and at all times throughout history (Fierke 2013; Ching-chang Chen 2015; Wulf 2016), including for those actors who subscribe to prior resemblance. Thus, the study of the BoR adds to the relational turn those cases where prior resemblance is lacking in general or inadequate in context. The BoR agenda studies the process of engendering Sinocentric resemblance embedded in some kind of invited Chineseness. It contains two dimensions: constructing the resemblance and ensuring the willingness to reproduce resemblance.

What follows in chapter 1 is a Sinocentric method for transcending both Sinocentrism and Eurocentrism. This method would regard a Eurocentric method of dealing with improvised resemblance as a natural ally that would craft a post-European theory. However, both could adhere to the general theory of a balance of relationships, which is thus not a Sinocentric theory. The discussion shows that the improvisation of resemblance can be a general analytical frame transcending the binary of China and the West. This book introduces those dimensions that define these categories of resemblance, how they are variously practiced, and why no one has total control.

Balance of Relationships and Bilateral IR

Analytically distinguishing the two different modes of relating nations that underline the allegedly Chinese and Western practices can transcend the binary of China and the West. While some are culturally prepared to enlist the one instead of the other, both modes are accessible to the world population anywhere. In other words, BoR is not about China replacing the West. The first mode is prior resemblance. It undergirds the primarily multilateral relations, whose members, with or without engaging in any interaction with one another, abide by the consensual institutional rules or discursive conventions, and operate within the same cosmological order that universally constitutes the otherwise differing identities of all. While prior resemblance can support dyadic relations, for example, a historical hierarchy between a suzerain and its vassal, it is volatile, given the negotiable nature of bilateral relationships. Prior resemblance enables multilateral relationality to the extent that it nurtures solidarity among the members and motivates all to care for and enforce its principles in the face of deviance (Kopra 2016; Johnston 2008).

The second mode is improvised resemblance, which facilitates the formation of a mainly bilateral relationship that is external to the commonly recognized rules or codes of conduct. Having a specific relationship with all other nations respectively requires a nation to address the peculiarity of each coupling relationship (Hagström 2005). Due to its practical nature, improvised resemblance is concerned with strategic relationships, making it a poor tool for multilateralism, that discourages peculiarity. Without a prior consensus on the rules or norms, the enactment of resemblance must rely almost entirely on gift giving of all sorts (Yang 1994). A properly devised benefit for the other state symbolizes and enacts the resemblance of certain role identities—for example, friendship, neighborhood, comradeship, brotherhood, and partnership—whose prior consensus is thin. In the ancient tributary system, for example, subjection to an abstract heavenly order and the derived common mission to reproduce the relationship between China and a remote vassal might be the only point of resemblance that served to enhance the internal legitimacy of each party (Ji-young Lee 2016; M. Liao 2012a, 2012b).

Improvised resemblance obliges unity in public stance, without which contrived resemblance ceases to exist and both constituted parties lose their relational identity as well as the sense of security embedded in mutual acceptance. Therefore, improvised resemblance requires the skill to create mutual roles in accordance with the situations. That is why BoR can appear too random to merit scientific interrogation.

Multilateral relations then articulate how nations already resemble one another and partially explain, as an independent variable, how consensual relations constitute self-identity. Bilateral relations, by contrast, reflect how nations strategically improvise resemblance and serve as a dependent variable to be partially explained by how nations choose to interact in accordance with their relational resources. Arguably, Christianity and capitalism contribute to prior consensual principles (Luoma-aho 2009; R. B. J. Walker 1993; Ruggie 1982), whereas Confucianism and the Chinese tributary system encourage improvised arrangements (for a detailed discussion, see

Shangsheng Chen 2015; M. Liao 2012a, 2012b; Zhang and Buzan 2012).[1] Multilateral relational thinking, however divided among the notions of field, pragmatism, network, practice, discursive possibility, and configuration, attends to a shared context of all situated actors and their interactions that have consequences for all (Jackson and Nexon 2019). In this light, minimal solidarity is spontaneous under prior relations, in which the members accept or even protect each being different otherwise. However, improvised relations impose unity as an obligation in context to downplay or even ignore each being different. A significant example is the notion of natural rights that define universal humanity. Insufficiency in prior resemblance may cause estrangement, misunderstanding, and even aversion, which could be solved through improvised resemblance bilaterally. Without its stranger-partners sharing the human rights tradition, for example, Washington can rely on economic, educational, and military aid to consolidate a mutual defense pact.

Widely noted, both Qin Yaqing's Confucianism and Zhao Tingyang's Daoism, in which an imagined common string—Tianxia—constitutes the identities of all of the actors, overstate the relativist side. For the purpose of discussion here, suffice it to define their Tianxia as *a system in which all are bound to be related* (in some way). Accordingly, strangers are by all means related, so they will naturally try to strike out a way to relate that can testify to their place in Tianxia. Finding ways to relate requires improvisation, reciprocity, and self-control. The highest level of self-control is expected of the prince, whose complete selflessness defines the state of benevolence, according to Confucianism. The rationale of self-control is allegedly that all who accept the prince may feel secure in growing and retaining their own crops. This rationale does not differ, qualitatively, from the logic behind signing a social contract, which allows Leviathan to protect people in exchange for them giving up their freedom, according to Thomas Hobbes (1588–1679). Confucius (551 BCE–479 BCE) specifically advised that the prince's mandate ultimately lies in the acceptance of the people, and hence, indirectly, is a natural contract (i.e., the Mandate of Heaven), based upon the prince's trustworthiness (信). If Leviathan's omniscient protection could provide a way to achieve equivalence with being trustworthily benevolent, Hobbes would be a Confucian. I will argue, however, that the Confucian way to achieve benevolence is to improvise resemblance through gift giving, as opposed to Hobbesian dominance. Nevertheless, the difference between a Confucian relation and a Hobbesian relation may be entirely methodic. In a nutshell, nature and the social are divided by the social contract for Hobbes; but they are not binary under Confucianism.

BoR offers two critiques of the dichotomization of Chinese Dao and Western natural rights. First, what the Chinese literature offers is actually a general argument about prior resemblance in terms of belonging to Tianxia, which arguably is the Daoist state of nature. Such imagined sharing is mistaken as an exclusively Chinese characteristic. Given that God is the creator, the Daoist state of nature, in which all are bound to be related, can be either Confucian or Christian. Dichotomy is inappropriate. Methodologically, all being related through commonly protected natural rights is an argument about the social contract; in comparison, all being related through the benevolence of the prince requires improvisation of the prince. Since the Confucian improvisation is to rely on the metaphor of kinship and the Mandate of Heaven, both are conceptually natural, too. Once recognized as an argument of prior resemblance, nevertheless, Confucianism-Daoism can be compared with Christianity or capitalism, each advocating a different set of values. Moreover, they need no longer be mutually exclusive civilizations, since it is always possible for people to learn different methods of relating—the social contract versus kin benevolence—to each other.

Second, Confucianism and Daoism are too thin to create a prior resemblance that can practically guide international relations. According to the IR scholars who address Dao on their agendas, Dao is pervasive and yet deliberately unsubstantiated (also Qin 2009; Ling 2014; Kavalski 2015, 2016a). It might imply caution against certain practices, such as squandering, killing, or taxation, but says little regarding how to act institutionally, in contrast with prior resemblance that implants an institutional preference for the protection of solidarity. Consequently for Daoists, everyone is to an extent a stranger to each other. Solidarity is not a presumed relation. This lacuna in the sophisticated prior obligation toward all other actors makes China a good case for studying how improvised resemblance works, how it obliges unity, and how it deconstructs solidarity. BoR is particularly keen to relations between strangers. Because it is based on Tianxia, all strangers are cosmologically related anyway and all those practically already related can revert to strangers where vital interests or perceived urgency arise. BoR therefore applies to all—strangers as well as potential strangers.

Qin and Zhao's respective critiques of Western IR for being interventionist indicate an alienation from prior rights and rules. Note that the prior resemblance implied in multilateral relations can risk the negligence of absolute strangeness that does not fit these relations (Nordin and Smith 2019). The advice of bilateral relationality is to improvise a relationship indifferent to alterity and thereby neutralize ontological stands. Even the strong side is dependent on the relationship with the otherwise unrelated weak side for the former to attain an integral self-identity that is now constituted by the relationship. This is a peculiar relation, where even absolute strangeness can be related through some improvised ostensible resemblance. Mutual acceptance, once achieved, ensures both parties' belonging to Tianxia. Whereas the assertion of absolute strangeness boosts the (self-centric) morale of the subaltern under suppression, mutually improvised resemblance shields absolute strangeness from interrogation or assimilation (T. Zhao 2004; Qin 2018). Which of the two strategies is appropriate for the subaltern population is a matter of perspective (Ling and Nordin 2019).

Prior resemblance supports the claim that relations come before states (Jackson and Nexon 1999), so that enforcing rules and defending norms enhances the self-fulfillment of relationally constituted states. Participation in multilateral processes sets states up for such endogenous self-creation. In comparison, improvised resemblance relies on an exogenous self-creation whereby one's relational quest strategically subjugates oneself to many rituals as well as role-play in order to link with a variety of others. Epistemological anxiety toward a condition in which two states share little prior resemblance induces each state to execute self-restraint toward the other by improvising resemblance.[2] Since improvised resemblance requires repeated external reconfirmation to overcome its transient characteristics, aborting reconfirmation by one immediately threatens the relational identity of the other. No third party will come to the rescue of the betrayed one, as improvised resemblance constitutes the identity of no one else. Therefore, a research agenda on how the bilateral relations embedded in improvised resemblance are able to proceed is a necessary step toward an inclusive relational IR without committing the binary of China qua non-West and the West. Post-Chineseness is designed to assist BoR in achieving that.

BoR addresses the dynamics of how two actors keep each other engaged in their imagined resemblance, improvised specifically by and for them in general and in face of a perceived incongruence in particular. The two central theses of the balance of relationships posit that a nation, regardless of its level of power, will either (1) continue to invest in an imagined resemblance to the other side in order to balance an almost revoked resemblance with it or (2) withdraw benevolence to jettison the corrupted relationship in order for another improvised resemblance to emerge (Huang and Shih 2014). History offers a rich repertoire for improvising kin-role relations to constitute the identities of both parties to a dyad. Marriage, for example, has been used everywhere as a relational mechanism. In Chinese history, for example, the court of the Song dynasty (1127–1279) could be either considered an elder or a younger brother, depending on the age of the emperor relative to the rulers of rival states that were stronger than Song China under them (Wan 2017; Feng Zhang 2010). For another example, the socialist "brotherhood" consistently appears in the narrative of the Vietnamese Communist Party calling on its Chinese counterpart but never characterizes the relationship between the two states (Thayer 1992).

Although multilateral resemblance is familiar to the legacies of Confucius and generations of his disciples, bilateralism possesses a far stronger history in practical lives. It divides social relationships into five types of dyad—between the emperor and his officials, father and son(s), husband and wife, elder and younger brothers, and oneself and one's friends. The relationship between a teacher and his students is also implicitly present. The members connected through each dyad do not conceive of their relationships as multilateral among individual members in the sense that a clan, school, village, and domain all have a leader. Rather, the head and his subordinates each have a bilateral relationship. Subjects are indirectly related through bilateral relationships with their common head. They would otherwise be strangers without prior concern for each other's natural rights. Such cultural practice parallels the tributary system, in which all vassal states negotiated with China on their own terms. Leading Chinese scholars find inspiration for their analysis of the contemporary relationship management of Beijing in the Chinese tributary practice of making concessions in exchange for relationships (Zhou 2011).

Although Marxism and internationalism once prevailed in the textbooks on diplomacy in the PRC before the 1990s (e.g., Xie 1999), the bilateral tendencies remain intact. Beijing's continuous adherence to bilateralism has several attestations. First, Beijing has painstakingly improvised specific "strategic relationships" with different countries, each with a different title. Second, Beijing insists that a better relationship with the US relies on mutual respect for each party's core interests rather than each yielding to a prior commitment to certain global governance norms. Third, the Belt and Road Initiative (or OBOR Initiative), contrived by Beijing in 2013 with the support of the multilateral Asian Infrastructure Investment Bank, proceeds through bilateral negotiations with each of the Belt and Road countries. Fourth, Beijing tends to deal with regional organizations—for example, ASEAN, the African Union, and the EU—as if it were in a bilateral relationship with these entities (i.e., with Beijing treating them as entireties). Fifth, Beijing has improvised different formulations of the one-China principle when exchanging recognition with different countries. Sixth, Beijing has consistently denied the legitimacy of uninvited intervention in failing states for the sake of enforcing multilateral rules in IR. Finally, Beijing insists on bilateral negotiations in resolving territorial disputes with smaller neighboring countries, wishing to avoid confrontation (e.g., Bhutan, Vietnam, Pakistan, North Korea, Mongolia, and Myanmar). By contrast, when dealing with equal powers, such as New Delhi, Tokyo, and Moscow, Beijing has appeared relatively ready to resort to confrontation.

Bilateral relationships are convenient, focused, yet flexible for any country. US president Donald Trump, for example, reconsidered bilateralism in 2017 to reflect the judgment that multilateralism does not benefit the US (Gertz 2017). The substitution of primarily the aforementioned second thesis of BoR for rule-based governance in his China policy testifies to the quest for improvised resemblance, in terms of reciprocal duty (Auslin 2020), and the implausibility of the China-West binary in IR relationality. In the case of China, without Confucianism or any substantive prior multilateral norms in mind, the question becomes, How does Beijing in the twenty-first century imagine a proper relationship with a target nation? The following discussion uses the anthropological notion of post-Chineseness to produce propositions regarding the balance of relationships.

Post-Chineseness as Relationality

Would not a binary of the Confucian and the liberal societies, between which a prior resemblance is lacking, be appropriate? To the extent that strangers accustomed to improvised resemblance are indifferent to the natural rights of the population under liberalism, they would appear threatening to, for example, the EU nations. The relational agenda of international relations will be incomplete unless a theory of how nations that dispense with prior resemblance, especially in terms of the legacies of European political thought, can relate is available. Such a theory will explain the forms of improvised resemblance. In the case of Chinese IR, the task is to discover how practitioners construct resemblance. For a weak China, practitioners may adopt, fabricate, or simulate a kind of Europeanness, Japaneseness, or Russianness in order to entice the recognition of relationality from Europe, Japan, and Russia. For a rising China, on the contrary, the confidence of the practitioners in constructing Chineseness in others apparently arises.

Post-Chineseness contributes to these processes by explaining the ways to improvise resemblance.

Reading Chineseness (or another post-identity) into the other's identity is key to understanding the BoR that manages to enact, reproduce, and repair resemblance. Given the impossibility of defining Chineseness, such improvised resemblance is always under negotiation; hence post-identities or, in our case, post-Chineseness. Post-Chineseness is about the claim to perceived Chineseness, the content of which is continuously evolving and practically varied. It involves the bilateral processes between the interacting actors of a dyad to identify the resemblance to each other's Chineseness, each time considering the context and purposes of the interacting actors (Hinde 1997). The same can be said about post-Asianness, post-Europeanness, post-Americanness, post-Indianness, and so on. The practice of post-Chineseness complicates the categories of social science without completely abandoning them. On the one hand, it records the practices of Chinese literature in constantly seeking to develop resembling Chineseness to overcome or prevent strangeness. On the other, it indirectly recognizes that all actors are capable of self-centrism in their efforts to improvise resemblance in the identities of the other side. This, in a sense, makes BoR equivalent to a balance of self-centrism, because improvised resemblance necessarily reflects one's self-identity as well as that of the other party.

Moreover, post-Chineseness is epistemological as well as methodological. Epistemological post-Chineseness is a metaphor enabling the appreciation of self-centrism elsewhere and subsequent mutual adaptation; hence, implicitly, intersubjectivity. Methodological post-Chineseness contrarily deconstructs self-centrism by recording incongruence, estrangement, and compliance on the other side, indetermination in one's internal policy-making, and changing contexts over time, indicating a self-centric deconstruction of China-centrism.

Consider two dimensions of post-Chineseness. The first resonates with the concerns of the relational IR literature with prior resemblance. It is about whether or not someone representing China judges that the other party already shares and practices certain Chinese characteristics, such as kinship, languages, conventions, territory, alliances, and so on. The construction of Chineseness that alludes to a target's Chineseness is both subjective and objective. Depending on how much confidence and comfort the groups making a judgment on a target enjoy in speaking and acting on behalf of China, self-declared legitimacy defines an insider's perspective. The most apparent insider group might be the Beijing authorities, but this is not absolute, as, during the Chinese Civil War, the rivaling Kuomintang used to deny such legitimacy to the Beijing authorities. Designation of post-Chineseness to a target by groups that *have the self-perceived legitimacy of speaking on behalf of China* is how this book defines the insider's perspective. Based on this dimension, the other party to a China relationship may inevitably acquire one of the three possible positions: (1) inside China, (2) some reconciled Chineseness, and (3) outside of China.

The second is linked to the degree of Sinocentrism. It partly comes from the long-held Confucian as well as Daoist propositions that Chineseness is primarily cultural and subjective in nature (Fei 1989; Liang [1905] 2011; Gu [1939] 2011). This is practically disputed in modern times, especially from the perspective of IR realism and Marxism-Leninism. Therefore, this dimension is related to whether the agent acting in the name of China is to judge the identity of the other party according to (1) the latter's ideational lenses (e.g., Chinese religions, ideology, customs, and norms) or (2) certain relatively objective lenses, such as Chinese citizenship, kinship, or class. Together, the dimension of prior resemblance and the dimension of China-centrism engender (3x2) six relationship strategies.

Relationships proceed in steps to ensure mutually agreed resemblance, reciprocal role performance, and periodical reproduction. Each entails rituals and gift-giving of a different kind. The BoR analysis defines gift-giving as *an offer of goodwill to oblige or abide by an expected relationship*. Under Confucian bilateralism, the failure to incur mutually corresponding Chineseness to show connectivity connotes the abortion of the relationship. This failure generates higher anxiety, anger, or alienation if the other party is already perceived as

Table 1.1. Post-Chinese BoR

Prior relations / Lenses of centrism	Insider	Reconciler	Outsider

Ideational criteria
  Post-Chinese type
  Emotion at abortion
	
	Moral
	Shame
		
		Hybrid
		Contempt
			
			Exotic
			Disappointment

Objective criteria
  Post-Chinese type
  Emotion at abortion
	
	Equal
	Anger
		
		Borderline
		Risk
			
			Utility
			Alienation

Source: author

an insider (Proposition 1). For Beijing, connecting to a perceived insider entails imposing a role obligation to comply. Therefore, Beijing will act as if the other already accepts the role expected by Beijing. By contrast, to connect to a perceived outsider, it is imperative for Beijing to convince the target to embrace a sense of Chineseness. This step leads to the enactment of the roles that Beijing preempts that the other expects Beijing to take. The success of role-taking relies on the judgment of the target nation. Being judged is not a pleasant condition emotionally. Therefore, in the long run, self-regarded Chinese have the incentive to conceptualize all of the rest as in-group targets (Proposition 2). This self-centric tendency is designed to avoid the emotionally stressful (re)connection with the perceived outsider. This proposition suggests that self-regarded Chinese prefer to consider the other as increasingly Chinese, allowing constantly improvised Chineseness. The increasing popularity of Tianxia (all-under-heaven), as an imagined world in which all are bound to be related (through pervasive and equalizing Dao, Confucian oneness in providing benevolence, or metaphoric universal kinship), in the Chinese IR discourses reflects such a desire to stay related to every other nation to avoid the embarrassment that would arise were they to reject the Chinese relationships (X. Yan 2015).

When a component of a possible shared ideational link in the target nation's identity is perceived, the target nation is expected to invoke resources to reinforce the link. The togetherness reproduced essentially constitutes China's identity. In such a circumstance, Beijing's incentive to demonstrate sincerity toward the desired relationship through customized concessions is strengthened. On the contrary, when Beijing identifies no such civilizational, philosophical, or ideational resources but sees primarily territorial, genetic, or legal relationality in the identity composition of the target nation/group, it probably finds communication less fruitful and so resorts to placing a more straightforward demand on the other to enact the perceived resembling Chineseness. For instance, Beijing can demand a show of conformity in various forms before it makes a concession to award the alleged relationship. In either case, the decision to begin with concessions or demand for clarification to reinforce a relationship is not conditional on China's relative power but dependent on China's identity vis-à-vis the target nation. Hence, the Chinese authorities concede to a subjectively defined target nation prior to the confirmation of a reciprocal relationship, whereas the authorities demand clarification of the relationship first in exchange for a reciprocal concession with an objectively defined target nation (Proposition 2.1).

Post-Chineseness and the Balance of Relationships

How Beijing improvises a resemblance to the other nation bears theoretical implications for how relations can emerge and evolve where prior resemblance is thin. To improvise resemblance, relating narrators identify resources available in the target nation that may connect them in the shared identity of a greater self, which their identified resemblance undergirds. Depending on how Chinese people in general are seeking a relationship to conceptualize the identity of China as well as that of the target nation, I propose six different post-Chinese conditions that engender six relationship strategies corresponding to each condition. These methodological conditions are conveniently named (1) moral Chineseness, (2) hybrid Chineseness, (3) exotic Chineseness, (4) equal Chineseness, (5) borderline Chineseness, and (6) utility Chineseness. The names of the six types are illustrative and can be entirely different from post-Americanness, for example. A nuanced division can evolve if a particular category sacrifices the epistemological complexity. In a nutshell, the two dimensions span civilizations, nations, and religions but the contents of the resulting six categories are geoculturally idiosyncratic.

Two issues remain: (1) How do the six post-Chinese processes balance relationships? (2) And why is China (or anyone else) conceptualizing Chineseness in a particular way in the target nation? Parts 2 and 3 will gather some of the answers to the second question. Chapter 1 addresses the first issue.

Post-Chinese strategies are those improvising perceived resemblance in the target nation. Defining authentic Chineseness is no longer possible, though. Each desired bilateral relationship carries its own particular affect, orients its own balancing strategy, and constitutes identities of China and its target nation peculiarly. It does not guarantee mutual liking. In fact, imposing obligations usually causes anxiety or even annoyance in both parties. To keep improvised resemblance in balance at a time when the other side challenges it, Beijing needs either to withdraw the benefits in order to improvise an alternative for the other side to stay related or contrive proper gifts to oblige the other side to return. This creates BoR that is both self-centric and intersubjective. It is self-centric epistemologically since relying primarily on China's own lens can judge the other side. Practically, however, it is intersubjective, as the other side holds the key to its workability, which affects China's judgment.

The section will proceed to define the six different types of post-Chineseness and consider their emotional tendencies and behavioral implications for the sake of illustrating the processual practices of the balance of relationships. Note the two caveats regarding these definitions. First, although they rely on knowledge of Chinese histories and cultures, other analysts can certainly define them differently according to different readings or analytical purposes. Others can also dispute the propriety of these definitions and suggest improvements. Second, however others determine their definitions and labels, these definitions and labels are unlikely to be suitable for another post-identity. In other words, the two dimensions and six categories are deductive and universal but their substance is interpretive and issue-sensitive. In fact, even the dimensions can be added or shelved, given more nuances or considerations added to the issue areas in question. The book employs these in the subsequent chapters, each by all means with some degree of revision, that is, recombination, redefinition, or further division, according to the issue area.

Post-Chinese Strategies

Moral Chineseness and BoR

When Beijing sees *an insider identity in the target group that shares a common reservoir of ideational resources with China*, the target group displays a post-Chinese opportunity, which the book defines as moral Chineseness. Moral Chineseness indicates the existence of perceived common historical, civilizational, or ideological trajectories of China and the target group that oblige the latter to take an indistinguishable role identity of being similar Chinese. The relationship strategy toward perceived moral Chineseness is to honor the target group ritually, practically, and frequently to preempt any second thoughts among the target group. Granting the perception of moral Chineseness, Beijing possesses confidence about winning understanding as well as sympathy, manifests a passion for repeated cycles of reconnection, and raises straightforward requests for support. The target group is also expected to acquire strong efficacy for joint endeavors through the enhanced, reassured spirit of unity. Moral Chineseness presumably reinforces nationalism or some moral disposition; for example, socialism. Beijing is likely to suffer shame, caused by the emotional sensitivity toward a kind of self-denial, if the target group fails to meet Beijing's expectations. Such shame almost guarantees strong, immediate disapproval by Beijing in the short run, frequently in the form of sanctions.

Hybrid Chineseness and BoR

When Beijing perceives a reconciler identity entrenched in Chinese ideational resources, Beijing explores the hybrid Chineseness of the target group. Hybrid Chineseness refers to *partially yet significantly shared ideational identities perceived in the common historical, civilizational, and ideational trajectories of China and the target group, with the latter and a third group likewise significantly sharing distinguishable ideational identities*. Hybrid Chineseness places Beijing in the awkward position of having to keep the target group appreciative of the Chinese resemblance. Concession is thus necessary to neutralize the other cultural component and reinforce the sense of cohesion of the target group. For sensible concessions or gift-giving, Beijing must discover what is expected of it or needed by the target group. Beijing would probably feel contempt either because the target group is unable to live up to Beijing's standard or because all of the maneuvering fails to engender any gratitude, which is expected of the target group in terms of openness to Chinese influence. However, according to relational coupling, the failure to be admired appears to be Beijing's own fault. The best solution to this is to withdraw benefits for the time being and work on other, similar targets. Contempt for the aborted relationship serves to offset, psychologically, the target group's tilt to the other side.

Exotic Chineseness and BoR

When Beijing cannot incur ideational resources in a target group embedded in its own distinctive civilization, relationality should emerge from Sinicization. Exotic Chineseness characterizes the *process of enhancing the readiness of the target group to attain a resemblance to China through influencing and receiving Sinicization*. Making China collectable to the other party, exotic Chineseness improvises for the paralleling civilizations to perceive no threat from each other. Similarly, this Chineseness places Beijing in the vulnerable position of being evaluated. Under this circumstance, the thrust of BoR is to convince the target group of China's broadmindedness and acceptance. Consequently, amid the atmosphere of the China threat, presenting China as a collectable treasure of civilization, as opposed to counter finger-pointing, dominates Beijing's relationship strategy. The target group is expected to show more curiosity than aversion to China in order to confirm its own goodwill. Beijing's failure to incur in the other side a sense of resemblance sufficient to confirm a relationship leads to disappointment, caused by the aborted chance to achieve a balance, which is initially considered possible. Little can be done apart from awaiting further access at another time.

Equal Chineseness and BoR

When Beijing sees *no prior resemblance of a perceived insider group, Chineseness is defined by extending citizenship-like status to its population or territorial sovereignty to the site*. This makes the target group and China objectively indistinguishable under equal Chineseness due to their lack of any meaningful distinction. Expectation is limited to a show of conformity from the target site or population. The strategy is straightforwardly to apply the same rules as are applicable to the self and dominate the relationship. Conformity is the expected response to the extension of equal citizenship. If conformity is lacking, Beijing can easily feel anger, which is caused by an unreasonable loss of that to which Beijing believed itself entitled. The population of Tibet or Xinjiang and, more recently, Hong Kong probably falls into this category, because legality creates a core of resemblance to elsewhere in China. Equal Chineseness has been applied in various other historical cases, such as vassal states, feudal domains, or even warlords, who dismissed cultural and kinship connections in their quest for independence.

Borderline Chineseness and BoR

When *a discernable site or population that shares little culture with China yet buffers Beijing from another major power that likewise exerts significant influence over the site*, borderline Chineseness arises. Borderline Chineseness holds strategic resemblance, characterized by uncertainty. Beijing's attempt to conduct economic and military exchanges and alert the other party when potentially unfavorable developments in politics and diplomacy occur defines borderline Chineseness. As long as the target population willingly allows the Chinese jurisdiction to access it, Beijing usually offers nominal protection from continuous intervention by a third party, probably including India, Russia, the US, and Japan. Beijing can further expect the quest for dependence in the target population. If dependence is unstable or even signs of defection are observed, then Beijing suffers the loss of relational resemblance caused by an exacerbation of the security risk scenario. Consequently, Beijing will probably resort to economic and political threats for a period of time to reassert control and influence.

Utility Chineseness

Most countries not immediately neighboring territorial China, ancient as well as contemporary, are typically considered alien in Chinese literature. Thus, these countries are unsusceptible to Chinese cultural influences. The result is that Beijing's relational concerns focus primarily on establishing friendship through beneficial treatment. For Beijing, China's contribution to those unfamiliar groups for them to breed resemblance must be primarily materialist in nature. Utility Chineseness emerges from *the perceived potential of China being instrumentally useful to the target group*. This phenomenon can mean alliance, commodity, raw material, technology, or sheer market. Utility Chineseness refers to something imagined as Chinese in the way of life of the alien population. The main theme of Beijing's relationship policy is to make China a "good bargain" on the premise that the target group willingly recognizes China's sovereignty over Beijing's own declared scope. From there, resemblance is expected to evolve from working together. If the target nation does not appreciate the improvised resemblance, the Chinese leaders will suffer alienation, caused by the impression of being unwanted or losing access. This alienation, however, can hardly arouse animosity.

Post-Chinese Affects

Considering that those targets that Beijing believes to be further away from the alleged scope of China engender fewer expectations from Beijing with regard to seeking specific relationships with them, Beijing will display higher patience toward those targets considered outside than China will do to other targets thought to be closer inside (Proposition 1.1). Likewise, consider that if those groups, believed by Beijing to own more shared ideational resources, presumably appreciate the politics of relationship better, then the Chinese actors seeking specific relationships with those targets of more ideational links will relinquish sanctions on them during a perceived breach quicker than those others owning less (Proposition 2.1).

Improvising a post-Chinese resemblance to China may backfire despite its bilateral alertness, because the choice relies on Beijing's own unilateral assessment of the situation. Under ideational Chineseness, Beijing's initiative can be either romanticizing or agonizing to the target group due to its imposing nature. In contrast, the Beijing authorities may desire objective Chineseness whenever the target group is indifferent. Beijing can resort to sanctions to assist with reinforcing its expectations. However, the target group can be so disregarding that Beijing might feel compelled to improvise a different resemblance by reconsidering the post-Chinese condition of the target group. For example, if Hong Kong and Taiwan appear hopelessly recalcitrant, then Beijing may decide that moral Chineseness is no longer applicable. The situation merits a reconceptualization of the two sites into hybrid Chineseness, with the US, Japan, and the UK as civilizational competitors. If the situation continues to aggravate, Beijing may simply wholly disregard the concept of ideational resemblance. This would mean that Beijing sees dominance as a fairer method toward other citizens, whereas equal Chineseness becomes the only resemblance to balance estrangement.

Such a shift is unlikely to be purely intellectual in nature, because it involves more than simply the selection of an applicable category. In addition, the unfulfilled quest for belonging, qua relationality, generates a negative affect. Two dicta follow. First, an affect-driven shift is more powerful than intellectual reconceptualization. Once a particular aforementioned negative affect—shame, contempt, disappointment, anger, risk, and alienation—is incurred, it prompts the selection of the corresponding post-Chinese strategy, although no further change arises in the target group. Second, the state of being evaluated consistently causes negative effects, since the China awaits the assessment of the target group. Aspects of contempt, disappointment, and alienation engender anxiety with regard to being judged. On the contrary, shame, anger, and risk trigger an enthusiasm for active coping.

Cognitive psychology confirms that the incurred affect is significantly efficient in guiding the strategizing and calculation to justify the affect (Neuman et al. 2007). Affective intelligence is a complex phenomenon. Affect preserved in the cultural memory makes an almost intuitive judgment regarding which category the target nation fits. Given that affects prompt one to select a post-Chinese identity on behalf of China, they provide better clues regarding which strategies to adopt immediately before the intention becomes clearer during a relationship crisis. Following this line of research on affect, as long as a particular affect can be incurred, the associated post-Chinese condition arises to direct the choice of the balance-of-relationships strategy (Proposition 3).

Since BoR proposes six types of affect to incur different kinds of Chineseness, a brief note on the features of each affect and its behavioral relevance is pertinent here. First, shame comes from openly denied morality and relationality, to which one belongs, and leads to narcissistic adjustment (Trevarthen 2005; Wurmser 1987). This affect leads to more and is correlated with an increase in nationalism, which compensates for the unfulfilled gap and devaluates the falsely honored target. Second, contempt reflects the emotional designation of the incompetence of the target nation to enhance Chineseness. Contempt causes avoidance rather than conversion (Bell 2013; Hutcherson and Gross 2011) and might lead to Beijing pushing for a reallocation of investment in a charm offense elsewhere. Third, disappointment connotes the emotional realization of the impracticality of making China attractive (Mauss et al. 2011; Craib 1994). Even so, disappointment may lead to further efforts to engender liking. Fourth, anger denotes the feeling of unexpectedly losing a relationship or an extended boundary that one previously assumed to own (Graham 2014; Mackie, Devos, and Smith 2000). Anger provokes the Chinese leaders' aggression and reduces their sensitivity to the target nation. Fifth, risk—as an alert to the potential of being betrayed by the target area to a third party—triggers action to control uncertainty (Slovic et al. 2004; Glendon and Clarke 2016). Finally, alienation emerges when friendship is denied. The Chinese leaders would experience powerlessness or meaninglessness in a relational void (Southwell 2008; Seeman 1983). To avoid losing face, further interaction is based on case by case need rather than control.

Conclusion

The anglophone literature on the relational turn does not treat Chinese relational thinking, while the sinophone literature asserts the uniqueness of the Chinese relational IR. This book disputes both practices. It instead defines relations as *a process of reproducing resemblance among strangers or potential strangers*, so that Chinese and Western relations are merely vicarious of two comparable modes. Chinese relational analysis contributes to relational IR by adding improvised resemblance to its agenda, which is mainly bilateral as opposed to multilateral. Being a vicarious variable that denotes bilateralism and improvised resemblance, the notion of China is heuristic rather than substantive. A Sinocentric method has been adopted to show how discovering Chineseness in the other actor is such an uncertain, processual practice to the effect that Chineseness is actually post-Chineseness. Six categories of resemblance are discussed in chapter 1 to show an international relation based upon the balance of relationships that differs from the balance of power or balance of interest. BoR evades the ontological pursuit and is tantamount to assuming ontological equality between actors of different sizes, and yet recognizes the intersubjectivity and changeability of their mutually constituted identities. It also reconciles the binary of China and the West.

Chapter 2

Into the Iron Brotherhood

Relational Epistemology

Theoretical Significance of the Sino-Pakistani Relationship

We do not know about ontology, although intellectually we can have ontological beliefs. Therefore, post-Chineseness avoids ontological questions. It is an argument about epistemology—all actors adopt relational lenses to understand the world and their identities, despite the possibility that they are ontologically autonomous. This chapter traces the evolution of relational identities of Pakistan and China and shows how a self-centric agenda actually reveals an intersubjective, as opposed to autonomous, process. Epistemologically, China and Pakistan are by no means self-centric actors to each other. The Sino-Pakistani relationship poses a challenge to international relations (IR) theory. In the twenty-first century, this relationship appears socially spontaneous and morally binding in addition to being mutually beneficial in political and economic terms. The Chinese media describe Pakistan as an "iron brother" (鐵哥). Pakistan, in turn, appreciates such a depiction and frequently reiterates her own passionate narrative of their relationship being "higher than mountains."

International relations theories, premised upon the ontology of a self-interested state, pale before such a relationship. It would not present a challenge, though, if one insists that the two actors simply use each other exclusively and separately, each for their own interest. In such a statist mode of analysis, even philanthropic acts are self-interested, designed to make one feel good or to be indefinitely profitable in the future. However, such a cynical view is problematic practically as well as theoretically. Theoretically, the conscious endeavor to enhance the welfare of another actor cannot also be consciously self-interested (Floler and Kam 2007; Brennan 1994; Meglino and Korsgaard 2004). This would otherwise result in the unlikely state in which one does not know one's own preference. Practically, the actor consciously acts with self-restraint to acknowledge the wishes of the other. In the case of Sino-Pakistani relationships, a peculiar collective identity is even emerging with the formation of the China Pakistan Economic Corridor (CPEC), which constitutes the self-awareness of both countries.

The sociological theory of social capital may ostensibly offer a solution by arguing that self-restraint to cater for a longer-term relationship is ultimately rational in that it keeps one from isolation in time of need (Lewis 2005; Joffe and Staerklé 2007; Tittle, Ward, and Grasmick 2004; Tirole 2002; Windsor 2006). The social psychological literature on friendship could further confirm that belonging to a stable relationship soothes one from anxiety about an uncertain future (Berenskoetter 2007; Myers 1999; Mayer 1957). Such arguments reproduce self-centered kinds of relationality in which relationships are instrumental, not constituent. Nevertheless, one does not know exactly what long-term benefits a relationship will accrue before they actually transpire or perhaps fail to materialize at all. Accordingly, sociologists are forced to agree that relationality conditions a rational society, at least epistemologically (Emirbayer 1997; Selg 2016; Dpelteau 2008; Jaggar 1995), if not ontologically. In this light, perceiving her world in relational terms is a social necessity for any reasonable actor at all times. Even the most adamant individualists must first identify others, from whose interference they intend to keep their calculus and with whose understanding they enjoy respect for individualism. Given that the state is relationally constituted irrespective of whichever ontology is truer—the self-interested state or the relational state—the change and continuity in its relationality call for a processual analysis.

This book defines relationality as *the condition of being related*. It pertains to the purposes and processes of relating that enable one to know one's world and one's own identity. Even self-consciously self-interested states know their interests through relationships. Instead of sheer instrumental relationships, therefore, relationality is the proper perspective to adopt regarding the evolution of the Sino-Pakistani friendship. The following discussion will trace the emergence of mutuality, togetherness, and a combined identity from the earliest point of their unfamiliar encounter in 1947 to the initiative of the China-Pakistan Economic Corridor in 2013–14, which transcends the paradigm of the self-interested state. There then follows a theoretical discussion of the notions of friendship, relational international relations, and bilateral identity, plus an illustration of these concepts through the Sino-Pakistani relationship.

The next step will enlist the notion of post-Chineseness to theorize about the evolutionary process of the mutual constitution of China and Pakistan and suggest a comparative agenda for future research. One could substitute post-Pakistaniness for post-Chineseness to appreciate the Chinese desire for recognition by their counterpart of their acquisition of a Pakistani identity. This would be a separate project, though. Finally, the discussion will draw implications and touch upon the "practice" and the "relational" turns regarding recent IR theorization. The discussion of this chapter points to an ignored mode of relationality—experiential Chineseness, indicated by mutual sympathy evolving out of increasing working collegiality. Experiential Chineseness may have no theory or ideology to represent due to the seeming contradiction in theory and ideology that China and Pakistan adopt respectively. However, working together is able to improvise a metaphoric brotherhood as if they resemble each other in terms of their social gene.

Into the Iron Relationship of the CPEC

Chinese premier Li Keqiang's famous quote, "If you love China, love Pakistan too,"[1] is by no means a typical statement by a self-interested state about its ally and hardly likely to have been uttered during the early years of the bilateral relationship. Although their bilateral relations improved dramatically following the Sino-Indian border clashes in 1962, this was still far from the same brotherly relationship that emerged and was consolidated in the twenty-first century. The evolution of their bilateral relationship has been no secret. Familiar topics between them include the factor of India, related disputes over Kashmir, Xinjiang, and Uygur issues, anti-terrorism, joint projects of all sorts (e.g., the China-Pakistan Economic Corridor, nuclear power plants, the related lessons from China's development model), and military cooperation.

Strategic concerns were apparent in the early days, although these were not exclusive. For example, Islamabad recognized the People's Republic of China (PRC) almost immediately after its establishment. This was completely unrelated to its war in Kashmir against India, and New Delhi had already offered its own recognition to China. However, on the Chinese side, this early recognition was deeply appreciated, along with a rare air link provided to the newly established PRC under siege. Beijing's appreciation was clearly understood in Islamabad.[2] Islamabad also facilitated the normalization between Beijing and Washington in the 1970s, indicating transcendence over ideology. Beijing's position and jurisdiction regarding Kashmir were never clarified to Pakistan, which stands in sharp contrast to how the kashmir issue later seriously poisoned Beijing's relationship with New Delhi. From the very beginning, the Sino-Pakistan and Sino-Indian relationships were on very different tracks; ironically, they moved in opposite directions. Although Indian Prime Minister Jawaharlal Nehru once held a highly positive attitude toward China, which remained even after the border clashes,[3] the Sino-Indian relationship deteriorated shortly afterwards. Conversely, the initial Sino-Pakistani strategic relationship, which was somewhat lukewarm in the late 1950s, warmed up dramatically during the Cultural Revolution.

In 1963, the two sides (China and Pakistan) resolved their disagreement over the Kashmir border issue in a mutually self-restraining manner, thereby forming a united front on India. In 1965, Beijing openly took sides in the Indian-Pakistani war. Although this was in line with Beijing's own grievances toward New Delhi, since 1965 Beijing has acted very carefully, such that no trace of inconsistency between Beijing and Islamabad is publicly noticeable. In other words, 1965 was not simply the reproduction of the realist strategy; that year also symbolized a premise that became clear only much later—that a collision with Islamabad's thinking and calculation were to be avoided as far as possible. This premise was not unilateral. Islamabad, too, has kept in mind Beijing's positions and interests elsewhere and carefully avoided displaying any sign of incongruence. One veteran opines, "Pakistan must cultivate China irrespective of other pressures. It must not bow to any pressures from the USA."[4]

Given that no point of negotiation specifically led to the exchange of favors on issues concerning each party (e.g., Xinjiang for Kashmir, Jet Aircraft and tanks for an air link, or a liaison in the Muslim World over a nuclear power plant), their care for each other's concerns probably emerged either from their own initiative or upon the request made by the other side for support, rather than from measured reciprocity. Pakistan singlehandedly spoke against UN sanctions on China in 1989, in complete defiance of the position held by its ally, the US, after the crackdown on Tiananmen Square illustrated an important sign of their friendship that was well remembered in China (Raymond Lee 2016, 2). In hindsight, until 1971, the relationship could already have been a binding identity in itself. Another indirect piece of evidence is that, later, Beijing even discouraged Islamabad from having problems with New Delhi.[5] This position removed India from being an essential factor in the bilateral relationship, but made no sense in terms of the balance of power. Rather, it indicated Beijing's assumption of a similar-minded Islamabad.

Other evidence better indicates the emergence of a collective identity, or "a greater self," in Chinese cultural terminology. Firstly, Beijing did not recognize Dhaka immediately after the partition that arose after a war between Islamabad and New Delhi. The latter supported the liberation of East Pakistan and the independence of Bangladesh, whereas Beijing was sympathetic to the resistance of its ally in West Pakistan. However, many Pakistani diplomats who worked with their Chinese counterparts were Bengalis. With Beijing refraining from intervening in the internal affairs of another country, these Bengali diplomats were nonetheless able to maintain an amicable network with Beijing.[6] China represented the spirit of liberation for many Bengali intellectuals and the relationships with East Pakistan were equally strong to those with the West.[7] Despite all these generally positive feelings between them, Beijing was opposed to the entry of Bangladesh to the UN and exercised its veto power in 1972. Beijing was only ready to offer its recognition of independent Bangladesh after Islamabad did so in 1974. This event constitutes early evidence that a different relationship gradually took shape between Beijing and Islamabad between 1965 and 1971.

Further evidence supporting the consolidation of a collective identity is Pakistan's approach to Chinese Xinjiang affairs (Yu-wen Chen 2016). The Pakistanis feel sympathy for the Xinjiang Uyghurs, probably due to their shared religion. Pakistani scholars on Xinjiang have portrayed the Chinese Xinjiang affair through three contending considerations: 1) the problem is a religious one that cuts across the Muslim world; 2) it primarily involves an internal ethnic affair between the Han and Uyghur; and 3) it manifests a Turkic nationalism that encompasses much of Central Asia.[8] Nevertheless, scholars are generally unsupportive of extremists. They believe that Pakistan should play a role in promoting China's national integration. In brief, the linkage between Xinjiang Uyghurs and the Muslim world elsewhere should be used to contribute to the CPEC instead of being detrimental to it.[9] Accordingly, Xinjiang is a principal component of the integration between China and Pakistan, and it obscures the distinction set up by national borders and between Han Chineseness and Islam in Central Asia.

A third piece of evidence of the self-restraint or collective thinking is the use of concessionary loans in the operation of the CPEC. China's loans typically carry low interest rates, definitively lower than those of the World Bank. Zero-interest loans are also not unknown in Chinese foreign policy elsewhere. These have been less frequent as the reform and openness substitute for the Chinese revolutionary and socialist world order. Nevertheless, for Pakistan, the loan interest could remain low, as little as zero-interest in some cases, after lobbying by the Pakistanis. In the operation of the CPEC, the list of Early Harvest items includes items of immediate concern for Pakistan, especially in its cotton industry; namely, the supply of electricity. Investment in transportation, which constitutes the major component of the Chinese billion-dollar investment in the Belt and Road Initiative (BRI), also includes investment in energy to meet Pakistan's development needs. In other words, rather than aiming primarily at the exploitation of resources in the light of China's own quest for multiple routes of energy supply, Chinese investment is the result of mutual consultation. Elsewhere, the relationship between China and Brazil is said likewise to illustrate a mutual relationship that avoids any exploitative implications (Cunha 2017).

Finally, no other nation in human history has ever invested as much in another nation as China has done as part of the CPEC in Pakistan. To some extent, this prepares for the transcendence of not only the sovereign estrangement that may linger on between China and Pakistan, but also an estrangement between traditional rivals, primarily Pakistan and India as well as China and India. In itself, the CPEC provides a base for identity and calculation, but it has no clear boundary in the traditional territorial sense. Its scope may extend continuously and its benefits reach far beyond Pakistan and China together, in the narrowest sense of sovereignty. The evolution of relationality (made possible by the emergence of the CPEC identity) engenders multiple relationships to counter the self-other frame that has plagued the regional relationality. The CPEC that constitutes the Sino-Pakistani relationship testifies against the possibility of purely unrelated national actors and in favor of the ubiquitous, albeit undertheorized, quest for reciprocal relationships.

The common relationality reflected in the self-restraint of both parties ascends to a higher level wherever affirmative actions, often unilateral, to support the other side in its need become intuitive. One such well-remembered action that Pakistan took during the Wenchuan earthquake in 2008 was to send all available temps in its strategic reserve, over 300,000 in total, to the earthquake area. The Chinese embassy (Embassy of the People's Republic of China in Islamic Republic of Pakistan 2008) in Islamabad collected the enormous appreciation of Chinese netizens and expressed China's sense of being "overwhelmed." An affirmative action is qualitatively stronger than self-restraint as an indicator of a relationship. This is similar to intervention by liberal countries in a so-called failing state in order to expand, improve, and enhance a global governance regime, hence reflecting a level of solidarity stronger than merely abiding by the rules.

The peak of the dyadic relationship that is clinched to the unitary or collective identity of the CPEC suggests that earlier strategic considerations were conducive rather than obstructive to relational development. If one assumes that they had walked on two separate tracks of interest calculus composed of materialist security and economic concerns, the trust and liking that ensued from years of working together would not have affected their respective calculi. However, the reality has proved otherwise. Since the signing of the China-Pakistan Free Trade Agreement in 2003, the significance of economic mingling has quickly replaced that of the security partnership. With both sides now identifying with the CPEC as a development actor for the entire region and even far beyond,[10] the epistemology of the self-interested state fails significantly. The metaphor of friendship is particularly relevant here (Nordin and Smith 2018). Friends do not usually become friends on first meeting, but friendship arises out of contact that breeds trust and liking (Bukowski, Motzoi, and Meyer 2009). In short, being relational actors, states are generally ready for relationships despite initially being unaware which relationships those are. Interaction is conducive to friendship even if it is not consciously mutual at first.

One metaphor recently drawn by Beijing is the historical voyages led by Ming dynasty eunuch Zheng Ho, who encountered, defeated, but never conquered the forces of resistance throughout today's South and Southeast Asia.[11] Whatever motivated his mission, his practice was to explore plausible relationships through abiding by the local customs. He left a Muslim legacy that grew into a convincing population that resides in Southeast Asia. Together, the metaphor and practice suggest that the self-interested state is merely the choice of a particular kind of relationship. In the words of Ali Shah:

> Regional commons derive strength from the eastern traditions of sharing and selfless service that culminate in horizontal distribution of benefits and discrimination in favor of the other rather than self. This prioritization of others over the self is the ballast of self-satisfied and symmetrical development, which in time leads to the comprehensive appreciation of varying needs

of different cultures and peoples passing through different stages of development. (Shah 2015, 25)

Relational IR, Chinese Friendship, and the Bilateral Identity

The relational turn, which criticizes realism and liberalism for overlooking the relations between states, offers a perspective that may help to explain the intimate relationships existing between states in general, and that between China and Pakistan in particular. However, I will argue that the relational literature is insufficient due to its obsession with the prior ontological processes of the system that constitute states. According to the relational agenda, relations at the systemic level come before states (Jackson and Nexon 1999). States emerged and evolved in a prior philosophical, linguistic, and historical resemblance to make their interactions practically meaningful to each other and conducive to their identities (Crossley 2010). Relational IR attends particularly to the self-restraint of states to abide by shared rules willingly (Adler 2008). This explains the intimate relationships between the Western European states and their common support for the liberal hegemony led by Washington, often at the expense of their immediate national interests. In this book, self-restraint refers to *the prioritizing of perceived common interests in general and the interests of others in context over one's own interests.* For nation-states that lack any significant prior resemblance, their relationships, which do not inspire self-restraint, would appear unlikely, dispensable, and unnecessary, if not counterintuitive. China and Pakistan are seemingly such stranger states.

Between China and Pakistan, indeed, no such tradition of shared rules exists. One strand of the relational literature stresses the point of entry into international society (Neumann 2011, 463–84), which may connect China and Pakistan, though only in the sense that both joined international society after World War II and moved immediately into the Cold War. Such a shared point of entry, which is defined by Euro-American rules, anti-colonial politics, and the quest for international recognition, could presumably overcome all the seeming odds blocking friendship between the two actors. Consider network theory, which composes an important dimension of relational IR (Nexon and Wright 2007; Slaughter 2009; Maoz 2011; Vaisey and Lizardo 2010). In many parts of the world, the networks that Washington established with various postcolonial states during the Cold War provided indirect routes for them to connect with each other—for example, Taiwan and Singapore, the Philippines and Japan, or Korea and South Vietnam. The same was true for the socialist bloc, through whose platform Mongolia, North Korea, or North Vietnam could connect with East Europe indirectly, thanks to Moscow, who built networks with both sides. Network theory would have actually downgraded the likelihood of a warm relationship developing between Beijing and Islamabad, since they squarely belonged to rival blocks, respectively led by Washington and Moscow. They actually were on different sides of the Cold War divide.

The other prior resemblance of the two actors points to the legacies of pre–World War II colonialism and imperialism that constituted the two newly independent states. At a slightly more nuanced level, China was never colonized by the UK, which ruled Pakistan prior to its independence. No specific prior resemblance could have brought China and Pakistan together. Nevertheless, there was an indirect clue. The British colonial legacies in the division of Pakistan and India made China's sharing of the anti-imperialist and anti-colonial legacies an obsolete relationality with South Asia as a whole. Imagine if the two states had never been separated by Great Britain. Without Beijing having to choose between the two postcolonial actors, the Indian perspective of China would probably have been completely different in the twenty-first century. Partially, therefore, their prior (imagined) solidarity as actors dominated and suppressed by the Western colonial powers first united China and India emotionally as well as intellectually and yet later engendered a strong relative deprivation toward each other due to the abortion of mutual sympathy. This abortion proceeded from the partition of Pakistan and India.

The only relevant resemblance of these two states was probably the quest for recognition that was embarrassed by their unfamiliarity with the rules of international society. This is obviously a relatively passive relationality. Sympathy for Chinese socialism, which was widespread among Pakistani as well as Bangladeshi intellectuals, albeit helpful for the forging of friendships, amounted to no more than one-sided romanticization, given the low level of interaction. In other words, the ontological bias of the relational turn could only damage the Sino-Pakistani relationship. There is, though, a practice turn within the relational IR that may remedy this ontological bias. According to the practice turn, national actors practice self-restraint consciously and execute their daily habits subconsciously (Pierre 1977; Bueger and Gadinger 2015). In this light, the actors collectively create a community of practices and individually adapt and improvise in their specific contexts. The challenge to the practice turn is that there were no prior relational norms and rules for the two actors to reproduce or change through practice (Neumann 2002; Adler 2005). In short, the community of practice required some shared rules prior to friendship, which was not there for Beijing and Islamabad, who engaged each other culturally only in a distant past.

Juxtaposed with relational IR, a Chinese relational turn emerges strongly in IR as well as in social psychology (Kavalski 2017a; Qin 2016b; Shih and Huang 2019, 2016). The Chinese narratives evade the issues of solidarity, duty, and consensual practices embedded in a systemic ontology. Rather, they value mutually beneficial arrangements that are improvised in various ways so that any dyad of actors could avoid encountering their potentially embarrassing strangeness in order to keep their interactions harmonious. This immediately adds a bilateral dimension to the overly multilateral sensibilities assumed in the relational literature (Shih and Chang 2017). In other words, the practical relationships between dyadic actors, which are idiosyncratic, are categorically distinctive and independent of the community of practice at the multilateral/systemic level, which is rule-based. Whether or not Beijing and Islamabad can develop a relationship away from an unfavorable relationality—for example, the Cold War divide, stereotyped religiosity in Islam as opposed to Confucianism and Marxism, the dissimilar colonial pasts, and so on—is a matter of both skill and motivation. China's habitual use of the term "friendly relationship" or "strategic partnership" to portray their diplomatic partner reflects its attempt to improvise a bilateral, as opposed to systemic, resemblance.

That said, with regard to the practice point of view, a question remains—one friend is obviously different from another friend; however, a friend today is never the same friend as before or after. The concept of friendship is conceptually insufficient in explaining change and continuity by itself. In fact, the reference to friendship within Chinese diplomacy reveals nothing about this friend. According to Chinese cultural norms, friendship is one of the five basic Confucian dyadic roles that keep the society integrated and harmonious. It is a dangerous role, though, because an overly developed friendship may easily break the rules and norms associated with other, far more fundamental dyadic roles, including those of the prince-official, father-son, husband-wife, and older-younger brothers. Confucius specifically warned against intimate friendship (Shih 2020). Instead, he preached about gentlemen's friendship, which can only last for a long time if it is as tasteless as water. He could not simply forego the role of the friend, apparently because the other four dyads could not cover a sufficient population to make people feel obliged to conduct the self-restraint that was essential for ensuring social harmony.

The combination of the practice turn (i.e., evolution and change) and Chinese relational IR (i.e., bilateralism and non-ontology) points to the importance of tracking the coupling of actors in order to identify how a specific style of friendship has been evolving. This enables the conceptualization of the practicing of a relationship without having to begin with a shared prior philosophical, linguistic, and historiographical resemblance. Accordingly, the Sino-Pakistani friendship is by itself, one of a kind. As a result, each coupling of actors has its own bilateral identity constituted by the prior practices between the two. These prior practices reveal the self-other imaginations that each party brings to the making of friendly roles. This is different from the naive encountering between a man and an alien under the Wendtian circumstance, where establishing some rule is the priority of making a community (Wendt 1992, 405). For the practice of bilateral IR, instead, some gift to take care of the need of the stranger is the way to start a relationship. The sense of being obliged to practice a set of intersubjective expectations as the formation of a "role relation" concerns an epistemological necessity to stabilize a relational self and oblige the other party to reciprocate.

Friendship is thus about an intersubjective dynamic of bilateral role identifications. It incurs the processes of prior other-imagining, practices of self-restraint, changes in role identification, mutuality, and the bypassing of a systemic ontology. To clarify further, ontology refers to *what constitutes actors/agents*. It does not change, so it does not explain changes in friendship or role identity. In addition, epistemology refers to *how actors/agents know*. This is linked with how agents acquire prior other-imaginations of each other, how they create expectations about the future, and how they evaluate. The notion of post-Chineseness or, for that matter, post-Pakistaniness, is the answer advocated in this book for one to approach changes.

Post-Chineseness against the Odds

Embedded Relationality

Despite their seeming differences in terms of religion, size, ideology, alliance, and level of development, as well as the contrast between a multiparty democracy and a one-party hierarchy, Pakistan and China have beaten all the odds against an intimate relationship and mutually imagine an Iron Brotherhood that is "higher than mountains and deeper than oceans." The challenge for IR theory is that this relationship evolved practically. In light of the fact that the IR tradition adopts the ontology of the self-interested state, for the self-interested state to become relational would be an ontological change (Müller 2004, 395–435), and this would be esoteric. However, advocates of a statist ontology could still maintain that the self-interested state necessarily incorporates relationality for its own self-enhancement. Nevertheless, given that relationality is no more than an instrument of self-enhancement, one must be able to appreciate and contribute to the benefit of the other in order to feel good about oneself. Hence, from the self-interested state perspective, even this process cannot be a change of ontology; it must involve at least a practice of relationship. This is why a determined ontology of the self-interested state continues to require an epistemology of relationality. In actuality, relationality must occupy an actor's agenda (Lieberman 2014).

Before 1965, the two countries felt less mutuality or togetherness. This was before they consciously considered each other's perspectives, acted on behalf of each other, or even thought from the perspective of CPEC as unitary actors. At that earlier point, depending on one's ontological position, one could argue either way—either they were epistemologically self-interested (i.e., thinking only about themselves) or they were epistemologically relational (i.e., related by thinking instrumentally about the other, who presumably thinks similarly). Conceptualizing both as two self-interested states or two relational states in search of an improved relationship was irrelevant to one's theoretical agenda in 1965. However, both the ontology and epistemology of the self-interested state appeared insufficient after their bilateral relationship adopted a far clearer mutuality.

Together, the relational and the practice turns and Chinese international relations have provided the alternative of the relational state as ontology (Qin 2016b; Zhang and Chang 2016; Zhang 2015; Shih 2013a; T. Zhao 2009). A growing body of literature insists, in one way or another, that states are mutually constituted (Kavalski 2017b; Bilgin and Ling 2017; Ling 2014a; Shih 2012; Jackson and Nexon 1999); hence, the relational state. However, the ontological debate is difficult to resolve. After all, we lack information. The Sino-Pakistani relationship offers an empirical case to move beyond this debate and rest upon relational epistemology, as opposed to ontology. That is, that relationship presents a case for tracing the evolution of relationality in different relationships without a decision on ontology. Relational epistemology demands research agendas that investigate how the actors become aware only through relations, regardless of ontology. Let the statist ontology continue to enjoy the benefit of doubt to argue that states can be self-interested throughout. Epistemologically, though, states are intellectually able, socially doomed, and psychologically pleased to acquire relationality for the sake of self-fulfillment. In short, relational epistemology, as a social necessity, allows one to avoid the ontological unknown but explain the rise and fall of the collective actor or "the greater self" between various forms.

Thus, the theoretical challenge is to gather different forms of relationships, observe the processes of adjustment, and explain the decisions to take and leave a relationship. In the early days of the Sino-Pakistani relationship, a shared interest was to balance India. This bilateral relationship was geopolitically inspired in a coincided realist interest. Since 2013, the officially designated Iron Brotherhood indicates the significant waning of the Indian factor and the obscuring of the geopolitical boundaries. The jump from unspecified relationality (in which the two explored relational potentials from mutually estranged positions that were imposed by the Cold War) to the transcendence of boundary in the CPEC covers the widest possible range of relationality. The changes in each side's mutual role identity result in the best test of IR theory.

In the following discussion, I will apply the anthropological notion of post-Chineseness to introduce and deduce the forms of relationship. This exercise enables one to trace the choices and shifts between the forms of relationship in accordance with the resources and processes to which Beijing relates or is related. This exercise concerns how to pull different strings of imagined Chineseness in order for Beijing and different actors to relate each in its own way. Over time, as the kind of Chineseness appropriated by each side adapts according to the choice of actors, a change in role identity takes place.

The Rationale of a Post-Chineseness Agenda

Reflections on post-Chineseness are indebted to Peter Katzenstein's work on civilizational politics and Gungwu Wang's writings on Chineseness, pertaining to Sinicization in particular. In his determined criticism of Francis Fukuyama's theme of the end of history and the late Samuel Huntington's notion of the clash of civilizations (Huntington 1998; Fukuyama 1993), Katzenstein insists that no civilizational expansion can be unidirectional.[12] Thus, he studies how interactions involving actors of Chinese identities have transpired to complicate both China as a category and Chinese civilization as a bounded civilization. China is under constant reconstruction even between Chinese actors—between the superior and the subordinate, the coast and the inland, any two neighboring ethnic communities, or different sides of borders. They have to negotiate the cultural meanings of anything imagined to be commonly theirs, as if they were engaging those without Chinese identities (Katzenstein 2012a; Shih 2013a). Katzenstein virtually comes to the point that China exists only in practice, which can neither conquer nor be conquered in actuality without manipulating symbols and discourses. This methodology renders irrelevant the Chinese threat, as well as the Chinese collapse. In fact, even speaking of China may become a dubious and suspicious act.

Echoing Katzenstein's deconstruction of expansionist and nationalist China, Wang's lifelong struggle has been to demonstrate that Chinese Southeast Asians or overseas Chinese cannot constitute a single category. Wang records the identity strategies of Chinese Southeast Asians that have produced vast differences among those called Chinese (G. Wang 2002; Ooi 2015). These indigenous Chinese possess cultural lives and social identities that are unfamiliar to, if not in conflict with, each other. Their responses to the rise of China have necessarily varied. Some are capable of re-Sinicization in their own peculiar way (Nyíri and Tan 2016; Ooi 2015). Others reconnect China and the communities to which they belong. As with Katzenstein, a significant political implication of Wang's research is the impossibility of the Chinese in Southeast Asia uniting to become a threat.

Sino-Pakistani relations can easily appeal to either Katzenstein or Wang on issues involving Xinjiang Uyghurs or the intertwined tracks of the Belt and Road Initiative (BRI). The challenge that the two pioneering constructivists bring forth is that any reference to China can commit false authenticity to the extent that China ceases to be a legitimate category. Such has never been the case in the interaction between Islamabad and Beijing. In other words, despite its constructive nature as a category, China continues to give meanings, discursively, practically, and emotionally. To cope with the dangerously simplistic and yet discursively fundamental category, post-Chineseness substitutes for China as well as Chineseness are included in the following discussion.

Based on the discussion in chapter 1, post-Chineseness connotes something from Chineseness but the latter is too fluid, contextualized, and individualized to have a name. Post-Chineseness avoids the ontological debate on how to define China. Instead, post-Chineseness refuses the imposition of any fixed meanings but allows the actors to continue to practice the name. As with Katzenstein, all actors (self-regarded as either inside or outside and elitist as well as subaltern) are epistemologically equal in enlisting China as an identity resource. Both Pakistanis and Chinese inevitably define Chineseness, and Chineseness constitutes their self-understanding in one way or another. As with Wang, differences in Chineseness call for comparative studies of the types of post-Chineseness and their behavioral implications.

Formally, post-Chineseness refers to *the processes incurred and the resources enlisted for one to relate to China or for China to relate to one*. In this definition, Chineseness involves practices in context that are contingent upon the purpose and the capability of the actors involved. As with chapter 1, two dimensions ensue. One is the self/other dimension. This dimension is imaginative and thought to be prior to an exchange that is taking place. The Sino-Pakistani relationships suggest that relationships, as they are imagined, can range from mutual estrangement (e.g., balance of power) to minglement (e.g., the CPEC). Another is the objective/subjective dimension. This dimension is likewise imaginative. Such dimension pertains to the imagined range of one's identity from entirely objective determinants (e.g., the Cold War alliance) to entirely subject assessments (e.g., brotherhood). A 2x3 typology can be drawn for each actor. Table 2.1 is for Pakistan, or anyone in an imagined position of facing China, to define the post-Chineseness of the PRC. Table 2.2 is for China, or anyone acting on behalf of her imagined China, to relate to Pakistan.

Let us consider the actors facing China, that is, those who do not have the legitimacy of speaking on behalf of China (see chapter 1 for the definition of insider and more in part 2). The columns in table 2.1 indicate whether their relationships with China are within the in- or out-group. Being motivated by their own purposes, they strategically enlist resources to relate China to enact their self-understood relationships. Self-perceived in-group relationships necessarily engender pressure to meet the expectations of those who interact on behalf of China as conceived. By contrast, the rows in table 2.1 answer whether the actors can imagine objectively what Chineseness stands for or whether they must consciously rely on the subjective views of the Chinese.

Table 2.1. China as the Imagined Object of an Incurred Relationship

Pakistan–subject / China–object	Subject inside	Subject in-between	Subject outside
Subjective China	2013– Cultural kind*		
Objective China	1971–2013 Experiential kind*		1950–71 Policy kind*

*Definitions of different kinds in an out-group perspective will follow in part 2.
Source: author

To trace the evolution of Pakistan's post-Chinese identities, I propose that the right lower corner is initially more relevant. It was during that time that an out-group actor was looking in China from an external perspective; hence the illustration of the extreme form of objective Chineseness. Objective Chineseness can be alternatively called physical Chineseness, scientific Chineseness, or policy Chineseness, depending on the context (see further in the chapters in part 2). The left lower corner, which became relevant with the passage of time, reflects the internalization of Chinese concerns and familiarity with Chinese practices by living together long enough, from the Pakistani point of view. I call this experiential Chineseness, which was gradually bred from long-term cooperation in the military, economic, and international spheres. One easily observes experiential Chineseness among journalists, expatriates, or anthropologists who acquire a knowledge of China by practicing or simulating the Chinese way of life as they perceive it.

Let us consider China in relation to other actors. The columns in table 2.2 indicate whether those self-regarded Chinese, that is, the insider's perspective, conceive of other actors as in-group or out-group actors. Contrary to the aforementioned situation of other actors looking in, I propose that in-group relationships enable them to feel justified to expect others' conformity, whereas out-group relationships place China in the awkward position of being assessed. The rows in table 2.2 answer whether, in their own understanding, the relationships depend on how self-regarded Chinese subjectively judge their relational roles or what Chineseness represents objectively, regardless of how they think. In practice, the initial years of interaction exerted less pressure on the Chinese authorities to show that China's values were superior rather than simply physically useful. As Islamabad attained

Table 2.2. China as the Imagined Subject of an Incurred Relationship

China–subject \ Pakistan–object	Object inside	Object in-between	Object outside
Subjective China	2013– Moral kind*	1971–2013 Hybrid kind*	
Objective China		1962–71 Borderline kind*	1950–62 Utility kind*

*See chapter 1 for the definitions of different Chinese from an in-group perspective.
Source: author

a possible role of being an in-between actor in the middle column, to mediate for Beijing on different issues, the pressure on Beijing considerably increased because a third party (e.g., the US or followers of Islam) could beat China in terms of civilizational as well as strategic attraction. That is why Islamabad's siding with Beijing in a US-backed UN resolution to sanction China in 1989 was thus tremendously soothing to Beijing, given that Cuba was the only other country to oppose the resolution. The left upper corner indicates moral Chineseness (see chapter 1) where the Chinese authorities would regard Pakistan as an in-group member that abides by the same rules of conduct. In resonance with Beijing's expectation of compliance with China's own civilizational criteria of brotherhood, self-regarded Pakistan's self-conceived internal role in table 2.1 would attach great importance to the relationships, ideas, and worldviews brought forth by China.

A Note on Post-Pakistaniness

From the dyadic role point of view, any two actors are epistemologically equal, since both must decide how to provide one's role identity to the other party and acquire the other's role identity in one's own practice. Post-Pakistaniness exists more vividly among those Chinese exchange scholars, expatriates, and businesspeople who have resided in Pakistan for a sufficiently long period. They amount to a rather insignificant portion of the Chinese population, though. This chapter adopts post-Chineseness instead of post-Pakistaniness for three reasons: (1) There is already an emerging literature on the post-Chineseness practiced and adopted by Hong Kong, Taiwan, the Philippines, and Vietnam (Clemente and Shih 2019; Shih 2018a, 2018b; Liao 2010), so the comparative potential is greater for post-Chineseness than post-Pakistaniness. (2) With the rise of China, it is intellectually more challenging and urgent to complicate the category "China" by showing how different actors can appropriate Chineseness for their own strategic purposes and consequently constitute a portion of their own identity. This results in complicated understandings of China amidst the anxiety of the mainstream literature to simplify China, each according to a particular ideological standpoint, strategic need, or political interest. And (3) by assuming that different Pakistani narrators have distinctive ways of combining and appropriating Chineseness, Pakistan achieves a level of intellectual power that is on a par with all of the others in the world who do the same as China and yet most of them in ways dissimilar to Pakistan.

Relationality Informed by Post-Chineseness

Post-Chineseness indicates, on the one hand, elements about China that Islamabad perceives as strategically useful for establishing a bilateral relationship and, on the other hand, elements about Pakistan to which Beijing perceives it proper to relate. If Islamabad and Beijing can perceive in each other identity resources in context to subscribe to (e.g., Xinjiang Muslims or the historical Silk Road), they resemble each other and belong to the same group. This type of Chineseness produces a moral pressure for each to comply with mutual expectations. If they lack imagined resemblance completely, the establishment of a relationship will rely on a show of goodwill. In the latter case, their respective understanding of Chineseness hardly overlaps. In this situation, relationships likewise rely on self-restraint. The self-restraint of an out-group actor suggests refraining from imposing one's will. If no relationship can be formed either because of an abortion of self-restraint or because of a mismatch between the actions of self-restraint, the maintenance of a relationship can lead to punishment, isolation, and self-transformation. These have not taken place in the cycles of the Sino-Pakistani relationship. One would need to look elsewhere for examples like these, such as to Vietnam, Korea, Mongolia, the Philippines, and Japan.

Post-Chineseness involves two qualities—how much pressure exists to comply with the expectation of the other and how much subjective assessment is required to determine the proper relationship. In the CPEC regime (which rests upon the same-group identity together with subjective choices of goals and values) two types of pressure are found. The first is the pressure for each to comply with the other. However, the norms to comply have been predominantly policy norms instead of cultural norms, because, culturally, the two have not been very knowledgeable about each other. These policy norms on the Chinese side have been about the one-China policy pertaining to Taiwan, Tibet, and the status of Uyghurs in Xinjiang. On the Pakistani side, these norms were Kashmir, nuclear development, and anti-terrorism. The second is the collective identity of the CPEC. This collective identity emerges in the regionalism of the CPEC that presumably supersedes nationalism.

Historically, for Islamabad to relate to China, it was initially self-regarded as an out-group member without any significant subjective access to Chinese civilization. Despite the fact that contemporary Pakistan once served as part of the ancient Silk Road, this civilizational network hardly rings a bell in contemporary history. In Pakistan, access to Chinese mainstream culture and the understanding of Chinese ideology are limited. China represented "a thing out there." Islamabad needed to decide for itself what China could mean to Pakistan. Islamabad began with a kind of gift-giving in 1950 that, in return, successfully oriented Beijing's subsequent approach to maintaining Islamabad's goodwill. Initially, Beijing also treated Islamabad as "a thing out there" to be related to in an unspecified relationship. The Bandung Conference was the first step toward a relationship away from physical traits, because both pledged to nonalignment embedded in a subjective choice rather than in sheer objective conditions. Following the Sino-Indian border clashes, Beijing began to view Islamabad potentially as an in-between identity that could connect China to the Muslim world and possibly the United States.

Beijing and Islamabad resolved the Kashmir border issues after the Sino-Indian border clashes. For Beijing, Pakistan was now a potential ally in the objective sense. Keeping Pakistan on China's side became an important agenda. The year 1971 witnessed both the Indian-Pakistani war and Islamabad's liaison for Sino-US normalization. Siding with Pakistan to oppose India could serve either as a balance of power against New Delhi or mainly a show of goodwill with Islamabad. Given Islamabad was already an important strategic ally and trustworthy partner for Beijing, pampering their bilateral relationship was a value in itself. Balancing India was comparatively a minor issue. In the eyes of Beijing, Islamabad further acquired a bridge role. This bridge role embraces a type of hybrid Chineseness because of its familiarity with the US-led alliance as well as Muslim affairs. To incur hybrid Chineseness implied a self-imposed social pressure by Beijing to care for the interests of Pakistan, because, if Pakistan jettisoned the role, the implication would be for Beijing to lose the contest to Washington. This compelled Beijing to maintain the relationship with special care to such a level that Beijing would not have reached under the circumstance of the self-interested state. China's competitor for a relationship with Pakistan was the United States. Thus, Beijing had to treat Pakistan better than Washington did.

The CPEC regime engenders newer norms. Both Beijing and Islamabad are obliged to enhance the prosperity of the population under the CPEC regime, which expands beyond their borders. It is a different type of post-Chineseness. Instead of Beijing feeling the pressure to meet the expectations of Islamabad, with Pakistan becoming an in-group member, Beijng became ready to impose its role expectation on Islamabad. In fact, the Iron Brotherhood, in Chinese terminology, carries cultural implications. According to Confucianism, the brotherhood is weighted with obligations.

We can predict that the expectation for Islamabad to assist the integration of Xinjiang will gain strength in the years to come. Other obligations associated with the CPEC include transcendence over rivalry with India through the economic sharing of benefits and the dissolution of terrorist organizations in due course. These goals have already been taken seriously by Islamabad. However, they now become obligations in the eyes of Beijing. In actuality, it infers the mutual obligation to make Islamabad and Beijing, now imagined as a single entity, more comfortable with Indian affairs. Consequently, facing India, both confrontation and compromise can come from a position of strength.

FORMATION OF EXPERIENTIAL CHINESENESS

One particular type of post-Chineseness, for Islamabad, is critical to the evolution of the Sino-Pakistani relationship, that is, experiential Chineseness (for more on this topic, see chapters 5 and 6). This type of Chineseness is not easily expressible discursively but known by heart because of the long-standing experience of living together. In addition to anthropologists, journalists and expatriates, diplomats, businesspeople, and students are among those who often possess experiential Chineseness. Experiential Chineseness engenders a same-group consciousness but does not rely on the subjective assessment of the targeted Chinese population to determine its existence. Once Chinese lives are understood with sympathy due to having lived together long enough, Islamabad knows how Chinese would feel and react. For Islamabad, whose leaders used to rely on physical Chineseness to explore a possible relationship, the move toward experiential Chineseness required a longer period of time.

In the relational literature, the notion of habitus comes close to experiential Chineseness (Bourdieu 1977). However, experiential Chineseness attunes more to capacity for mutual sympathy than common habits that the notion of habitus investigates. Even so, they both attend to disposition and familiarity established over time through practice. Experiential Chineseness is an important source of imagined resemblance because it relies not on abstract theorization, but on a binding relationship that culminates in the reciprocal calling of brother and investment in a corridor belonging exclusively to the couple sharing some kind of social and political gene. This speaks to the core of the balance of relationships (see chapter 1), namely, experiential Chineseness is between the two, for the two, and by the two.

Experiential Chineseness explains why the Pakistanis, who have limited contact with Chinese civilization, can eventually cultivate in themselves a same-group consciousness. Chinese moral support during several military conflicts against India equipped the Pakistanis with a collegial spirit. Beijing's efforts to keep Islamabad on its side reinforce the bilateral relationship. The all-round interactions between them forge a deep working relationship. Although all interactions carry some strategic and national interest calculus, after so many joint projects over such a long time period, what eventually matters is that the trusting atmosphere is usually sufficient to develop a friendship. In other words, experiential Chineseness, embedded in living and working together, for whatever divergent purposes, can produce a trust emotion that transcends interest calculi (Wheeler 2013). Being disadvantaged in Chinese civilizational knowledge, Pakistanis can still grasp the Chinese way intuitively. They can appreciate the gravity of the one-China principle and hope for a better-integrated nation for China, especially in terms of the Xinjiang issue. Most vividly, they can feel the suffering of the Chinese during disasters, as they did during the 2008 Wenchuan earthquake.

Experiential Chineseness explains how these two seemingly separate actors can ultimately act in union in the CPEC. If one fails to adopt the epistemology of relationality, one cannot acknowledge the current state wherein the Pakistani people can feel for the Chinese people as if they were not two distinct actors. The long-term process of mutual constitution that experiential Chineseness generates parallels how strangers who share no common traits can still become friends despite their initial interaction resting upon respective strategic calculi. These seemingly separate strategic concerns indicate a specific relationship that is embedded in physical Chineseness. The evolution of physical Chineseness to experiential Chineseness encounters no ontological transformation. It is relational epistemologically throughout.

Conclusion: Implications for International Relations Theory

Chapter 2 argues that the Sino-Pakistani relationship illustrates a truly relational identity, albeit only on the positive end of it. It is significant because international relations do not expect positive relationality. It involves two relational selves constituting each other and the formation of the CPEC independently constituting each of them. The chapter further claims that both the study and presentation of this relational identity are only possible under an epistemology of relationality, as opposed to the epistemology of the self-interested actor. Chapter 2 proceeds with the anthropological notion of post-Chineseness, which typologizes relationality in accordance with how Islamabad and Beijing identify each other in their strategic choice of relationship. The evolution suggests that China has moved from its expectations of stranger Pakistan as being an owner of utility Chineseness, through hybrid Chineseness, ultimately progressing to moral Chineseness under the CPEC. By contrast, Pakistan's self-positioning vis-à-vis stranger China has shifted from the owner of policy Chineseness, via experiential Chineseness, to moral Chineseness. Among them, Pakistan's experiential Chineseness and China's experiential Pakistaniness are the most relevant common elements for explaining the evolution.

Relational IR has an ontological tilt toward systemic or multilateral processes that cannot make sense of the practical relationships evolving from two mutually out-group actors into one of bilateral identity. The relational sensibilities in bilateral qua Chinese IR contribute to the extent that the practicing of a role identity does not require any prior constituted norms and rules. Bilateral IR attends to the skill of building mutually obliged relationships in order to transcend any differences of two strangers in ontological imagination. However, Chinese IR has not answered the question regarding through which mechanism the national actors go about mutually obliging each other. Chapters 1 and 2 have developed the notion of post-Chineseness in order to demonstrate the two decisions—in- or out-group and subjective or objective criteria—that an actor can make in order to make roles for each other. Post-Chineseness is a major dimension that defines the parameters of a bilateral role identity, and post-Pakistaniness is the other.

In brief, the Sino-Pakistan relationship exhibits a spontaneous rise of intimacy or friendship, made possible by a long-term process of a collegial working relationship. That said, it is by all means plausible to study from the perspective of post-Pakistaniness if one's interest is to compare with an imagined Chinese perspective how those carrying Malaysian, Indian, or Bangladeshi identities see through relationships embedded in unsynchronized Pakistaniness in order to understand their worlds and identities. Unfortunately, students of international relations are either negligent of or uninterested in theorizing the Sino-Pakistani relationship because of an insufficiently developed epistemology of relationality in favor of the epistemology of the self-interested state.

The notion of experiential Chineseness not only challenges the epistemology of the self-interested state but also contributes to the relational turn and the practice turn in international relations. Experiential Chineseness uncovers the blind spot in the epistemology of the self-interested state, which disallows the breeding of togetherness and mutual concerns through security or economic cooperation. Because such an epistemology fails to provide a link between the self-interested state and the relational state, the sense of togetherness can at best be conceived as either political rhetoric or false consciousness. In contrast, experiential Chineseness echoes the call for processual analysis of the relational turn. It makes possible the comparison between those practices that reflect mutuality, for example, the CPEC, and others that do not, for example, an alliance to balance India. In brief, pure cooperation alone is sufficient to trigger the shift from one relational state—physical Chineseness—to another—experiential Chineseness. This is how even strangers can become friends in daily life. Nations are no different.

While strategic concerns continue to undergird the bilateral role identity of the Sino-Pakistan relationship throughout the twenty-first century, they are not the same concerns as existed in the 1960s and 1970s. In the early days, Islamabad and Beijing considered China and Pakistan respectively in objective and policy terms as a potentially stranger state becoming useful. However, the Cold War relations defined their togetherness at the systemic level in a peculiar way—their common enemy, India, required them to defy the Cold War norms so that they were ready to move beyond the Cold War divide at the start of their encounter. The role identity of the iron brothers has dramatically changed the calculus to the extent that they must first consider the strategic togetherness between them. They have practiced their emerging togetherness by substituting developmental for military joint force. Consequently, despite India being a lingering security issue for both, their bilateral relationship has gained its own life, exempt from the India factor. In short, the strategic interests associated with different role identities acquire different bases for calculation and mean different things to both China and Pakistan, who are now obliged to think on behalf of each other.

Chapter 3

Up from Subaltern Identities

Strategic Nonessentialism

Colonial International Relations and Taiwan

"Asia's East," or the "Asiatic East," hereafter "Yadong" (亞東), has been a lost category that used to refer to *an unspecified group of nations and societies in East Asia*. It conveys a nonbinary message, in which politically distinctive entities in the geographical area of East Asia imagine that solidarity exists between them in one way or another (Shangsheng Chen 2015). This contrasts with East Asia (dongya東亞), which is a familiar term in the security discourse (Arase 2016; Park 2014; Cho and Park 2011; Bernard 1996). In practice, Yadong is particularly keen to a collective sense of being victimized by imperialism. The mutual sympathy is pervasive despite Yadong people suffering due to the dominance of different and usually contending imperialist powers. Targeting no particular colonial power, Yadong aborts any focused political struggle. Solidarity even encompasses portions of the population belonging to the colonial powers. Yadong is accordingly a concept that spans identities across the region. It so de-emphasizes national uniqueness that nationalist and revolutionary May Fourth leaders in Republican China were contented with its use. For example, May Fourth leader Chen Duxiu (1879–1942) even suggested that Yadong should be the name of an activist/internationalist bookstore/library (Yongqi Cheng 2016), which adopted it accordingly in 1903. In this regard, Chinese nationalism in the Yadong discourse was by no means anti-Japanese.

Yadong embraces a peculiar style of Chineseness. It is not embodied in theoretical bilateralism (chapter 1) or decentralized dyad (chapter 2). Rather, it is a discourse that relates China to unspecific others in the vast land and sea of Asia. Given post-Chineseness is a practice of imagining Chineseness in an alter identity and adjusting, it is not a proper analytical concept to trace the evolution of relation with many at the same time. To relate to multiple alters simultaneously, an alternative relation that can apply to many and yet is elusive enough to allow differences and fluidity such as Yadong is called for. A geocultural relation of this sort—borderless, unsubstantiable, and yet with solidarity—has been rare in the literature as well as in the practice of international relations. Even so, Yadong is a noticeable practice of post-Chineseness in the multilateral setting. Its rise and fall illustrate the difficulty of narrating post-Chineseness and the vulnerability of post-Chinese practices in face of the ontology of binary in international as well as national politics. Chapter 3 argues that the disappearing reference to Yadong, as opposed to East Asia, in Taiwan's post–World War II political history is a harbinger for the implausibility of decolonization in Taiwan. Taiwan's apparent post-Chineseness is discursively silenced by the Cold War.

The Cold War, pertaining especially to the American intellectual intervention in the conceptualization of the world through the fault line of containment, contributed greatly to the substitution of East Asia for Yadong. Chapter 3 argues that, in the linguistic practice of Sun Yatsen (1866–1925), Yadong is a geocultural lens, while East Asia connotes strategic purposes of various kinds. The notion of East Asia provides each of its members with ostensibly autonomous identities. However, such sited identities reproduce the binary of the self and the other in their respective encountering with imperialist powers as well as their neighboring relations. In theory, all were independent. In practice, though, they perpetuate the dependence and inferiority of the former colonies, which were too weak to defend themselves against a communist invasion (Rozman 2013; Shih 2012; Ikenberry 2004; E. Goh 2008). Decolonization could not help but fade away.

The backfiring of sited identity suggests that the adoption of "strategic essentialism," spawned and disputed by the cultural critic Gayatri Chakravorty Spivak, to defend the sense of difference can be counterproductive to decolonization. Spivak interrogates whether or not an essentialized collective self-identity can inspire the colonized people to resist the invading forces.[1] She minds the danger of suppression associated with the politics of essentialism, however (Spivak 2008, 260). Therefore, essentialism is legitimate only if the leaders who enlist it understand that its purpose is strictly strategic for resistance. However, there are at least three caveats: strategizing and essentializing are paradoxical practices; essentialized identities undermine the solidarity between victimized nations; and they reproduce the division between victimized and dominant populations and the inferiority of the former.

I will first retheorize decolonization as a relational project. Then, I will show how empirically the intellectual demise of Yadong as a relational as opposed to essentialist discourse emerged with the proceeding of the Cold War. This indirectly testifies to the impracticality of decolonization in Taiwan as well as the value of the post-Chinese agenda.

(Re)theorizing Decolonization via the Relational Discourse

Decolonization anywhere is necessarily political and institutional, with the initial goal of the colony achieving self-governance (K. Chen 1998; Strang 1991). However, this is insufficient for the postcolonial population to normalize respectfully and incorporate indigenous relations, conventions, and norms in its ways of life. Nevertheless, harder and deeper ideological, discursive, and psychological struggles to cleanse colonial legacies almost certainly backfire practically as well as logically (Tuck and Yang 2012; Kohn and McBride 2011; Louis and Robinson 1994; Marglin and Marglin 1990). Practically, the postcolonial elite typically maintains colonial relations in education, kinship, economic production, and lifestyle that engross the postcolonial population in those values that easily reproduce the superiority of the former colonizing population. Logically, thorough self-independence, that picks the postcolonial against the colonial, reinforces a discursive binary of mutual estrangement that may silence already intimate relations and harm the self-respect of all sides (Schiwy 2007; Scheffler 1981).

I define decolonization as *a process of reducing the dominance in postcolonial relations*. This definition can be further elaborated: (1) dominance arises from *the unequal distribution of mutual influence* between the former colonizing power and the colonized population, among the elite, and between the elite and the subaltern; (2) postcolonial relations refer to *the perceived resemblance between the former colonizing power and the colonized population that enable them to exert an influence over each other or represent each other*; (3) resemblance exists in ideology, values, worldviews, ways of life, kinship, alliances, production, interests, identity, memories, loyalty, and so on. According to this definition, political and institutional decolonization via a power shift is relatively easy. And, yet, subsequent decolonization proceeds in complex relations. It involves improvised practices that are sometimes barely distinguishable even from recolonization. The emphasis on revitalizing indigenous values, for example, can inadvertently reinforce the dependence on the former colonial power for contemporary education. Dominance is inevitably chronic if decolonization focuses exclusively on the unlikely mission of cleansing prior colonial relations.

This reflection brings one to the quest of a broader relation that empowers the colonized population to place postcolonial relations in alternative contexts so that decolonization is exempt from binary. Such transcendence over binary contributes to decolonization in the sense that former colonial relations are neither privileged nor silenced where both parties share a greater, longer trajectory that involves third parties/identities/civilizations. Consequently, all sides necessarily adopt post-identities. Yadong illustrates this broadened trajectory. However, it will take conscious construction for such post-identities (i.e., post-Chineseness, in our case) to achieve representation discursively.

"Can the Subaltern Speak?"[2]

To justify the discussion on Yadong as opposed to East Asia, the section critically reflects upon the notion of discursive power or discourse as power for the sake of decolonization. Discursive power has been a key point of struggle in its efforts to re-present the subaltern identities in the study of international relations (Blaney and Tickner 2017; Koschut 2018 Miskimmon, O'Loughlin, and Roselle 2017). Postcolonial IR manifests the power of discourse during the Cold War. It formulates the *problématique* and the anti-communist agenda everywhere and determines the allocation of strategic resources accordingly (Hammond 2004; Moore 2017). To assert subaltern voices in order for a change to occur in the postcolonial order, the struggle for discursive reconstruction enables (1) the realization of the subaltern participation as well as influence in the making of the alleged world order; (2) the rediscovery of sited trajectories inexpressible in the current IR; (3) the critical assessment of the evolving postcolonial conditions affected by such participation, and 4) the reimagination of the colonized self in parallel space (Aydinli and Biltekin 2018; K. Smith 2017; Bilgin and Ling 2017).

Ultimately, in this vein of thought, resistance appears plausible and even desirable because the indigenous subjectivity of each population can grow in a site-sensitive narrative. Such rise of indigenous subjectivity ought to pluralize the ontological terrain that used to succumb to a synchronized kind of existence, that is, sovereign, self-centered, and strategic nation-states. In other words, with an indigenous contribution, any group is entitled to a certain sovereign scope, territorial or not, in which the form and meaning of association are exclusively of its own making. All ontologies appear equal and independent under this discursive circumstance.

That said, there is a logical caveat and practical possibility that are not considered in this quest for subaltern discourse; specifically, that such a pluralist terrain continuously privileges the strong. A discursively distinctive identity that does not belong to the imperialist or colonial order may lack practical attraction. Consequently, subaltern discourses suffer irrelevance. An identity that cannot sustain its morale of resistance can reproduce colonial dominance in the long run. Therefore, the remedy points to the analysis of discourse not as power, but in relational terms—as "relations," which neutralizes power.

The overlooked caveat is that colonial discourses that silence subaltern voices are epistemologically almost all the same as the essentialist discourses of resistance in the sense that both the colonizing and colonized forces seek to narrate and represent mutually exclusive selves, be they autonomous individuals or independent nations. The appearance of the subaltern population as ontologically different continues to rely on a self-other binary. This binary thinking becomes the ultimate and only lens shared by all sides. As a result, the recovered site of difference can repeat epistemological reductionism in the binary thinking to become just another sovereign, self-centered, and strategic actor (Shih and Ikeda 2016). The overlooked possibility is that discourses that overcome subaltern status do not have to engage in resistance.

This nonbinary style leads to self-interrogation, instead of self-assertion. To that extent, discourses serve two deconstructive purposes—(1) the deconstruction of the imposed hegemonic exclusionary values such as rights, wealth, or power, and (2) the deconstruction of the reasserted sitedness of the subaltern actor informed by either nationalism or fundamentalism. The following discussion will reconsider the possibility of decolonization not as a project of power, but as a relation.

Discourse as Power Reconsidered

To begin, while discourse as power may inspire revisionism or even revolution, at the same time, it risks homogenizing or synchronizing a population to a territorially based ontology. Since discourse as power celebrates the resistance of the colonized population, it necessarily breeds a binary-consciousness, which is often, although not inevitably, territorial. Where the former colonial power abides by the same discursive binary, it usually enjoys a higher capacity to recruit and protect the formal colony as a strategic ally. Worse, it can resort to physical conquest where resistant discourses appear too powerful to realign. The subaltern discourse of difference could be merely an object of political consumption that authenticates colonial relations (Dirik 2002, 1994).

The discursive re-presentation of the colonized site through a differing identity easily incorporates some geocultural sensibility. Such an identity is, at the same time, a statement of boundary to discriminate and alienate another colonized site. Given their different relations with the same colonial power, however, their solidarity of some kind, as opposed to mutual alienation, could have complicated and potentially reconstituted the identity of the former colonial power. Instead, the discursive power to celebrate how all the past colonial parties each contributes to the process of international relations distinctively reveals not only (1) the reproduced division between the colonizing and the colonized worlds, but also (2) the differences between all colonized worlds in themselves, as well as (3) the differences between the postcolonial national actor and the cross- or subnational actors (Sajed 2018; Thomas 2018; Larramendi 2018; Narváez 2017; Lowe and Tsang 2018). The multiplying of reimagined sited identities can reduce the level of self-empowerment of all of the postcolonial sites taken together. Sharing the same religious belief, the global south identity or past colonial system cannot sustain with each to claim distinctive identities. Therefore, the strategic essentialism of the postcolonial sites can even result in the actuality of collaborative essentialism, where differences are comfortably and even profitably ghettoized in the postcolonial relations.

Discourse as Relation

Relational discourses avoid appealing to distinctive identities. Rather, they seek points of association as well as resemblance (Dépelteau 2015; Donati and Archer 2015; Szlachcicowa 2017; Rojas 2016). Such relationality depends on the two-way creativity of reading otherness into a Chinese self or Chinese selfness into the other. Frequently, this proceeds through imagining the shared history or fate of a greater sphere based upon (1) a cultural memory that preserves an intuitive sense of intimacy, for example, the Commonwealth between Canada, Australia, India, and the UK, or (2) cultural resources that can strategically trigger a mutual liking, for example, in professional sports, anti-imperialist activism, and pop music. They, thus, contrast strategic essentialism directly in their promotion of mutuality, reciprocity, and togetherness in a greater scope that encompasses all. This indicates "strategic de-essentialism." If self/empowerment requires a sense of subjectivity, the discursive power derived from a constructed self-identity would be a key to effective decolonization. However, a relational discourse can be empowering where the sense of togetherness of a greater community relieves the fear of isolation, the anxiety toward superiority/inferiority, and depression arising out of an inability to control.

Reverse empowerment through an enhanced sense of belonging to a relational, greater community usually comes at the expense of the immediate interests of each relational party because they spontaneously consider the interests of the other relational party. They perceive a resemblance to each other in terms of the concern for the interests and identity of their greater community. Spontaneous concerns and a willingness to offer support enact bonded relationships. One frequent practice of small states is to couple with a much stronger party in order to foster sympathy, fondness, and the obligation of the latter toward the former (Auguste 2010; Claremont 2018). The seeming disappearance of the distinctive identity of the postcolonial actors thus keeps them from becoming targets of suppression and even enables them to discipline the colonial power occasionally. This is unlikely if the postcolonial actor insists on a self-other ontology in face of the past colonial power. In contrast, an imagined greater community grants the colonial and the colonized populations an equal relational prerogative to act and speak on behalf of the greater community. All members of the greater community are entitled to equal membership. On the contrary, binary postcolonial relations can easily reduce the relations to an instrument of control that reproduces the past dominance.

Further away from strategic essentialism, relational discourses turn off the binary, resistant, and essentialist voices either to romanticize or convert differences. The function of discourse is to transcend binaries so that no one can or should be the target of anyone else on behalf of any allegedly universal rules. In this regard, multiple mutuality substitutes for difference in relational discourses in order to oblige former colonial powers to sympathize with subaltern perspectives. Discourses serve to reconfirm togetherness instead. Essentialism would be counterproductive, as it connotes the impossibility of togetherness. Some extent of self-sacrifice/restraint/discipline to reciprocate between relational actors ensures that decolonization is a collective project. Having obscured the boundary, relational discourses may dissolve the ambivalence toward the dependent and independent desires of the former colonized population when encountering the colonial power. Without ambivalence, the cycle of submission and resistance of the colonized population and that of the discrimination and responsibility of the colonial power can lose momentum.

In short, given that both strategic essentialism and strategic de-essentialism resist imperialism as well as colonialism, the former relies on multiplying any mutually exclusive subjectivities, while the latter obscures them all, Western as well as subaltern. Under relational discourse, all seeming failures, successes, and experiments simultaneously belong to all. Once rule-policing gives way to relations, not only is the conversion of the former colonies into compliers with the regime irrelevant in the end (Whyte 2017; Huang and Shih 2014), but any attempt at the self-strengthening of a postcolonial site would also be immediately appreciable by relational others.

Two subaltern modes of discursive empowerment coexist: (1) empowerment to assert one's difference and capacity to simulate, revise, and reimagine the hegemonic order for one's own ever-changing purposes (Paolini 1999); (2) empowerment to engender relations that obscure the however defined binaries required to support or resist any universal order (Ling 2018). Both essentialism and de-essentialism are strategic to engage in resistance. Chinese nationalism exemplifies essentialism and yet post-Chineseness records de-essentialism. In the same vein, whereas "East Asia" exemplifies the essentialism embedded in sited binaries, resistance to the colonial other aborts decolonization. "Yadong" reversely embraces de-essentialism to encompass the colonial and postcolonial for decolonization in a greater sphere of imagined common fate.

Resistance involves supporting the suppressed subaltern, while transcendence entails avoiding the reemergence or reproduction of the previously plaguing kind of order, value, or identity in the aftermath. In the relational discourse, resistance on behalf of a sited identity must involve collective decolonization that cuts across binaries and borders. To that extent, the decolonization of the former colonial power is equally, if not more, important. Relational resistance demoralizes any civilizing projects that a synchronizing regime of universal norms preaches. It deconstructs the colonial power. No fixed subjectivity is necessary for anyone; hence a spirit of resistance is supported by strategic de-essentialism. Presumably, all readily exercise self-restraint to abide by relationships rather than power. Relational discourses ritualize a mutual constitution to oblige the decolonization of all.

Yadong as Relational Discourse in Sun Yatsen's Narratives

Given its colonial and sited sensibilities, Yadong is apparently a geocultural identity, but peculiarly not fixed with a demarcated site. There is little systematic study of the term, reflecting as well as reproducing its freedom from the nationalist narration. Its origin is also mysterious. However, there are a few noticeable features about Yadong. I will employ Sun Yatsen's narrative to show that, in comparison with East Asia, Yadong is more of a relational term than a geographical term. Neither unified nor divided, Yadong actors are mutually adaptive and dynamically related. The intangible concept of community is an appropriate metaphor for Yadong. East Asia is contrarily a tangible concept. East Asia policy typically conceives of it as a reshapeable object, geostrategically either unified or divided, depending on the decisions of all relevant actors.

Discursively, as induced from Sun's narratives, the conditions of any Yadong actor could symbolize, indicate, or project the conditions of all of Yadong. Yadong made a quintessential case of post-Chineseness in hindsight. For example, China's backwardness, progress, or victimization was Yadong's at the same time. A reference to East Asia, in comparison, is appropriate for an analysis of how autonomous actors conjunctively shaped its conditions. This contrast suggests that Sun intended that Yadong should connote a prior relation that dissolves binary thinking. It could be a prequel to Asiaticism or pan-Asianism.[3] As for East Asia, he used it where he saw uncertainty due to the autonomous decisions of different actors and wanted to convince them jointly to craft a desired order. In a nutshell, Sun's Yadong was spontaneous, but that of East Asia artificial.

Secondly, Yadong also contrasted with the "Far East" to the extent that it represents a self-perspective rather than an other-perspective taken from a remote angle in Europe, despite their geographical overlapping. The Far East has been a concept that is notoriously colonial (Keay 1997). Thirdly, Yadong incurred a differential self-image from South Asia and thus implies a prior relation or cultural memory of the tributary system (Hamashita 2008). Fourthly, Yadong was initially a frequent reminder of a difference with Europe, the West, or Christianity. Last but not least, Yadong recognizes no superior status of China regarding other actors in the neighborhood. China is ancient, and imperial perhaps, and yet vulnerable. In brief, despite their overlap in terms of geographical scope, Yadong alludes to a resemblance of the fate of being victimized between its members, as opposed to other notions that mainly attend to the loss or rise of agency of individual actors inside as well as outside the territorial scope in question.

Yadong as a Relation

Given the impossibility of defining Yadong, we could nonetheless consider Yadong as a sphere that includes China and its neighbors, where each member resembles China in various different ways. Imagined resemblance manifests in discourse as well as practice. It needs neither scientific nor experiential proof for its subscribers. For strangers in a liberal society to care about each other's natural rights, they already expect each other to behave in a certain way before an event takes place. Consider how people do not behave in the same way in reality. Thus, practical resemblance is somewhat imagined and imagined resemblance can be one-sided. In the Chinese case, it is one-sided to the extent that the Japanese narratives of Yadong perceived different kinds of resemblance to China. A Chinese narrative on Yadong might expect Japanese support for Chinese revolution. A Japanese narrative on Yadong might expect China to succeed in bringing forth a world revolution. A Vietnamese narrative, to further complicate the argument, might expect that Chinese revolution could provide a lesson for Vietnam. In any case, they could all easily empathize with one another due to the pressure and the wish for transformation in the face of Western imperialism. The lack of ideological strings and the relatively casual reference in the reference to Yadong in everyone's narrative has privileged it as an easily accepted term anywhere.

From Sun's messages to his fellow countrymen at the turn of the twentieth century, the major resemblance that made Yadong a meaningful greater relation for its members was exactly their shared fate. This is not to say that culture, society, and history were insignificant in relating them. There, nonetheless, used to be a tributary age, from which they all sprang. The arrival of the West destroyed the tributary system, though. All past tributary actors, high and low, faced the same fate of being transformed, with the noble strata facing the danger of revolution and uprooting the indigenous culture.

Japan was peculiar in this regard due to its fast, effective Westernization and determination to become Western. The first issue of the *Yadong Times*, established in Japan in 1898 to create the grand strategy for Asian revival, set the mission to converge the Chinese and Japanese minds (Jiang 2015). Having been torn between the indigenous and Western systems, the sense of crisis and peril defined the common fate of all sites in Yadong. In the arts, as another example, *Yadong Print and Paint*, which was also published in Japan between 1922 and 1924, included Mongolian camels in its photo coverage. The imagined resemblance of fate rendered the past history and culture practically irrelevant for the Chinese. It was inappropriate to appeal to the obsolete, defeated common past. However, it was this common past that engendered the perception of common peril, to which neither the hierarchy of the suzerain and vassal states, nor the center-periphery imagination of the civilized versus the barbarian, nor Confucianism could ably address and offer solutions any longer. Yadong became a substitute to recap their relations, at least in the narratives of a high number of Chinese and Japanese intellectuals.

The notion of Yadong was not particularly visible before 1895, the year when Japan forced China to yield Taiwan after the latter's losing of the Sino-Japanese War. Ironically, Taiwan's transfer seemed to trigger a stronger sense of common fate among those previously Confucian circles. The discursive practice of Yadong had, since its beginning, been exempt from the sovereign binary that divides the nations into mutually exclusive entities. Sun Yatsen's references to Yadong, for example, always assumed a mass of subaltern population to face the West. For Sun, a nonessential binary existed in either race or civilization, which he intended to combine. Nonetheless, the use of Yadong and East Asia was not always distinguishable until the Japanese expansionists' appropriation of East Asia in an exclusively geostrategic discourse—the Greater East Asian Co-prosperity Sphere. Contrary to the call for self-strengthening and the mutual support of Yadong people, who faced imperialism together, East Asia in this new usage assumed an integrative sphere under the leadership of Japan alone. Power is its concurring discourse. A change in the balance of power could immediately implicate a different geostrategic configuration for Japan's East Asia. Yadong differed sharply to the extent that the shared sense of being victimized was deep, strong, and persistent.

Sun Yatsen's Yadong and East Asia

Yadong consistently adopted a subaltern perspective. Anxiety, uncertainty, and activism characterized the emotional states of Yadong, in addition to a feeling of togetherness bonded by a West-inflicted fate. Sun's first recorded reference to Yadong dates back to 1897, where he saw Yadong about to open up only to be greeted by Europe and the West with jealousy and suppression (亞東閉塞, 甫見開通, 而歐西之妒燄, 已起而相迫; Y. Sun 1989, 2:193–223 [1897]).[4] In the same year also appeared his famous quote that Yadong was a yellow race, ready to cleanse their shame (雪亞東黃種之屈辱; 2:398–99 [1897]). On the eve of the Republican Revolution, Sun incurred Yadong in anticipating mutual support between China and Japan to achieve progress (提攜共圖亞東之進步; 4:157–58 [1911]). After the revolution, Sun lauded the Republic as the first of its kind in the sphere of Yadong (共和之制, 亞東首出; 9:556–57, 564 [1912]), but reminded that Yadong was the name of a sick man (病夫; 9:239–49 [1904]; 6:35 [1912]). In 1912, Republican China seemingly felt self-centric satisfaction at being the first in Yadong (造成一偉大中華民國, 雄視亞東; 3:56 [1912]). In fact, he was ready to praise Japan's openness as a model for Yadong (因開放門戶, 遂成亞東強國; 3:122 [1912]). Sun urged the two countries to strive for joint happiness (共同謀亞東大陸之幸福; 3:141–46 [1912]). In 1919, he praised Thailand for being the other truly independent country in Yadong (亞東一完全獨立國; 1:382–87 [1919]), together with Japan. He recalled, in his final years, that the rise of Japan in Yadong had stopped China from becoming divided (日本崛起於亞東之海隅, 而瓜分之謀又不遂; 5:490–94 [1923]) by the imperialist powers.

A few features stand out. First, the condition of any individual actor informed the conditions of Yadong as a whole. Second, Yadong was a communal as opposed to statist sphere. Third, Japan was of particular importance to Yadong. Fourth, Japan's rise was a blessing to China. Fifth, Yadong was a victim of imperialism. Sixth, it was not about policy. And, seventh, Yadong was racial to a significant extent. One might disagree with Sun's use, but Sun must have believed that his use of Yadong made linguistic sense to his audience. Most importantly, the above nonbinary messages were entirely unclear in the East Asia discourse, according to its usage in Sun's narratives.

East Asia connotes something delicately different for Sun. Its references reflected the implicit tension existing between the national actors pondering on their relationships. The pressure to choose between political integration and mutual estrangement was always between lines as if no shared fate had already constituted both. A quick examination of all of the references to East Asia in Sun's entire career yields a number of syntaxes. The earliest reference expressed a wish for the convergence (同化) of China and Japan (2:193–223 [1897]). This echoed some of the earlier thinkers in Japan during the Meiji and Taisho periods. However, increasing references to East Asia conveyed a wish for or disappointment at Japan's policy on China. This was linked to Japan's expansive tendency, reserved attitude toward Sun's political parties, and lukewarm support for China's strengthening (3:605

[1912]; 3:138 [1913]; 2:496 [1913]; 3:140–41 [1913]; 3:159 [1913]; 4:310–13 [1914]; 4:523 [1917]; 5:57 [1918]; 5:182–84 [1919]; 5:219–21 [1920]; 2:547–48 [1921]; 2:559–60 [1922]; 5:490–94 [1923]; 9:616–17 [1923]; 1:3–12 [1924]; 3:535–42 [1924]; 3:542–45 [1924]; 2:642 [1924]; 5:570–71 [1925]). These conveyed Sun's consistent advice that Japan must support China and Sun's "party of the people" (mindang or 民黨) in order to save East Asia (dongya baoquan or 東亞保全; 2:237–41 [1903]) from the Western division (分割; 2:237–41 [1903]) or invasion. East Asia stood out as a theater or arena where policy consequences for the whole area, either better integration or further weakening, would emerge.

One of the policy consequences was peace in East Asia (和平; 3:137 [1913]: 2:495–96 [1913]; 4:296–97 [1913]; 3:149–50 [1913]; 4:300–301 [1913]; 4:491–92 [1917]; 4:523 [1917]; 4:527–28 [1917]; 4:543 [1917]; 5:6 [1918]; 5:219–21 [1920]; 5:490–94 [1923]; 5:572–73 [1925]), which Sun regarded as essential for the rise of the entire area and the spread of happiness in East Asia (dongya xingfu or 東亞幸福; 3:138 [1913]; 2:496–97 [1913]; 4:294 [1913]; 5:260–61 [1920]).[5] More frequent references were as general as the grand situation (大局), macro trend (大勢), crisis (危局), or common future (前途) (4:155 [1911]; 3:137 [1913]; 3:159 [1913]; 4:310–13 [1914]; 6:147 [1917]; 4:491–92 [1917]; 4:527–28 [1917]; 4:543 [1917]; 5:7–8 [1918]; 5:49–50 [1918]; 5:56–57 [1918]; 2:155–56 [1924]; 5:564 [1924]; 2:628–31 [1924]). Where the anticipated consequences were specific, the references to East Asia pointed to the presumed rise of China as Japan's faithful ally (3:146, 159 [1913]; 4:300–301; 5:7–8 [1918]; 3:226–33 [1921]; 3:281–306 [1921]). Sporadically this had implications for the effect on civilization (wenming or 文明; 2:7–8 [1909]; 4:499–500 [1917]). This last use of East Asia was dubious because civilization had little to do with nation state, policy, or international politics, but nor was civilization about a common fate.

In one particular narrative, East Asia and Yadong coexisted in the same sentence (3:141–46 [1912]), suggesting that Sun consciously distinguished between them. He referred to Yadong when he mentioned that China had joined the pursuit of happiness on the Yadong continent after the Republican Revolution. He directly referred to East Asia when he said that China and Japan were the common owners (主人翁) of East Asia. The distinction in Sun's eyes was revealing. On the whole, Sun's references to Yadong usually recognized all relevant actors, for example, China, Japan, and Thailand, simultaneously with Yadong. His references to East Asia reversely recognized China and Japan as autonomous, national actors whose decisions would influence the fate of East Asia.

Taiwan's Lost Opportunity for Decolonization during the Cold War

The decolonization of Taiwan encountered bottlenecks from the very beginning (Chang and Chiang 2012, 29; Kuang-hsing Chen 2010; Chuang 2016). First of all, it was the Kuomintang that assumed a decolonizing agency after World War II. The indigenous population neither took over governance nor confiscated colonial properties. This was frustrating. The KMT did not, as a noticeable example, destroy the colonial government's building. Rather, it took it over and used it as its own office. For the colonized population, the building symbolized the dominance of an alien regime. For the KMT, it was simply a trophy for the victorious party, which the KMT believed included the colonized Taiwanese, to appropriate.

Second, the Kuomintang expected to see in Taiwan a Chinese population welcoming the return of a Chinese regime. There was no urgency for decolonization or appreciation of the need to demonstrate the regained independence of the colonized population. No indigenous or spontaneous campaign was available to prepare a subject engaging in critical self-reflection, nor did the school curricula challenge the colonial modernity. Rather, the attitude toward the colonial past was one of contempt and ignorance. The colonized population felt no pride after colonialism left, although it adopted equal Chineseness (see chapter 1) under the migrant regime. Some were able to capitalize on equal Chineseness, but others felt alienated from it. In principle, though, nonessentializing relations were unavailable. Under the circumstance of the Civil War, the KMT was battling to display its own Chineseness by having to silence any postcolonial experiences.

Third, there was the Chinese Civil War, so the KMT perceived mainly the threat of Communist agitation rather than nostalgia for colonial modernity among the postcolonial elite and returning soldiers, who remained loyal to the colonial identities. The Kuomintang was impervious to such alienation. Consequently, for the postcolonial elite, the only vehicle for self-respect was to rely on colonial modernity that placed the Kuomintang in an inferior position (M. Lo 2002a; Liao and Wang 2006; Ching 2000; Heylen 2004). The Civil War and colonial modernity created two binaries—the KMT versus the CCP and the modern versus the inferior—that plagued the opportunity for a nonessentializing relation between the colonial Japan, the postcolonial Taiwan, and the motherland China to consolidate on the eve of the Cold War. China could have acted as a potential intermediary in reconciling Japan and Taiwan but, contrarily, became an alien regime in Taiwan as the Civil

War and Cold War broke out. The postcolonial population was concerned with its post-Japaneseness instead.

Ironically, those soldiers, and civilians as well, who were loyal to Japan during the war immediately attained the status of winners by becoming Chinese citizens upon the return of Taiwan to China. This legal conversion exempted most of them from standing trial for war crime. The fact that they joined forces with victorious China partially explained why the Chinese Kuomintang failed to understand how they could remain nostalgic regarding the colonial past. In fact, though, many could recall the loss of the war without the shame or responsibility that veterans in Japan probably experienced. The nostalgia for war among the colonized population, together with the pride of possessing colonial modernity, and the Kuomintang's own migrant perspective that neglected a postcolonial identity, contradicted the mission of decolonization. Decolonization was not a priority on the Kuomintang's agenda anyway.

On the positive side, the Kuomintang provided equal education, economic opportunities, and citizenship to the postcolonial population. On the other, it cooperated with the former colonial Japan to battle against communist China. The return of Yadong spirit, indicated by the recurring references to Yadong in Taiwan before Tokyo shifted diplomatic recognition from Taipei to Beijing and Washington handed Ryukyu to Tokyo, could contribute to the quick melting of the war animosity. The binaries between the colonizer and the colonized, the migrant regime and the postcolonial population, and the two World War II rivals were initially blurred. Nonessentializing decolonization could have succeeded in Taiwan if equal Chineseness provided to the postcolonial population had occurred for long enough to recruit and acknowledge the Japanese contribution to the rebuilding of war-torn China. Nevertheless, through the geostrategic redefinition of East Asia as a divided security zone, the on-going Cold War removed the opportunity for a relational decolonization to take root at various relevant sites.

TAIWAN'S POSTCOLONIAL DISCOURSE

Yadong is an imagined prior relation that renders any member legitimately representative of the community. Accordingly, an allegedly progressive actor and a backward actor were epistemologically equal in their respective reflection of Western imperialism in the fate of Yadong. This imagined common fate constituted the resemblance between them, despite their differing roles in war or in colonial modernity. In the same vein, the Kuomintang, in its capacity as decolonizer, was neither higher nor lower than the colonized population as well as the former colonial power. If the Kuomintang could have faced Japan and Taiwan from an imagined Sino-Yadong perspective, the Kuomintang could have continued to represent China indirectly by representing one aspect of Yadong, which constituted China. However, under Cold War circumstances, this was the perspective of neither the former colony nor the former colonizing nation because they were given no opportunity to unlearn the binaries embedded in colonial modernity.

Due to its obsession with being the legitimate ruler of China, the Kuomintang was the only actor in East Asia that could cross the Cold War binaries between China, Taiwan, and Japan. Decolonization would not be a matter of examining, interrogating, and converting the colonial Japan or the postcolonial Taiwan. It would have instead incurred an imagined common fate that would have held the colonized population together with the defeated colonial power as well as the war-torn China. In consensual reality, the Kuomintang was no China, which was ruled by a communist regime having no relation with the decolonization of Taiwan. For the Kuomintang, the postcolonial population naturally owned moral Chineseness (see chapter 1). The party would have represented meager Chineseness otherwise and lost the legitimacy to claim rulership over the whole of China. Decolonization that assumed the loss of Chineseness of the Taiwanese population under colonial Japan would have been political anathema.

Alternatively, East Asia appears to be an empowering discourse. It allows any actors in search of a distinctive identity to imagine a reconfigured territorial identity to dichotomize the inside from the outside. In fact, East Asia was exactly the discourse that Japan once used to reconfigure the territorial order before and during World War II. With the migrant Kuomintang unsympathetic to the coloniality of the Taiwanese population, the indigenous elite, in quest of respect, easily reconnected their fate to the former colonial power after the Cold War. Throughout 2020, they increasingly and intensively rely on prior colonial relations contrived by Japan to testify to independent statehood from China (Kingston 2018). In fact, a pedagogic reform substitutes the category of East Asia for China in the textbooks on humanities. Aborted decolonization thus led to a revived nostalgia for colonial modernity in Taiwan that is territorially distinctive and more modernized than China.

In addition, the postcolonial elite sided with Japan in opposition to Beijing's People's Republic of China as well as their own Republic of China on Taiwan after coming to power in the 1990s. For example, some assert that Japan owns the Senkaku Islands, which both Beijing and Taipei claim (B. Chen 2017). Some urge Japanese leaders to visit Yasukuni Shrines where war criminals are worshiped. Some even visit the shrines themselves or, alternatively, contribute signed statutes in the capacity of retired president or president-elect (Yamaguchi 2007). Some reinstall Troii to revive Taiwan's Shinto spirit. Some refuse to celebrate the end of World War II, because they argue that they belonged to the loser, qua Japan. Some refuse that Taiwanese comfort women in the Japanese military were all sex slaves, because there must have been a few volunteers (Stolojan 2017; Yao 2018). In 2018, the Ministry of Education in Taiwan formally determined that East Asian history should replace Chinese history in the middle school curriculum. This echoes the discursive dissolution of China into a Greater East Asian Sphere during the early Shōwa period (1926–89).

The Cold War reinforced the complexity of Taiwan's postcolonial conditions. The US containment policy grouped Japan and Taiwan into a geostrategic alliance that further obscured the need for decolonization. Containment restrained the Kuomintang from enforcing its pledge to return to China. Without a chance to return to China, the Kuomintang was, at best, a pseudo-Chinese regime in Taiwan. Containment that targeted a backward communist China coincided with the contriving of an inferior China from the colonial modernity point of view. As long as China was inferior, the pseudo-Chinese Kuomintang would have to be inferior, too (Chih-huei Huang 2003).

As a result, the discourse of East Asia served multiple functions for Taiwan. It provided Taiwan with a distinctive, sited identity. It reinforced the ideological and power divides between Taiwan and China under communism. It prioritized the Cold War over decolonization on Taiwan's political agenda. It perpetuated dependence and hierarchy as the parameters of postcolonial Taiwan in the essentially territorially based ontology of East Asia—a weak actor relative to Japan, China, and the US. Taiwan's sense of inferiority has no exit. East Asia crafts binary. Binary engenders essentialism. Essentialism reproduces inferiority.

COLD WAR INTERVENTION IN TAIWAN'S DECOLONIZATION

East Asia almost always emerges in a geostrategic discourse. In fact, at the beginning of the Cold War, references to East Asia in Taiwan were probably associated with anti-communism, directly as well as indirectly. Consider 1951, for example. The first reference that appeared on the *United Daily* data bank (http://udndata.com/ndapp/Index) associated East Asia with "the world's free market" (September 16, 1951, p. 5), the second cautioned against the "Soviet influences" in the area (September, 17, 1951, p. 2), and the third urged Japan to "sign a peace treaty" with the Kuomintang China (September 19, 1951, p. 2). In fact, in the entire year, references to East Asia were predominantly associated with the theme of anti-communism. A number of exceptions involved either a narrative on the realignment of Taiwan with Japan economically or a warning against the notorious Japanese war slogan of the Greater East Asian Sphere. As the Cold War proceeded, the national-security oriented Institute of East Asian Studies came into being in 1968. Its only mission used to be training China experts that served the intelligence sectors. East Asia was increasingly a self/other discourse to face communist China.

Such a discourse demoralized decolonization in various ways. It realigned two war rivals, the Kuomintang and the Japanese conservatives, which made decolonization too embarrassing for them to be appropriate. Without decolonization, the tension between the Kuomintang's war memory and the postcolonial nostalgia for the colonial modernity accrued. Japanese right-wing intellectuals looked to Taiwan's reviving colonial sensibilities for post-Japanese inspiration (Y. Hwang 2010). The postcolonial Taiwanese elite and contemporary Japanese right-wing developed a mutual bond. In the twenty-first century, the substitution of East Asia for China in Taiwan's school curriculum recollects the same colonial project that dissolved China into regenerable objects during World War II. China is no longer even a given ontological category. Rather, a self-centrist Taiwanese identity has powerfully emerged to reduce China to an outsider, at best owning policy Chineseness (see further in chapters 5 and 6).

Earlier during the Cold War, for the Kuomintang, Yadong continued to serve as a connecting discourse among the actors, presumably through sharing a prior fate of being dominated by the West and currently threatened by communism. Yadong presumably included actors of various kinds, at various levels, and in various networks. Consider the basketball tournaments—Sino-US Military Basketball Contest of the Yadong Region (亞東區中美軍事籃球錦標賽)—that continued for seven years between the Taiwanese and American troops, including those stationed in Korea, Japan, Ryukyu, Taiwan, Vietnam, and the Philippines on the guest side and Army, Navy, Air Force, and Quartermaster teams on the host side. The tournament was finally terminated upon Japan's recognition of the PRC and the return of Ryukyu to Japan in the early 1970s. The tournament was noteworthy because (1) it indirectly reflected the Yadong sense of a common fate of being dominated by the US qua the West; (2) there was a taste of nationality but the games were not national in the sense of the typical Yadong custom of complicating the identities of the teams, crossing the colonial, the Western, and the colonized boundaries; (3) their practical interactions were internal rather than involving the othering of an external communist target; and (4) equal relationships existed between teams from very different constitutions, including the dominant West that represented other Yadong actors vicariously and simultaneously.

Japanese Yadong thinkers struggled to transcend the Cold War divide, too. The East Asian Friendship Association, which actually used Yadong in the title as a Han character, emerged in 1949, initially under the name of the South China Club. The second name it adopted in 1970 was the Yadong Industrial and Business Association. Yadong likewise echoed the history of the Kuomintang. The Kuomintang included Yadong in the title of the consular organization—the East Asian Relations Association (in English)—which succeeded the official embassy after Tokyo recognized Beijing and severed diplomatic relations with Taipei. The association changed its name to the Taiwan-Japan Relations Association in 2017, ahead of and along with the use of East Asia to replace China in the history textbooks of high school, to signal the equal sovereign status between Taiwan, China, and Japan. This ended any hope for decolonization in Taiwan but extended the colonial hierarchy and need for dependence.

Yadong was almost ignored in the *United Daily* data bank after the mid-1970s, except in the comments of the consular office, while the references to East Asia greatly increased. It was the Cold War that engendered the discursive consequence of keeping the double binaries under East Asia—that of communism versus anti-communism and that between national security nations. These constitute the foundation for re-incurring colonial modernity to dichotomize inferior China and modernized Taiwan. The Cold War discourse easily took advantage of the notion of East Asia as a shapable object that rendered decolonization an irrelevant responsibility for both the colonizing and the postcolonial actors. The use of Yadong throughout 2017 in the name of Taiwan's consular agency in Japan was nonetheless a symbol of solidarity between the two, who no longer maintained a diplomatic relationship. However, this solidarity was futile, as, practically, it only meant common caution against a potential China threat. Yadong could not sustain such a confrontational connotation. It was eventually replaced by "Taipei" in the new name of the agency in 2017. This happened when Tokyo was ready to restore its broken relationship with China, so maintaining Taiwan's anti-China stance appeared necessary. In short, the East Asia discourse has completely overshadowed Yadong for the former colonial Japan and the postcolonial Taiwan in practice.

Conclusion

Decolonization would have a better chance under Yadong, but the Cold War had imposed East Asia. The notion of East Asia provided multiple self-centric lenses for decolonization to fail. Amid the atmosphere of binary thinking that reproduces dominance and inferiority, improvised resemblance in terms of some post-identities between Taiwan, Japan, and China yields to strategic essentialism. In practice, therefore, the notion hindered decolonization. Decolonization requires a discourse that neither reproduces the colonial relations nor commits binary thinking. The binary thinking disallows mutual sympathy. A relational discourse of a greater scope to hold the former colonies and former colonial powers is crucial to crafting a decolonization agenda that is exempt from power as well as identity struggle. This chapter proposes an epistemological lens to substitute discourse as a relation for discourse as power. It questions the adoption of strategic essentialism to resist the continuing dominance of past colonialism. A relational discourse obliges the colonial and postcolonial to improvise a resemblance between them and feel for each other in their common, albeit unequally born, fate.

Yadong, as opposed to East Asia, exemplified such a discourse. Despite their almost identical literal meaning, the practical uses of the two terms meant that they reflected very different relations. Yadong connoted a community consciousness with its various actors sharing the same fate of being victimized by Western imperialism or colonialism. Experiences of victimization would have constituted a hybrid kind of Chineseness of postcolonial Taiwan. However, East Asia acquired geostrategic rationality, informed by the binary discourse of state sovereignty or anti-communism. Taiwan's decolonization could not appeal to the Yadong relations because the outbreak of the Cold War re-incurred East Asia as the dominant discourse. The discourse of East Asia compelled its actors to choose between integration and division. The Cold War further pushed Taiwan to contrast, confront, and estrange China and rely exclusively on the US and Japan. Japanese colonial modernity remained superior for postcolonial Taiwan while their common fate in a greater sphere had no foundation at all under the Cold War situation.

Chapter 4

Beyond Fundamentalist Faith

Cultural Nationalism

Amid the rise of religious tension in the twenty-first century, nationalist leaders and fundamentalist activists rely on and employ religious resources willingly and without hesitation. However, this does not seem to reflect developments in the PRC, despite CCP leaders likewise resorting to Chinese nationalism in their attempts to reinforce the legitimacy of CCP rule. By complicating the categories of "China," the "Chinese," and "Chineseness," chapter 4 aims to produce a trivializing analysis of the role of religion in the reconstruction of cultural as well as political nationalism in China. It shows that, when moving out of bilateral and multilateral relations, China cannot exist autonomously in the form of national self without its scope and constituents being disputed, reconstructed, or even denied. In a nutshell, post-Chineseness is inside of any religious version of China. China can only be post-Chinas.

Despite Marxism, the Communist Party state of China has witnessed a revival of religion (I. Johnson 2017; F. Yang 2011; Marsh 2011). Even President Xi Jinping has resorted to Buddhist wisdom, along with Confucianism as a practical religion, in his public speeches. Many Chinese leaders have been known for their faith since the beginning of the Republic (Katz 2014). For example, Chiang Kai-shek and former president of the Republic of China Lee Teng-hui in Taiwan were dedicated Christians and consistently nationalist leaders. Chiang and Xi are apparently Chinese nationalists, and Lee is a determined Taiwanese nationalist. Nevertheless, religious beliefs have not intervened in the formation of their nationalist sensibilities, given the largely secular inclination of the Chinese population compared with the ethnically hybrid Indians (Veer 2013). To that extent, the role of religion in the Chinese politics of nationalism is different (Faries 2010; Bovingdon 2010; Katz and Rubinstein 2003). To say the least, the nationalist leadership did not intend to relate to religion beyond the level of self-discipline.

Chapter 4 regards religions mainly as faith. Abiding by certain sacred texts, religious nationalism is conceived as *the belief in a presumably common faith in order to build, reproduce, or protect an imagined nation.* Religious nationalism has not been a common practice in either historical or contemporary China, though. Consider Chinese religions as *supernatural beliefs and related practices.* Their practical aspect tends to reinforce those secular purposes coming outside of religious values and practices instead of deriving from the gospel or apocalypse (Y. Zhao 2013). Thus, religion constitutes Chinese selfhood in two mundane ways. First, religion provides an imagined relationship between believers and their gods, as if gods are obliged to bless the believers who worship them (Sutton 2003). Religiosity distinguishes the believers from others mainly sociologically. Second, religion reminds and urges self-sacrifice and self-discipline at the individual level to sustain the virtue of perseverance, devotion, and benevolence in a relational habitus that encompasses believers (J. Yu 2012; Rošker 2016; Tang 2016; Keenan 2011).

Thus, Chinese religions are neither inevitably nationalist nor provide outright resistance to nationalism projects. They promote a peculiar kind of cultural nationalism, shared by a population beyond any definitive territorial scope or, where territoriality prevails, motivate a kind of soft resistance to an encountered and presumably stronger rival via the sporadic construction of an unyielding volition for some and a feat of endurance for others. Equally importantly, cultural nationalism in China is not entirely compatible with statist nationalism embedded in territoriality.

This chapter tackles how the improvisational character of post-Chineseness informs the cultural function of Chinese religions and, as a result, the ineffectiveness of statist nationalism in the religious sphere. As defined in the previous chapters, post-Chineseness embodies the processes of relating between those who are considered Chinese. Whether or not the target group of connection/reconnection acknowledges its Chinese trait is a different matter. Ancestor worship, for a noticeable example, is a trait usually regarded as a Chinese practice, but Chinese overseas who practice it may not identify with themselves being Chinese, despite others' designation. Therefore, post-Chineseness can be either reciprocal or unilateral. Cultural nationalism, here, refers to *the process of reconnecting or networking between populations by incurring the imagined sharing of the same cultural practice,* which, in the religious realm, includes the worship of ancestors, Buddha, Jesus, or earthly Gods. Cultural nationalism is not the consequences of the common faith, though. The subscription to the same faith serves to reinforce the sense of being related, but this hardly necessitates nationalism. Rather, shared faith can similarly reinforce other existing relationships, for example, family, political party, school, project, and so on, embedded in prior cultural practices of Confucianism, partisanship, scholarship, and professionalism respectively.

As populations at different sites improvise their connection or disconnection differently, post-Chineseness enacts differing social networks that engender wide-ranging cultural nationalism for different constituencies, which resemble Wittgenstein's (1986, 31) notion of family resemblance that defies any definitive scope. Post-Chineseness is, in other words, about romanticization of one's belonging (or aversion) to a collective identity that likewise inspires many others. As with the bilateral case of Sino-Pakistani relations and the multilateral case of Yadong, post-Chineseness can improvise various kinds of relationships between members and their nation. Given the multireligious traditions of Chinese culture, Chinese religious nationalism enables a self-relation for its members to embrace a kind of Chineseness being ontologically unquestionable and yet epistemologically undefinable, culturally unproductive, or socially unstable. The coexistence of multiple religions in the Chinese context individualizes cultural nationalism for believers. It allows them to become or remain related while preserving their own self-identity. Their supernatural world reinforces existing relationality as well as inspires new practices.

Cultural Nationalism as the Purpose of Post-Chineseness

Post-Chineseness, as the embodiment of connection between self-recognized and other-designated Chinese groups, can rely on religious resources. Chapter 4 discusses three of these religious resources; namely, Buddhism,

Table 4.1. The Cultural Nationalism of Post-Chineseness

Relationality \ Purpose	Pure	Hybrid
Temporal	Cultural Chineseness Religion as culture	Cosmopolitan Chineseness Religion as cross-culture
Spatial	Political Chineseness Religion as statehood/ethnicity	Postmodern Chineseness Religion as sitedness

Source: author

Christianity, and Confucianism (examples of folk religions will be briefly mentioned where relevant). After merging and revision of the post-Chinese categories in earlier chapters, a 2×2 table comes forth. On the purposes of networking through a cultural resource, there can be (1) discovering a shared Chinese trait of another Chinese group, that is, the quest for purity, or (2) exploring the potential of a non-Chinese group to acquire a Chinese trait, that is, the quest for hybridity. (Alert readers may have noted that this second purpose combines the two categories of the in-between group and the out-group, which the previous chapters separate.) Depending on one's self-identity, constituted either by an imagined national being as in political nationalism to reproduce a definitive scope or by a process of constantly becoming as in cultural nationalism to transcend a definite scope, one can identify one's own relationality as constituted by (1) spatiality defined by a physical scope, such as a body, a kin network, a site, a security community, a tax regime, or a sovereign border, or (2) temporality embedded in an evolutionary trajectory, such as a common origin, an overlapped historiography, a joint civilization, or a shared cultural identification.[1]

Cultural Chineseness in a Multireligious State

Cultural Chineseness reflects a nonterritorial national identity that supports an imagined resemblance among the audience and worshipers (Kuehn, Louie, and Pomfret 2014). Intended maneuvering of cultural symbols to connect the audience does not necessarily contribute to the nationalist consciousness, whereas unintended cultural sharing might (Katzenstein 2012a; Louie 2004). The following discussion on cultural nationalism attends to the process of producing and enhancing the conscious resemblance of a population. Thus, cultural nationalism can either reinforce an extant nonterritorial national identity or produce a relationship between those not already constituted by a collective identity. For a population of multiple religions, an agency to craft imagined resemblance on behalf of the imagined cultural nation can rely on religious beliefs and transcend borders and ethnicities. In this regard, an annual ritual presided by the president in Taiwan to worship Confucius, for example, reproduces a romanticized civilization to which all Chinese subscribe. It has been only proper for the president to refrain from presiding after Taiwan determines to pursue a non-Chinese national identity.

The nuances of religious practices remind and distinguish between groups (Clayton 2010). Religious practices that have no recorded historical origins make a consensual origin that is easily imagined by appealing to a sacred text, a school or scholar, a god, or a site, which constitute and connect contemporary disciples (Thurman 2011). The incurrence of a religious belief or practice embedded in imagined historiography to reconnect with other Chinese overcomes the obsession with territorial Chineseness. Such reconnection transcends territorial borders (Yao and Zhao 2010). Cultural nationalism can pose a challenge to the political leadership wherever its scope does not overlap with political Chineseness to include and exclude certain populations and can be embarrassing for the connected group who politically owns a separate citizenship. For example, Taiwan's Genghis Khan worship can be embarrassing to Mongolians who see no shared kin with the Han Chinese in Taiwan.

Reconnections for the sake of the inclusion or exclusion of the targeted groups are all about one's agency of reimagining and reconstituting one's own relationality (Shih 2015). Therefore, reconnection is strategic in consequence, if not by nature. Goddess Mazu worship, for example, can be a cultural strategy for the Chinese authorities on China's southeast coast to engender a resemblance to Taiwanese believers in order for their relationship to become conducive to a sense of shared Chineseness (Yang 2008).

Political Chineseness in a Multireligious State

Within a multireligious scope of territory, religious beliefs that support political nationalism, either in terms of statist or ethnic identity, are difficult to attain because disciples inevitably spread across borders, which undergird a kind of contemporary political membership that is usually rendered irrelevant by religious connection. Instead, religious beliefs inspire by their peculiar manner of instilling devotion, concentration, and determination into individual leadership. Political Chineseness in religion is only relevant where leaders that subscribe to political nationalism acquire strength from their conviction that they have the support of the supernatural spirit. Religious inspiration takes place at the agential level, rather than the communal or national level, but the members of the community can understand leaders' self-empowerment because they share certain prior cultural and historical relations. For example, Xi Jinping's Buddhist encounter earlier in his life can be an appreciable story despite no one else having had the same experience. Thus, the individual faith of leaders and organizations disregards mundane concerns in the pursuit of their own political nationalism that does not arise directly from religious beliefs. Rather, the perseverance revealed in their pursuit benefits from their faith in God (Formicola and Morken 2001).

Nationalism and religion are two relational trajectories in a multireligions condition. Even so, any faith leader can derive strength from her religion. Leaders of different faiths can cooperate to pursue or resist Chinese nationalism not because their religious beliefs are identical but because a shared political identity with Chineseness or counter-Chineseness connects them. Religious faiths are conducive to their post-Chinese connection only indirectly, because they provide self-confidence in whichever political ideology they choose (e.g., Cagle 2016; Ahmad 2015). Two relational effects are noticeable. A demonstration effect is revealed as disciples subscribing to the same religious belief acquire a political mission to actualize the strength of their faith. A mobilization effect exists as politically neutral disciples elsewhere may come to assist because of religious brotherhood/sisterhood. One example of this is the leaders of the Boxers in the late Qing period who inspired anti-foreign nationalism through the use of Daoist superstition. In this regard, the faith leadership provided by religious organizations is an indirect and yet plausible source of nationalism (Cismas 2014).

Cosmopolitan Chineseness in a Multireligious State

A peculiar but usually overlooked religious practice that can engender Chineseness is about cosmopolitan Chineseness. Cosmopolitan Chineseness emerges in the reconnection consented to by putative out-group individuals who seek reconstitution of their selves through owning Chineseness. Relying on religious resources to connect with others can reconstitute the individual identity to the effect of engendering relations across fixed boundaries (Yeh 2000). This cosmopolitan Chineseness reflects the pursuit of self-fulfillment at the individual level. Religious resources are conducive to bridging politically and culturally distinctive groups. Consider the Society of Jesus. Bridging is necessarily the choice of individual Jesuits seeking transcendence. Encountered groups imagine a resemblance to each other through the media of religious agency of the Jesuit sinologists, who introduce and translate cultural meanings that are incomprehensible or even unnoticeable without the religious media. Cultural exchanges through religious means can be either threatening due to their, at times, obscuring effect on the orthodox positions or relaxing due to their lack of an immediate or specific political intention.

For noticeable examples, post-Chineseness spread to Europe through the abovementioned media of the Christian missionary, to South Asia through the media of Buddhism, and, in the twenty-first century, through the establishment of the Confucius Institute, to the younger generation everywhere.

Even where a Western believer in Daoist shamanism is attracted to a spiritual medium in another Chinese society, a peculiar kind of cosmopolitan Chineseness can ironically emerge to reflect connectedness. Thus, the religious reconnection between Chinese and non-Chinese groups is more effective with an agency that is culturally familiar with both sides (Yu Liu 2015). The other groups, who became more comfortable with Chineseness, tolerate the first few members who begin to appreciate, enjoy, and own Chineseness to make the scope of Chineseness truly open-ended.

Postmodern Chineseness in a Multireligious State

Culturally for this book, postmodern Chineseness is about the reconnection of individuals at a conventional site who evoke religious resources to improvise and reproduce resemblance among themselves. Reconnection through the mutual recognition of a shared religious practice at a certain site, amid the appreciation of some dubious common Chineseness, informs the pursuit of nuanced self-identification. This indicates improvisation of solidarity between members of a kind of support group. For example, a Zen group meeting and mediating together in a remote mountain village can develop solidarity to support its members each in their own real-life pursuit. These nuanced pursuits can either embrace a variety of individualized claims of each being differently Chinese or facilitate a sited ethnicity that conveniently performs being different collectively. For example, the Kokang people in Myanmar that have received no stable recognition in any modern system have found in Confucianism a self-sustaining spirit.

The ethnic practice of religion that constitutes individual identities enables a claim to distinction from others. To resist religious synchronization across sites, the actors of sited identities view those religious resources that encompass the encountered groups with suspicion. This explains the failure of Chinese Buddhist relic diplomacy in Myanmar or Sri Lanka, where the population distinguishes the supernatural from the political. In contrast, to construct a sited distinction, the religious resources are open-ended, since all sites can appropriate these resources in their own ways, resulting in boundary spanning (Carlson 2009). A sited religious identity, such as Islam in a county of Hunan far away from Xingjiang, exists in postmodern Chineseness as a condition of curiosity toward exotic differences (Israeli 2007), as opposed to national unity. Ironically, the purpose of reconnection in the postmodern context is to expound on how and why reconnection cannot and should not be integrated or assimilated.

The practice of postmodern Chineseness occasionally risks overemphasizing the differences embedded in territoriality. For example, Tudigong (Lord of the Soil) worship, which cannot be shared outside its site, always accepts outsiders passing through to mimic indigenous worship. Thus, postmodern Chinese reconnection fulfills the function of differentiating outside Chinese without resorting to causing estrangement. Therefore, legitimate othering aims at reciprocal recognition as opposed to the orientalist construction of an inferior other. The appropriation of the post-Chinese nuances on a particular site can proceed through political, economic, or cultural vehicles, depending on what composes the agency for difference (Hirono 2008). Thus, an economic agency consumes religious resources to meet the desire for individuality and subjectivity to resist developmentalism, growth, or mercantilism; a political agency mobilizes religious resources to reproduce sited consciousness as a way to resist war in general and invasion in particular; and a cultural agency appropriates religious resources to inspire following to resist discrimination.

Post-Chinese Buddhism

Historically, Buddhism has assisted its followers in various incompatible ways. In areas neighboring China, Buddhism has been the only religion that enabled its followers to resist powerfully the suppression of external and internal controls (Harris 2013; Benn 2007). Examples include the resistance by the Vietnamese, Cambodian, and Burmese to the Confucian court of Vietnam, the Chinese invasion, and the American puppet regime in Saigon during the Cold War. Buddhism has attained emperorship in history but has rarely been devoted to nationalism. Buddhism assists in the

Table 4.2. Buddhist Mechanisms of Post-Chineseness

Purpose / Relationality	Pure	Hybrid
Temporal	Cultural Buddhism Master Hsing Yun	Cosmopolitan Buddhism Suma Ching Hai
Spatial	Political Buddhism Master Taixu	Postmodern Buddhism Buddhist tourism

Source: author

Confucian adoption of modernity by providing the theme of transcendence so that, philosophically, modernity does not reduce Confucianism to sheer materialism in its resistance against Western imperialism. Similar to Confucianism, Buddhism is not conducive to nationalism despite its occasional rescue of Chinese nationality. No historical experiences in China have tied Buddhism to a particular nationalist position (Tan 2015; Sen 2003). Circumstantial passion and sympathy for the masses can nevertheless inspire Buddhist intervention.

Cultural Chineseness and Buddhism

Chinese Buddhism is less territorially or ethnically bound than in Sri Lanka, Myanmar, or Thailand. Buddhism neither owns nor defines Chineseness, and, today, PRC China does not own Buddhism. Chinese Buddhist priests are concerned with Chinese followers and understand their conditions better, as also applies to Tibetan priests and their Tibetan followers. Nevertheless, Tibetan Buddhism that enhances ethnic consciousness is not territorially bound (Smeyer Yü 2014). Rather, Tibetan Buddhism is culturally ethnic (Goldstein and Kapstein 1998). In addition, a string of secularized humanist Buddhism (人間佛教) has emerged from Taiwan and has now spread all over the world, including within Chinese communities everywhere. Disciples actively spread blessings and provide benevolence regardless of their identity. A major leader, Hsin-yun (1927–), has been keenly aware of the reality that, although his current base and strength arise from the devoted Chinese community in Taiwan, the continuous growth of Buddhism lies in the return of Buddhism to mainland China. Thus, the future of Chinese communities staying together harmoniously in politics becomes a religious mission.

Buddhism across Chinese communities, for example, the circulation of Buddha statues/images/representations to different sites, helps Chinese across different borders to reconnect and engenders a pressure on politics to refrain from mutual estrangement. Hsin-yun is particularly worried that the pro-independence leadership of Taiwanese nationalism will hinder Buddhism's prospects by inhibiting its quest for a reconstituted Chineseness of a broader scope.

Political Chineseness and Buddhism

During national crises, history shows that followers of Buddhism can always join forces with other fellow patriots to defend the nation, even to the extent of committing "compassionate killing" (X. Yu 2011; Walton and Hayward 2014). Historically, Buddhist interventions in national defense took place in Korea, China, Japan, Vietnam, and contemporary Tibet (Woeser 2016). Taiwanese Buddhism has been associated with Taiwanese and Chinese nationalism. A well-known modern example in China was Master Taixu (1890–1947), who supported the anti-Japanese war. He was able to inspire his followers to demand reform.

Dispensing benevolence to demonstrate transcendence over mundane politics is conducive to the formation of a reciprocal relationship between the givers and receivers (Pittman 2001). Political Buddhism possesses a privileged position that allows it to take advantage of its apolitical image and selfless sacrifice if it chooses to support nationalism (Tikhonov and Brekke 2013). The purpose of Political Buddhism is either to overcome the subnationalism of a differently religious ethnicity, as in the case of Sri Lanka and Myanmar, or resist suppression, as in the case of Tibet. Political Buddhism is presumably transient and yet hinders reconnection with differently religious Chinese.

Cosmopolitan Chineseness and Buddhism

Buddhism can spread around the world to develop new worshipers because its transcendent views of the world inspire new subscribers who seek alternatives to the promise of modernity (Crook 2012; Guruge 2005). People outside the Asian Buddhist circles do not usually become Buddhists through being the providers or receivers of benevolence. They become followers to contemplate or listen to Buddhist wisdom, which leads to an image of this world that is unreliable and transient and in which mundane interests cease to provide incentives. One well-received nun, Master Ching Hai (1950–), who comes originally from a Vietnamese community, uses different languages with different audiences in the West and explains the wisdom of simple zen in a straightforward manner so that the audience will be enlightened and released from the burden of mundane life (Ching Hai 2011). Ching Hai has a colorful career, thought, and outlook, which stand in sharp contrast to simplicity. Consistently, her preaching is intentionally cosmopolitan in nature. Her disciples in the West seek her advice individually, as opposed to her benevolence extended to a worshiper of Chinese societies. The themes embedded in the imagined afterworld that they share with their Chinese followers inform their post-Chineseness.

Postmodern Chineseness and Buddhism

The representation of Chineseness through Buddhism is common in China wherever historical Buddhist temples exist. Given that praying and tourism in Buddhist temples have flourished, Western and Chinese worshippers frequently mingle with tourists (Chau 2008; Granoff and Shinohara 2005). Each temple usually has its own glorious history. Tourist trips to China would be incomplete without visiting at least one characteristic temple (Shepherd 2013). However, Taiwanese temples are usually not historical but postmodern, as they are the earliest to adopt electronic technology, such as laser beams during family funerals and to attract tourists' interest. Tourism has become so powerful in Chinese Buddhism that worshipers complain that tourism has reduced Buddhism to no more than an economic instrument. In addition to the commodification of Buddhism is Xi Jingping's habit of citing Buddhist sayings. For example, Xi urges the Communist cadres to look beyond mundane interests in their service to the nation (Lim and Blanchard 2013). Communism and capitalism coexist in the sense that Buddhism is their common retreat. In other words, Buddhism can become an easily consumable representation that provides an otherwise dry position with a characteristic identity so that one remains connected in one's secular Chineseness shared by all benevolence-seekers.

Post-Chinese Christianity

Judging from the fact that Anson Burlingame (1820–70), the first Chinese ambassador to Europe, was an American priest, it can be argued that Christianity constituted at least part of the Chinese image. Robert Hart, an Irish Christian who worked for the Qing dynasty for half a century, single-handedly built the Chinese custom system and composed what John King Fairbank called the Manchu–Han–West synergy. The Church joined imperialism to rob Chinese land and wealth and topple the Qing Empire but intervened in the subsequent nation-building. China was the single most important nation to be saved in the practices of the American churches. For example, Chiang Kai-shek's renaissance movement evolved into a Christian campaign under the supervision of Mme Chiang, who came from a Christian family. Her baptized elder sister, Song Qingling, was the only woman who became a member of the national leadership of the People's

Table 4.3. Christian Mechanisms of Post-Chineseness

Relationality \ Purpose	Pure	Hybrid
Temporal	Cultural Christianity Chiang Kai-shek	Cosmopolitan Christianity The Jesuit sinologists
Spatial	Political Christianity The Taiwan Presbyterians	Postmodern Christianity Three-Self Patriotic Church

Source: author

Republic of China. Despite the devastating interlude during the Cultural Revolution, more Chinese have been converted in the twenty-first century, thereby making China a plausible candidate for being the largest Christian state in the world (Stark and Wang 2015). However, for the Chinese, Christianity as a religious identity is not spontaneously a cultural identity, because Christianity is not intended to unite Chinese. Rather, Christianity constitutes individuality more than collectivity (Madsen 1998). Exempt from the pressure of choosing a collective identity for China, Christianity is an uneasy, yet accessible resource for believers to transcend the political rivalry between Chinese communities plagued by the politics of identity and ease post-Chinese reconnection wherever a wish to reconnect exists (Fulton 2015).

CULTURAL CHINESENESS AND CHRISTIANITY

Although Christianity is not, in itself, a national identity for the Chinese, Chinese political rivals that subscribe to Christianity can set aside their struggle against each other in the context of a common faith in God, hence constituting a quasi-cultural group. It can support a collective identity that is broader than the nation state. For example, Chiang Kai-shek was able to keep his faith in a greater Chinese nation that has never been unified since the Republican Revolution. Chiang's conviction in the Chinese nation was not only sustained by historical experiences, but also by the soul he acquired through the Church that supported him throughout (Kyounghan 2009). His scope of the nation extended far beyond territorial China. From an imagined string of successions embedded in the spirit of the Confucian Dao, Chiang considered himself the latest carrier of a line that could be traced back to the emperors Yao and Shun of primordial time. This half-racial, half-philosophical perspective has little to do with

Christianity as a religion (J. Taylor 2011); however, Christianity supported Chiang to overcome spiritually the political failure and continue believing in his moral appeal to every Chinese person in the world (C. Wang 2014). To that extent, Christianity is more a psychological than a cultural base to withstand his cultural nationalism.

Political Chineseness and Christianity

Creating nationalist consciousness out of religion, as is the case in Catholic Poland, is unfamiliar to China (Zubrzycki 2006). Similar to the psychological strength required to make cultural Chineseness a convincing project for Chiang, political nationalism can acquire strength from the faith in God to drive a realistically questionable project of nationalism. Political nationalism is most clear in the case of the Presbyterian Church in Taiwan (see further in chapter 10), which has been an ardent advocate of Taiwan's independence and Taiwanese nationalism (Coe 1980). Nevertheless, another separate Presbyterian Church division in Taiwan supports a strong reconnection with the Chinese mainland, which indicates that the church is able to reduce the political tension among its politically divided followers in Taiwan (V. Hsu 2016). Moreover, the pro-independence Taiwanese Presbyterians continue to interact with Chinese Presbyterians in their common world organizational frame, which indicates that the church can contain the political discord. Although the political reality disallows the quest for the statehood of Taiwan to succeed, Taiwanese Presbyterians could register their volition in the spirit of resistance that is embedded in the Presbyterian tradition (Coe 1993).

Cosmopolitan Chineseness and Christianity

Jesuit sinologists, who were able to interpret China and the West for each other, best illustrate cosmopolitan Christianity. The Churches retreated from China on the eve of the Communist Revolution. Many stayed in Hong Kong. They further withdrew in the face of the coming return of Hong Kong to China and moved to Taiwan (Morrissey 2008). The Jesuit fathers who were simultaneously trained sinologists never stopped learning about Chinese culture and politics. A notable example is their publication of *China News Analysis*, which used to rank as one of the most consulted intelligence works for Chinese experts globally (Heyndrickx 2005). Their interpretation of events in China was derived from their observations of local affairs and cultural perspectives engrossed in their sinological training (Domes 1990).

Their professional dedication was intellectually prepared under the church system of pedagogy and financially sponsored by the church. Thus, they could serve as cultural translators between China and the world. Their staunch anti-communist beliefs, propagated by the church, made them all determined researchers (Lin and Shih 2018). Cosmopolitan Christianity aimed to integrate Chineseness and Christianity.[2] Pope Francis, the first Jesuit pope, has worked steadily toward mutual recognition between the Vatican and the People's Republic of China.

Postmodern Chineseness and Christianity

The nationalization of Christianity has been the official line since the Communist Party came to power in 1949. The subsequent reorganization of the churches in China resulted in the establishment of the Three-Self Patriotic Movement Church (i.e., self-govern, self-support, and self-preach) in China, which emphasizes the independence of Chinese Christians from the influence of the pope. The Communist Party tolerated only patriotic Christians. Thus, notwithstanding the Marxist aversion to religion, church dogma and pedagogy were still permitted. Coexisting, alternative house/family churches were ostensibly illegal but still realistically practiced (Lian 2010). With the end of the Cultural Revolution and the revival of folk religions, family churches reemerged strongly, particularly following the spread of urbanization (J. Kang 2016). Patriotic and house churches can operate only within China, because patriotism refers exclusively to Chinese patriotism (Entwistle 2016; Shan 2012). Nevertheless, the Vatican and international churches outside China actively seek a reconnection with any Chinese Christians inside it (Baugus 2014; Hirono 2008). Such a reconnection compels the connection seekers to reassess how they would accommodate Chinese patriotism to constitute Christianity as they fulfill their duty as workers on behalf of God. By contrast, Chinese churches must build their strategies on the newly acquired international relationality in the process of reconstituting Chinese Christianity.

Post-Chinese Confucianism

Confucianism has inspired two particular modes of thought that can indirectly contribute to Chinese nationalism; namely, unification and self-strengthening.[3] Unification specifically refers to those splinter regimes or lost lands that subscribe to Confucianism that is embedded in imagined kinship;

thus, it is usually oriented toward a certain kind of poetic territoriality (Han 2011; J. Chan 2001; C. Hsu 1991). Moreover, kinship is dubious because the common practices of mixed blood and political marriage disallow any definitive scope. Imagined resemblance exists because of the myth of common ancestors enacted by the ritual of ancestor worship that, together with the national worship of heaven and sagehood, allows Confucianism to be categorized as a religion (R. Taylor 1990). If successful, then the practice of mixed blood requires no resistance to alien regimes, whose leaders could adopt ancestor worship through cultural assimilation. A highly motivated leadership can engage in self-strengthening to restore an allegedly authentic Confucian regime (Roetz 1993, 160–65). In the twenty-first century, PRC neo-Confucianists even advocate a revival of the Confucian state. Although self-strengthening can make an ethical inspiration to the effect of fighting alien invaders, cultural mingling remains a viable strength of Confucianism. The string of Confucian nationalism continued on both tracks of value—assimilation and self-strengthening.

Cultural Chineseness and Confucianism

Confucianism most vividly contributes to contemporary cultural nationalism in sinological studies (Makeham 2008), particularly among Southeast Asian Chinese intellectuals. Veteran Chinese Southeast Asian scholars describe the scholarship as "living sinology" (Shih 2014a). A typical sinological agenda covers classic humanities during the millennia or dynastic China; thus, Southeast Asian sinologists endeavor to record the evolving strings of classic humanities in the writings of the migrant scholars of the Chinese diaspora. Their sinology continues to live and develop in sharp contrast to the lifeless classics, on which

Table 4.4. Confucian Mechanisms of Post-Chineseness

Purpose / Relationality	Pure	Hybrid
Temporal	Cultural Confucianism SE Asian living sinology	Cosmopolitan Confucianism Confucius Institute
Spatial	Political Confucianism Xi Jinping	Postmodern Confucianism East Asian Confucianism

Source: author

sinologists elsewhere work. A genealogy that leads to the contemporary scholarship establishes a sense of longevity and infinity of Chineseness that enhances the self-respect of the Chinese population facing the indigenous Southeast Asian populations that continue to practice ethnic division. Living sinology reconnects the Southeast Asian Chinese population to a dubious China but distinguishes itself through its imagined living characteristics. Living sinology can enable a nuanced claim to the distinction of indigenous Chineseness from China and can alternatively inspire the population to embrace various routes of re-Sinicization during the rise of China (Hau 2014).

Political Chineseness and Confucianism

Given that Confucianism is historically alienated from territoriality, its contribution to political nationalism is, at best, ambiguous. During the crisis of modernization, Confucianism has been a major target for blame. One may trace, from the beginning of the Republic of China in 1912, a series of anti-Confucian campaigns, which include the May Fourth Movement and, far later, the Cultural Revolution. Confucianism can contribute to nationalism to the extent that it offers a sense of difference because of the highlighted contrast with Western civilization (Chang 2008). Nevertheless, Confucianism finally restored its recognition in 2012 as emerging Chinese president Xi Jinping intensively cites Confucian classics in almost all of his public speeches. Xi means to incorporate Confucian values in his effort to revive Chinese civilizations (Fenzhi Zhang 2015). Xi has been keen to raise the moral consciousness of his cadres. His quest for national greatness and the associated China dream are registered within the Chinese sovereign borders, rather than among Confucian disciples (Terrill 2016). Therefore, his use of Confucianism primarily focuses on individual ethics regarding how to be a good Communist.[4] Making Chinese citizens a disciplined population for the sake of state building is a peculiar kind of post-Chineseness. However, in practice, no discursive or philosophical restraint exists regarding how a conscious use of Confucian wisdom will evolve, even to the extent of becoming alienated or critical of the Communist leadership (G. Wang 2002).

Cosmopolitan Chineseness and Confucianism

In practice, the state-sponsored Confucianism spills over territorial borders in the twenty-first century to produce post-Chineseness beyond definitive borders. The establishment of the Confucius Institutes all over the world, staffed by language teachers sent and paid for by China, is a policy premised upon the Confucian indoctrination of these teachers who are expected to introduce Chinese culture through their teaching (Kluver 2014; Li, Mirmirani, and Ilacqua 2009). Neither teachers nor their alien students can be immune from cross-cultural exchanges in their encounters. Students attend at will and are clearly interested in a future career that may be related to China (Hartig 2015). Teachers learn the local values and practice the local lifestyles (Ye 2017). Students fulfill their own localized or individualized decisions in the process of becoming familiar and even comfortable with Chinese civilization and language (Hartig 2012). Confucianism constitutes their new identity indirectly, each in her own way. The post-Chineseness of the Confucius Institute secularizes Confucianism, where it connects the students and teachers at the expense of a widely considered Confucian ritual trait. However, such a loss in the process of expansion guarantees a kind of cosmopolitan post-Chineseness, embedded in individualized trajectories that are unrestricted by borders.

Postmodern Chineseness and Confucianism

Multiple Confucianisms become an imperative in the postmodern condition to preserve the local identities of those societies to protect their own Confucianism from any totalizing definition. This quest for a distinctive identity can easily find a shelter embedded in mutually exclusive sitedness that cannot be shared. The East Asian Confucianism, which stresses the common origin but different trajectories of improvised hybridity due to sited genealogy, represents the postmodern Confucianism that combines Chineseness, Western modernity, and indigeneity (Ivanhoe 2016; Chun-chieh Huang 2015). All can appreciate the Chineseness of each other, whereas most remain sensible to their own differences (Barmé 2005).[5] How Confucianism continues at several sites is premised upon an imagined common origin that ensures the othering of one another to proceed in a mutually appreciated manner. A hybrid and special mode of Confucianism is possible because the relaxation on ancestor worship, together with the pedagogy offered by international Confucian scholars, can create post-Chineseness that enables all sides to practice different Confucianism.

Conclusion

Chapter 4 complicates the essentialist understandings of Chineseness by enlisting religious cases and identifying the nuances in their application to the understanding of Chinese nationalism. While Chinese nationalism is a prior relation for contemporary Chinese anywhere to develop a self-understanding at both individual and group levels, no national self-conception of China can sustain the intersection with religion without having the boundary of China and the Chinese nation spanning, disquieted, and even disintegrated. Their supernatural worlds reinforce denationalized relationality as well as inspire new connections across boundaries. Thus, post-Chinese religiosity preserves the dynamics of a "self-in-relations" that adheres to no single nationalism.

Once disquieted, Chineseness evolves into multiple strings of post-Chineseness, which constantly reconstruct Chineseness via all sorts of strategic reconnections, enacted by those self-regarded cultural Chinese. In this sense, cultural nationalism is the practice of reconnection. Chinese cultural nationalism involves parallel attempts at reconnection with an imagined Chinese population. Religions can contribute to Chinese cultural nationalism in various ways. One incurs different types of religious resources to achieve a reconnection so that an imagined resemblance can be engendered or reproduced. In this sense, cultural nationalism practically denies the plausibility of mutual resemblance agreeable to all those presumably belonging to the same Chinese nation.

Amid the atmosphere of China rising, cultural nationalism contributes to political nationalism only indirectly, where the agents attain psychological determination from their religious conviction to pursue state or ethnic nationalism. Cultural nationalism hinders political nationalism because culture is necessarily cross-boundary in the Chinese case of multiple religions, and thus fails to fit with any territorial identity. Religious resources that serve the imagination of reconnection in the multireligious context vary in their implications for behavioral consequences. In this manner, post-Chineseness reinforces the image of ethnic and Sinic Chinese nationalism but actually, due to the evasive ontology of Chineseness, neutralizes its development, embraces cyclical dialectics, and restrains any steady contribution from religion.

PART 2

STRATEGIZING CHINESENESS

Relations from the Outside In

Other nations, represented by leaders, scholars, journalists, businesspeople, ethnic and cross-border communities, or simply consumers, are related to China and interact with their imagined China in certain co-constituting relations, in which all people examine each other's post-Chineseness. Sinologists are of particular relevance in these processes as they provide a repertoire of identities of China and Chinese to enable their communities to choose and craft a certain resemblance to China. The improvisation of post-Chineseness proceeds in international sinology, involves the strategizing of bilateral identity, and always incurs disputes, anxiety, and cycles. International sinology indicates the relevance of non-Western sources of the imagined China. All decisions on the use of a certain Chineseness to preempt relations with an imagined China are doomed to be unstable in the long run in these non-Western and post-Western relationalities that are embedded, as part 2 will demonstrate, in cultural, colonial, and ethnic memories as well as geostrategic considerations.

Succinctly, part 2 contains one national site for each of the four chapters, including a case of cultural relations of Vietnamese sinologists, a case of colonial relations of Taiwanese scholars of China, a case of ethnic relations of Chinese-Filipino scholars of China, and a case of geostrategic relations of South Asian scholars of China.

Chapter 5 analyzes the attempt of Vietnamese sinologists to portray an outsider China that has actually been a constituting component of Vietnamese identities. The production of knowledge is intrinsically a choice of national role and a strategy for imposing an alter role of China. In comparison, chapter 6 examines how Japanese colonial history and Chinese culture co-constitute Taiwanese identities. The situation of China studies in Taiwan is thus more complex than Vietnamese sinology. The attendant constituting component of China studies in the Philippines in chapter 7 shifts to the ethnic conditions of Chinese-Filipino scholars, who are either in the Philippines, in a third country, or moving between the Philippines and a third country. Opposed to common sense, the indigenous scholars are relatively ready to imagine a position of watching that is internal to China. Chapter 8 compares a number of think tanks located at various Global South national sites in terms of the methodology of their China watching. Singapore has strategically created a position that is external to China by mimicking its counterpart in South Asia for the purpose of stabilizing the relationships with its Southeast Asian neighbors.

Chapter 5

Cultural Self Rebalanced

The Vietnamese Practices of Sinology

Introduction

Part 1 interrogates the implausibility of any national and, for that matter, de-national perspective to present China and Chineseness. According to the chapters in part 1, China is not simply something that can be intellectually owned or excluded. Nor is China fictional, undefinable, or nonconsensual. Indeed, there is a national China, the name and the discourse, that contains many Chinas coexisting in practice, in context, and in time. The book maintains, however, that taking a China-centric premise can ironically be a critical method to enable transcending China-centrism. This is not only applicable to the deconstruction of Chinese perspectives (in part 1) that reproduce particular kinds of China, but also to the deconstruction of non-Chinese perspectives that presumably look in from an imagined position in the outside. Thus, for those of us (in part 2) whose relational identities depend on strategic uses of Chineseness, post-Chineseness is likewise a way to engage in emancipation.

While a China-centric method can certainly explore the Chineseness of others through presumably Chinese lenses, it can likewise interrogate how self-regarded others practice different kinds of Chineseness in accordance with their own relational lenses. The following chapters in part 2 seek to complicate the category of China or Chineseness from an allegedly external position of the observers, meaning, according to chapter 1, having insufficient legitimacy to speak on behalf of China and therefore can only define China's post-Chineseness according to their imagined relations with China. These chapters are not about a self-regarded agent of China looking out as with chapters in part 1. Rather, by enlisting a few selected oral history interviews of South and Southeast Asian China experts and sinologists, these chapters review how others relate China by appropriating Chineseness.

The scope of "others" in this and other chapters in part 2 includes at least two peculiar groups: (1) those, such as Chinese overseas, who are outside of a China that has been consensually defined in their own groups, for example, the territorial PRC, the Chinese race, or the tributary relations; and (2) those, such as Sinologists, who perceive themselves being regarded as non-Chinese by the Chinese whom they study. Their inclusion allows the possibility of someone presumably taking the external perspective also to claim belonging to the same Chinese group. When this happens, they own the counterpart of moral Chineseness, which part 2 calls "cultural Chineseness." Cultural Chineseness enables the legitimacy of judging someone else's practices of Chineseness on behalf of China.

The book argues that all can practice and even own certain kinds of Chineseness by strategically enlisting specific intellectual resources. Different kinds of Chineseness enable different people to connect those Chinese who are most relevant to their purposes. Similarly, the same processes can serve the purpose of disconnecting China. Chapter 5 takes Vietnamese sinology as a case. Along with the chapters in part 1, it provides two dimensions to understand the regression of the positions and roles that define the sinologists' relations with China or Chineseness: insider versus outsider and temporal versus spatial resources. Together, they enact six kinds of post-Chineseness. Examples of each kind taken from the Vietnamese discourses are present in the second half of the chapter.

Defining China or Chinese from an imagined outside position is an impossible mission, and the validity of this statement becomes apparent if one recollects the intellectual histories of China studies, Chinese studies, and sinology, which have respectively produced the scholarship on China, Chinese people, and Chinese civilization. Nevertheless, borrowing the notion of family resemblance from Ludwig Wittgenstein (1986, 31), one still finds that scholars can practically identify their research scope despite their incapacity to reach any consensual definition. Such practical Chineseness hints at socially recognizable traits and turns Chineseness into a role identity instead of an involuntary, fixed, or shared quality, innate as well as acquired (Thies 2010; Thies and Breuning 2012). Chineseness accordingly carries expectations that impose a duty to perform either on those who strive for recognition of their Chineseness by others or on those whom others recognize as the owners of Chineseness.

It is strategically sensible for people who intend to interact with those whom they identify as Chinese to demonstrate their possession of a certain similar Chineseness in order to achieve connection, reconnection, or disconnection that serves their purposes. This is not about any objective or correct Chineseness. Rather, it involves relying on intellectual resources to enable the politics of relation. Chapter 5 gathers from the reflections of the Vietnamese sinologists as well as inducts accordingly various conceptual routes for them to be intellectually connected with Chineseness. Such practices of intellectual Chineseness may deconstruct any discursive foundation for a self-regarded Chinese population to claim a stable or definitive identity.

Nonetheless, studies on China, Chinese people, and Chinese civilization, combined, make Chineseness an epistemologically plausible and discursively expressible identity. To the extent that it is impossible to monopolize its substance, it attains the characteristics of a social role. Given that roles can be denied or claimed in contradiction to expectations, owning Chineseness necessarily involves a political process that has contextual behavioral and policy implications. Thus, a Sinologist may have studied Chinese topics so extensively and intensively that his or her intellectual capacity and psychological capacity to take the role identity of Chineseness can be far stronger and even more willing than the people whom she studies, obscuring the distinction between sinologists and the Chinese they study. As a result, all can potentially speak and act in the capacity, or on behalf, of Chinese as long as one can purposefully perform the duty expected of such a role in its context. Post-Chineseness is the concept that characterizes the indefinite practicality of Chineseness as a role identity.

Looking at China's Post-Chineseness

In contrast to chapter 1 in terms of one's position vis-á-vis China, part 2 mainly reviews cases where groups that do not claim the legitimacy of speaking on behalf of China, including Vietnam, the Philippines, Singapore, and postcolonial Taiwan, try to practice post-Chineseness. In the lenses of those who adopt an imagined position of looking at China, post-Chineseness refers to *the cultural preparation and political process of mutual acknowledgment among those who consider themselves to resemble one another in terms of (some kind of) Chineseness*, practically defined according to the context and its trajectories, each time and each site. The important skill is to evoke relevant resources to establish a mutual sense of familiarity, cooperation, and sympathy, reproduce or confirm an extant relationship, and recover from estrangement. In short, for the relevant parties to discover the kind of Chineseness in the other side that can resonate with their own identities, the key to successful balance of relationships is to be reciprocal. Consequently, in the long run and at the macro level, Chineseness can thus have various, if not entirely irrelevant, meanings.

For example, Chineseness in the Confucian Northeast Asia may indicate one's imagined degree of cultural centrality (Shih 2010), whereas it mainly triggers the politics of differentiation among Chinese Southeast Asians (Wang 2000, 2002), which denies the possibility of cultural centrality. Centrality implies a shared quality among a set of population, a proportion of which may have a higher degree of the shared quality than others. By contrast, the politics of differentiation in Southeast Asia rejects it. In Hong Kong and Taiwan, for example, Chineseness may bifurcate into pursuits of both ethnic difference and cultural centrality because of the mixed postcolonial culture bred by the UK or Japan and Confucianism introduced by generations of migrants. Chineseness can likewise negatively include those who strive to achieve non-Chinese identities through the same process of mutuality, constituting a dyadic contrast. In other words, post-Chineseness refers to the intellectual capacity of people to use the cultural resources within their reach for reconnecting (or disconnecting) with one another as Chinese.

Reversely and implicitly, there is likewise post-Vietnameseness. Both of these strategic identities are imaginations of how one thinks others are who they are and uses them to reconstitute one's own identity for strategic reasons. In these intersubjective processes, one makes roles and also takes roles to oblige others to reciprocate (Harnisch 2011, 2012). Repeated role-playing may result in role identities with which one identifies in order to contrive one's purposes (the chapter will not pursue the line of post-Vietnameseness for the same reason as it will not do post-Pakistaniness. Please refer to chapter 2 for a further explanation.)

An example of post-Chineseness is given to illustrate what it means. If ancestor worship is considered Chinese, then the people who are able and willing to recognize Chineseness in one another through their shared learning, practice, or teaching of ancestor worship are exercising a vague kind of Confucian Chineseness (one can make the same argument about Confucian Vietnameseness, which ancestor worship constitutes, too). Similarly, those who deny Chineseness while practicing ancestor worship can likewise be exhibiting Chineseness in the sense that they deliberately distinguish the non-Chinese nuances of their ritual from that of others who are allegedly Chinese. The behavioral and policy implications of this particular example include a will to connect, or disconnect, presumably with a separate Chinese population to reconcile a dispute, grasp an opportunity, trigger sympathy in an incident, and fulfill self-enhancement, among others. They try forging a scope of the greater self, which is defined by a perceived common ancestor or ritual life.

Post-Chineseness in Vietnam is distinctive because of (1) the long history of the political merger between Vietnam and dynastic China, (2) the shared religious and cultural beliefs of the Vietnamese with the Chinese, and (3) the recurrent migration as well as the resultant kinship across contemporary borders. Vietnamese intellectuals have relied on different kinds of post-Chineseness to make sense and use of their relationship with the encountered Chinese in order for the former to select and determine the mode of self-understanding, the purpose and a strategy to reconnect, and the normative criterion to assess and manage the relationship. The Vietnamese are allegedly different from other East Asian communities in their relations with the Chinese. For example, there are significantly fewer Chinese-Vietnamese than Chinese-Malaysians, Thais, and Indonesians in the national population. The history of Vietnam is, for another example, considerably closer to that of China than that of Korea and Japan in terms of the length of the merger.

Note that Vietnamese people's strategic acquisition of post-Chineseness reproduces certain kinds of imagined Vietnameseness, which presumably constitutes a deeper identity than the strategic practice of Chineseness. On the other hand, there are likewise self-regarded Chinese, plausibly in Guangxi, which is on the other side of the border, who are eager to connect those who, in their eyes, are Vietnamese by simulating Vietnameseness in various ways; hence, post-Vietnameseness. The latter can make a separate research project, epistemologically equalizing those communities of identity of different sizes. In short, post-Chineseness and, for that matter, post-Vietnameseness are about successful or unsuccessful strategizing rather than about being right or wrong. The rest of the chapter will review how different Vietnamese sinologists' discursive formulations can incur different categories of post-Chineseness, despite these formulations being possibly unpopular, controversial, or punditic.

Post-Chineseness as Intellectual Practices

Post-Chineseness, given its strategic characteristics, thus has no definitive content or scope, even if all who claim a certain kind of Chineseness must ostensibly share post-Chineseness. Self-identified Chinese are *those who share different Chineseness with different other self-identified Chinese in context*. As a result, Chineseness is more a processual and even tautological notion than a substantive one; however, it still appears definitively in the context in which two can recognize in each other a shared Chinese feature. Thus, all Chinese must be post-Chinese because they uniquely share something with different Chinese, but no such Chineseness can be shared by all. Given that owning or losing Chineseness has an equal likelihood, someone not considered Chinese in one context is potentially an owner of Chineseness in another, as long as such recognition of her assuming Chineseness is mutually agreeable. Similar processes of post-identification certainly apply to Vietnameseness, Americanness, Tibetanness, and so on.

Consider a prolix logic. A Tibetan, a Taiwanese, or a Chinese-Malaysian can similarly claim post-Chineseness where they achieve mutual recognition with someone else, even if the Tibetan, the Taiwanese, or the Chinese Malaysian culture may not be shared by others who claim to be Chinese. They are in between different identities and images to the extent that their mutually recognized Chineseness only partially constitutes their selfhood. They can also claim that the Chineseness that they own is not shareable with others not living and growing up in the same geocultural background; therefore, Tibetans, Taiwanese, and Chinese-Malaysians are arguably different. They cannot recognize in each other any familiar Chineseness, each having evolved on a peculiar trajectory. This kind of differentiated Chineseness denies any other self-claimed Chinese belonging to their group and makes their own a kind of culturally isolated Chineseness.

Ironically, if they insist on being non-Chinese outsiders, as many Tibetans, Taiwanese, and Malaysian Chinese are inclined to do, they are still entitled to a kind of epistemological Chineseness informed by their own civilization or methodology, which enables them to recognize, understand, and connect with the Chinese people who may or may not see Chineseness in Tibetans, Taiwanese, and Malaysian Chinese. To claim a complete distinction, they must know how to represent or practice Chineseness in order to show how their respective Chineseness is unique or outside. The political or intellectual elite probably prepares the population to imagine such uniqueness. This intellectual capacity to know Chineseness is the basis for reclaiming a connection if so desired in a different context.

In a nutshell, the post-Chineseness of sinology, the topic of the ensuing discussion, describes how a China scholar strategically positions herself through scholarship on China so that the proposed relationship between her community and China is intellectually sensible.

Altercasting Embedded in Post-Chineseness

Post-Chineseness, which is registered in the cultural preparation for, and the process of, reconnecting any two populations considered owning Chineseness, is inevitably altercasting as well as reflexive altercasting (Epstein 2012, 135–45; Wehner 2015, 435–55). Altercasting occurs when a Chinese group incurs a particular component of its alleged Chineseness, which the alter-Chinese group is perceived to share by the former; consequently, the latter is obliged to respond positively to the former. The alter group's obligation to respond reflects the role expectation imposed on it (Harnisch 2011, 2012). However, even if practiced by the same group, the alleged Chineseness can differ in accordance with the context of the encounter. For those who espouse "the Chinese Dream," they conceive of Chinese Southeast Asian as same Chinese; for example, the food or Chinese language of Chinese-Malaysians could represent their Chineseness; thus, Chinese-Malaysians are expected to eat rice together and speak Mandarin. By contrast, as neither the food nor use of Mandarin conveniently applies to the Tibetans, suffering from the same British imperialism could be a trigger. This imposes an obligation on the Tibetan population to embrace Chinese nationalism. To that extent, altercasting has the function of socializing alters.

Reflexive altercasting emerges when an actor relies on the strategic use of Chinese cultural resources to meet what is perceived to be the alter group's role expectations of her (S. Walker 2014). For example, a Tibetan who desires an educational opportunity may stress her Chinese citizenship and proficiency in Mandarin. Alternatively, she could pledge opposition to Tibetan independence for the sake of national unity. This strategic role-taking might have an acculturation effect; however, it does not take away her intellectual capacity to revert in another future context. Reflexive altercasting for a self-regarded non-Chinese group works in the opposite way. For example, the same Tibetan group who promotes Tibetan independence would deliberately abort the duty of national integration imposed by the PRC authorities. Those who belong to this group could walk out to join Dharamsara or insist on the superiority of religion over politics. Reflexive altercasting in the last example proceeds to counter-altercasting, which generates the self-role expectation that the Chinese authorities would punish it.

The pressure on reflective altercasting is particularly strong for actors seeking recognition for their Chineseness. In this chapter, when one declares the ownership of Chineseness shared by a Chinese alter group, one's role identity of being Chinese arises from an internal perspective of the imagined scope of Chineseness and is called an insider's Chineseness. This perspective necessitates reflective altercasting among those who see themselves as owners of Chineseness because they need to meet the role expectations of their Chinese alter group. In Vietnam, for example, many sinologists believe that understanding the Chinese culture is essential to the understanding of the Vietnamese culture.[1] Being appreciative of their own Chinese cultural embedding thus enhances the comprehensiveness of Vietnam's distinctive culture and, consequently, promotes self-respect. Even so, such distinction is conditioned upon the approval by an alter Chinese group.

By contrast, for those whose identity is internally determined by their fellow citizens, their identity rests on the sense of difference from China. In this chapter, this kind of Chineseness is outsiders' Chineseness. Asserting and basing their own identity on their knowledge of what differs from China, these actors' ownership of Chineseness is generally contradictory. Such negative kind of Chineseness cannot be rewarding to their self-understanding or even confirmed at all. The Chinese alter group is expected to avoid treating them as either Chinese overseas or Chinese culture subscribers. Altercasting is essential to an outsider's identity-based Chineseness, in which China could represent an achiever to emulate, an interest seeker to avoid, or a grasping power to defend, among others. In this lens, Vietnam's national identity comes primarily from deliberately excluding the perceived cultural components that they share with China.

Between being an insider and an outsider, a hybrid identity of being both an insider and an outsider exists. This hybrid identity requires support from both the Chinese alter group to recognize one's Chineseness and one's own group to partially achieve an identity of being non-Chinese. The question of whether the role consciousness more strongly faces the Chinese alter group than the non-Chinese alter group is contingent. In the case of

Chinese-Vietnamese, one could more strongly identify with Chineseness to reconnect with the Chinese motherland during a political crisis in Vietnam. In this case, reflexive altercasting would be dominant to achieve recognition from the Chinese alter group. Alternatively, the Chinese role consciousness for Vietnamese sinologists to present Vietnam's contrast could be stronger when facing Chinese counterparts in order to achieve equal status. In this case, altercasting instead of reflective altercasting is the appropriate pattern, because Vietnamese sinologists would offer lessons about Vietnamese deviations for the uninformed Chinese sinologists to learn.

Note that the following uses of oral history scripts of senior Vietnamese sinologists available to the public do not validate the cited and referred interviews. Sometimes, the referred opinion may not represent the majority or stereotyped views and each has its own context. The methodology of the chapter is to use whichever reference that can illustrate the incurrence of a category of post-Chineseness. Neither is there the assumption that an incurred category can define the entire identity upon its utterance or dominate the social and intersubjective being of the experts. They merely show the discursive route to a post-Chinese category.

Memory versus Resource in Role Identity

Whether or not one assumes an insider's perspective and strives to gain recognition from the Chinese alter group is often an acculturated decision, which is almost intuitive although mutable. One's cultural memory, acquired through socialization, prepares one to accept what is immediately rational for one to position one's cultural self (Assmann 2006, 210–24; Erll 2011). Under the influence of cultural memory, the decision on one's cultural position is not entirely one's own choice. Nonetheless, it is a kind of choice for two reasons. First, the decision on one's position must be a prior choice collectively made by the earlier generations and taught to the contemporary members to reflect the evolutionary wisdom. Second, resocialization in consideration of the new evolutionary pressures eventually facilitates a change in cultural memory; that is, everyone participates in adjusting the cultural memory. The cultural memory prompts an intuitive and emotional reaction to achieve a purpose constituting post-Chinese identities. This attunes to the notion of habitus that constrains the actor's capacity of improvising resemblance to the other party (Bourdieu 1977).

Table 5.1. Post-Chineseness in the External Perspectives

Resource \ Memory	Subjects inside (role)	Subjects between (role identity)	Subjects outside (identity)
Temporal object (becoming)	Cultural reflexive altercasting	Sinological altercasting	Civilizational altercasting
Spatial object (being)	Experiential reflexive altercasting	Ethnic reflexive altercasting	Scientific/policy altercasting

Source: author

What action to take with one's position or what position to take with one's action are questions on using cultural resources instead of cultural memory. The selection of the cultural resources to use depends on how one conceptualizes the Chinese alter group, being a constant process of becoming or a discernable scope of being. In this regard, two approaches that parallel the division between the humanities and social sciences decompose the strategic practices of post-Chineseness into temporal Chineseness and spatial Chineseness. In part 2, temporal Chineseness, defined as *Chineseness that has an evolutionary trajectory under constant reconstruction, relies on the knowledge of the history and philosophy of the alter group to be able to empathize with the emotional and epistemological characteristics of this group.* Spatial Chineseness, defined as *Chineseness that has a discernable scope, is based on the combination of structural, comparative, and local intelligence*; this combination is independent of the intervention of alternative emotions or epistemology already adopted by Vietnamese observers.

The process of becoming embodies temporal Chineseness, which one can trace through a significantly broader and longer trajectory from the past. Three types of temporal Chineseness emerge according to the self-positioning of one's role identity. The first is "cultural Chineseness," in which members belonging to the same Chinese group are able to perceive their resemblance in terms of cultural identity because they live together long enough to understand the relationships, issues, and emotions of one another in ways that out-group members cannot fully appreciate. The second type, "sinological Chineseness," possesses culturally in-between perspectives of both China and Vietnam in order eloquently to translate and make sense of both sides. The third type, "civilizational Chineseness," presupposes mutually estranging ontological identities between China and Vietnam, as an out-group, and allows the latter to learn, assess, and handle Chinese identities. This last type exemplifies a thread of counter-resemblance that enables self-designated strangers to understand each other as a kind of nonself.

Spatial Chineseness exists in its being and is defined by the corresponding site and presumably objective conditions. Spatial Chineseness requires a discernible scope, so that one can gather intelligence to speculate about its conditions as well as behavioral pattern. In the spatial formulation, no pressure exists to attribute Chineseness to knowledge revealing the past. As temporal Chineseness, spatial Chineseness has three types according to the positions of Vietnamese observers. According to chapter 2, "experiential Chineseness" speaks of an in-group self-consciousness, resulting from living and working together with a recognizable Chinese group, with concomitant consensual role obligations to act with mutual sympathy. An actor possessing "ethnic Chineseness" usually shows some Chineseness in front of a Chinese alter group to improvise a sense of resemblance, tends toward reflective altercasting to win respect, and demonstrates more resemblance to Vietnamese characteristics in front of their fellow citizens to enable reflective altercasting in another direction. "Scientific Chineseness" demonstrates one's intelligence gathering on the Chinese alter group, such that objectively analyzing a Chinese alter group and epistemologically distancing it from one's own group simultaneously testify to the identity of an external collector of Chineseness. The criteria Vietnam evokes to examine China reflects the latter's resemblance to Vietnam in terms of the imagined essence of the state that constitutes both China and Vietnam.

Altercasting and Vietnam's Practices of Post-Chineseness

Vietnamese who perceive Vietnam or Vietnamese as Chinese are usually considered nonexistent or irrelevant. However, the succeeding discussion shows that Vietnamese actors who grew up in a Chinese cultural environment, owing to their family traditions, are prepared to view the Chinese alter group as, at times, lying within the boundary of a greater self, which simultaneously includes their own. This leads to either cultural Chineseness or experiential Chineseness. In case the Vietnamese actors are consciously outside, the resources for them to reconnect with the Chinese alter group include civilizational Chineseness and scientific Chineseness, depending on whether the enlisted identity of the Chinese alter group is considered a process of becoming or a scope of being. A process of becoming incurs the subjective attitude toward an evolving and exotic civilization, historiography, or ideology. A process of being involves the objective intelligence gathering and analysis abiding by Vietnam's own national interests. In case both Chineseness and Vietnamese characteristics constitute the actors' identity that is in-between, the cultural resources include either sinological Chineseness, which translates meanings for both sides, or ethnic Chineseness, which strives for recognition from both sides.

For Vietnamese intellectuals and those actors who perceive Vietnam as an insider, consciously or less consciously, and who apply cultural norms either to assess China and its performance or reflect on their own problems in the form of China's self-criticism, they engage in reflexive altercasting. Criticism is significantly more powerful than assuming an outsider's position, because self-criticism can reveal the weakness of Chineseness, which an outsider can rarely do. The pressure of reflexive altercasting is reduced whenever one takes an in-between position, which is supported by the knowledge of both sides that neither side fully understands. However, when an actor self-positioning in between the insider and the outsider ends up in a situation in which both sides can claim knowledge of her identity, for example, ethnic Chineseness, she is reduced by both sides altercasting the in-between actor who has no discursive identity of her own in the middle.

Altercasting and Civilizational Chineseness

Vietnamese who apply Vietnam's perceived civilizational standards to identify, evaluate, and absorb Chinese civilizations, specifically from the perspective of differentiation, are exercising civilizational Chineseness. Differences constitute the civilizational identity of Vietnam that forms Vietnam's distinctive identity. Themes that emancipate, demonize, romanticize, patronize, historicize, or merely relativize China illustrate this type. Under civilizational Chineseness, learning from Chinese experiences shows no signs of assimilation. The Vietnamese geoculture, evolving out of the local history as well as indigenous religions, will undergird such civilizational borrowing. Confucianism, Daoism, and even Buddhism are first assimilated into or transformed by indigenous cults. Civilizational Chineseness stresses two distinctive trajectories—China and Vietnam, intertwining but independent.[2] The purpose of owning civilizational Chineseness is to separate it from Vietnamese identity.

Altercasting leads to the expectations of China refraining from enlisting civilizational resources to restore the metaphors of the Middle Kingdom or all-under-heaven during the time of its rise to a major power. China should not act as the sole origin of Vietnamese civilization or consider Vietnam a student exclusive of the Chinese cultural sphere. China should not expect Vietnam to exchange political favors for China's beneficial treatments that grow out of China's expanding scale of economy. China should instead maintain its role as just another civilization with a different past and future to be liked or disliked. Civilizational Chineseness motivates Vietnam to assert civilizational uniqueness. Civilizational Chineseness could lead to a soft resistance of Vietnam by restricting the spread of Chinese civilizational commerce in Vietnam. Intellectual narratives could alert nationals to the arrogance or misinterpretation of Vietnam's civilizational history in Chinese discourses.

Vietnamese society is inclined to watch and assess China, positively and negatively alike. Web information about China typically receives more frequent hits.[3] If this curiosity originates from a sense of a distinctive perspective, it represents civilizational Chineseness. For example, the curiosity toward Vietnam's path to Marxism is normally accompanied by a comparison with the Chinese path.[4] This comparative consciousness is keenly applied to the quest for Vietnam's history of philosophy, widely acknowledged to be heavily grounded on Chinese philosophies. Mutual learning indicates civilizational Chineseness. In fact, Chinese students in Vietnam have been observed to adapt to their study environment and, in general, learn more effectively than other foreign students.[5] Nevertheless, one interviewee suggests that Taiwanese are better sinologists because of their Chinese background, which reveals Vietnam's external position.[6] Another interviewee opines that, the more one knows about China, the more one appreciates how different China is from Vietnam.[7] However, this does not preclude Confucianism or sinology from being a universal value for other civilizations to adopt, according to yet another interviewee,[8] suggesting that being Confucian is not the same as being Chinese.

One interviewee expresses the view of instrumental Confucianism, whereby people access Confucianism with different calculi of interest. Although they share Confucianism and other cultural traditions with the Chinese, Vietnamese who hold a negative attitude toward China exhibit a clearly opposing attitude. One explanation is that the Chinese embrace a strong Han-centric sensibility.[9] This triggers Vietnamese nationalism, sometimes to the extent of people refusing to learn the Chinese language.[10] When the political atmosphere becomes extreme, the studies of China and sinology can be entirely halted. Although most people clearly distinguish the

Chinese people from the Chinese government, alienation from the Chinese government can be so considerably intense that many Vietnamese allegedly remain constantly alerted by any move that the Chinese government takes.

Altercasting and Scientific Chineseness

Vietnamese scholars who rely on a presumably objective scale or policy agenda to study an alter Chinese group as a discernible site or body that others can describe, explain, and compare are exercising scientific Chineseness. Institutionalists, Marxists, as well as think-tank analysts illustrate this type. Scientific Chineseness treats China as conditions of capacity, demographics, social structure, and policy orientation with which Vietnam must cope. Scientific scholarship allows Vietnam, as an intellectual site, to contribute to China studies because of Vietnamese sinologists' empathetic capacity to compare, supported by sited intelligence, familiarity with Confucianism and Daoism, alliance experiences, war history, the same party-state system, common Russian pedagogy, and the Chinese language skill. Unique, if not more comprehensive, China expertise in Vietnam results in a peculiar kind of comparative studies, in which the approach to Chineseness is universally applicable.

Altercasting leads to the expectations that the same values and rationality that Vietnam considers common and normal must constitute Chineseness. The strategic implication is the presentation of a nondistinctive China that is ready to cope with Vietnam through power play, an exchange of interests, or a monopoly of influence.[11] China is expected to appear in Vietnam only as strategic opportunities or threats, resulting in a bilateral relationship that is plagued by uncertainty, mistrust, and competition. China is expected to oppose the multilateral as well as global intervention, because China can dominate in the bilateral situation. Vietnam expects China's policy to be a carrot and stick. In scientific Chineseness, the Vietnamese detect the calculus of China's national interest.

Most forms of scientific Chineseness treat China's behavior as composed of characteristics that everyone else similarly owns or understands. However, Vietnamese scholars do not adopt this prevailing perspective. Internally, these sporadic scientific identities analyze the Chinese leadership style.[12] Externally, they regard China as a player of international politics facing Vietnam, which prefer a multilateral over a bilateral frame when dealing with China. A major component that influences Vietnam's national self-identity is the reference to China as a big nation to the effect that an asymmetric relationship constitutes Vietnam's nationhood. For those who grasp scientific Chineseness, Vietnam preempts China's expansion, but Vietnam has no intention of initiating confrontation with China or expectation that the ASEAN could actually stop China.[13] Neither will Vietnam's alliance with either the US or Japan, if successful, be ultimately useful in opposing China nor will Vietnam romanticize China's historical support for Vietnam. Scientific Chineseness breeds the belief that superpowers do what is best for their own interests. In general, though, Vietnamese sinologists are unenthusiastic about practicing this kind of scientific Chineseness, which certain other nations can easily own.

Scientific Chineseness actually features alienation from classic Chinese studies. During the time of confrontation, one interviewee recalls that many sinologists left their agenda behind and switched to other subjects.[14] Consequently, knowledge about China originated primarily from Russian materials. Scientific Chineseness about China required peculiar Vietnamese perspectives to adopt Russian social science discourses (Dinh 2019). For almost a decade and half after the 1979 war between Vietnam and China, more general subjects substituted for Chinese learning: philosophy and Marxism on the one side, and Vietnamese culture and the Russian language on the other. Western China studies flourished and appeared to study China objectively; thus, one's knowledge of China need not depend on the Chinese literature.[15]

Altercasting and Sinological Chineseness

Vietnamese scholars who can describe and explain the different functions and values of the Chinese and Vietnamese cultural beliefs to the members of each group are practicing sinological Chineseness. Non-Chinese Confucians in general, and church sinologists in particular, illustrate this type. Sinological Chineseness in Vietnam stresses the need for a deep understanding of China so that Vietnam can learn from China what is useful and deal with China without the support of a third party. Such learning comes from empathy, or even sympathy, rather than the uninformed romanticizing dominant in civilizational Chineseness.[16] Sinological Chineseness identifies Vietnam as assuming the role of an intellectual who understands the social, political, and psychological difficulties that Chinese leaders suffer and reads with confidence between the lines the policy messages from China. Owning sinological Chineseness is, therefore, accompanied by a duty of double-sided communication, including uncritically showing the negative side of China.

Altercasting leads to the expectation that China and Vietnam will be reciprocal, willing to share, and appreciative of each other's relationship. Once the interpretation of one party's consideration is revealed to the other party, the latter has the role obligation to show sympathy and patience. During difficult negotiations, China is obliged to prevent the situation from escalating to an irrevocable level. China is also expected to exert patience and accept a nonsolution as a solution in a kingly manner, which has been preached and praised in sinological classics as well as among their contemporary disciples.

Sinologists are emotionally involved in their works of translation.[17] Good translations of the Buddhist texts, literary pieces, scenes, and philosophies are essential to the learning of Chinese culture.[18] Several sinologists have never been to China but can develop a deep empathy toward the Han characters through the texts. Others are worried, though, that isolated translators could miss the needed touch in their translation because they fail to capture the spirit of the time due to their lack of living experiences in China. For example, a student of *The Forbidden Female* expounds the challenge of translating the contemporary novel to convey the triad of a universal human rights message, a gender equality message, and the reform and openness message. The exact choice of Vietnamese words to convey the delicate messages and the flow of the episodes presupposes an intricate appreciation of the Chinese narratives.[19] Overall, sinological Chineseness encourages a general sense of duty to both their political leaders and schoolchildren. Sinologists intend that their leaders understand China correctly and their pedagogy enriches the curriculum so that reading about China in Vietnam can avoid an inherent bias caused by a short-term rift.[20]

Sinologists are used to the suspicion that they are overly pro-China during Vietnam-China conflicts.[21] From the point of view of sinologists, they explain this image as being caused by their profound knowledge of China. According to a think-tank scholar, recommendations from the perspective of sinological Chineseness can sometimes be acceptable to the government.[22] A well-trained sinologist learns the Chinese classics by heart that they reflect humanities in them. Sinology enables one to transcend mundane affairs and regard wars as merely a transient phenomenon. An interviewee finds himself in complete agreement with a Chinese counterpart regarding the assessment that China and Vietnam have no good reason to fight.[23] Well-equipped scholars can not only translate texts, that is, Buddhist and Confucian texts and literary pieces, but also convey the spirit so that each party is able to appreciate the mood and temper of the other party. For example, an interviewee discovers an either/or mentality plaguing both parties. This mentality is caused by a shared style of nationalism—either to praise the other side to the extreme or to despise it to the extreme.[24] Nevertheless, most sinologists seem to believe that the Han culture features open-mindedness.

Reflective Altercasting and Ethnic Chineseness

Those Vietnamese who can describe and explain the different functions and values of the nuanced ways of life embedded in a certain cultural or geographical space that overlaps with a discernible Han Chinese domain are practicing ethnic Chineseness. Han or other ethnic Chineseness in Vietnam or on the borders that are capable of communicating with both Vietnam and China, as well as within their own groups, illustrates this type. Ethnic Chineseness is strong among those Chinese-Vietnamese who escaped at the end of the Vietnam War to live abroad. It is equally evident among the Kinh Chinese in Guangxi, China. Others, who are neither Han nor Kinh Chinese but nonetheless on the borders, such as certain divisions of the Yao people, travel culturally in between, too. The ethnic Chineseness of these populations, whose densities are high within a territorial scope, can be more evident in case they adopt distinctive religions, dialects, diets, and clothes, making their difference a political statement of identity. In comparison, those Han as well as Zhuang Chinese in Guangxi looking for business opportunities in Vietnam and acquiring the Vietnamese language are practicing ethnic Vietnameseness.

The identity of ethnic Kinh Chineseness in Guangxi, for example, is necessarily hybrid and can easily cause misunderstanding or stereotyping by either Chinese or Vietnamese. The life task resulting from ethnic Chineseness is for the population or its sympathetic scholars to remain acceptable to both sides and, therefore, impose on their members a certain pressure to shift and adapt in accordance with the context. Confrontation between China and Vietnam is their nightmare.[25] Reflective altercasting is a survival skill. However, reflective altercasting can lead to different strategies, with some simulating the same identities in compliance with their Chinese or Vietnamese counterpart, whereas others resist it to establish a social space to which they are entitled.

Vietnamese Chinese are called Kinh Chinese, many of whom reside in Guangxi—the three islands outside the city of Fangcheng. The Kinh Chinese population speaks both Chinese and Vietnamese. A good number of them make a living by daily crossing the River of Beilun to the city of Mong Cai (or Mangjie) on the Vietnamese side, where casinos are allowed.

Interviewees embrace a Chinese identity despite their ethnic Kinh status that will link them to the major nationality of Vietnam. However, in their work, they primarily receive and entertain Han or Zhuang tourists from China. A particular nostalgia for Mao Zedong-Ho Chi Minh friendship sweeps over the three islands. On the one hand, the Kinh Chinese community is disposed to their Chinese citizenship to avoid historical discrimination inflicted by the Han population. On the other hand, they act superior to the Vietnamese. Numerous legends relate the contribution made by the early Kinh Chinese generations to the Chinese nation-building. This population complains about the Vietnamese policy, which allegedly aggravates the relationship between both sides during the border clashes. Resistance to China is rare among the contemporary Kinh Chinese.

By contrast, few signs of resistance among the Chinese-Vietnamese have been evident. First, during the American War, some Chinese Vietnamese in the south dreaded the conscription by the Saigon authorities to fight the North. The aftermath of the unification in 1975 is the large outflow of Chinese-Vietnamese to escape the communist rule.[26] Some of the migrants who have settled in the US have continued to hope that the US would support the democratization of Vietnam. On the contrary, Chinese Vietnamese staying in Vietnam tend to have an isolated mentality.[27] They have resented the public-sanctioned certificate for those who speak a second language because they consider Chinese their mother language.[28] Chinese Vietnamese in general are fond of Ho Chi Minh. They show a significant support for nation building in Vietnam.[29] Their operating languages are Chinese dialects, which differ from Mandarin. Chinese consciousness,[30] together with support for Vietnamese nationalism, produces a hybrid identity with uncertainty as well as incapacity in gaining recognition from either Chinese or Vietnamese in-group members.

Reflective Altercasting and Experiential Chineseness

Scholars who mingle with a self-identified Chinese population within a discernable boundary long enough to present, explain, and interpret Chinese lives from the sited viewpoint are practicing experiential Chineseness. Anthropologists, travelers, and migrant scholars illustrate this type, as well as people living in regions that do not distinguish between the two peoples,[31] in historical official families running a Chinese lifestyle,[32] and in circles in which intensive intermingling occurs.[33] The Chinese lifestyle includes both traditional and socialist lifestyles, resulting in the intuition that their experiences are mutually exchangeable.³⁴ Experiential Chineseness enables people to view China as their own group and willingly conform to the norms and institutions practiced by the Chinese population. However, a hatred may arise during conflicts with China, given that the Chinese are presumably like one's own folk; thus, a strong sense of relative disappointment is felt.³⁵

Reflective altercasting to fulfill the role of being Chinese-like and practicing certain lifestyles does not negate one's self-awareness of being Vietnamese. The pressure to retain the familiar in-group recognition from the Chinese population sharing the same life experiences and values induces the anxiety of being associated with the different lifestyle adopted by Vietnamese elsewhere. Confrontation between the Chinese and the Vietnamese immediately causes a twist of identity, in which Vietnam, rather than China, appears to be more culpable. Reflective altercasting leads to the mitigation of the conflict happening in high politics and the expectation that the conflict will inevitably pass.³⁶ An expectation that the Vietnamese side would concede also exists. Under experiential Chineseness, anything that happens to China is considered likely to happen to Vietnam.

Experiential Chineseness occurs most naturally in the family, neighborhood, and school as seniors exhibit an unreserved practice of Chinese culture and religion for the younger generation to emulate.³⁷ Many Vietnamese sinologists could recollect certain family traditions. Some of these traditions have proceeded from the past imperial officialdom, usually from a grandparent who is wholeheartedly engrossed in Confucian teachings, as well as the classic literature.³⁸ Fathers are even more important if they have been determined sinologists.³⁹ Teachers are equally important in some cases because they reinforce the interest and aptitude of a traditionally grown child for sinological scholarship.⁴⁰ With an embedded childhood, some sinologists continue their studies all by themselves outside the formal curricula. They are naturally self-disciplined and so can continue a tradition they gradually consciously represent in their selfhood. This family tradition may, at times, include the legendary incidents of historical fights with China, as if the wars were family feuds, not to be considered alarming, as civilizational or scientific Chineseness would assume.

Beyond the intellectual dimension, experiential Chineseness is present among the rank-and-file who are exposed to Chinese soap operas, movies, and novels that spread logics and values familiar to the Vietnamese audience, who automatically accepts Chinese narratives as its own.⁴¹ In fact, Chinese narratives easily attract Vietnamese viewers exactly because the lifestyle, rhetoric, and social relations all echo the Vietnamese experiences.⁴² Vietnamese who mingle with the Chinese population in their neighborhood or during their studies in China similarly and typically have desensitized the sense of difference at the basic levels despite a distinctive national identity.[43] The linguistic and cultural environments that enable the Vietnamese to transcend the sentiment that nationalism easily monopolizes are the major facilitators of mutual empathy.[44] However, those presumably in-group Chinese who deviate from the expected pattern or the consensual reality deny the value of Vietnamese members and cause anxiety as well as retaliation.

Reflective Altercasting and Cultural Chineseness

Scholars who study or practice Confucianism or any other perceived Chinese cultural, religious, or political belief system in their lives and apply this belief system to their understanding of Chinese phenomena are practicing cultural Chineseness. Cultural Chineseness forms a certain imagined mutuality exclusively between Vietnamese and Chinese.[45] It enables people to take advantage of the classic wisdom accumulated in the shared cultural memory confidently and comfortably. Cultural Chineseness is more intensive than experiential Chineseness to the extent that the former develops from a long-term association and familiarity with Chinese discourses and, therefore, is more appreciative than the latter's mere practice of the same lifestyle, which does not necessarily reach the intellectual level. Compared with sinological Chineseness, which introduces China to Vietnam, cultural Chineseness focuses on Vietnam's self-enhancement.[46] It can facilitate a powerful criticism of China by appealing to the values and norms to which China presumably subscribes. It can even serve as a methodology for how to search and use Chinese beliefs that are not immediately available.[47]

Looking for clues from Chinese examples on how to deal with a similar situation exemplifies a kind of reflective altercasting.[48] Chinese examples are intuitively relevant, as if the success and failure of the Chinese are similarly reproducible in Vietnam, once the same response to a similar situation is attempted (N. Nguyen 2014, 139–56). Moreover, an understanding of Chinese culture is believed to promote an understanding of Vietnamese culture,[49] as if the cultures of both sides are the same, despite the fact that Vietnam is a different country with a distinctive past,[50] so that how one understands Vietnam would be a matter of how one understands China.[51] A sense of reflective altercasting similarly exists in the criticism of China, as if criticizing China is tantamount to self-criticism.[52]

Vietnamese Han Nom characters have set the foundation for cultural Chineseness.⁵³ They not only allow the Vietnamese literati to comprehend and teach Chinese classics and Chinese thought but also leave a tradition of poetry that prompts a number of Vietnamese sinologists to declare their superior grasp of Chinese culture compared with their Japanese and Korean counterparts (Shih, Chou, and Nguyen 2017). The Nom system provides a specific methodology for a senior to assess how well the younger generation has preserved their own culture.⁵⁴ In addition, Buddhist beliefs comprise another powerful foundation of cultural Chineseness, as renowned Vietnamese priests may travel to serve temples in Guangxi. The argument that keeping rather than averting cultural Chineseness is the key to Vietnam's own cultural subjectivity simply means that Vietnamese culture is heavily indebted to Chinese culture.⁵⁵ Appreciation for one's culture is how self-respect evolves;⁵⁶ thus, appreciating the Chinese cultural legacy is how Vietnam can develop cultural dignity.⁵⁷

Vietnam must protect cultural Chineseness not merely because of self-respect and self-confidence. Cultural Chineseness is also Vietnam's proud intellectual capacity to read between the lines the mind of the Chinese leader, given the similar cultural calculi of both cultures. In addition, Vietnam is able to see the moral problem of the Chinese leadership precisely because Vietnam is aware of how China violates its own cultural norms or alleged behavioral patterns.⁵⁸ Vietnamese intellectuals and political leaders know how not to abandon their moral ground and yet cope with the encroaching China on the rise by relying on both their shared cultural pattern and political party system.⁵⁹ All of these Chinese norms are simultaneously Vietnamese norms and patterns. An interviewee goes as far as suggesting that Vietnam is the little brother who occasionally fails to address the need to save the face of the big brother in accordance with their shared system of propriety.⁶⁰ Another interviewee who frequently contributes to opinion columns in newspapers under a pen name explains that he decided to use the pen name lest his real name should embarrass his Chinese counterpart, with whom he has had a long relationship.⁶¹

Policy Implications

The capacity for fluidity, embedded in complex cultural memory and history, in terms of self-positioning between an in-group identity and an out-group identity, suggests that human decisions ultimately produce the act of positioning and relationality. For example, individuals owning sinological Chineseness always have the potential to shift toward the position of an outsider who subsequently yields their resemblance of Confucian standards for Western realism when assessing China's Vietnam policy and preparing for realignment in international politics. As a result of the shift, the role identity of sinological Chineseness, originating from the duty to translate between and improvise for Chinese and Vietnamese, evolves into a unilateral identity of scientific Chineseness, defined by the necessity to manage China. Furthermore, someone owning ethnic Chineseness to meet the expectations of both Chinese and Vietnamese may revert to the role of a cultural successor of Confucianism and enter a high profile, demanding the reconstitution of Vietnamese identity with a clearer respect for a cultural resemblance to China. Another plausible scenario is that some individuals will initially feel comfortable about undistinguishing Vietnamese and Chinese ways of life under the condition of experiential Chineseness; they could suddenly realize the lack of morality in the experiential Chineseness and support civilizational distinction, which exposes the negative image of Chineseness, as if Vietnam has been the sole successor of a moral culture, which China aborts.

The volatile nature of owning Chineseness inevitably prompts uncertainties in policy. The coexistence of different kinds of resembled Chineseness is the norm and spirit of the new century. Accordingly, a South Vietnamese scholar's use of traditional Chinese characters, which seemingly convey a pro-Taiwan disposition toward civilizational Chineseness, may succeed in improvising cultural Chineseness due to its efficiency in linking Han Nom and the Chinese classics. Accordingly, cycles, as a methodology, fare better than a typical evolutionary or linear historiography. Cycles of cooperation, teaching and learning, realignment, suppression, sharing, and aversion, combined with a variety of emotional characteristics, such as opportunism, enthusiasm, anxiety, anger, happiness, and hatred, demand an epistemology that is not obstructed by linearity, consistency, structure, or parsimony. A quote from a sinologist veteran who strives to avoid making an impossible choice could be a good harbinger for the coming age of consciously mixed Chineseness:

> Zen scholars in Vietnam often advocate the difference between Vietnamese and Chinese Zen, pointing to the former's national spirit and its perseverant continuity. In my view, this is incorrect.

Zen is no more than simply Zen. Vietnamese Zen and Chinese Zen are identical. The national soul is a matter of historiography. For example, [Emperor] Trần Nhân Tông [1258–1308], who led troops to fight Mongolian invaders, was a historical character. Do not confuse his two roles. The role of emperor obliged him to fight. His other role as a Buddha required him to follow religious practices. His leadership in fighting was not derived from being a Buddha. One could not argue, in his case, that the Vietnamese Buddha was [a] nationalist. Do not confuse two roles in order to reflect one's own desire for national independence and autonomy. Zen is most alert to dichotomy. Zen is a spirit of selflessness. How can Zen promote self-independence? Vietnamese scholars have a habit of reading the patriotic spirit and love for Mother Nature into Zen, but people from all other countries also love their country and Mother Nature.[62]

Chapter 6

Colonial Cleavages

Japanese Legacies in Taiwan's Views on China

Introduction

After Japan's defeat at the end of World War II, the Allied Forces returned Taiwan to China, which was at that time represented by the nationalist Kuomintang. The KMT was then, in turn, defeated during the Chinese Civil War and retreated to Taiwan in 1949. Consequently, because decolonization did not proceed from an indigenous consciousness embedded in precolonial Chineseness (Cumings 2004, 279; Chang and Chiang 2012, 28–29), which was equivalent to borderline Chineseness (see chapter 1), Taiwan became a peculiar postcolonial as well as post-Chinese nation.

The exiled KMT, a latecomer to Taiwan, attempted to implement Taiwanese decolonization from its own perspective of moral Chineseness (see chapter 1). Its migrant characteristics, however, alienated a significant portion of the indigenous population from the decolonization project and induced it to perceive the KMT as the successor of an estranged civilization that was inferior to Taiwan's colonial modernity (Thiele 2017; Louzon 2017; Chen 2002; Takeshi 2006). In the eyes of the KMT, this colonial modernity indicated enslavement at best, which failed the role expectations in accordance with moral Chineseness. In contrast to the KMT's claimed Chineseness, indigenous Taiwanese scholarship on China looked primarily on Mainland China, instead of Chineseness of Taiwan. Owning no legitimacy to speak on behalf of China, such a colonially prepared outsider's position of Taiwan informs most of the contemporary perspectives on China.

In the first part of the chapter, I will argue that this unfulfilled decolonization explains why Taiwan differs so much from most other postcolonial societies, where attitudes toward the former colonial powers mark one of the main locations of social cleavage. Under the KMT, attitudes toward a differently imagined China, as opposed to colonizing Japan, instead, have increasingly marked the main social cleavages. The KMT Chinese Civil War agenda, together with its self-righteous moral Chineseness, substituted for decolonization. With the KMT losing the Civil War, the reemerging colonial modernity undergirds Taiwan's own identity away from the insider's position as well as the associated sense of moral Chineseness imposed by the KMT. The former colonial relation with Japan has, oddly, become the dominant intellectual resource to support Taiwan's identity strategy regarding Chineseness.

The chapter will then illustrate how Taiwanese intellectuals born before the end of the Japanese colonialism have grown and developed their perspectives on China in later years. It applies the theme of post-Chineseness to complicate the notions of China and Chineseness. Essentially, the analysis will show that those who find a resemblance to China a challenge to their self-respect allow colonial modernity to constitute either their scholarship or their social relationships (Lee and Chen 2014). In contrast, those who reimagine resembled Chineseness in Taiwanese perspectives are inclined to remain critical of the Japanese influence in their presentations of China.

Colonial Relationality of Modernity and War

Up from Colony

The chapter defines colonial relationality as *the conditions of being related through shared colonial history* (Sealey 2018; Shih 2016; M. Lin 2016). (See chapter 3 for a technically longer definition.) Colonial relationality distinguishes the arriving KMT from the Taiwanese indigenous population, who has either directly experienced colonialism to some extent or internalized indirectly colonial experiences through interaction in later years with the elderly who have direct experiences of it. Colonial relationality enables discursive congruence among those who once practiced colonial rules, participated in colonial modernity, and learned colonial values despite incongruence in their moral assessments of colonialism (Heller and McElhinny 2017; Harvey 2015; Chow 2014). The most important aspect of colonial relationality for later generations to develop their imagination of China is that a significant portion of the Taiwanese elites accepted the conversion of their own identities into a Japanese one. Wherever the Civil War regime failed to treat their colonial relations with respect, nostalgia for colonial modernity in the postcolonial period was bound to arise (Raychaudhuri 2018). Consequently, the images of China would be alien and negative.

Consider colonial modernity as *achieving characteristics of modernization that make the colony useful to the colonizer* (Takeshi 2006; Aguir 2011; Shin and Robinson 1999). Some praise it as an instrument to contrast against the backwardness of the KMT or China; others denounce it as mechanism of exploitation (Morris 2017; Heylen and Sommers 2010). With decolonization, colonialism usually becomes perceived as exploitive, as has been the case in, for example, the formerly Japanese Korea and British India. In Taiwan, though, the colonial modernity brought by Japan provides, to date, an intellectual foundation for those who strive for dignity before the disapproving KMT who, at the time of its arrival in Taiwan, lacked a similar level of modernity (Barclay 2016; H. Tsai 2009). On the contrary, for those indigenous people who did not go through conversion or suffered relative degradation due to the arrival of the KMT's Civil War regime, a lingering Chinese consciousness may lead to suspicion toward colonial modernity despite the readiness to take advantage of it when convenient or strategically beneficial. In fact, the KMT likewise recruited Japanese advisors to engage in its Civil War.

One key development of colonial modernity in Taiwan was the so-called Kominka (Japanization) campaign, which coincided with the beginning of Japan's expansion into China. It included a language campaign and surname reform so that the entire population would eventually enjoy a cultural resemblance to Japan. However, the key component of the campaign's cultural aspect was religious in nature (Peng and Chu 2017; Lee, Mangan, and Ok 2018; C. Lee 2012). It involved the installation of the goddess Amaterasu as the highest spirit that was fungible for previously worshiped ancestors. Migrants in Taiwan used to conceive of their own selves as racially Chinese. After Kominka, people officially became Japanese, which was a spiritual thing and, hence (Ching 2001; Henry 2016), arguably, metaphorically similar to the situation that the protestants celebrated after winning the Reformation wars in Europe—that is, they no longer needed to go through the medium of Catholic churches and could now pray directly for God's blessing.

To ensure the absolute loyalty of colonized people toward Japan (Wong and Yau 2013 W. Chou 1991), the earlier cultural campaigns went hand in hand with material incentives. For instance, the more successfully assimilated families received privileges in education, recruitment for public office, and rations. Physically bowing to the emperor at fixed times composed the daily body politics, especially in schools. The post-Kominka situation transformed the earlier designation of the colonized population as "the slaves of the (barbarian) Manchurian nation," which had implicated a status lower even than barbarian. With Kominka, however, they became direct subjects of the emperor. Consequently, as the Pacific War intensified, over 120,000 Taiwanese voluntarily joined the Japanese military to fight against the Allied Forces. Officially serving the imperialist army was considered an honor in general. Even the ultimate defeat could not reduce the sense of pride. This is underscored, for instance, by the fact that, even as late as the seventieth anniversary of the end of the war in 2015, pro-Taiwan independence forces in Taiwan insisted that Taiwan only memorialize the defeat in order to contrast itself against the self-regarded winner, China. They did so to prove that Taiwan is not Chinese (Amae 2011; Liao and Wang 2006).

The KMT after the takeover perceived itself as enacting the role of "liberator" from Japanese colonization (Louzon 2017; Hui 2019; Jacobs 2014; M. Lo 2002b). However, its migrant nature inhibited it from seriously understanding colonization in the Taiwanese context. Therefore, the KMT's decolonization was only superficial, through providing equal citizenship and unifying patriotic education for the postcolonial population. Resistance by those remaining loyal to Japan was mistaken as Communist infiltration or still part of the Chinese Civil War. The KMT failed to catch the sense of relative deprivation that its rule brought for the indigenous population, which was the result of the following four factors: (1) the population had (partially) internalized the Japanese view that the KMT regime belonged to a lower civilization; (2) it perceived Japan's defeat primarily as a result of American atomic bombing rather than the combat skills of the KMT; (3) the KMT governance was far less efficient and more corrupt compared with the Japanese colonial administration; and (4) the KMT was, in itself, a loser of the Chinese Civil War. In short, nostalgia for the former colonial identity provided the convenient, effective reference to reverse the KMT Civil War ideology.

Yet, the fact that Japan's legacy remains particularly strong pertains additionally to the fact that the postcolonial Taiwanese population was not held accountable for the war. The defeated Taiwanese soldiers as well as civilian collaborators loyal to Japan received the arriving KMT regime without becoming subjected to war crime trials. As Japan renounced ownership of Taiwan, the population automatically assumed their citizenship of the victorious side—the Republic of China (ROC)—at the moment of defeat. Peculiarly, the returning Taiwanese soldiers felt no military defeat and yet maintained a sense of colonial superiority. As the bizarre winners of the Chinese war against Japan, they escaped the pressure to reflect upon the Japanese war of invasion of which they had been a part. Neither did they jettison the civilizational imagination behind the enthusiasm for war. As a result, seventy years after the end of the war, there is the increasingly vociferous assertion that Taiwan should only celebrate the loss of the war since Taiwan belonged to Japan during the war. In other words, the fact that they officially became "Chinese" citizens provided the pro-independence force in Taiwan with a shield to remain exempt from punishment and a shadow of loss, while also enabling them comfortably to assert an un-Chinese identity.

Practically, though, colonial modernity had its limits (Chen and Shimizu 2019; T. Cheng 1989; Shih 2007). First of all, a vast portion of the population had not undergone Japanization, and this part of the population's nostalgia for colonial modernity was less powerful (Chu 2016). Second, with the KMT wielding political control in the postwar period, those who had experienced Japanization were able to take advantage of social mobility in economics, education, and even public administration. Third, the KMT was able to deliver economic growth for a prolonged period of time to distract from political tensions. Fourth, identificational exits became available in the United States, where educational as well as career opportunities started providing an alternative route to regain the self-respect lost under KMT rule. Fifth, electoral democratization since the mid-1990s facilitated a rising national consciousness in Taiwan (Jacobs 2013). Last but not least, the KMT engaged in decentralization, indigenization, and democratization in the 1980s to accommodate the coming legitimacy crisis that would inevitably emerge with the demise of its first generation (Sumei Wang 2009).

In the meantime, the Japanese colonial contempt for the "inferior" Chinese civilization was able to find a natural substituting target in communist China, which was economically backward and politically authoritarian. With the last generation of the Japanized population coming to power in Taiwan through the KMT's internal channel (e.g., presidency of Lee Teng-hui) and then the next generation following up through winning electoral campaigns (e.g., presidency of Chen Shui-bian as well as Tsai Ing-wen), colonial modernity, colonial identity, and Taiwanese identity reemerged powerfully in Taiwan (Corcuff 2012a; Lynch 2004). Ironically, China's rise in the twenty-first century and confident calls for reunification with the island only bring back memories of the deprivation brought about by the KMT after World War II.

Post-Chinese Possibilities Embedded in Colonial Relationality

(Post)colonial scholarship in general and the writing of China in Taiwan in particular involve strategic choices. For instance, regarding the primary sources and the methodology on which one relies, the language of (re)presentation, and the audiences one intends to address necessarily incorporate as well as affect one's purposes and strategies of research and writing (L. Smith 2012; Kovach 2010). To the extent that indigenous research anywhere must be relational in both the social and political sense (S. Wilson 2009), purposes can evolve and multiply accordingly. This is especially the case when considering that a postcolonial scholar on China can receive educational training in homeland Taiwan, in Japan, in an Anglo-European country, in China, or in another post-colonial country, such as India, Hong Kong, or Singapore. Owning some mixed (educational) background is common among scholars, too. In fact, senior China scholars usually received mixed training in China, Japan, the United States, and Taiwan.

The embracing of particular approaches or the consultation of certain sources implicate one's intellectual and identity distance from specific audiences (Tanaka 1993). In other words, one can measure the distance of a scholar from China and indicate her identity by looking at the methodology that she adopts and the audience to whom she intends to establish resemblance (Matsumura 2018; Golovachev 2018; Lomová and Zádrapová 2016). If, for instance, one intends to distance oneself from the audience that is already at a deliberate distance from China—for example, by enlisting a supporting Chinese source to interact with a pro-Taiwanese independence audience—one probably identifies more with China than one's audience does. On the contrary, if one uses Japanese sources to mingle with the same audience, one would probably identify less with China. In other words, if one intends to shorten the distance from such a pro-independence audience, one may reflect an implicit purpose of keeping resemblance to China minimal. However, the identity strategy is more complicated than any universal rule can describe. To name another example, by enlisting a British source or an American methodology, one might intend to take a neutral position between Taiwan and China—that is, presumably through being "objective." The international style of scholarship could likewise support the quest for higher status in the face of the Taiwanese domestic audience or targets in China, both of whom are arguably less international (Shih 2014b).

Taiwan's situation is reminiscent of Hong Kong. Hong Kong is different from other British colonies but comparable to Taiwan in the sense that the main liberator is an external power that failed to empathize with the identity crisis of the former colony. Both Taiwan and Hong Kong face an identity choice between the colonial motherland, Japan and the UK, respectively, on one hand, and the Chinese motherland or the indigenous site, on the other hand (Hou 2018; S. Lin 2018; Y. J. Cheng 2017). This makes the situation in these two localities more complex than the situations in Korea or India. For India, the choice is between the colonial and the indigenous. However, Korea and Taiwan are comparable to the extent that their similar positioning during the Cold War and all-round dependence on the United States add an alternative to their former colonial motherlands (Cho 2015). With regard to facing China through multiple perspectives, the situation in Taiwan seems most complicated. This is particularly the case since Taiwan has the possibility to pursue either a psychologically higher but linguistically neutral scholarship on China embedded in Anglo-American methodology, a higher but anti-China scholarship embedded in the Japanese colonial perspectives, or a higher but pro-China scholarship embedded in the classic humanistic perspectives. Specifically, the use of the Anglo-American methodology, which keeps Chinese voices from intervening, can fulfill multiple purposes—for example, it can be used as a tool to move beyond the scope of influence imposed by the former colonial Japan, to apply as a standard estranging the presumably politically superior China, or to win the respect of fellow Taiwanese who worship the American.

In short, the above can be boiled down to two dimensions: (1) position, whether or not one understands China from a self-imagined internal perspective or an external one; and (2) source, whether or not one allows Chinese perspectives to determine what constitutes Chineseness. As regards the first dimension, there are internal, external, and in-between positions where one consciously decides between being Chinese, non-Chinese, or partially Chinese (and thus partially non-Chinese). For the second dimension, one can rely on either Chinese sources or allegedly objective sources in order to approach China as well as Chineseness.

The above two dimensions produce (3x2) six possibilities, already familiar to readers who have reviewed chapter 5, which the book calls post-Chinese possibilities—cultural Chineseness (internal/Chinese), civilizational Chineseness (external/Chinese), sinological Chineseness (in-between/Chinese), experiential Chineseness (internal/objective), scientific or policy Chineseness (external/objective), and ethnic Chineseness (in-between/objective). The practices or shifts toward a certain post-Chinese identity reflect someone's strategic choice in a context, which implicates upon her attitudes and policies on her China.

The first approach on the source dimension is to rely on those perceived Chinese perspectives. To reiterate briefly, three categories divided by self-positioning emerge. First, those writers who consider themselves practitioners of Chinese cultural lives in one way or another own cultural Chineseness. Cultural Chineseness could be practiced, for instance, through ancestor worship, specific food diets, advocating patriotism/nationalism, speaking Mandarin/provincial dialects, adhering to the lunar calendar, or anything that reproduces a trajectory of relationality in which a resemblance to other self-identified Chinese could be improvised. Second, people who are able to mediate between Chinese and other cultural lives possess sinological Chineseness. Such Chineseness reflects self-confidence in understanding both sides and explaining each to the other. Third, civilizational Chineseness describes an embedded self-consciousness that identifies China as a distinctive other. In this regard, China refers to religious, ideological, or cultural resources to be learned or borrowed for exotic purposes, on the one hand, and despised and rejected for exclusionary purposes, on the other.

The second approach to the source dimension is to adopt a presumably objective standard and divide the post-Chinese possibilities into the same three introduced in the previous chapter. Paraphrasing it quickly, first, experiential Chineseness is owned by those self-regarded insiders who have spent enough time with Chinese so as to practice and support the same pattern as well as stance acquired through experiences from living or working together. Second, ethnic Chineseness contrasts with sinological Chineseness in the sense that people who possess it are not embedded in Chinese cultural or civilizational perspectives. Rather, it comes from an awareness of being physically related in one way or another to both the Chinese and the other side. Ethnic Chineseness compels conformity of its owners to expectations from both sides and incurs anxiety of all sides toward undecidable results. Third, scientific/policy Chineseness points to the analytical practices of those self-designated outsiders who approach and claim knowledge of China based upon certain selected, presumably objective, criteria, regardless of how those perceived Chinese under study may respond. These criteria could include size, level of power, type of institution, gene, borders, and anything that is functional to defining China as an object of a research agenda that makes most sense to the narrators.

Six Illustrative Stories of Colonial Relationality

Hsu Chie-lin's Practices of Cultural Chineseness

Hsu Chie-lin was born in Hsinchu in 1935 and received his primary education at Kitashirakawa Elementary School, a school established in memory of Prince Kitashirakawa Yoshihisa, who died during the war of conquest over Taiwan.[1] Hsu later attended a different school to escape from American bombardments. He was bilingual to the point that he wrote his doctoral dissertation in Japanese. After Japan's defeat, Hsu's Chinese teacher was suspected of infiltration and executed by the KMT. Hsu's academic career began at the National Taiwan University. During his time there, the professors who impacted upon his intellectual growth the most were mainly the exiled Chinese ones. Although Hsu does not come from a wealthy family, after college, a fellowship from the Japanese government enabled him to enroll in the University of Tokyo to study under the guidance of a leading sinologist, Naoki Kobayashi. Hsu is proud of his training at the University of Tokyo. Although in his 70s now, Hsu still actively publishes on Manchuria, Taiwan, and Japan regularly in Japanese journals.

Hsu's later career demonstrates cultural Chineseness. Despite the deep Japanese influence on his intellectual growth, he still remained critical toward Japan. This was mainly because, coincidentally, the Japanese professors he studied with during his time in Japan were predominantly reform oriented. However, Hsu himself primarily attributes his critical aptitude to the difficult conditions he endured during his childhood. Because of his critical stance, he was disappointed at Taiwan's submission of intellectual independence to the US and Japan. He insisted that, since Taiwan had officially returned to China in 1945 and in the light of their converging civilization, reunion with China should be the natural path to follow. Hsu's initial agenda in Japan was Taiwan studies, which he intended to serve as a stepping stone for a longer-term agenda of China studies. Both Hsu's professor in Japan, Naoki Kobayashi, who was a constitutionalist and peace activist, and his professor earlier in college in Taiwan, Sa Meng-wu, who was a reputable institutionalist, had a profound influence on his thinking. This influence was highlighted by the heavy indebtedness to their institutionalist viewpoints in Hsu's doctoral thesis, which explained why Japan's Westernization had succeeded but China's failed. Hsu currently still stresses the importance of political thought and argues that China's adherence to classic Chinese thought most powerfully explained its abortion of Westernization. In addition, he finds history extremely important but overlooked by political scientists. He considers his utmost contribution to the Taiwanese academic field his research on the political history of Taiwan.

Hsu's China studies correspond to his cultural Chineseness, that is, understanding China both culturally and historically from an internal perspective. For instance, he explains the success of Deng Xiaoping's reforms mainly through the influence of Deng's thought reforms, which he believes paralleled the thought reforms implemented during Japan's Meiji Restoration. He criticizes the preference for behaviorist methods in social science. Instead, he accepts the Japanese sinological tradition that relies on the classics. Besides his dissertation, another of his major projects was to assess China's economic conditions through the Japanese academic literature. Here, he owns sinological Chineseness as well as a kind of Japanological Japaneseness, too. Moreover, he was also the founding father of the China studies team at National Taiwan University's College of Social Sciences. In principle, though, his China studies proceed through the China connections in Taiwan's political history. In this light, he begins his China studies project with the year of Taiwan's colonization by Japan and compares it with that of China during the Opium Wars, so that he is able to see the different influences of UK and Japan on China. Over the years, he has invited a good number of leading sinologists to NTU to engage in exchange programs. Nishida Masaru has been his latest cooperator. They edit a journal together.

Yeh Chi-cheng's Practices of Sinological Chineseness

Yeh was born in 1942. His grandfather was thirteen years old when Japan colonized Taiwan. His many old-fashioned Chinese classic collections fascinated his young grandson.[2] Yeh's father, though, collected a good number of Japanese books, whose pictures as well as sporadic Han characters likewise intrigued young Yeh. The three generations inherited different civilizational identities, breeding in Yeh a liking for both Japanese music and Chinese opera. In school, Yeh met the children of the Chinese migrants who had followed the fleeing KMT. Their languages did not mingle well, which often led to fist fights. Yeh, therefore, became sensitive to the differences in birthplaces very early. He then realized that even Taiwanese had taken multiple paths, with some being born or schooled in China during childhood before returning to Taiwan. He also encountered migrant Chinese who were victimized by KMT rule. After he started college, his intellectual growth as well as career was heavily indebted to migrant scholars, whose nostalgia for China easily reminded him of his father's nostalgia for colonial governance. In fact, he noticed his own nostalgia for the past the moment he encountered a Japanese soap opera.

Yeh demonstrates a kind of sinological Chineseness. For instance, he dreamed of saving China while in high school. However, throughout his adulthood, he felt alienated from the KMT rule as well as its propaganda and rituals. He acquired a high degree of political consciousness from his father. Yeh feels sympathetic toward migrant Chinese soldiers who ended up in Taiwan often unexpectedly. His critical attitude, career development, and academic engagement benefited enormously from various migrant liberals, some of whom he felt obliged to support despite their general opposition to Taiwanese independence, which is his wish. Although he is aware of his marginal position, he is ready to criticize both sides for failing to empathize with each other or for their typical hypocritical practices. He uses his coexisting trajectories of intuitive love for Japanese songs and Chinese instruments as a metaphor to illustrate how life experiences can be apolitical and yet distinctive. Once politicized, however, the indigenous and migrant populations in Taiwan are compelled to confront each other.

Yeh's scholarship is accordingly alert to ironies, ambivalence, and dialectics. What particularly alerts him is the incapacity of academics to resolve the widespread dichotomic incongruences in human society in general and in China as well as in Taiwan specifically. One such incongruence is that between modernity and tradition, which is obviously a challenge not just for China or Taiwan. Behind this incongruence lies the conflict between the West and East and, more profoundly, between dependence on and a fear of the West/East at the psychological end and between being or becoming the West/East at the ontological end. It is unlikely for Taiwanese scholars, Yeh insists, to tackle this issue without themselves being situated both in Western intellectual history and engrossed in Oriental wisdom. In order to do so himself, Yeh seeks insight from Newtonian calculus, which originates from the Hobbesian notion of endeavor and produces repercussions in conceptualizing continua in human phenomena. Self-reservation thus contrasts with Chinese thoughts. Moreover, Confucian officials of the late Qing period provided Yeh with a contemporary *problematiqué*, from where he discovered the rationale for the sinicization/indigenization campaigns in social science. This has led to Yeh's ultimate quest for "self-cultivation" as the last resort of transcendence in his own academic discipline—sociology.

Shih Ming's Practices of Civilizational Chineseness

Shih Ming was born in 1918 and passed away in 2019.³ His father had a college degree from Japan and was associated with leading activists promoting political participation for the Taiwanese people. During his childhood, Shih Ming himself went to a private teacher to study the Chinese classics, which his mother also understood well. Although his father was accustomed to the indigenous folk dramas performed for the gathering masses at local temples in Taiwan, he went on to learn music in Japan. Shih Ming was then smuggled into Japan to study when he was nineteen. He recalled no discrimination against colonized people. He entered Waseda University and enjoyed its liberal style. He mingled well with classmates off school, usually in bars. He also participated in study groups, where he encountered Marxism. Later, he found that Marxism allowed him to understand China in a relatively objective way. He was able to travel to China in order to support communism. In actuality, he mainly ended up mingling with the Japanese in Shanghai instead. No Chinese police or Japanese security bothered to watch him because he looked so Japanese. Nevertheless, he sympathized with China and felt regret at not being able to join the fight against Japan when it invaded China.

Shih Ming's perspective on China increasingly resembles civilizational Chineseness, despite him having learned the classics at an early age. This is because his socialist perspective on China romanticizes a future that is available neither in Taiwan nor in Japan. After Japan surrendered, he prepared himself to join the Civil War in China. First, he went to Lianhe University in Beijing where the studies involved serious self-critique sessions as well as the learning of anti-Japanese thought and Marxism. After returning to Japan, Shih Ming began to contact the pro-Taiwan independence organization. He simultaneously reflected upon the meaning of Taiwanese being Chinese from the perspectives of Marxism and materialism. This Marxist view supported the formulation of his theory of Taiwanese nationalism. Japan played an indirect but rather significant initial reference point. It was the contrast with Japan, as well as Japan being the Taiwanese beneficiary of colonial modernity, that Shih Ming used to make sense of the backwardness of China while at the same time conceptually defining China as a "class-based nation."

In his legendary publication—*Modern History of Taiwanese in 400 Years*—he divided the Chinese in Taiwan into five different types according to Marxism: (1) the ruling class that included both the Manchus and later the

KMT rulers; (2) the comprador class; (3) the proletarian class in Taiwan during the Qing dynasty; (4) the deceived Taiwanese under the KMT that included those Chinese migrants who followed the fleeing KMT to Taiwan; and (5) the sober Taiwanese. For Ming, China is no longer a home of socialism and Japan imposed no suppression on Taiwan after World War II. Rather, China as an entirety contains a suppressive national class (i.e., the ruling class). This explains how the Taiwanese population in its entirety is a suppressed class and why Taiwan is, necessarily, a separate nation. In this light, the KMT represents the Chinese nation that suppresses Taiwan. In other words, the colonial suppressing class of the KMT has victimized the Taiwanese as a colonized and suppressed class. Hence, for Shih Ming, the appeal to a shared Han identity in China and Taiwan is no more than an illusion.

CHEN PENG-JEN'S PRACTICES OF EXPERIENTIAL CHINESENESS

Born in 1930, Chen Peng-jen's ancestor followed Ming general Zheng Chenggong (Koxinga) to Taiwan seven generations ago.[4] During his childhood, Chen knew that he was from Fujian, China. Besides, he recalls that, when he noticed that the Japanese emperor had no surname, he felt puzzled and perceived himself as absolutely different. As a child, he took courses in Japanese for six to eight hours a week. He even won a Japanese speech contest in elementary school. However, he was barred from entering a higher-level competition because his family had kept its Chinese name during the Japanization campaign—even though this was because the campaign had not reached the remote countryside where Chen's family resided. Still, he recalls a neighbor hiding a statue of Buddha in a barrel filled with excrement to avoid it from being confiscated and burned by Japanization campaigners. He also points out that those very few who went through Kominka were nicknamed "three-feet-sons," people in between ostensibly four-footed Japanese and two-footed human beings. Nonetheless, Chen later realized that the Japanese teachers were devoted wholeheartedly to education, as opposed to the Chinese migrants who had fled to Taiwan and primarily taught for a salary. After his primary education, Chen went to Japan as an adolescent worker, all the while hoping that Japan would lose the war so that he could return home.

Colonial relationality did not lead to a Japanese identity in Chen's consciousness, although he was almost the best-connected Taiwanese among the Japanese high circles, which included a few former premiers. Rather, very early in his career, he had the good fortune to encounter a number of senior migrant officials affiliated with the KMT and received their consistent support. Even though Chen did not tour China until it was opened up in the 1990s, he attained a strong experiential Chineseness due to his daily life spent with migrant Chinese politicians and intellectuals. Consequently, he understood perfectly well how attached these senior migrant politicians were to China, the KMT, and its Three Principles of the People. Chen himself even embraced the KMT due to his faith in the Three Principles of the People. He was also anti-communist, probably because he had internalized this KMT stance. Chiang Kai-shek himself decided that Chen ranked as high as number four in the KMT. With regard to Chen's intensive mingling with the KMT elite throughout his career, his relationship with the KMT senior politician Ma Shu-li particularly stood out. Ma, who was in charge of overseas affairs and later became general secretary of the KMT, was very fond of Chen and treated him like a son. Ma later served as Taiwan's representative to Japan for over a decade.

A major contribution of Chen's scholarship is his translation work. In his translations, he was always sensitive to human characters and paid detailed attention to nuances. In his work, a few apparent themes particularly stand out. For example, specific Japanese and Japanese government attitudes toward China, revealed by words and deeds, alerted him. Moreover, complying completely with his given role, he was always prepared to criticize Japanese imperialism, Taiwanese independence, and communism. Consistently, these were the enemies of the KMT during the reign of Chiang Kai-shek as well as Chiang Ching-kuo. In addition to the political scholarship, he was preoccupied with storytelling. Among his nearly two hundred published books, people and their social relations always formed the core focus of his stories. All this made him highly qualified to take up the post of director of the history department of the KMT. Chen's achievements during his term included his acceptance of manuscripts submitted from the PRC, the opening up to the public of party historical documents, the raising of funds to establish a civilian foundation, and, most importantly, the sending of research delegates to the PRC without the approval of the KMT.

Shih Che-hsiung's Practices of Ethnic Chineseness

Shih Che-hsiung was born in 1942 and was not formally educated in the colonial system at all.[5] Neither was his family indoctrinated under the Kominka campaign. Shih Che-hsiung followed the KMT educational system through college, after which he entered the Graduate Institute of East Asian Studies at National Chengchi University as part of its first cohort. The institute was the first pedagogical institute of China studies in Taiwan under the KMT. Its mission was to remedy the lack of objective analysis of China, which suffered from serious political biases in the hands of the military and intelligence staff. President Chiang Ching-kuo was so concerned about its development that he even met in person with the first six students whom the institute recruited. Shih Che-hsiung would continue his career as student, assistant, lecturer, and even director of the institute. Along this long career path, he developed all kinds of interests regarding CCP politics, revolutionary history, ideology, demography, social welfare, the PLA, and so on.

Shih Che-hsiung is consciously aware of his position in-between Taiwan and China. However, he does not act upon any inclination to choose sides. Instead, he stresses the importance of both sides knowing each other. His ethnic Chineseness is reflected in his readiness to adjust himself in order to remain connected to both sides. He has many different friends throughout China and can always call somebody wherever he visits the country. Moreover, he claims that, among his relationships with many of his good friends in China, not a single problem has arisen. He observes that distrust is used to create problems for academic exchanges. However, he underscores the importance of these exchanges, because they are conducive to mutual understanding and making friends. Nevertheless, in times of distrust, he still endeavors to keep both sides informed. He does so, for instance, through pointing out directly to Chinese officials that there have been too many restrictions from the Chinese side. Moreover, he recommends that the hosts in Taiwan should act in a straightforward, sincere manner in order for the other side to gain trust in them. He also highlights the critical importance of acknowledging the need for face-saving by both sides.

In his own studies of China, Shih Che-hsiung relies intensively and extensively on field research. Not only did he belong to the first cohort of professors who led graduate students to visit China, but he was also a frequent visitor to various different sites in China himself. One of his famous skills of communication is deftly to recite all kinds of doggerel that he has gathered from villages all over China either to enhance his acceptance at different sites or to provoke the curiosity of his students. Another skill is reflected in his determination to collect a large number of books each time he visits China, which enables him to update his perspectives on situations in China socially as well as culturally. During his professorship, he has visited all thirty-one provinces in China. His approach primarily takes the form of humanist geography, since he always begins by investigating the history and ecology of the site that he is visiting. Now, at his retirement, he is a little unsure about whether or not his site-oriented scholarship has kept him from developing his own system of China scholarship.

Parris Hsu-cheng Chang's Practices of Scientific/Policy Chineseness[6]

Parris Chang was born in 1936. His father was an appointed county leader during Japanese colonial rule. Now, in the twenty-first century, the official post of the Xikou County leader is still provided by the same family at the same site. Chang is the head of the Xikou association in Taipei. His brother studied agriculture in Japan before returning to attend college at the postwar National Taiwan University. Chang moved to Tainan to attend a better high school. Many of his close classmates and friends at the time—such as Luo Fu-ch'uan (1935–), Hsu Shih-hsian (1908–83), and Trong Tsai (1935–2014)—decades later, became leading pro-Taiwan independence activists. Hsu, for example, encountered Sun Yatsen's thought while studying in Japan. She recalled that Sun's nation-building schemes had fascinated her. The KMT executed some of Chang's relatives and neighbors after World War II, and his family suffered during the subsequent land reforms. Moreover, he was able to recollect various stories about the jailing of his acquaintances. Chang learned about politics early on, because important local political figures came to visit his father frequently. Unlike most Taiwanese families who feel alienated from politics, Chang decided to major in politics. He also passed the diplomats' qualification exams at the age of twenty, making him the youngest student ever to do so.

Chang entered the field of China studies through Robert Scalapino (1919–2011), whom Chang was introduced to by a KMT connection because Chang's political position appeared to be anti-communist. However, he formally chose China studies as his career path, thanks to Doak Barnett (1921–99). Methodologically, Chang's academic training made him a fervent comparatist. Consequently, he adhered to the method of comparative communism throughout his career. This made him a devoted practitioner of scientific Chineseness. His analyses have continuously been heavily indebted to Harold Lasswell's frame of who gets what, when and how. Moreover, Barnett supported him to engage in China watching in Hong Kong. This allowed him to meet with Chinese from various backgrounds who were fleeing from China. Chang was able to establish himself as an expert on Chinese factional politics, which facilitated his worldwide connections, including in the former Soviet-bloc nations. Equally informative to scientific Chineseness was his conscious decision to avoid any involvement in activist campaigns for Taiwan independence. Despite several invitations by close acquaintances, he remained organizationally unconnected to them and contributed to the promotion of Taiwanese independence in his own professional way.

Chang's comparative approach enables him to broaden the base of the analysis to enlighten his audience through cases that would be otherwise unthinkable. As a member of the first group of overseas scholars who met Zhou Enlai in 1972, for example, he was able to counter Zhou's call for reunification by referring to Switzerland as a model (of neutrality) for Taiwan's future, catching his host completely by surprise. Categorically, this model also differed significantly from other pro-Taiwan independence advocacies, which mainly argued for Taiwan to become part of the US or Japan. Tellingly, he was able to continue his field research in China in the subsequent years, collecting information about the Great Leap Forward and the Cultural Revolution. Another example is that, in his testimony at the US Congress, he promoted the "Singapore model" for Taiwan, meaning a Chinese state that did not belong to China. By this, he alluded to a softened position on Taiwan's ownership of cultural or experiential Chineseness as well as the lack of legitimacy of the KMT to claim to represent China. His comparative scholarship on China has been easily accepted by think tanks and government agencies in India, the US, and Russia, among others.

Conclusion

The colonial relationalities left by Japan continue to constitute Taiwanese identities and constrain the KMT from improvising a sufficient sense of resemblance to the colonized population. Instead, the binary of China and Taiwan as two distinctive political entities constitutes the primary source of cleavage. Colonial relations ironically provide the intellectual resources to support the strategizing of various approaches to a practically undefinable China. Chapter 6 argues that this irony developed because the KMT substituted the Chinese Civil War ideology for decolonization and, in the process, overlooked a significant portion of the Taiwanese whose identity had been constituted by Japanese colonial modernity. The KMT thus neither decolonized the indigenous population nor caused it to apologize for its participation in the Japanese war of invasion. This was probably linked to the fact that the exiled KMT regime once considered Japan's legacy inferior. However, as this chapter has shown, this same legacy has enabled others to own a sense of superiority toward a China that is often imagined in different ways.

Given the overwhelming existence of colonial relationality in Taiwan, the postcolonial population can act upon it in various ways. The backgrounds of different people analyzed for this intellectual history chapter informed their intellectual agency for insistence, resistance or reconciliation. In this chapter, I only reflect on the more conspicuous of these—Hsu and Chen are relatively critical of Japan, while Shih Ming and Chang are more critical of China; Yeh is critical of both, and Shih Che-hsiung is critical of neither. This underscores how colonial relationality has an overarching impact upon the direction of desired resemblance and types of identity available within a specific context and thus influences how a postcolonial population understands China, Chinese civilization, and Chinese people.

Given that defining and understanding China, rather than Japan, has been the primary source of binary and cleavage in postcolonial Taiwan, chapter 6 applies the same six categories of post-Chineseness and proceeds to complicate China and Chineseness so that writing on China can reveal the agency of the writers themselves. However, these are intellectual categories. Actual human beings are able to combine, reconcile, and cyclically retrieve them. The notion of post-Chineseness sheds new light on the tentative and strategic nature of the Taiwan-China binary. However, one can anticipate that a specific pattern of behavior ensues once one can trace the emergence of a particular kind of post-Chineseness—cultural Chineseness embraces, experiential Chineseness follows, sinological Chineseness mediates, ethnic Chineseness answers, civilizational Chineseness divides, and Scientific Chineseness compares. A more nuanced categorization is possible and actually appreciable for the sake of tracing threads of resemblance that have been improvised. In order to provide this, though, more sophisticated types of disposition and behavioral consequences first need to be empirically observed.

Chapter 7

Ethnic Role-Making

China Watchers in the Philippines

Introduction

Along with chapter 5, the current chapter likewise relies on the anthropological notion of post-Chineseness to appreciate the perspectives of the Philippines' China watchers. However, chapter 7 further interrogates the strategizing of identities among ethnic Chinese-Filipinos. The relevance of the social psychological notion of altercasting is more apparent in chapter 7 because, compared with sinologists in Vietnam, Filipino scholars additionally have an ethnic relation to mind. Therefore, the identity strategy strongly involves an individualized preference for indigenous identity rather than a collective pursuit of national relation with China.

The study in this chapter uses the case of China watching in the Philippines further to argue that the desire to move from the internal position is social and psychological. The reflections of the Philippines' China experts reveal a politics of identity that most would consider irrelevant, given the effective integration of Chinese-Filipinos into the indigenous community. However, ethnic Chinese scholars continue to ponder how the integration of Chinese-Filipinos can be further improved, for example, by seriously considering the interests of the entire Philippine nation or contributing to the welfare of the indigenous population, in addition to caring merely about the benefits provided for the Chinese-Filipino community. Integration can be perceived by some Filipinos as incomplete as long as distinctive routes of reconnection with Chinese elsewhere, with PRC Chinese probably being the most significant, are registered among Chinese-Filipinos.

Such presumably distinctive routes of reconnection conspicuously exist in other Chinese Southeast Asian communities, alluding to a significant challenge posed by the project of integration (Callahan 2004). This chapter will argue in the ensuing discussion that the trained adoption of a sympathetically internal perspective for the West to understand China, lauded as China-centrism (P. Cohen 2010) as opposed to an otherwise imagined externality, is not the same as watching China from an innately internal position, because an exit is relatively easily available to the (Western) former. Their dual ability to bridge and disconnect distinguishes them from ethnic Chinese scholars.

Basically, the case study suggests that the attainment of the sympathetic capacity to understand China can enrich the knowledge of those China-watchers coming from an external position. However, adhering to an internal position of China watching may lead to backlashes in the indigenous community. Therefore, in the long run, the trend is for all ethnic scholars to navigate internal and external perspectives in watching China.

A Role Analysis of Post-Chineseness in the Philippine Context

The social positions of scholars and scholarships are key to understanding human knowledge and our knowledge of humans. This notion is true in modern China, which challenges not only the existing knowledge of the Chinese nation, Chinese people, and Chinese civilization but also the identity or self-identification of China-watchers with these positions (Brook and Blue 2002; Culp, U, and Yeh 2016; Hillemann 2009; König and Chaudhuri 2016; Manomaivibool and Shih 2016; Vukovich 2012). In other words, the identity of those who watch China, the Chinese people, and Chinese civilization make a difference to our understanding of the subjects and their objects.

The challenge is surely different for watchers who watch China in an imagined external position and those who possess a certain type of self-perceived "Chineseness." Another challenge for the latter is if they watch China outside the territorial, legal, and institutional barriers of the PRC, hence no felt legitimacy to speak on behalf of China. The emerging identity crisis in postcolonial Hong Kong and Taiwan in the twenty-first century seemingly indicates a trend among those possessing Chineseness to seek an epistemologically external position. However, the lingering identity politics pertaining to a culturally, territorially, and economically diverse Chinese population in Southeast Asia illustrates no such definitive trend (Tagliacozzo and Chang 2011; G. Wang 2002).

Contrary to the effort to establish an external position of watching, American, Japanese, Vietnamese, and Russian watchers of China, as a few noticeable examples, have been reflecting on their epistemological capacity to understand China from within. Instead of the issue of transcending the Chinese identity of (once) self-regarded Chinese scholars, the epistemological hurdle in studying China, the Chinese people, and Chinese civilization elsewhere is to overcome the imagined difference, which causes some to see "Orientalism" (Katzenstein 2012a; Shih 2013a; Tanaka 1993). Japan's China studies appear to be a successful case of epistemological migration out of the Chinese intellectual trajectory after 150 years of study, evolving the identity of Japan from a sinological state into a nation state by itself. Ironically, the call by late Mizuguchi Yuzo (1932–2010) to move beyond the Japanese national conditions while studying China suggests his regretful reflection of such epistemological migration.

Comparatively, altercasting and reflexive altercasting in Vietnamese sinology takes place between the corporate actors, Vietnam and China. In the case of China watching in the Philippines as well as Taiwan, it takes place between scholars and their communities. Accordingly, this chapter continues to use the concepts of post-Chineseness and altercasting, including primarily those adopted by individual Filipino scholars, to study the intellectual perspectives on China and the Chinese people. Post-Chineseness not only informs the variety of Chineseness but also considers the choices of identity strategy made necessary by individualized post-Chinese conditions. As with chapter 5, altercasting in the current chapter indicates the role expectations of China or anyone acting on its behalf to adhere to such a role that arises from the enactment of reconnection (Epstein 2012; Wehner 2015). For those watchers who culturally or politically identify with China, such as Chinese-Filipinos who mind their Chinese identities, altercasting is actually reflexive altercasting, which induces a role identity to satisfy a Chinese alter group and improvise a stable self-identity.

In the peculiar case where the external scholars see themselves as belonging to a greater Chinese identity, they are epistemologically similar to the majority of those possessing the PRC nationality, watching China from within. Chapters 5–7 nevertheless consider them watching China from an external position because they understand that those Chinese people whom they study usually consider these overseas and postcolonial scholars watching China from an external position. In other words, the legitimacy of speaking on behalf of China is not registered among the China scholars whom chapters in part 2 study.

In theory, China-watchers unilaterally discover some type of Chineseness in the population under study that they identify or connect with in relation to their own conditions, socially as well as intellectually. In practice, post-Chineseness triggers mutual relations across all types—directly between watchers and China, and indirectly between different watchers, and between watchers and their readers everywhere. Although the conventional ownership of Chineseness everywhere is predominantly premised on some imagined kinship, post-Chineseness allows anyone who owns nonracial Chineseness, which is agreed upon reciprocally, to enact reconnection. One such example could be European sinologists who faithfully subscribe to Confucian values and can make an intellectual history subject out of cultural China. Given that Chineseness can either symbolize cultural centrality in the Confucian condition or ironically sensitize differences between Chinese populations in an ethnic condition, post-Chineseness enacts strategic reconnections between anyone as well as everyone through altercasting for whatever incongruent and inconsistent purposes (Nyíri and Tan 2016; C. Wang 2014).

Altercasting is the process of encouraging another Chinese person to express Chineseness, recognized as such, to maintain social relationships (Michalski and Pan 2017; Thies 2015; M. Wong 2010). The narrator should be able to communicate with the other person such that the latter self-identifies with such Chineseness (Callero 1994; Thies 2012; Wasson 2015). Reflexive altercasting, for example, conveying the message that a Chinese person like me should or should not be doing something, is the process whereby China-watchers imagine an expectation of their own role by the studied population and conform to such expectation (Hasting 2000; He and Feng 2015; Valenta 2009). Reflexive altercasting occurs when China-watchers are themselves self-regarded Chinese who watch China from an internal position. Under this circumstance, China watching reconnects China-watchers to their target population as a single group. In other words, reflexive altercasting reproduces cultural Chineseness in China-watchers.

In line with the previous chapters, post-Chineseness is related to whether the improvisation of resemblance between different Chinese groups comes from a self-regarded in-group actor or out-group actor. Any Chinese Southeast Asian narrator whose loyalty is toward one of China's Civil War rivals is an example of a self-regarded in-group actor. An improvisation initiated from an external position similarly re/constructs a role identity that unavoidably brings forth expectations that are informed to a degree by certain out-group perspectives, thereby altercasting. An in-group re/connection fulfils the function of reconfirming one's sense of belonging in particular ways and entails a role identity that necessarily generates self-expectations, thereby becoming a type of reflexive altercasting.

Figure 7.1 reiterates the same six categories of table 5.1. The notion of post-Chineseness thus engenders a research agenda that studies how Chineseness (1) as an unquestionable ontology is reproduced through its constitution of either in-group or out-group self-identity anywhere; (2) as an unsynchronized epistemology is supportive of contradictory identity strategies everywhere temporally and spatially; (3) as a cultural methodology is destabilizing to nationalist mobilization; and (4) as an intellectual project is necessarily composed of individualized cycles of life. The following discussion will rely on the oral history interviews of senior scholars of China and Chinese studies in the Philippines to gather different intellectual paths that reflect identity strategies of various types pertaining to Chineseness.

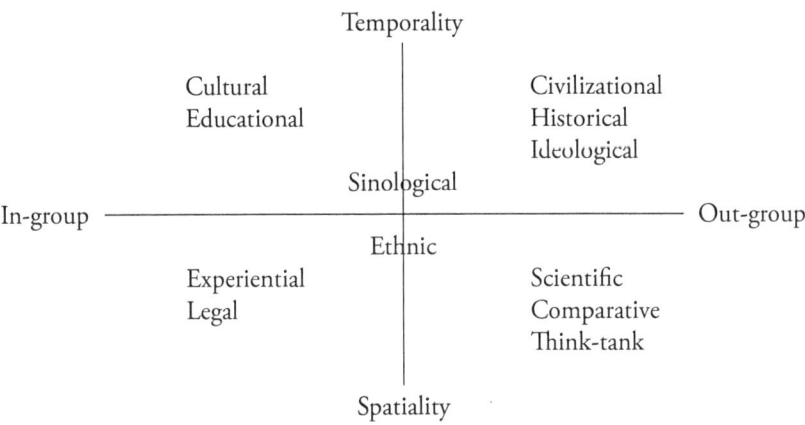

Cultural Chineseness: Enacted by imagining a shared culture and values
Experiential Chineseness: Enacted by recalling past living with Chinese
Sinological Chineseness: Enacted by bridging the differences between China and another
Ethnic Chineseness: Enacted by caring expectations of both China and another
Civilizational Chineseness: Enacted by assessing China on a subjective scale
Scientific Chineseness: Enacted by treating China as a comparable object

Figure 7.1. Two dimensions of Post-Chineseness.

Theoretical Propositions of Post-Chinese Agency

The social psychological literature does not confirm the designation of a positive emotion or affect to a relationship constituted by the greater self. Within the scope of Chinese social relationality, the greater self is literally a Confucian notion of collective identity, the contents of which vary depending on the encountered social context (Ho and Chiu 1998; K. Hwang 2012; Hwang, Francesco, and Kessler 2003). The social psychological translation of the greater self points to the incurring of the relational self such that the roles taken by one constitute one's self-identity (Barbalet 2014; Qi 2011). The greater self is therefore a sociological necessity everywhere, despite the fact that the Chinese culture injects a distinctive moral significance into the conscious celebration of its prevailing (F. Hsu 1971; Yang Kuo-shu 1995).

Nevertheless, social identity theory consistently demonstrates that the mere belonging to an artificially constructed group is sufficient to incur behavior that favors the in-group and discriminates against the out-group (Oldmeadow and Fiske 2010; Stephan and Stephan 1985). This condition partially explains the rationality of constructing a greater self and securing one's membership regardless of context. The greater self-consciousness is thus not uniquely Chinese, although the Chinese culture pertaining to the greater self is arguably more sophisticated than the Western one. Feeling for others is nonessential to the enactment of role identities; on the contrary, feeling concerned with how others regard the fulfillment of the role identity maintains social harmony and order (Barbalet 2001, 108). The emotional stress incurred renders the relevance of the indigenous population, because migrant and minority groups, with their imagined difference, are a target of loyalty or merit check.

The literature contrarily suggests that, under the condition of the relational self, the emotional aspect of role identity is easily registered in anxiety or stress (Burke 1991; Simon 1992). The self-discrepancy in one's performance of a role, as evaluated by the counterpart, is a major source of anxiety (Higgins 1987; Roseman 1984). Moreover, symbolic interactionism and dramaturgical sociology concur with the observation that significant others hold the key to one's emotional state of stress (Turner and Stets 2006, 26–32). The relational turn in psychoanalysis similarly points to the important subject of separation anxiety (Dimen 2001, 396; Renolds 2007), thus implying the dreaded loss of a role partner.

In addition, studies of Chinese psychology note the critical function of relationships in the maintenance of mental health (Hwang and Chang

2009; Lin, Tseng, and Yeh 1995). A role, in multilateral and bilateral settings, is constantly examined externally, which causes stress (J. Hsu 1985, 100). Accordingly, a stable relationship might momentarily generate a positive effect, but this situation is a rarity, especially for anyone acting on behalf of a national actor. On the contrary, relationality as a process of constant adaptation is the condition of altercasting and reflexive altercasting.

From the emotional aspect, Chineseness that is imagined as essential engenders a different type of self-identity in comparison with Chineseness that is artificially acquired. A self-image of innate Chineseness compels one to assess one's own performance from an imagined internal Chinese perspective and reproduces the difference between Chinese and non-Chinese. A greater self embedded in shared values and rituals exists to encompass mutual role expectations between one and other in-group members (D. Ho 1998; K. Hwang 2012; King 1985). Reflexive altercasting becomes inevitable as Chineseness is registered in the duty of being a member. For self-regarded Chinese, an effect of anxiety is immediate wherever Chineseness is incurred.

The same was most apparent during World War II, a period during which many Chinese Southeast Asians supported China to resist Japan. Anxiety is strong in the situation of a split in the greater self because the split compels one to choose sides and to work on reintegration, without which the selfhood constituted by Chineseness, qua greater selfhood, becomes void. This effect was observed during and after the Chinese Civil War, which resulted in the division of Chinese Southeast Asians as either pro-communist or pro-Kuomintang.

Self-regarded Chinese may face another pressure of reflexive altercasting as they interact with indigenous communities, because they may perceive a role identity vis-à-vis the indigenous population, a role identity that they believe reflects their higher status economically as well as culturally, and interact accordingly. In other words, they think that local communities expect Chinese to be socially and economically advanced. In summary, two processes of reflexive altercasting simultaneously occur. One induces the self-regarded Chinese Southeast Asians to act patriotically toward China, and the other induces this group to differentiate their identities from the hosting communities. Both processes generate psychosocial pressure to perform in order to release the worries that the perceived motherland, that is, China, or the indigenous population may consider them doing lower than expectations.

By contrast, acquired Chineseness complicates one's self-identity through learned or practiced values, rituals, and languages, among other things. Such complication gives rise to an intellectual capability to understand and interpret both sides. Such intellectual capability, if exercised, similarly complicates the criteria of self-evaluation of both sides once a different set of criteria is introduced to them. In the process, one's own standing in either group may be jeopardized if neither side appreciates one's effort to bridge the gap. In the situation in which one's in-between position is acquired, for example, in the case of a sinologist, an anthropologist, an expatriate, a China-based journalist, or a diplomat, the wide discursive scope attained may enable the narrator to achieve strong self-confidence. On the contrary, in cases in which such an in-between position is socially imposed, for example, in the case of a migrant citizen, she may suffer incompatible role expectations coming from both sides.

A migrant or an ethnic citizen is, in one sense, similar to self-regarded Chinese to the extent that both carry identities that are given, except where the actor is an ethnic citizen, in which case she has more than one given identity. An ethnic Chinese Southeast Asian faces double altercasting. Unlike sinologists, who preach to both sides about how the other understands the world, ethnic citizens are not discursively prepared to preach. On the contrary, the situation can be embarrassing if they have to meet the expectations of both sides. Double reflexive altercasting does not reproduce the same sense of difference as it does for a self-regarded Chinese who can perform consistently, although anxiously, in an environment such as Chinatown/Binondo (Kwong 1996). For ethnic citizens living in a large group, they ought occasionally to perform inconsistently to meet the inconsistent expectations caused by their in-between positions. If one standard to be met already causes anxiety, then double altercasting can only aggravate the situation.

The contrast of the sinological and ethnic types suggests that the former is ultrastable, whereas the ethnic type is ultra-unstable. An ethnic narrator can improve her discursive position by taking an in-group position that privileges the Chinese identity and yet reproduces a mutual discriminatory condition in the midst of the indigenous population. A frustrated narrator in the mainstream condition could strategically choose to take shelter in Chinatown, whereas others may opt for a determined struggle for equal citizenship. This condition is nearly true everywhere, such as in the United States, Southeast Asia, or even Chinese Hong Kong and Taiwan.

By contrast, a sinological narrator may face similar double pressures from both sides but is able to understand their limitations. She is intellectually confident and discursively prepared either to refute the one-sided criticism or simply remain calm without feeling the need to engage in political correctness. However, in the long run, the return to Chinatown guarantees no continuous reward unless one runs into a new age of the PRC China that may give new meanings of belongingness to a distinctive Chinese category.

On this basis, the chance of reverting from an out-group position to an in-between or in-group position exists in cases in which the politics of identity retrieves unpleasant memories of discrimination, stereotyping, and stigmatization or, with the rise of China, reconnection with PRC China triggers a sense of enhancement, familiarity, or relaxation that revitalizes a silent and silenced cultural memory embedded in an imagined string of Chineseness. However, this condition is difficult, because citizenship denoted by pragmatic considerations of rights and equality is always locally oriented.

Anxiety is not a comfortable emotion, and the intellectual capacity, cultural memory, and social distinction of the later generations of a migrant population to retain the in-group cohesion necessarily diminish over time; thus, one can predict a historical trend that moves away from the positions that require reflexive altercasting as incurred by the imagined belongingness to China or the Chinese people. Such a trend indicates the objective to adopt an out-group position such that one's assessment of the Chinese

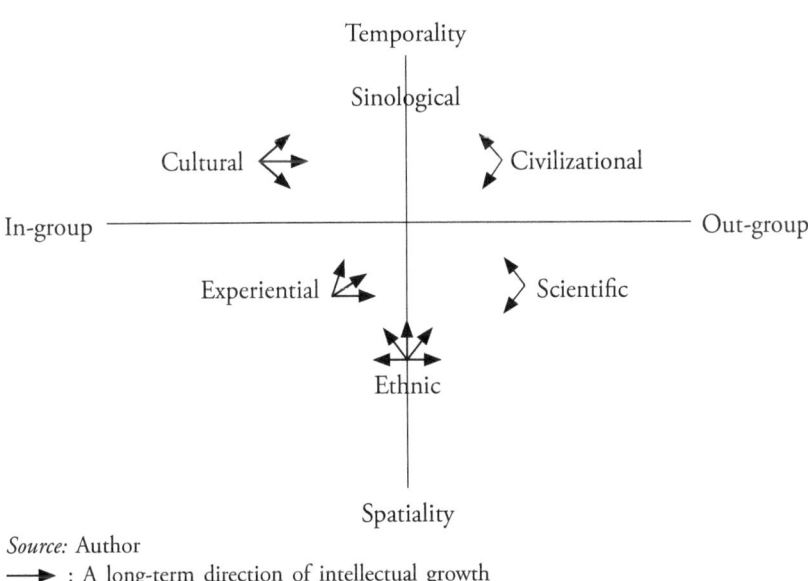

Figure 7.2. Post-Chinese Evolution in the long run.

nation, Chinese civilization, and Chinese people simulates indigenous Filipino perspectives.

The Chinese relationality that constitutes the identity of a self-regarded Chinese or an ethnic Chinese-Filipino evolves into an object to be assessed from the vantage point of the Philippines' national interests, as well as a certain Philippine historiography. In this development, the enthusiasm or calm of being able objectively to reconnect with Chinese targets, be it a sovereign state, a social network, or a cultural asset, substitutes for the anxiety caused by the in-group consciousness. On the other hand, the sense of belonging to the indigenous group may engender another source of reflexive altercasting, though.

Accordingly, a few plausible propositions, particularly individualized tracks, emerge to assist in the reading of the evolution of intellectual history in general. Chapter 7 contends that these propositions can be generally applied to any place where non-Chinese identities prevail in the mainstream, although the later section relies primarily on Philippine interviews.

> **Proposition 1.1.** The general trend is for any narrator to shift from an in-group perspective to an out-group perspective in the long run.
>
> **Proposition 1.2.** The auxiliary proposition is that the movement from an out-group perspective to an in-group perspective is impractical.
>
> **Proposition 1.3.** The third-order proposition is that the movement from an out-group perspective to an in-group perspective is only possible in cases where re-incurred discrimination compels a narrator to carry an ethnic stigma again. (This proposition is absent in the case of the Philippines.)
>
> **Proposition 2.** The sinological perspective is ultimately stable. A sinological type of narrator will not shift to other positions.
>
> **Proposition 3.** The ethnic perspective is the least stable. An ethnic type of narrator always seeks opportunities to practice an in-group or an out-group perspective.

Epistemological Shifts Illustrated

The scholars of Chinese studies in the Philippines include indigenous scholars who study China, and Chinese-Filipino scholars. They create two ostensibly ethnic groups. Chineseness constitutes their self-identities professionally and culturally. The three propositions suggest that the evolution of China watching for Chinese-Filipino scholars moves toward an out-group position. To illustrate how categories of post-Chineseness enable a scholar to position her relations with the object of study—China, Chinese, and Chineseness—the following discussion attends primarily to how positions remain static or shift. Categories are, therefore, the result of strategic positioning according to the choice of the scholar at the time. They are not given structures that constrain choices continuously. Categories do not apply to individuals, accordingly. Categories emerge from narratives. It is only proper to surmise how scholars choose between categories, not how categories fix scholars. After all, post-Chineseness is processual, fluid, and political. It reflects agency. It does not label people.

PROPOSITION 1.1: IN-GROUP CHINESENESS MOVES TOWARD OUT-GROUP CHINESENESS IN THE LONG RUN

Theresa Cariño (2016) is a Chinese-Singaporean moving to the Philippines. She has been intensively involved in development projects affiliated with a religious foundation and in the development of the curricula for Chinese studies in higher education. Unlike her experience in Singapore, she realized that being Chinese made a difference in the Philippines after her arrival. However, she has not attempted to enter a hybrid position to introduce her own Chineseness into her career. In fact, her perspectives on China shift from ideological to scientific Chineseness, with the former registered in Maoist romanticism when she was far younger, such that China had acquired an exotic ideological understanding, although on the positive side. Her later involvement in exchanges with Chinese NGOs and Chinese development projects has led to a scope of observation defined by the state boundaries of the PRC. She cautions against the cultural explanation of economic success in Confucian societies by looking at economic policies. In international relations, she recommends a pragmatic policy to cope with the China-Taiwan rivalry. These approaches are not ethnic in the sense that Cariño's analysis is not guided by how either China or indigenous politics assess her.

A case of experiential Chineseness moving toward scientific Chineseness is vividly present in the interview with Jaime FlorCruz, whose advice for the contemporary, after living in China and becoming "mature and patient," is to "spend time in understanding China. And then, share it with the population" (FlorCruz 2015,13). What this advice implies for the population is "to go and visit China even though for a short time because I experienced myself what a big difference it made to see it, to feel it, to smell it, and to personalize China" (8). This is exactly the same aforementioned argument (in chapter 2) for mutual sympathy out of working and living together to transcend ideologies under the circumstance of experiential Chineseness. He also warns against racism and advises, with noticeable comparative objectivism, "strip away the ideology or the color of the skin, or the shape of our eyes, we Filipinos and Chinese are all the same" (8). His own task is to report on China, providing timely, accurate information. However, his experiences in China win him trust as an in-group member such that he always speaks, inquires, and sits in on behalf of a large international media group in China. The Chinese audience of his lecture welcomes him because he can compare modern China with the China of forty years ago, witness the changes taking place, and appreciate the "incremental" as opposed to a drastic speed of change (13). As he is a China-watcher who "never miss[es] an appropriate chance to say that I am a Filipino," his scientific Chineseness seems spontaneously to arise from his experiential Chineseness:

> For over 30 years, China has been successively my refuge, my training ground, and my home. Living and working in China pose genuine difficulties: language barriers, culture shock, pollution, bureaucracy, and home-sickness. However, China has an inherent charm that draws me to stay on. Its diverse culture and long history is a bottomless mine to explore and study. It is a huge country in a state of flux, and watching it change—and even experiencing the changes myself—is exhilarating as a China-watcher. On a personal level, what draws me to China are "three Fs": friends, food, and foot massage. (FlorCruz 2015, 12–13)

The pressure of ethnic Chineseness to generate self-role expectations from both sides can be reduced if one can physically evade the supposedly monitoring environment. Despite the monitoring by the Kuomintang and the anti-Chinese attitude resulting from the Philippine nationalism, Caroline

Hau's (2015) journey from Binondo, to Filipino communities, and then to the United States and Japan eases the potential tension of being ethnic. She is aware of owning some Chineseness, and thus feels in no position to speak for China because of her lack of knowledge. She is determined to understand her Chineseness. However, this goal creates no self-assessing pressure. On the contrary, she reverses the usual schema of understanding Chineseness from the PRC standpoint by appreciating the fact that PRC Chineseness is adaptive and nuanced in itself through her own path of becoming differently Chinese. Hau similarly enjoys visits to the Philippines despite her academic awareness of an anti-Chinese potential at home. She discovers that internationalization is conducive to the alleviation of such potential.

Hau's ethnic Chineseness causes a distinctive example of relaxed ethnicity. Reflexive altercasting is particularly weak in her self-reflection because she could calmly hope that someone else who understands Chinese positions will clarify the situation regarding the South China Sea, assist in the Chinese-Filipino integration without committing activism, and be exempt from the usually intense exchanges while engaging in public identity debates. In other words, she lacks a bridging sensibility that is often observed in sinological Chineseness. Hau shows no urgency in preaching to each side how each side perceives the other. She learns from both sides through visiting China and the Philippines but transcends the anxiety about recognition. This behavior is closely linked with her adoption of a comparative perspective through an exit in Japan, where she enlightens her target of research regarding each of the countries' historically shaped and changing identities. This characteristic actually illustrates a derivative of civilizational Chineseness attained in an ethnic Chinese identity.

PROPOSITION 1.2: OUT-GROUP CHINESENESS DOES NOT MOVE TOWARD IN-GROUP CHINESENESS

Aileen Baviera (1959–2020) represented the epistemological stability of an out-group watcher in international relations, a task she enjoyed while watching China, being defined territorially by the sovereign borders. She was concerned with the formation of the coherence in the Philippine foreign policy sectors, composed of analysts and policymakers (Baviera 2016). In the Chinese counterparts, she cautioned against too much intellectual investment unless the other side demonstrated open-mindedness. She showed a slight intention to bridge the gap or preach to the PRC Chinese scholars about the outside world to connect their perspectives. With her expertise regarding Chinese foreign policy, her involvement in the Philippine Association of China Studies, composed of experts on Chinese-Filipino studies and overlapping with the Kaisa Para Sa Kaunlaran (Kaisa), fit the Kaisa's overall goal of breeding an integrated and national consciousness among the Chinese-Filipinos. Consistently throughout her career, she realized the importance of China to the Philippines. Curiosity and pragmatism appeared to echo the spirit of her agenda.

Chito Santa Romana similarly demonstrates the stability of an out-group perspective, initially leaning toward civilizational Chineseness, as his evaluative schema has been Maoism. He started with an ideologically romantic view of China with a strong comparative sensibility. In his fifteen years in China, he discovered that ideology is irrelevant for him to understand China. In retrospect, he compares China and the Philippines to bypass the thinking of the China model completely. The issue is not "whether we can use the China model" but rather "to see what we could learn from China" (Santa Romana 2016, 15). According to Romana, "Filipinos are a little more spontaneous and freewheeling. The Chinese, on the other hand, are ritualistic and Confucian values are very strong" (11). In addition, he finds "certain aspects of Filipinos' religion, culture, and politics, which make it difficult for authoritarianism to take root" (11). Moreover, "they are a mainland or continental country, while we are an archipelago" (15). Romana warns against any quick judgment from the surface:

> You have to see the situation from there; and the bottom line is that you have to understand that human beings are influenced by all these cultural and historical forces. We are the same but yet we are different. We have our own culture and our own history. It is just that I do not expect it to be easy to understand China. I mean you could experience it yourself. If you live in China, there are certain things you have to get used to, which is not so easy. Basically, we have to find our own way of understanding and navigating in China, but also need to consider their experiences. (Santa Romana 2016, 15)

Romana's experiences in China have retrained him to reconnect China through a mix of civilizational and scientific sensibilities. His job as a foreign journalist, who had to explain the situation in China to an international audience, reinforces this tendency objective while gathering information and reporting the news. He is consciously "an outsider" who enjoys a "detached view" while benefiting physically from being an insider who "got to know people's sentiments and talked to them" (12). In addition, an insider detects forces not within the media and reads between the lines. However, his reconnection with China is more through information gathering, analysis, and explanation than bridging or engaging in Chinese affairs. After a long career as a journalist, his scientific Chineseness tilts toward Sinological Chineseness:

> It taught me to be a little skeptical. That you should never accept what's on the surface. You may know about it, but it is almost like the art of reading tea leaves. It is never easy. That is why China watching actually became part of my life. First is because I lived and worked there, and then I worked as a foreign journalist who had to explain what was going on in China to an international audience. (Santa Romana 2016, 12)

Proposition 2: Sinological Chineseness Is Stable

Richard Chu (2016), whose family came from Binondo, was once identified as an "Intsik," which he considers to have derogatory undertones. He considers himself a Filipino, due to having received a Catholic education. This dual identity led him to reflect on the historical conditions that caused ethnic conflict. Free from much fixation on Binondo, he initially acquired the intellectual faculty through scientific learning, with the purpose of bridging the distance between China and the Philippines. Then, he achieved the sinological position in a scope far broader than a usual bilateral sinologist. Considering his root in Minnan very early in his career, his

> motivation for going to China was partly personal, which was to seek my roots back in China and learn more about Chinese culture, the country, and its people, and about my own family's background. But it was professional as well, in the sense that I wanted to work in the field, where I could help bridge the people of China and the Philippines. (Chu 2016, 6)

However, he had a strong wish to become a priest. Nevertheless, he was ready to transcend ethnic Chineseness. The training in Chinese history provided him with the intellectual tools to study China and the Philippines simultaneously from an external perspective, thereby connecting him to a wide academic world; thus, he has cut across many different disciplines to create a new self-identity of being "transnational" (Chu 2016,12).

His scholarship is consciously marginal to China studies in general but intertwined with Asian American, Chinese diaspora, and the Philippine studies. Chu illustrates a journey from initially being an owner of ethnic Chineseness, through attaining scientific Chineseness, to practicing sinological Chineseness, thereby exempting from "nation-based narratives, where there's a thirst for either-or propositions" (Chu 2016, 15). This sinological Chineseness extends from not only a communicator between China and the Philippines but also an epistemologically illuminating correspondent for the United States and the Philippines, as he specifically wishes to "create research that will be applicable and relevant to both countries" (Chu 2016, 12). Such a sinological style of teaching and writing in between nearly resembles a priest determined to preach between communities, bridge new encounters, and proceed by

> always trying to figure out where I am in my life, personally and professionally. Professionally, this means in terms of how and where the field leads me, including which scholars I get to interact with, and whose work energized me. I think this is so important to me. That's why even if the Chinese Cemetery and Chinese hospital projects are not part of my next book project, I still want to undertake them; because they bring me again into contact, and into conversation with, all these other scholars. (Chu 2016, 13)

Scholarship combined with activism has produced the sinological Chineseness of Teresita Ang-See (2015) in her preaching to both sides regarding the necessity and routes for building an integrative nation in the Philippines. In her earlier career, See took a double learning path first in Binondo and then in the higher education among her Filipino classmates at the University of the Philippines. She found that continuous loyalty to China is impractical for the Chinese who live in the Philippines. In her endeavor to move beyond such cultural embedding, she embarked upon a journey to adopt ethnic Chineseness.

Ethnic Chineseness, that is usually focused on working for recognition rather than self-assertion, immediately faces the challenge that the traditional Chinese identity turns hostile to such a strategy while the mainstream is unsure of how even to think of an integrative agenda, if not at all reacting suspiciously. See escalates her discursive power by engaging in activism where she benefited from her knowledge of both sides, such that she could enlist culturally sensitive communication in her attempt to enlighten the migrant and hosting communities. Given such sinological Chineseness, she has never ceased preaching.

Once integration has been considered achieved and Kaisa was established to reflect the benchmark of integration, See's perspective on China, without Binondo acting as China's vicarious enclave, is presumably from the vantage point of the out-group. In fact, she does not consider herself a China expert. In actuality, her style embedded in sinological Chineseness triumphs institutionally nonetheless, as she not only heads the Philippine-China Development Resource Center to bridge mutually beneficial experiences between the Philippines and China but also in her leadership capacity in the Philippine Association of Chinese Studies. The sinological sensibility is clear in her design of leadership training for students that ensures "the input is also how to be a bridge and then how to be proud of your being Chinoy."

Sinological Chineseness exists similarly in her bridging between China and the Philippines, aiding Xinqiao that arrived in the Philippines during the Cold War as the newest wave of the vicarious China, and the PRC Chinese think tanks that know little about the Philippines. She recalls,

> China politics, geopolitics, China relations and everything. Um, we seem to have a better group of people who can really be the bridge. In fact, yeah I saw one of the questions, the advantage of this group of China experts is that they really focus on China studies, and they know a lot about China. . . . It was the Chinese experts who were all surprised at the inputs of the Philippine experts. Uh, maybe it's very understandable because at that time the Philippines loomed very far from their consciousness. That's why they did not pay attention to Philippine studies and knowing the Philippines. They were surprised a lot by what the inputs of our China experts there [*sic*]. (Ang-See 2015, 15)

From being an out-group member fascinated with China, Eric Baculinao (2016) has lived in China for over forty years and so has gained experiential Chineseness as an in-group watcher. He works both in China and the United States, thereby benefiting his own curiosity in acquiring views on China "from different perspectives and different scholars around the world" and focusing on "finding the intersection in common interests and decoding the intentions and apprehensions of China's bureaucracy and Western media for both sides." His practice of sinological Chineseness thus began. His take on the Philippine-China dispute over the South China Sea is relatively calm accordingly, emphasizing "more debates" in the Philippines to highlight "more different opinions" on China. He hopes that

> all these debates will lead us to the conclusion that being complacent or even narrow-minded about our understanding of China will not lead us to the correct strategy that would mean a victory for national interest that would be of benefit to the people. The conflict would only drag on, and that's not victory. (Baculinao 2016, 9)

A sinological type of warning is particularly powerful as he insists that a Filipino "distinguishes between advanced studies about China, and the influence of geopolitics that restricts [us from getting] a far more balanced, up to date, objective understanding of China" (Baculinao 2016, 9).

Other than sharing his understanding of China whenever needed by the local Philippine communities, back home, and in Toronto, Baculinao discovers that the legal knowledge among Chinese scholars is limited and that the Philippines may help by facilitating academic interactions. The Philippines is misunderstood as "the puppets of the Americans," such that an appreciation of history, in which "Philippine independence has developed so much and deserves to be understood," is sorely needed (Baculinao 2016, 15). His goal is to "close that gap" of mutual understanding. His in-between position advises that the difficulty depends on nationalism and national interests:

> I think maybe it's because nationalism is an important factor. It's natural to encounter resistance, especially if you challenge conventional positions; you run the risk of being called anti-nationalist or unpatriotic, even if it's not the case. I think the main difficulty of breaking through our restricted understanding of China is the fact that we are so passionate about our national interest—which is a very positive thing—that sometimes we neglect to see the weaknesses of our own positions, of our own understanding, which then leads us to very weak strategies or tactics; weak in the sense that they cannot conceivably lead to a peaceful negotiated outcome of our disputes. (Baculinao 2016, 15)

Proposition 3: Ethnic Chineseness Is Unstable

Go Bon Juan (2016) reveals the pressure of remaining ethnic and argues that the study of China and the Philippines should take an integrative approach by studying the Philippines in its entirety rather than the components of each of the nation separately. In addition, one should study the Philippines by comparing the country with other Southeastern countries. He retrieves the historical paths, where the Chinese sacrificed during World War II, split after the Chinese Civil War, and became a policy problem. His thought is deeply ethnic in style to the extent that he is keen on a type of self-assessment that advises how the Chinese and Filipinos should learn and practice how to integrate better. He is similarly conscious of how China as a perspective perceives, or misperceives, integration as an example of the "overseas Chinese" problem. He appeals to "utang na loob" ("the debt of gratitude") to oblige the Chinese to move beyond hometown nostalgia:

> You would think that in the hundreds of years since the Chinese arrived in the Philippines—and that this is not our place—but we were allowed to live here, live, develop, and have become so successful, there should definitely be some form of utang na loob. Doing good things for the country is not saying that you are just helping the people, it is utang na loob. It is time to pay back to the country. (Go 2015, 6)

Go urges the Tsinoy community to simulate the national perspective but blames his people for being concerned about themselves alone. Instead, he promotes a "broad knowledge to solve Philippine problems, we need [to know about] the Philippine history, economy, [and] society" (Go 2015, 16). Chinese-Filipinos usually learn about the Philippines through self-study. His methodology is historical and external in that he believes that in-depth historical research will show that the Tsinoy and Pinoy communities are already integrated. For example, his research showed that, in 1782, fifty mestizos were included on a list of on hundred serving as Catholic priests under the Archdiocese of Manila. The distinction between local Chinese and mainland Chinese is even politically essential as he could not imagine "how many anti-Chinese racial riots there would have been" if they had not been differentiated. He thus suggests, to let the Chinese and Filipino mainstream society discover that the relations are so tight. All in one. That we are in each other's lives and cannot be separated. Hundreds of years of history already show that. This helps very well in promoting integration. Why do we need to say/differentiate you from us? There is no need to do that. We realize that we are close. We avoid the concept that the Chinese are no Filipinos, or that you are Filipinos [and] we are Chinese. If we cannot resolve this identity issue, then the two peoples cannot become close, racial problems cannot be resolved. (Go 2015, 17)

Florencio Mallare (2016) illustrates a contrary shift from ethnic Chineseness to cultural Chineseness. He has been preoccupied with his early encounter with the Chinese Exclusion Act, which grants the authorities the power to deport Chinese and was practiced in history. He was himself once detained, despite adopting a Filipino name. He anticipates the pressure from the indigenous society for him to defend his citizenship. His sensitivity toward the ethnic status and focus on the vulnerability of the Chinese communities attracts his attention such that he has endeavored to answer the question, "What is my role now?" (Mallare 2016, 3). He has not tried to bridge the gap between the Chinese and the indigenous communities as others do in the ethnic position. By contrast, his effort is to remind the Chinese-Filipinos of the inferior legality incurred by their ethnicity.

However, the rise of China seems to have provided a sufficient boost to his morale as he finds that the claim of the Philippines in the South China Sea disputes has no ground and the Chinese expansion mimics the Monroe Doctrine or other Western practices, thereby legitimized by the Western standard. Such perspective-taking can engender a sense of duty to preach the Tsinoy community, whereas it may empower one to face the regime of Chinese exclusion.

A further return to cultural Chineseness enables Mallare to speak with enhanced certainty of his identity. His suggestion to the younger generations of Tsinoy conflicts with the trending advocacy of indigenization. Specifically, he believes that the retrieval of one's own path, that leads one's ancestors to migrate from China to the Philippines, which presumably reproduces one's Chinese in-group consciousness, is conducive to a comprehensive self-understanding for the Tsinoy community. He then detects a "lack of continuity" in the Chinese studies in the Philippines and suggests the adoption of a cultural approach:

You have to know who are you. . . . Identify yourself. . . . Who are you? . . . How did you come about here? . . . Why are you in the Philippines? Why is your surname Mallare? And then you begin to think. The passion is so intense that I went back to China specifically to look at it. . . .

Like the Chinese will exist; will still continue . . . just like encyclopedia . . . continuously . . . you go and understand the Zhou Dynasty, the ancient times in China . . . you know your history. (Mallare 2016, 29)

In comparison, Charlson Ong's (2016) reliance on cultural Chineseness illustrates a different style, although similarly rejects the pressure of external examination imposed on ethnic Chineseness. Ong demonstrates a historical sensibility that tracks a life in its origin in China, but he uses cultural Chinese not to reconnect with an essentialized China, but to trivialize and therefore broaden the scope of a collective identity. In other words, Chinese origins and their individualized contributions to the life of the Chinese-Filipinos deserve recognition as a component of the Philippine nationality. Based on the ethnic identity of the Chinese-Filipinos, Ong contrives the representation of the nuances of each life that renders any monotonous criterion irrelevant in assessing or transforming one's identity:

The idea is to broaden or to deepen the idea of nation and community. I think that's the main work—to deepen and broaden the idea of community, of the nation, of ethnicity, to problematize it, and then to broaden and help people understand it. I think that's the work. As far as China is concerned, I think right now, a lot of the traffic is [happening in] both ways. There are many Filipinos working in China now, so I think it's going the other way. The labor movement is going the other way. Filipinos are working in China. (Ong 2016, 16)

Allusion to a Comparative Agenda

Ethnic Chineseness adds complication to the practice of balance of relationships that necessitates a choice of post-Chineseness and the cyclical changes of the choice afterwards. There are multiple levels, including one of ethnic and indigenous scholars, another of scholars and their Chinese objects represented by people, villages, the government, and the nation, and yet another of the Philippines and China, as well as the complexity of involving another actor both at the level of the multinational corporation such as NBC and the level of another hosting society such as the US or Japan. The decisions regarding to whom to give the priority of improvising a resemblance and which resources to evoke for that purpose have to be contingent, intersubjective, and strategic.

The first half of the chapter argues that reflexive altercasting is not a psychological home in the long run for the people who only view themselves from certain in-group perspectives and impose self-role expectation in accordance with several imagined standards that define their group identity. People can be strategically reconnected with an imagined Chinese internal perspective in many ways to attain opportunities, dignity, or security. They may judge incorrectly and suffer. They may also detect changes in the historical conditions and adapt accordingly. In the long run, a lure to an out-group position is therefore expected to result in re-incurring cultural resources to reconnect with China differently. Presumably, this condition leads to the adoption of an out-group position.

The second half of the chapter uses the interviews with the Philippine China experts and scholars of Chinese studies to illustrate this general trend toward an out-group position. An alternative exists in which one complicates cultural Chineseness by attending to practical nuances that render any definitive scope of cultural Chineseness unavailing.

The Philippines is a harbinger for what one may similarly discover elsewhere. Specifically, at the national level, shared Confucianism and other cultural Chineseness in Vietnam, Taiwan, and Hong Kong have prompted epistemological practices that can construct their out-group positions, as a sovereign state, a different nationality, a liberal democracy, an agent of containment, and a non-Chinese colony. At the individual level, the discourses and knowledge produced along these lines of thinking creatively arise from the scholarship on China. Their politics of post-Chineseness uncovers the unnoticeable linkage elsewhere between those in the out-group position and their target of watching; for example, in Southeast Asia, where Chinese Southeast Asian scholars who watch China from the outside are actually each practicing a kind of reconnection with China.

For another example, China experts in Europe or America who adopt the scientific or civilizational approach similarly constitute their identities with scientific Chineseness, although with purposes different from those of the Chinese Southeast Asian. In fact, the relationships of the Chinese

European and American narrators with the mainstream in their societies immediately expose the strategic choices of all, and they are aware as well as unaware of China as a constitual component of their identities (Shih 2013a). The case of the Philippines is only one of many cases that provide information on post-Chineseness as a process and a choice.

Chapter 8

Geopolitical Distancing

Think Tanks in Southern Neighborhood

Chapter 8 relies on the same post-Chinese possibilities that inform the previous chapters in part 2 and analyzes the think tank watching of China in Singapore in a comparative perspective. However, this chapter records a whole-of-national-identity strategy of Singapore to control the intensity and the ethnic and cultural kinds of resemblance to China, and the chapter poses a contrast to the individualized tracks of intellectual history gathered in chapters 5, 6, and 7. Rather, the improvised Chineseness of Singapore is a practice of reflexive altercasting to meet the expectations of Southeast Asian neighbors. I will show how strategically the main China watching think tank deliberately gives up its sinological Chineseness as well as cultural Chineseness to distance Singapore strategically from China. It even avoids ethnic Chineseness and civilizational Chineseness, presumably ensuring the implausibility of reconnection with China. The only post-Chinese possibility that China-watching adopts is scientific or policy Chineseness. This strategy contradicts the self-identity of Singapore as a civilizational bridge. It neither echoes the strong component of ethnic Chineseness in both Singapore and neighboring Malaysia nor, unintentionally, groups Singapore with think tanks in South Asia to the effect that Singapore loses its credit as a civilizational bridge. Chapter 8 is, therefore, an ultimate statement of how China is, at best, an intellectual project as opposed to an objective research agenda.

Civilizational Bridges qua Former Colonies

Colonial and postcolonial relations have always constituted sites of knowledge production in the Global South (Nyanchoga 2014; Beigel 2013; Kanu 2006; Taiwo 1993). This condition is particularly noticeable with regard to the production of knowledge of the self in the Global South vis-à-vis the West (Sylvester 1999; Spivak 1992; Dirik 1997). However, the literature has not seriously investigated self-knowledge production in the Global South with regard to non-Western others (Shih et al. 2020). With Brazil, Russia, India, China, and South Africa (BRICS countries) now becoming significant others, this issue becomes increasingly relevant. If the colonial relations of the Global South have not been dominant in crafting perspectives on China, then what styles of self-knowledge will emerge in its southern neighborhoods? This chapter focuses on China from the perspective of its neighbors. Instead of critiquing how Western academics misrepresent China (Vukovich 2012), the study examines China from the perspective of the Global South (Ling 1996). Specifically, it analyzes how the production of knowledge independent of the former colonial relations can contribute to the quest for self-identity in China's southern neighborhood, especially in South and Southeast Asia.

Arguably, Singapore, Nepal, and Bangladesh are comparable in a crucial aspect (Zheng and Lye 2015; Mitra 2013; PTI 2016; Kashinath 2016). They each have a desire to bridge the difference between China and its potential rival in India, the West, or both. Bhutan may likewise have an unspoken wish to bridge the cultural distance between Tibet and the rest of the world. Their names are incurred here not to suggest that they are ontologically autonomous or they exist and act by themselves. Rather, the notion of civilization bridge indicates their being aware of their relational constitution and attentive to the adjustment of their relational conditions. As relatively small nations neighboring major powers (Muni and Yong 2012; Penjore 2014; Snedden 2016), their value and image can be enhanced if they are able to provide a platform for competing neighbors to explore cooperation. China appears always to create a side of the gap to be bridged in order for China effectively to connect to another country.

Singapore's cultural familiarity with and ethnic proximity to the Chinese society resemble its South Asian counterparts' cultural familiarity with India. Singapore enjoys an apparent advantage in understanding and presenting the PRC's situation. China similarly holds strong cultural sensibilities toward the Chineseness of Singapore. Singapore's submission to Asian values and hierarchical governance as opposed to liberalism even inspired the Chinese

Communist Party's method of reform (Huei 2016). However, in contrast to Nepal's view of China as leverage over India, Singapore regards China as a force to be balanced by the United States (Roy 2005). Singapore thus creates a sense of relative deprivation and even anxiety among its China-watchers (Feng Zhang 2016).

This chapter begins with an analysis of how the role identities of these nations inspire them to serve as civilizational bridges. It then discusses how Singapore consciously subdues its cultural connectivity to China, such that it has to rely on social science discourses to frame its China watching (Yew 2017). This situation is tantamount to self-quarantine from Singapore's arguable cultural sensitivity toward political and cultural nuances, which could have made a qualitative difference to Singapore's knowledge of China with respect to its South Asian counterparts. Such a lost qualitative difference leads to a methodology in which visits, consultations, and the exchange of intelligence are shared instruments. China scholars adopt a common epistemology of watching China from the outside, where no legitimacy of speaking on behalf of China is claimed. For comparative purposes, the chapter further considers Chinese studies in Malaysia, where bridge sensibility is not apparent but Chinese-Malaysian intellectuals are equally productive with the support of their occasionally incurred in-between Chineseness.

Relying on published interviews with retired diplomats, think tank experts, and established scholars, this study discusses how Singapore's style of bridging its differences with China aborts civilizational sensibilities and restricts Singapore's role. These interviews are open-access scripts gathered from a transitional project on the comparative intellectual history of China studies. The teams that conducted these relevant open-ended interviews include the Department of Chinese Studies at National University of Singapore, the Association of Asia Scholars in New Delhi, the Institute of Chinese Studies at the University of Malaya, and the Department of Political Science at the National Taiwan University. Given that the notion of a civilizational bridge has been rarely discussed in the literature, the interviewers who referred to it inspired the thinking underlying this study. The argument and analytical frame of the study were initially obtained from reading these references to a bridge.

Four Possible Roles of a Bridge State

The Anglophone literature pertaining to civilizational bridges, though limited, consistently treats civilization as a process (Elias 2000; Katzenstein 2010; Lawrence 2010). In other words, the literature treats civilization in itself as a bridge metaphor, through which exchanges take place. Consequently, civilizational bridges necessarily divert and evolve. In contrast, in the Islamic and Confucian worlds, the notion of civilizational bridges usually considers civilizational entities, instead of processes. In this light, two strings have emerged. One discusses the role of the former colonies in bridging the West and the indigenous (Hashim and Langgulung 2007; Bradley 2004; Tibi 2012) and the other how Japan, Turkey, or Russia, which have not been colonies, provide bridges between the East and West (Kösebalaban 2008; Tanaka 1993; Fogarty 2013). Despite their difference regarding colonial experience, these actors face the same challenge of connecting to the West, which they perceive as distinctive and imposing (Dhavan 2019; Shih 2012). This immediately reveals that becoming a civilizational bridge is an intellectually contrived role identity for a population that is plagued by imperialism or colonialism to restore a sense of independence, equality, and dignity. Accordingly, a bridging narrative coming from the East (or "non-West") should convince the West that there exist essential matters that must be learned from the East (Nayak 2007).

The literature has not treated a particular string of thought on civilizational bridges; namely, the one that does not take the West as a significant party of the two sides. In the absence of the West, there is no sense of inferiority registered in being a civilizational bridge. Actors consciously act between India and China as well as Islam and China. Good examples include South and Southeast nations, such as Myanmar, Malaysia, Singapore, Nepal, Sri Lanka, and Bangladesh. Their notions of the civilizational bridge are not stuck in the system of sovereignty. Instead, in practice, Buddhism, Confucianism, socialism, third world identity, and British colonialism can all contribute to their points of connection. These nuances in the background, combined with the exemption from inferiority, allow for a comparative study that shows how bridging roles exclusively in the context of the Global South can exist.

The role of a bridge between two great forces usually benefits from a kind of in-between identity. This in-between identity either makes one comfortable with both sides or allows one to be made comfortable with both sides so that differences, misunderstandings, or collisions can be either dissolved in a mingling context or reinterpreted in an appreciative discourse (Wallace and Oliver 2005; N. Johnson 2012; Chellaney 2012). In other words, a bridge role player can actively mediate between two sides or passively accept its hybrid condition without needing to take sides. The former is an interpreter state that breeds empathy between two sides (Ling 2019). Exemplifying the chapter 5 kind of sinological Chineseness, an interpreter state relies on the intellectual capacity of knowing the history, culture, and contemporary situation of both sides and strives to clarify matters for both. Its knowledge is civilizational to the extent that learning and assimilation are considered possible but not threatening. The latter resembles a buffer state whose survival requires acceptance by both sides. Embracing the chapter 7 kind of ethnic Chineseness, a buffer state is territorially sandwiched, practically inconsistent, and intellectually tolerant. Interpreter and buffer states can be bridge role-players provided that they are conscious of their in-between position. Accordingly, a bridge role may have different versions and may need to compete with nonbridge roles (Kaya and Kentel 2005; Lesser 1994).

Bangladesh and Nepal are familiar with Indian cultures and practices, but the same cannot be said regarding their understanding of China. With this imbalance in the level of familiarity, operating on one side of the bridge is easier than operating on the other. An in-between identity is flawed in an imbalanced condition, because, for both bridge role players, the resemblance to China is too weak to claim the existence of a shared prior relation. Nepal is slightly more advantaged intellectually than Bangladesh because of its shared belief in Buddhism with China. However, seemingly shared religiosity does not contribute to the confidence about knowing China from an internal perspective. Nepali experts on China continue to lack a culturally sympathetic perspective to make China studies intellectually engaging, despite the acknowledged style of noninterventionism that is consistently demonstrated in China's Nepal policy.

Accordingly, four types of bridge roles can be derived from South Asian experiences according to whether a bridge has a balanced relationality and is formed in an interpreter or buffer state. An interpreter state with a balanced in-between consciousness can portray China and India in an appreciative narrative. A buffer state with a balanced in-between consciousness can absorb the differences between China and India to alleviate the urgency to resolve them. On the one hand, the roles of appreciation and absorption player are difficult to play for both Nepal or Bangladesh, because they know far less about China; thus, India feels obliged to monitor China's involvement in Nepal and Bangladesh. On the other hand, China has significantly less intimacy with both nations. The resulting expectation for them to comply with China's needs is neither strong nor specific. (See Proposition 1.1 in chapter 1.) By comparison, Singapore can fare well as a balanced interpreter state because of its sinological resources and social and cultural connection to China (Lim 2016). Equally important are Singapore's knowledge of the Anglosphere, possession of trust by Western countries, and modernity of social life.

Table 8.1. Role-Playing of a Bridge State

Identity \ Relationality	Balance	Imbalance
Interpreter state (active) (as sinological Chineseness)	Producing appreciation	Incurring stereotypes
Buffer state (passive) (as ethnic Chineseness)	Absorbing differences	Gathering intelligence

Source: Author

An imbalanced in-between identity causes an interpreter state to rely on existing perspectives embedded in civilizational stereotyping, which might emerge from religions (e.g., Buddhism or Islam), ideologies (e.g., socialism or capitalism), or even issues of international politics (e.g., the Cold War, China's rise, and contested transnational waters). A buffer state that is imbalanced and tilted toward India (or the West) needs to determine China's expectations and wants based on its own experiences so that it can endeavor to meet such expectations, and mutually acceptable and beneficial exchanges can take place. For a composite example, the literature on the Association for Southeast Asian Nations (ASEAN) regards all four bridge roles as appropriate for ASEAN. ASEAN can be a passive but imbalanced bridge trying to connect the isolated communist state of Vietnam (Leifer 2013). It can likewise serve as an active and balanced bridge, attempting to force an isolated Myanmar and the rest of the world to empathize with each other (Fan 2013, 16). By contrast, ASEAN can also serve as an active, imbalanced bridge, aimed at romanticizing the region for potential investors (Yong 2014), or, alternatively, a passive yet balanced player exemplified by the so-called ASEAN way that absorbs conflicts (Majumdar 2015).

Nepal and Bangladesh can become intelligence players to the extent that knowledge on China primarily originates from visits, statistics, exchanges between think tanks, and the encountering of travelers. According to Bhaskar Koirala (2016), on the one hand, Nepal lacks expertise on Chinese poetry, calligraphy, the classics, and painting. On the other hand, Nepal is a plausible stereotyping player due to its historical and religious background, constituted by contact with the Chinese. If Singapore decides to purge sinological resources from its intellectual repertoire, then its only function would be that of an intelligence player as well.

Role Identities of Nepal and Bangladesh

The rise of China, together with the recent Belt and Road Initiative, has compelled the country's South Asian neighbors to reflect on their relational roles with China. China's political image in Bangladesh has been consistently positive, although China sided with Pakistan during the independence war and used to veto Bangladesh's entry to the United Nations. China's socialist and revolutionary image has been inspiring Bangladeshi intellectuals since 1949. China's post-1978 reform success also impressed its neighbor that had become ready to develop. China's political relationship with Nepal has been particularly warm because of the mutually appreciated Buddhist religiosity of the bilateral relationship. Even when anti-Chinese activities increased in the past decade because of the Tibetan issue, China refrained from making an intervention. No Chinese prime minister has failed to visit Nepal, including the cautious Wen Jiabao, who prudently urged his host to attend to activities against China. Mohan Lohani (2016) notes the delicate interaction among India, China, and Nepal on the Tibetan issue:

> With India we share the same culture and language. Geographically, we are very close to the Eastern side of India and culturally too we have a lot in common. Moreover, Delhi is just an hour's flight away from Kathmandu, while to reach Beijing it takes at least five hours. Even for medical reasons, Nepalese fly to India for treatment. Quite a large number of Nepali students are studying in various Indian universities. Despite this, some politicians and scholars continue to look upon China as Nepal's reliable neighbor. We are close to the Tibet Autonomous Region of China. Tibet is a soft underbelly of China which becomes sensitive when Tibetan refugees engage in anti-China activities from Nepalese soil.

Nepal and Bangladesh are intensively connected to India in an all-round manner, although the political ambivalence toward India is apparent. Unlike China's political innocence, the Indian influence in Nepal and Bangladesh has been overwhelming, and escape from an interventionist image and the resultant uneasiness is virtually impossible, according to the Bangladeshi and Nepali interviewees. For example, one Nepali interviewee specifically complained that India had disrupted the political integration in the country (Ghimire 2016).

Similarly, India does not hesitate to show its displeasure about the political situation in Bangladesh. All of the interviewees believed that India has its eyes on China while coping with Nepal and Bangladesh. Nevertheless, no apparent intention exists to choose a side in Nepal or Bangladesh.

In Nepal, many China-related actors find the notion of a triangular relationship attractive. For example, Ramesh Nath Pandey (2012), the former foreign minister of Nepal, specifically acknowledged, "We, in Nepal, see ourselves as a part of a large triangle." He points to the reality that "Nepal has an open border with India and a very long border with China" (Pandey 2012). Therefore, he believes that "Nepal is in between India and China and will continue to be of strategic relevance both for India and China." Such a triangular conception is a harbinger for Hiranya Lal Shreshtha's analysis of "trilateral development" (Pandey 2012). He explains:

> Nepal desires a strong neighbor in the south and a strong neighbor in the north. . . . We do not want to create annoyance between the two. We want to be neutral and keep the two large neighbors, India and China, in harmony. This is in Nepal's interest. . . . China is investing in other countries, including India. This could be an important area for a trilateral partnership to emerge. Thus, we need to take this through trilateral investment. (Pandey 2012)

The same triangular consciousness appears to be registered in Chinese and Indian perspectives, thus rendering the bridge role substantially plausible. Mohan Lohani (2012) cites Prime Minister Baburam Bhattarai, who believes that "instead of Nepal being a small yam, it can actually be [a] vibrant bridge between India and China." Lohani states:

> Nepal has tried to keep a balanced relationship with both countries. Interestingly enough, we have been advised by Chinese leaders to maintain good relations with India. Similarly, when our Deputy Prime Minister was in India, he was advised by the Indian Prime Minister Dr. Manmohan Singh that Nepal should have good relations with China. . . . We are a small country yet of strategic importance for our two big neighbors. (Lohani 2012)

In comparison, the self-role conception for Bangladeshi intellectuals is less enthusiastic, if not inconsistent. Suspicion of Bangladesh's bridge role comes from the incapacity of the country to influence the two great neighbors. For example, Ehsanul Haque (2016) believes that the course of India-China relations has its own path. However, if Bangladesh manages its bilateral relationships well, then certain trickle-down effects can be anticipated. Humayun Kabir argues that

> we do not want China and India to compete with each other because that itself works as a negative element for us. As we are thinking about Bangladesh in the 21st century, it can be a bridging nation in the region. For example, it can be a bridging nation between India and China. It can also be a bridging nation between South and South East Asia and also between South Asia and China. Bangladesh looks at itself as a bridging nation. . . . We believe that the Indo-Chinese relationship will make Bangladesh realize its larger objective of becoming a hub in the interregional collaboration.[1]

Delwar Hossein (2016) is highly optimistic and indicated that the highly active role of Bangladesh in global governance issues can be successful everywhere. In his portrayal of the future, he states,

> If you think the kind of relations Bangladesh has with India or with China, with more confidence and with more trust at some point of time, Bangladesh can play this role. . . . So there is an opportunity for Bangladesh because its foreign policy and discourse is moving towards the direction that Bangladesh feels that we need a strong South Asia under the leadership of India and we also need a strong Asia where China has its own strong role and India and other powers. The kind of vision will . . . help maintain some relations, some type of informal role to reduce mutual mistrust between India and China. (Hossein 2016)

China Watching in South Asian Bridging States

Think tanks on Chinese affairs whose experts do not rely on sinological resources are keen on observational methods of gathering intelligence, in addition to the stereotyping necessity, when encountering an alien civilization. Where observation is pertinent, events and daily lives can reveal deep structures or preferences that are not apparent without observation. Nepali and Bangladeshi experts on China are conscious of the best and most convenient methods to establish knowledge on China, and these include visits, exchanges, and statistics. Coincidentally, Yew also observed that, in Singapore, the "works produced [by think thanks] in the 1990s read more like an insider's accounts of the going-ons in China than scholarly analyses, relying heavily on personal experience and press sources and interpreting the speeches of political leaders."

One can begin with event-watching physically to observe and learn about China. The events mentioned by the interviewees include the border war between China and India in 1962, the prodemocracy movement of 1989, the NATO bombing of the Chinese embassy in Belgrade, the clash of an American EP-3 reconnaissance aircraft with a Chinese J-8 fighter, and the 2008 Beijing Olympics. The domestic events that repeatedly emerged in the Bangladeshi interviews include the independence war fought in 1971, the subsequent vetoing of China in the UN over Bangladesh's membership in 1975, and the assassination of Sheikh Mujib in the same year. For Nepal, a common concern is Premier Wen Jiabao's visit, in which he urged that the rising anti-China activities in Nepal should be handled appropriately. Another concern is the transition from monarchy to democracy. In relation to this concern is the reference to India's intensive involvement in Nepal's domestic politics. All of these events and issues lead concerned observers to create impressions or expectations regarding China.

In addition to events, issue areas are relevant to the framing of an analysis of China. One across-the-board issue for Nepali and Bangladeshi interviewees is China's dubious role in the South Asian Association for Regional Cooperation. The area of China's participation can be in multilateral and bilateral issues, but each nation or even scholar can have a different perspective. With the competitive relationship between Pakistan and India, China's formal membership would serve as a balancer against India. However, numerous local scholars wish to see China's full participation, primarily in order to benefit from China's increasingly rich resources. Nevertheless, event and issue areas incur analyses that position Bangladesh and Nepal in an outsider's role rather than as an in-between player.

Civilizational and political dispositions affect China watching in a reverse manner. Instead of watching practices to infer knowledge on China, civilizational and political dispositions guide the approach to China regarding the things to watch and the ways to answer. This observation is particularly pertinent in the case of Nepali Buddhism, which has extensive exchanges with Chinese Buddhism. Chinese visitors to Lumbini and investment in the infrastructure of the location to facilitate Chinese tourism testify to the significance of the shared religiosity between the two countries. The same claim is less credible for Bangladesh, which is mostly Muslim, despite the fact that ancient Buddhism was transmitted to China through contemporary Bangladesh. Alternatively, the Bangladeshi perspective on China is primarily due to a romanticized image of anti-imperialism, which is so powerful that even China's siding with Pakistan during the independence war did not offset the positive feeling toward China among the Bangladeshi population. The unofficial diplomatic links were never truly severed. In addition, the capitalist development in China inspired Bangladesh to adopt a similar reorientation.

Nonetheless, a positive disposition is insufficient for good research. Methodologically, South Asian countries rely on visits. Ramesh Nath Pandey (2012) specifically said that "for studying China, it is important that one visits China and that would be a great learning experience." Given that a large proportion of Chinese experts come from the diplomatic circle, they benefit from their period of service in China to witness the development and policy style of the country and the personality of specific political leaders (Pandey 2012). Iftikhar-ul-Karim (2013) recalled his experience and stated that he "was surprised to say the least. We did not encounter any of the perceptions that we had of the communist leaders of China." Humayun Kabir was similarly impressed upon hearing the Chinese counterpart candidly "admi[t] that they did not know all the tricks to manage the unfolding tensions" in the South China Sea and East China Sea.[2] Ramesh Nath Pandey (2012) is able to portray Zhou Enlai's humble character from their encounter. Furthermore, Harun ur Rashid, who met Mao Zedong before the Cultural Revolution, compares the leaders in person:

> I thought outwardly Mao Tse-tung looked like a primary school teacher: very calm and composed. One could not ignore a big mole on his face. Little did I realize from his face that he was planning the so-called "Cultural Revolution" next year. Chou En-lai was smart and very alert. Marshal Chen Yi was a smiling diminutive figure with whom you could easily relate to, and Chu The was a reserved person. (ur Rashid 2013)

Academically, visits have been and are increasingly emphasized. An increasing number of students go to China for their higher education. The interviewees mentioned that academic exchanges have been very helpful. Simply seeing is, by itself, a dramatic learning process compared with reading statistics and web news. Delwar Hossein (2016) found that, on the Internet, pieces of "information are not always correct. They do not give the right perspective." Harun ur Rashid (2013) and Iftikhar-ul-Karim (2013) obtained inspiration from the transportation condition that they witnessed and the change during the interlude to their subsequent visits. The latter stated,

> Tiananmen was a distant memory, and the energy of frenetic economic activity was palpable everywhere. I remember in 1988 standing outside the Diaoyutai State Guesthouse for 40 minutes observing the cars on the road. I could hardly see 10 cars while the whole city seemed to be on bicycles, and almost everyone was wearing Mao suits. In 2002, the sight from the same complex of the guesthouse was completely different. Both sides of the road were full of cars, and there was a traffic jam for 45 minutes; there was hardly any bicycle, and no one was in [a] Mao suit. (Karim 2013)

Changes are always easy and important to watch whenever one visits China for a second time, and these include the "change in the lifestyle of the people" (Pandey 2012). Iftikhar-ul-Karim (2013) then discovered changes amid the continuity: China "had become more open," but "otherwise things were quite similar." Lailufar Yasmin (2016) similarly attends to changes. She encountered shy children who were able to greet her in English with their parents' encouragement ten years after her first visit, when no Chinese seemed interested in learning English at all. She narrates why traveling and meeting with people creates an essential method of China watching:

> If you do not go to a country and mix with the people, you will have all sorts of wrong perceptions, and not only that you can have some of your perceptions actually confirmed. . . . Whenever I would ask them a simple thing in English, they would stare at me and start laughing with an impression that she doesn't know Chinese. That made me think that they still think that they are the middle power, that they are the center of civilization or the center of the Earth. (Yasmin 2016)

Singapore's Role-Making and China Watching

Aside from their resembling bridge role, Singapore is different from other neighboring countries in many ways. An example is that Singapore and

Bangladesh do not share a border with China, whereas Nepal and Bhutan do; thus, India is compelled to consider China primarily as a competitor in the latter territories. In another example, India wields overwhelming political influence over Nepal, Bhutan, and Bangladesh but much less over Singapore (Thapliyal 1998; Chowdhury 2013; Jain 1959; Singh and Rahman 2010). Furthermore, Bhutan and Nepal are intrinsically part of the Tibetan issue because of their proximity and shared religiosity (Mathou 2004; Kumar 2010; Shneidermann 2013), but Bangladesh and Singapore are not. In addition, the strategic competition between China and India in Nepal and Bangladesh is conscious and conspicuous (V. Wang 2011; Rehman 2009; Pant 2007; Hong 2007). In contrast to Singapore, the capacity of Nepal and Bangladesh to serve as a bridge is limited intellectually in the sense that their civilizational underpinning is more attached to India than to China.

Given the extreme sensitivity of the Chinese identity issue since its independence from Malaysia (Reid 2009), Singapore has endeavored to avoid becoming a Chinese nation. Socially, Chinese-Singaporeans and Chinese-Malaysians continue to stereotype "Chinese-Singaporean and Malaysian" (新馬華人) into a single group, which is a challenge to the nation-building of Singapore regarding the boundary of its nationality. A few complications have arisen due to Singapore's nation-building process. To begin with, Singapore must face a suspicious, if not inimical, atmosphere from neighboring Southeast Asian countries where ethnic Chinese account for a significant portion of the population. Singapore must cope with communist infiltration during the Cold War because the majority of Singaporeans of earlier generations were patriotic Chinese. It must maintain the loyalty of a quarter of non-Chinese citizens and gain support from the US to enhance its prestige among its citizens and neighbors.

Singapore's cultural policy, embedded in its national security concerns, has effectively bred a double role for Singapore over the years. This is about Singapore's role as a geostrategic port for the US and its selection by many international firms to host their Asia Pacific headquarters and manage steady foreign direct investment. The cultural policy that institutes English as an official pedagogical language in schools looks to a long-term survival strategy. Given Singapore's significant Chinese ethnicity, its natural allies would be either the People's Republic of China (PRC) or the Republic of China in Taiwan. Both have appeared to be shaky supporters, with each struggling with their own survival under the pressure of the Cold War and Chinese Civil War. The choice of a credible ally left for Singapore in facing its Muslim neighbors is the Anglophone world. Despite the fact that its being a US ally alienates China, the prestige that this alliance brings to

Singapore, along with a much higher level of income in comparison with its neighbors (e.g., an estimated US$103,717 for Singapore, US$32,454 for Malaysia, and US$14,019 for Indonesia in 2019, respectively)[3] that have resulted from its international business activities, effectively builds its hard power in Southeast Asia.

On the soft power side, the National University of Singapore (NUS) is among the world's top universities and is consistently ranked first in Asia and usually in the top twenty worldwide on various scales. Coming to support for research, Ching Hwang Yen (2012), a Chinese-Malaysian scholar teaching in Australia, finds the Chinese collection at NUS better than that at the Australian National University. It also hosts the most comprehensive and productive institute of Southeast Asian studies in Southeast Asia. This condition underscores Singapore being international as opposed to being sinological. An infliction felt by Chinese intellectuals in Malaysia and Singapore was the purge of Nanyang University due to its intensive Chinese legacy (Ngeow 2020).

In the new century, Singapore has worked hard to attract Chinese migrants, initially from Hong Kong and later from China, to maintain its current ratio of ethnic composition. The government also encourages the sustainment of spoken Chinese to take advantage of the economic opportunities in China. These moves enable a balanced role and point to a national grand strategy of distancing from China and Chinese cultural bearing while instrumentally improving the utility of Chineseness that preserves Singapore's function as a bridge for international communities to enter China from a safe distance. John Wong (1929–2018) recalled the wisdom of Lee Kwan Yew (1923–2015):

> Foreign leaders who visit Singapore do not ask about Singapore. They invariably ask about China whenever they open their mouth. This is because we are friendly neutral. We represent an objective view. They will not seek advice from either Hong Kong or Taiwan. In Taiwan, what one says about China always foregrounds one's partisan connection. (John Wong 2016)

Anticipating China's future rise, Lee Kwan Yew established the Institute of East Asian Philosophy in 1983 to study the role of Confucianism in economic development, which he found to be relevant to the success of Japan and Taiwan (John Wong 2016). However, the influence of civilian intellectuals was consciously excluded. The institute evolved into the East

Asian Institute of Political Economy in 1990 to reflect the fast changes in China and rapidly turned into the East Asian Institute. The orientation of EAI has been specifically non-Western and non-PRC so that the government can produce objective reports (John Wong 2016). According to Wang Gungwu (2007, 2010), the request is for the government to have access firsthand to the most recent developments in China. To ensure this access, reports should be written in English, be presented in the shape of social scientifically framed analyses, be exempt from policy recommendations, be immune from systematic influences by any particular source, and thus be inclusive of as many perspectives as possible.

EAI is not distinct from South Asian think tanks, given that Singapore was also a British colony that comfortably embraces its postcolonial connection with the West. Singapore easily substituted colonial English for Chinese education in schools. However, after the reform and opening up of China in 1978, Singapore quickly realized that a reconnection with China could be essential to its continuing welfare. For Singapore to benefit from the return of China to world capitalism, it has selected a bridging role for itself so that the world can come to Singapore to gain professional and trustworthy access to China. This choice means that Singapore gains credit for its objectivism by owning the knowledge of all sides. EAI, testifying quintessentially to this self-designated objectivist role, deliberately recruits Western-trained Chinese scholars who are methodologically and rigorously Western yet practically well-informed Chinese (Lim 2016).

By contrast, local sinologists in Singapore and Malaysia are inclined to make judgments or learned guesses whenever insufficient intelligence is available, because they are cognitively prepared to empathize with an internal Chinese standpoint (Tanaka 1993; Shih 2018b; Cohen 2010). However, sinological resources readily available in Singapore have never made the list of consultants. Rather, sinologists remain, at best, half-institutional as scholars of Chinese humanities, novelists, dramatists, and poets who receive minimal support and only serve in public teaching posts occasionally (a typical example is Yoon Wah Wong 2012). Sinologists contrarily find an increasingly systematic demand for services from neighboring Malaysia, where Chinese communities struggle with their own private efforts to keep the Chinese cultural lineage alive. Veteran Chinese scholars who, during their childhood experienced the end of the anti-Japanese war, find their history and values uninspiring for the younger generation in Singapore, but, to a certain degree, these values continue to trigger a sense of pride among the neighboring Chinese-Malaysian population (a typical example is Yee Hean

Gwee 2010). Similarly, Malaysian Chinese sinologists who continue to observe the rise of China and readily provide the intellectual foundation for reconnection have little to do with the think tank research on China by the mainstream indigenous academics in their country.

Chinese Legacy Denied a Bridge Role

Such strong sinological traditions in the noninstitutionalized intellectual circles of both countries make Malaysia an informative case for comparison. In reality, Singaporean and Malaysian sinologists make up a community that supports Chinese education in Malaysia. Academic writings on China by Muslim scholars are perplexingly meager. The postcolonial educational connection with the UK prepares Malaysian experts on China to rely primarily on English sources. No sense of urgency is registered in Malaysia to produce local-language knowledge on China. Sinophone scholars continue to research and publish in Chinese. Their agenda is composed of Chinese Malaysian studies, Chinese humanities, and the history of Chinese migrants. Segregation of this sort thus results in a situation that disallows deep interaction with Muslim scholarship. The Cold War history further cautioned against communist infiltration among Chinese-Malaysians, thereby intellectually reinforcing the segregation effect. Among the twelve senior scholars of Chinese studies in Malaysia interviewed by a renowned oral history project,[4] eleven are ethnically Chinese. Without the involvement of national security concerns, no attempt, as in Singapore, to create a state-controlled agenda of Chinese studies is noticeable.

Ironically, Chinese-Malaysian communities, whose number amounts to about one-fifth of the entire Malaysian population, are able to keep the legacies of Chinese humanities far deeper than in Singapore, where ethnic Chinese account for more than 80 percent of the population. According to Wang Gungwu, this upkeep is related to the ethnic tension in Malaysia that has made the preservation of the Chinese language an issue of ethnic survival; in Singapore, it has evolved into a national security issue that contrarily demands a move away from Chineseness (G. Wang 2007, 2010). When the language issue creates a political agenda, keeping the mother tongue becomes imperative for all groups. The mutual compromise reached in Malaysia allows Chinese communities equally to organize Chinese schools up to the level of high school to avoid aggravating the cleavage (Voon 2012). Therefore,

Chinese students going on to college easily consider international education more desirable than domestic universities operating in the Malay language. Students who eventually pursue academic careers prefer to stay at a US, UK, Australian, Singaporean, or Hong Kong institute. This situation is especially true for students who lack confidence in their Malay skill or ethnic impartiality.

China scholars in Malaysia have other disincentives and grievances regarding conducting teaching and research on China. Yen (2012) observed the lack of curiosity in the Malay academic circles regarding comparative studies. Even Southeast Asian studies fail to attract research interest. Predominantly, scholars of social science study Malaysia (Yen 2012). China studies fare worse because of anti-communist sensibilities. The library collection that supports contemporary China studies is poor, because the collection was banned at the moment of national independence (Voon 2012). China studies predominantly refer to classic humanities or ethnic Chinese studies in Malaysia. Malaysian students usually feel intimidated about taking Chinese-related courses, where many of their peers are Chinese-Malaysians who possess an existing skill at the native level and background knowledge of Chinese history at the high school level (Poh Ping Lee 2013). Ethnic Chinese scholars in Malaysia and Singapore are well-prepared for humanities studies. The government of Singapore consciously wants to play a bridge role, whereas its Malaysian counterpart has only a slight engagement with contemporary China studies. Ironically, the role of ethnic Chinese scholars in the EAI's China agenda remains consistently marginal.

Crafting Objectivism at EAI

Wang Gungwu, the head of EAI, reveals that the objectivist policy of EAI is not intended to affect or lead international views on China, and should be available for all to use (G. Wang 2007, 2010). He specifically mentions the interests of Indian scholars in EAI reports. To achieve such objectivity, Wong, the former head of the research department, used to read every draft prior to its submission to the government to ensure that Chinese visiting analysts do not act defensively on behalf of China. Chinese sources are imperative, but the reports written by Chinese scholars are often methodologically flawed and full of political positions, according to Wong. He explains that this is the reason why he has been keen to recruit Western-trained Chinese scholars for short-term services (John Wong 2016). By any standard, the sinological resources available among Chinese-Singaporean intellectuals are beyond remedy for EAI, given their use of the Chinese language, potentially pro-China feelings, and lack of social science methodology.

In comparison with South Asian China experts, who grieve about the lack of access to Chinese humanities, the institutional philosophy of EAI deliberately advises scholars to avoid connection to any Chineseness that is embedded in the humanities. EAI could have found a learned audience and a rich repertoire of human capital otherwise, but could have risked yielding on its pledge to objectivism. As matters stand currently, EAI is institutionally and intellectually separate from the Chinese-Singaporean population. In fact, Chinese-Singaporean scholars live in an intellectually active environment. Cross-border Chinese intellectual circles actively exist. Their research significantly involves ethnic identities, records of community history, and humanities, and many are creative writers (S. Wong et al. 2015). They are China-watchers by any standard, because they read Chinese literature, speak Chinese dialects, and follow Chinese affairs.

Singapore has been deliberately doing this kind of self-renouncing after carefully considering its national interests. EAI evolves based on the assumption that Singapore is inside and outside China; that is, between East and West (Lim 2016; Wong 2012). However, in practice, the Singaporean authorities have been alert to sinological components. These components mainly belong to a population that tends to romanticize their Chinese ethnicity. As with Malaysia, during the Cold War, Chineseness connoted vulnerability to Chinese communist infiltration and, therefore, posed a national security threat. The establishment of EAI and its aftermath witnessed strong caution against Chinese relations. This caution, among other concerns (Silver 2005), led to the termination of the official sponsorship for Chinese language education in the country. As a result, the organizing principle of EAI has been self-quarantined to ensure the immunity of the population to any access to intelligence on China.

Watching China from a culturally estranged angle, based on the gathered information from Chinese scholars and within a social scientific frame, EAI could not interpret Chinese affairs through a cultural lens. Therefore, its perspective is a kind of intelligence similar to that of a peculiar stranger, struggling to make sense of Chinese phenomena. Methodologically, EAI similarly relies on exchanges, visits, and interviews, although on a larger scale and with significantly better language skills than Bangladesh and Nepal. It has minimal interest in sharing Singapore's knowledge of the West with China, despite the fact that retired EAI leaders, including Goh Keng Swee

(1918–2010) and John Wong, used to be busy advising the Chinese government at various levels everywhere. In other words, they are intellectually capable of playing the interpreter role but institutionally and consciously fail to do so. The institute is open to sharing its policy analyses with the rest of the world. However, this act is similar to a translation aimed not at enlightening but at engendering a sense of familiarity among Anglophone readers with a subject beyond their comprehension. No attempt is made to bring the Chinese perspective to the outside world. EAI is a bridge that contributes not to mutual understanding, but to Singapore's own identity as an intelligence site that treats differences as objectivism.

What would an agenda of Chinese studies dispossessed of sinological underpinning look like? The South Asian neighbors of China offer the best case for comparison, because they can regard their own country as a bridge of difference between China and India, with themselves being familiar with the Indian intellectual traditions and political social conditions. Granted that short-term-employed Chinese scholars at EAI are generally far better informed about Chinese affairs than international scholars, they suffer an epistemological eclipse familiar to their South Asian counterpart, in the sense that they are merely informants to a hosting institution that is self-quarantined outside China and is, therefore, an ineffective bridge for the Chinese side. This observation is ironic for Singapore, which is presumably culturally capable of winning the trust of the Chinese side.

Reviewing the methodology of think-tank Chinese studies in the South Asian neighbors of China is useful for appreciating their styles, which EAI unknowingly emulates, and also for understanding the sinological lacuna from which EAI consciously makes itself suffer to enact its objectivist identity. Considering the similar strategies adopted elsewhere in East Asia, especially in communities associated with intensive Chineseness, cultural as well as ethnic, Singapore is no exception. Taiwan and Hong Kong also resist a connection with China. This occurred after they witnessed the rise of indigenous consciousness, ironically supported by their alien or postcolonial identity in relation to Japan and the UK, respectively. Nevertheless, such identity reconstruction fails to echo the survival strategy of Singapore, where Chineseness threatens the neighbors in Malaysia and Indonesia more than the Singaporeans, while Chineseness would question the quest for a separatist statehood in both Taiwan and Hong Kong. Nonetheless, Taiwan's think tanks likewise shy away from the rich sinological resources available in academic circles and turn to the social sciences and strategic calculus in their studies on China (Shih 2014b).

Conclusion

The bridge role is a rare sensibility in the postcolonial critique of the West. The post-Chinese approach of this book uncovers such a sensibility. Watching China from its Global South neighborhood incurs such an agenda. In this chapter, Singapore is the primary concern, and Nepal and Bangladesh are crucial points of reference. Does an intelligence player serve Singapore's interest or identity better than, say, an appreciation player? Given that Singapore possesses an appreciative knowledge of Chinese poetry, calligraphy, or painting, the self-quarantining of EAI from these rich intellectual resources cannot easily erase the potential of cultural return. This silenced potential of sinological or even cultural Chineseness could engender anxiety regarding the possibility of cultural reconnection and thus prompt the need to remain alert constantly for any such signs. As a result, Singapore's function as an intelligence state and its intended bridge role contradict each other, although its credit with China's rivals or with Singapore's Muslim neighbors may benefit from this. In this epistemological context, the West is an identity instrument, rather than a purpose or destiny, in strategizing Singapore's position vis-à-vis China.

In the whole-of-nation approach, China does not expect Nepal or Bangladesh to show sympathy toward its position beyond that allowed by the existing reciprocal relationships that it has developed through its anti-imperialist history, the Buddhist legacy, and contemporary economic investment. However, China used to hold significantly higher expectations toward Singapore because of its cultural and ethnic Chineseness and, to a lesser extent, the demonstration effect of Singapore's exhibition of a successful authoritarian style of governance. Singapore's anti-communist stance is similar to what was exhibited by Bangladesh during the independence war to the extent that China was not turned away from either country because of political distance. In the case of Nepal, one can hardly imagine what would be left if the nation deliberately confined the Buddhist components in its bilateral relationship with China. Would China's becoming a complete stranger win Nepal additional credit with India and promote Nepal's bridging role between India and China? Probably not. Alternatively, would this reduce Nepal to appearing a puppet state of India?

Accordingly, the methodology of China watching can either reflect or incorporate an identity strategy. The methodology of Nepali and Bangladeshi experts combines a small extent of stereotyping, which is embedded in their Buddhist and political orientations, respectively, and a large extent of intelligence, relying on visits, exchange, and statistics. For Nepal and Bangladesh, the methodology reflects the limitation of their tilted, although not always positive, relationship with India. Nevertheless, several individuals intend to plan a bridging role for their nation for India and China to appreciate each other mutually slightly more than before and leave the bridging role state to a peaceful environment. Neither Bangladesh nor Nepal can interpret China for India well, and both must struggle with their own understanding of China. Therefore, their bridging role is only possible as an imbalanced, absorption state. Such a bridge state serves to exempt India and China from demanding a solution to their contradictory positions.

Singapore's in-between identity could have been balanced between China and the West at large. However, Singapore has opted to become imbalanced in order to cope with its own identity and its regional relationship. Therefore, Singapore's methodology of China watching incorporates a consciously contrived identity strategy. Nonetheless, Singapore could be a good intelligence state, because its experts can digest intelligence effectively and quickly. However, Singapore has no disposition for conflict resolution and does not attempt to make China well-accepted by the West or vice versa. It pursues a reputation for handling China well on behalf of the West. However, it alienates China and, therefore, loses empathy, intellectual appreciation, and the ability to serve the West in the long run. Nepal and Bangladesh are in a better position than Singapore, because they are not compelled to turn away from China culturally.

PART 3

BELONGING TO CHINESENESS

Relations from the In-Between

Chineseness is most unstable in those postcolonial-Chinese contexts—that is, Hong Kong, Taiwan, and, arguably, Singapore—where the international ethnicities and their reconstructions are consciously flexible, constantly interrogated, and yet pervasively interventionary. The threads of resemblance to an imagined China as well as an imagined West in these post-Western and postcolonial intersections are too rich to allow any consensus that does not cause anxiety in someone. The decisions are inevitable, though, at a given moment on a given agenda, albeit not easily honored on a different occasion. They can be as transient, sincere, detached, or ironic as, in part 3, the former colonial powers, the Western hegemony, and the rising Chinese influences together make an almost permanent junction of three roads.

Succinctly, part 3 testifies to the implausibility of defining China. It analyzes cases of undecidable identities in the cultural, religious, academic, and political spheres that mainly take place in Taiwan, Hong Kong, and, comparatively, Singapore.

Chapter 9 contrasts a Hong Kong experimental drama director who deconstructs any canonic Chineseness with a Singapore director who seeks to retrieve a certain lost Chineseness. Both adopt a composite of Western and Chinese techniques in their products, yet with different inspirations. Chapter 10 discovers an atypical style of promoting Taiwan's independence (from China) in the Presbyterian tradition to the extent that it has not been anti-Chinese at the same time. Such a nonconfrontational quest for statehood has its origins in a desire to transcend the Japanese colonialism.

Chapter 11 compares Taiwanese migrant scholarship with Western migrant scholarship in Hong Kong and finds that the choices of scholars in terms of their relationships with China affect their theoretical orientations. This results in an array of perspectives that multiplies China. Chapter 12 explores the pressure of the mainlandization of Hong Kong and Taiwan under the circumstance of both sites having been subjected to simultaneous Westernization and colonization. Such pressure engenders a fluid identity strategy that also destabilizes any alleged contents of Chineseness.

Chapter 9

Me Inside and Outside

Performing for Hong Kong and Singapore

Prescribing Post-Chineseness for the Community

In the situation where a self-regarded external group is caught between China and another identity, chapter 5 makes a significant distinction between sinological Chineseness and ethnic Chineseness. The former is shown in actively preaching to both sides about each other, and the latter, in questing recognition from both sides. This chapter reviews the same in-between identities/post-identities in Singapore and Hong Kong, but the ethnicity is Chinese in both places rather than an external Vietnamese ethnicity as in chapter 5. How to justify a local Chinese identity in Singapore and Hong Kong as a different or same Chinese identity testifies to the quintessential politics of post-Chineseness. The development of experimental dramas directed by the late Kuo Pao-kun (1939–2002) in Singapore and contemporary Denny Yung (1943–) in Hong Kong illustrates how they each want their communities to be respectively recognized by China and perceived in the role of alter in the context of the rise of China and decolonization.

There is no doubt that some kind of prior Chineseness constitutes the identities of both directors and their communities. How they can and should belong, however, is the common agenda that reveals their ambivalence. Kuo intended to prompt the audience to connect culturally with something Chinese that can reconstitute their individuality. For Kuo, the crisis is the loss of cultural subjectivity, and the improvisation of imagined resemblance to the people of greater China can enable a Chinese-Singaporean to recollect this. For Yung, cultural subjectivity is no longer a question after the return of Hong Kong to China. Acknowledging that epistemologically Hong Kong perspectives do not represent China, Yung painstakingly seeks to encourage and generate the volition and capacity of individual Hong Kong people to have faith in their own ways of transcending any version of the entirety of China.

Chapter 9 gathers, between the two sites, a possible dichotomy within the representation of China: China as a collective same-group to accommodate the changing world and China as an individualized trait that emerges from each narrator's chosen perspective. The two directors and their successors have each struggled to preach their versions of communal identity in face of the rise and arrival of the influences from the PRC. While Kuo tried culturally to shift the "outsider" Singapore to a somewhat "insider" position by recalling its resemblance to Chineseness, Yung has endeavored the opposite by balancing a prior resemblance to Chineseness.

Postcolonial artists in Singapore and Hong Kong face a challenge regarding the positioning of their creative work between their indigenous identities and Chinese identities due to the vicissitudes within the image of China at their respective sites and their respective understanding of Chineseness (G. Wang 1981). Constantly reformulating or recombining cultural identities at each site into different possibilities makes experimental theater a pertinent medium for their expression. Challenges are both ontological and epistemological, since both societies are culturally dynamic and politically vulnerable. Ontologically, they must decide whether the creative work should come from an acknowledged Sinic tradition, albeit constantly adapting to changes in an environment over which they have no control, or be intrinsically exempt from any such tradition to allow for an absolutely decontextualized reappropriation and reassociation of cultural resources. This ontological dilemma alludes to the extent to which cross-cultural subjects should accept, rather than transcend, their differing resemblance to Chineseness (Liu and Wong 2004; Suryadinata 2007; 2002).

Epistemologically, since a creative work makes sense to its audience because it is embedded in a prior relation that its author shares with the audience, the author must decide whether the creative work should attract a sympathetic audience or prescribe a legacy in the thought process of subsequent generations.[1] The creation of a particular mix of market and educational considerations in a particular creative work is a conscious process.

Chineseness and Cross-cultural Representations

Kuo was born in 1939. He migrated to Singapore with his family after the Communists rose to power in 1949. He began his performing arts career at the age of twelve and received his professional training at the National Institute of Dramatic Art in Australia between 1962 and 1965. He returned to Singapore and established the Academy of Performing Arts in 1965. In 1976, he was prosecuted for participating in a left-wing demonstration and was deprived of his civil rights. He was released from prison in 1980. In 1990, he received the Cultural Award from the government and had his civil rights restored within two years. The academy was renamed Theater Practice in 1996. In 2000, he began a pedagogical curriculum, "Training and Research for Theater Practice." He passed away in 2002 and has been dubbed Singapore's "father of modern theater" worldwide.

Kuo was similar to most first- and second-generation Chinese migrants to Singapore. This group of migrants consisted of a strong patriotic first generation that had recently emerged from a hard-fought anti-Japanese war. A twenty-first-century oral history project of Chinese intellectuals in Singapore yields two evolving prior relations of his time (see J. Wong 2013; Pi-chun Chang 2009). The first prior relation involves the changing political identities of Chinese-Singaporeans, a change that began in the 1930s along with the emerging socialist and indigenous consciousness and resurfaced after Singapore gained its independence (for more discussion, see Quah 1995). Thus, the second generation gradually experienced a transformation in the image of China from a familiar "motherland China" to simply another country. The latter image has prevailed among the third and succeeding generations, who are accustomed to an English-speaking environment and, along with their school curriculum, certain foreign (Western) perspectives on China. Singapore becomes a complete outsider.

The second prior relation is the largely patriotic (toward "motherland" China) and pro-socialist sensibilities of the first two generations that suffered from the anti-communist governance in Singapore, the cultural reassociation with anti-communist Taiwan, and the nascent rise of pro-capitalist China. Kuo arrived in Singapore in 1949 at the age of ten. The historical trajectory that emerged from the aftermath of the anti-Japanese war carried with it the popularity of anti-Japanese dramas. Patriotism drew modern dramas away from former feudalist arts, such as the Beijing Opera, that was popular during the war (H. Yan 1992). Modern dramas fit the political need of the time, particularly because they could be expediently staged for the gathering masses. The mobilizing function applied in Singapore to the anti-colonial movement and to anti-Japanese patriotism. Modern dramas were certainly popular in Chinese language schools, just in time to shape the beginning of Kuo's intellectual life. Their propagation of social movements directly answered the immigrant Chinese circles in post–World War II Singapore. Kuo's early career emerged from exactly the same historical trajectory, only to encounter the arrival of the Cold War and the entry of the anti-communist tide.

Anti-communism, physically and politically, censored the Chinese in Singapore with regard to patriotism for their perceived motherland; leftist dramas, which echoed Chinese socialism, were considered a politically incorrect mode of expression. Before Singapore's independence, however, the revolutionary change in China did not readily surrender to the gradual indigenization of the local Chinese community. This situation explains the second generation's undying nostalgia for China in the ensuing decades. In fact, many Malaysian communists, who retired from their revolutionary career upon the decision of Deng Xiaoping to honor a rapprochement between China and Singapore, chose to reside in Singapore during their later years.

Chinese consciousness received the first significant blow from the national strategy of the newly independent Singapore, whose authorities mindfully managed the racially and religiously sensitive Southeast Asian neighborhood (G. Wang 2005; Aljunied 2009; Chua 2009). In a nutshell, the reshuffling of the local pedagogy to substitute English education for Chinese education after 1965 bred a third generation that has been increasingly estranged from the Chinese cultural legacy (Purushotam 1998). The authorities were determined to enact an identity that is definitely outside China, with the consequence that "utility Chineseness" (see table 5.1 and figure 7.1) became the only appropriate feature to impart the Singaporean identity, with "ethnic Chineseness" (see table 5.1 and figure 7.1) being the maximal relation to China allowed. Ethnic Chineseness points to multicultural and multiracial components of the country, each with a cross-border connection. The complex politics of identity cautioned against any art experiment embracing potentially discriminatory content. The aftermath of Kuo's imprisonment indeed led to him making several attempts to utilize multilanguage narratives. The independence of Singapore has, therefore, been unfavorable regarding the reception or preservation of Chinese consciousness from its connection to the motherland. This state of affairs was very different to that in Hong Kong, which incorporated a migrant society that was geoculturally and racially subsumed to (Han) Chinese dominance.

Denny Yung, the "father of art and literature" in Hong Kong (Tsoi 2012), was born in 1943 in Shanghai. His family migrated to Hong Kong in 1948. Since childhood, he has been conscious of a transcultural environment and has deviated from, while being aware of, the politicization of cultural symbols. He lived through the Chinese Civil War, the assassination of John F. Kennedy, the radical late 1960s, and the Cultural Revolution during his schooling in the United States, and experienced, more recently, the handing over of Hong Kong to China (Chung 2002). He does not totally reject politics, though; in fact, he has willingly participated in creating cultural and art policies both before and after the handover. Experimental theaters are officially supported by the authorities in Hong Kong, which allowed Yung to acquire skills and connections from all over the world. Yung's running of Zuni Icosahedron (2013) for over three decades has taken full advantage of Hong Kong's lenient policies. Deliberate depoliticization is an additional necessity for him in light of Hong Kong's divided ideologies. Even the adoption of a cultural theme could inadvertently involve one in unwanted political polemics. Yung's creativity in form, for which he is renowned, is in itself a statement of politics, due to his conscious detachment from the demand for political correctness and decontextualizing of China for each to access it in its own way. As sticking with form begins as a way to avoid direct engagement with the integrated image of China in order to accommodate variety, this method might well end up with preserving China in an open-ended interrogation that is acceptable to all (Chow 1993).

In hindsight, the emergence of Hong Kong's return to China in 1982 and the completion of its return in 1997 significantly affected the evolution of dramaturgical thinking in Yung's philosophy of directing. The political and cultural anxieties in Hong Kong primarily involved the anticipated monopoly of statist China (Abbas 1997; Liu and Kuan 1988). If political independence is unlikely for a Hong Kong used to the comfortable and even lofty position of watching China from somewhere outside, a certain form of cultural independence engrossed in Hong Kong's Westernized governance and multicultural mix provides a plausible clue to imagining an alternative route that will transcend its nascent political subjugation. In contrast, the same anxiety toward Chinese dominance in Singapore comes strongly from outside the Chinese community. Being apprehended by the perceived alienation from the Chinese cultural tradition among the third and future generations, intellectuals of the second generation of Chinese Singaporeans welcome a reconnection with China.

The cross-cultural experimental theater in Singapore that arose from a mutually alerted ethnic and national environment has experienced constraints imposed by an estranged system of governance. The 1949 communist takeover in China and the anti-communist politics in Singapore forced the indigenous Chinese who identified with China into primarily private-sector endeavors. This Chinese consciousness carried by first-generation migrants originally benefited from the Chinese teachers who, for the early years following the Japanese occupation, guaranteed the quality of the Chinese language education. Sympathy for socialism likewise persevered, mainly in the literature and art sectors. As time passed, more help with the Chinese teaching and literature curriculum came from Taiwan, whose government's anti-communist stance and alleged representation of a genuine Chinese nation fit Singapore's political conditions. The blow was most serious when the government closed the Chinese language schools in 1965, substituting English for Chinese as the first language. The education policy bred future generations with primarily Western perspectives on China, leading to the impression that artistic creativity mainly stems from Western sources and China is considered exotic (Heng 2012; Quah 2009).

The danger of losing cultural subjectivity in Singapore's Chinese community is, therefore, different from that of Hong Kong. In Singapore, if private endeavors cannot hold their own, multicultural integration will only encourage estrangement from any imagined Chinese cultural legacy. Without an imagined subjectivity as guidance, the creative mix of multiple cultures and their forms has no prior standard of appreciation except that it should be a marketable mix; commercial promotion prevails easily under the circumstance of this technically required mix. The government's deliberate inattention to Chinese cultural preservation reinforces the sense of crisis among passing generations, which explains why the cross-cultural environment incurs a sufficiently strong sense of urgency among this generation to trigger a desire to restore a Chinese cultural subjectivity and develop Chinese multiculturalism. The new epoch has begun, as mainland Chinese have again started migrating to Singapore since the Communist authorities adopted the open policy in the early 1980s. However, the newcomers' competition with local Chinese in Singapore does not necessarily favor reconnection. The Chinese language program survives only to serve instrumental, rather than cultural, functions. The sense of crisis lingers among the passing generations.

Compared to Singapore, Hong Kong's fully-fledged reconnection with China in the process of returning to China threatens to eliminate Hong Kong's distinctive in-betweenness (Kam 2010; Lui, Ng, and Ma 2010; Chow 1998). Note that Hong Kong has accommodated generations of refugees from China. Reconnection entails political discomfort. The cross-cultural strategy for a distinctive Hong Kong will, accordingly, be one of qualified, vis-à-vis enhanced, Chineseness. The capacity to re-present Chinese culture in ways that do not subsume a Hong Kong identity will recontextualize Chinese culture. Based upon the Chinese consciousness of its residents, the cross-cultural experimental theater targeted at Hong Kong's identity is destined to rely more on creative form than on substance (Lilley 1998). The preferable Chinese identity that contributes to a different Hong Kong identity points to the capacity to appropriate Chineseness for a far wider, and usually external (Western), audience by using the techniques familiar to the latter. Hong Kong can achieve an imagined sense of uniqueness (and even superiority) by disengaging from a fixation with any cultural resemblance (Chow 1993).

Accordingly, two different notions of China are distinguishable in the cross-cultural theater. The first China supports the imagined resemblance of cultural subjectivity, based upon which one can improvise cross-cultural forms and techniques of art. The enhanced resemblance of cultural subjectivity prescribes the expression, quest, and reflection of cultural adaptation to a level of communal revival. In this particular vein, the authors and directors practice the recombination of cultural resources to enable like members of the same community to appreciate their past, understand their current conditions, and choose their future orientations. Only if China is conceived of as constituting elements of one's own subjectivity can experimental theaters prescribe perspectives on the cultural adaptation that is meaningful to the community itself and to its cross-cultural environment. Such prescription, if successful, might enable Singaporean intellectuals to attain sinological Chineseness (see table 5.1 or figure 7.1) and substantiate the official platform of making the nation a civilizational bridge (see chapter 8).

The second China is not unlike a cultural repertoire that supplies endless objects for re-presentation via various creative forms. Creative re-presentation seeks emancipation, recontextualization, and transcendence. It moves any particular Chinese community beyond the quest to represent China as a whole. China will lose contemporary meanings at the national level, because sites will be politically free to recombine multicultural techniques that will dissolve any challenges posed by any assertion of one entire China to the Chineseness of the authors or directors producing from sites of their own. The second China is no more than a creative use of Chinese symbols. A symbolically individualized, seemingly broken China is, in Hong Kong, more acceptable and even vibrant in the longer run than a discursively integrated entirety of China. Historically embedded in anti-communism, neither the insider's moral Chineseness in the Confucian context nor the outsider's civilizational Chineseness in the Christian context could sustain Yung's reformulation. Instead, an insider's exotic Chineseness (table 1.1) exclusively belonging to Hong Kong when facing the international audience and the outsider's ethnic or civilizational Chineseness when facing the fellow citizens of the PRC provide better balances to the prior resemblance in terms of belonging to a nationally united China.

A summary and comparison of the cross-cultural experimental theaters in Singapore and Hong Kong consist of at least three different levels: (1) At the sovereignty level, Singapore considers China as another nation whose cultural legacy is only one component of Singapore's own national culture. Utility Chineseness prevails. In comparison, adopting the same-group role of an insider, Hong Kong practices either moral Chineseness of anti-communism or equal Chineseness of citizenship. (2) At the cultural level, the Chinese community in Singapore perceives a religiously and racially oppositional surrounding, whose populations, in the eyes of Singaporeans, own (negotiable) utility or (hostile) civilizational Chineseness, whereas the Hong Kong Chinese face cultural resemblance in their mingling with China. And (3) at the theatrical level, which is critical and resistant, the restoration of cultural subjectivity is in Singapore a method of producing cross-cultural experimental theater that rehabilitates sinological Chineseness. However, the danger in Hong Kong is an overwhelming Chinese culture that may ironically backfire and call for a theater to obscure Hong Kong's insider Chineseness. Therefore, two comparable agendas emerge. The first agenda deals with how to restore insiders' Chineseness as a community for Singapore. The second agenda involves how we each improvise Chineseness in our own way that collectively results in outsiders' civilizational Chineseness for Hong Kong.

New challenges are also emerging. First of all, the mentality of independence has been gaining momentum in Hong Kong in the 21st century, especially among the Hong Kong-born generation (Zheng & Wong 2002; Lui 2010; Wong & Wan 2007). They shocked the world in 2014 and 2019 respectively by their generally anti-China Umbrella Movement and Anti-Expedition Campaign. Secondly, new waves of Chinese migrants continue to arrive in Hong Kong and Singapore. They are either socially dependent residents or economically rich consumers in Hong Kong but, in Singapore, they are primarily competitive professionals. The functions of writing and directing scripts on China in cross-cultural theaters may diverge at both sites.

Kuo Pao-kun's Quest for Cultural Subjectivity

Kuo gained firsthand experience of the Western form of theater while studying in Melbourne and Sydney. The Western theatrical form first entered the Chinese context as early as the May Fourth Movement of 1919. Chinese artists in Singapore concurrently adopted it. Alongside Nobel laureate Gao Xingjian in China, Kuo spearheaded the second wave of Westernization that took place sixty years later. He introduced Western art theory and methodology to the presentation of Chinese topics and was the most advanced and active individual regarding the application of Western artistic techniques. The excitement generated by the freshness of the new technique and form led to Gao's assertion that substance is constituted by form (Gao 1998).[2] A period of experimentation with new forms of theatric performance began. However, this period did not proceed without political implications.

Kuo consciously brought Western realism into the Oriental style of spontaneity (寫意). The concentration on the form of art nevertheless neutralized, if not extricated, in effect, the ideologically laden time of anti-communism. Considering that he had recently been freed from prison and was still suffering the loss of his civil rights, one can appreciate this choice of form over substance to the extent that substance would have been incompatible with his concerns for China. His estrangement from the politics of the time via his focus on methodology paralleled similar attempts by Gao Xingjian (1940–), who likewise needed a method to cope with the post–Cultural Revolution anxiety regarding the lack of meaning of life.[3] Form is the instant representation, requiring no beginning or end. This form-driven tide was a harbinger for Hong Kong artists as well, who were preoccupied with the expression of a sited understanding of their Chineseness in face of the upcoming handover.

In the aftermath of Kuo's release from prison in 1980, the artistic form of traditional theater or street-level dramas no longer sufficed. Kuo encountered a tremendous challenge involving blooming artistic methods and needed to reflect on his style. His choice was, nevertheless, filled with cultural sensibilities, which were manifested in his preference for scripts that carried ethical messages. With Singapore loosening its control on its relationship with the PRC and the irrevocable opening of China in the 1990s, Kuo's concerns for the loss of identity of Chinese communities, nevertheless, attained a strong technical dimension. Toward the latter part of his career, he collaborated with both Gao Xingjian, originally from China, and Denny Yung, originally from Hong Kong. The popular novelist Long Ying-tai, originally from Taiwan, was also in the loop.

Artists from various Chinese cities found the coalition fruitful for several reasons. The coalition could, ironically, signal a transnational Chinese subjectivity to inspire Kuo or a multisitedness of Chineseness to comfort Yung. Long and Yung were more in line with each other, because they both relied on China as inspiration while simultaneously attempting to transcend the image of an integrated China. Long's ambiguity sprung from her two-front battle against the anti-China trend in the pro-independent politics of Taiwan and the unpopular push for the reunification of China with Taiwan. The common mission was to accept and make sense of their Chinese cultural roots without playing into the hands of the Chinese government. In contrast, Kuo's task was to integrate Chinese identity from a culturally and racially alien environment.

In Singapore, Kuo's major concerns in practice included tracing the presumably Chinese cultural origin in his directing of drama.[4] Numerous cross-cultural scripts in the Chinese market appeared to be classic Western dramas, rewritten for the Chinese audience. The text could alternatively be an appropriation of Chinese cultural symbols for a Western audience looking for an exotic performance that is comprehensible within their Western style of presentation, which could have been Kuo's choice of theatrical form during a low point in his life. His sense of urgency to restore the Chineseness of the Chinese community remained strong in the early 1990s, though. His aim was to reconnect with his Chinese legacy, which was often critically conducted, as shown by his sensitivity toward the inability of Chinese culture to cope with postmodern conditions.[5] Kuo's practice of culturally showcasing Chinese origins is imperative for his experimental theater to achieve meaning.

Kuo's quest for cultural subjectivity can be broken down into two dimensions: methodological and substantive. He methodologically sought ways to aid the survival of Chinese drama in the face of new generations and the challenges posed by globalization. He appeared to have benefited greatly from certain Western sources in his struggle to return to the mainstream through Western methods. However, he was consciously aware of the earlier genealogy of the Western methods rooted in the Chinese context. He also consciously and substantively imbued Chinese elements in his narratives, presumably in order reconnect new generations to their Chinese subjectivity.

Kuo was influenced by his leftist activities from his early years, when he wrote narratives particularly for Chinese workers and immigrants from the lower social echelons.[6] This legacy constrained him from immediately participating in the postmodern form of artistic expression, which serves a consumers' market. However, he longed for a return to the masses. Therefore, he focused on an artistic refinement that was previously untapped in his earlier work, which targeted the lower classes, with the hope of attracting a wider audience. He looked to Western theory for inspiration. His new work particularly resembled that of Danish director Eugenio Barba (1936–), who demonstrated how a multicultural system of artistic performance is possible. Barba utilized various Asian sources, particularly Indonesia, Japan, India, and China, for his system components. Kuo believed that he could similarly combine Asian elements into Western forms if the Western directors were able to succeed in this.[7]

The Western creation of the hybrid system contrasts with the Chinese practices, because Chinese dramaturgical forms usually lack an interpretive theory in the first place. Chinese dramas are popularly perceived to be preoccupied with body techniques, whereas Western dramas are concerned with the expression of feelings. In Western dramas, the meanings that directors convey to the audience are mediated by the performance of the characters, which are associated with individual roles and actors. In Chinese drama, the meanings are largely standard, in accordance with the solid body techniques adopted. Chinese actors are given little room for interpretation or reinterpretation. The essential secret to the success of Chinese theater is the solid training in body techniques and the improvised, rich use of these techniques by the actors. In contrast, individualized role-based meanings are essential components in Western theater.

Today, methodology is an intrinsic element of Western dramas on a scaled modern stage, where facial expression fulfils, at best, a limited function, and spatial arrangements, sounds, color, and lights must support the eclipsed expression of individualized meanings. In comparison, traditional Chinese dramas are usually exempt from spatial techniques and methodology, because the audience expects to see skill rather than dramaturgical techniques. Kuo needed to adapt, because the third-generation Chinese in Singapore were becoming increasingly accustomed to the Western form of theater. He borrowed vanguard art techniques from Europe and America to communicate with the Westernized audience. However, he remained adamant in his desire for his combination to transcend the market-oriented production of sheer Western favor.

Kuo Pao-kun's Unspeakable Methodology

In his later career, Kuo incorporated a large amount of traditional Chinese elements in his directing—substantively in his scripts and methodologically in his artistic technique. *Lao Jiu*, for example, introduced traditional puppetry art in a story about an adolescent love for puppet drama. The narrative is about nostalgia for traditional puppetry art. The quest for freedom by the innocent Lao Jiu, who opens the music drama by speaking in a dream, ironically points to the return of tradition instead of freedom from tradition. In *Descendants of the Eunuch Admiral*, traditional Chinese punch music is naturally present when the story begins with the surfing outwards of ancient immigrants. Kuo's works differ from the exotic combination of Chinese and Western artistic components. Kuo challenged his audience to interrogate their own cultural subjectivity in form (e.g., punch music) and substance (e.g., puppetry art).

However, a deep-rooted constraint seemed to prevent Kuo from developing a methodological discourse. He preserved widespread Chinese practices in his later dramas, which confront the focus of Western methodology on individual actors. For example, a voice-over or something similar would periodically remind the audience of what the director would like the audience to keep in mind as they continued to watch. This side narration is usually performed by the actors, who temporarily leave their roles to have a direct conversation with the audience. Side narratives are not even present in the script. Such side narratives present a presumably objective standpoint to the audience to disallow the reduction of the audience into a mere sounding board for the actors. In *Lao Jiu*, the titular character introduces himself at the beginning of the drama. Similar to the audience of the traditional Chinese drama, who is conscious of its evaluative position and even expressive of its appreciation during the show, Kuo's audience is expected to make a judgment based on its own perspective during the show.

This continued application of a voice-over underlines Kuo's pursuit of cultural subjectivity to a certain extent. The voice-over allows the director to provide the audience with an exit from the narrative, the overwhelming performing techniques, or the interpretation of meanings and expression of feelings by the actors. The contents of the narrative in a voice-over and the form of using the voice-over reflect the cultural sensibilities in Kuo's attempts to create a new dramaturgical form. The sheer application of the form suggests that it is the duty of a director to keep the audience coolheaded. Kuo's directors perform an educational duty for the audience and its society by providing the asides, despite the fact that the director's voice-over can only be indirectly related to Chinese cultural subjectivity.

In practice, Kuo's voice-over carries significant cultural sensibilities. The cultural messages instilled in Kuo's voice-over substantiated his painstaking defense of the Chinese identity of Singapore. In light of the unfeasibility of social movement since independence, Kuo created dramas that told stories of familial passions in his attempt to use the Western dramaturgical form. Familial passions were essentially cultural topics. However, he also began to place additional emphasis on the performing art of the actors and became slightly obsessed with the aesthetics of his work beyond the class-minded or nationalistically embedded determination. Kuo was dissatisfied with the method-laden turn in his career and searched for a methodological discourse. His seemingly unsuccessful quest was indirectly answered by Gao Xingjian, when the latter called the narrator of asides "a neutral actor."[8] The performance of the "neutral actor" temporarily renders aesthetics irrelevant by her neutrality to the cross-meanings within the roles enacted by the dramaturgical actors. The theme of the "neutral actor" could potentially be that of Kuo as well.

Kuo's neutral actor is, notably, often played by an actor who temporarily exits the context of the drama to provide the voice-over. When actors are given the chance periodically to distance themselves from their roles, they similarly retain an evaluative position in their performance. This symbiosis of action and evaluation allows the actors to retain their real-life perspective and enables them to enact their roles through a cultural subjectivity that is prior to the narrative and directing. The actors achieve cultural subjectivity by acting out their own cultural experiences as well as shifting between acting and evaluating (Quah 2002). After Kuo's time, the Japanese director Susuki's assertion of "culture is the body" (Susuki 2002) methodologically captured the symbiosis of pre-drama cultural subjectivities (Susuki's culture) and in-drama actors (Susuki's body) and somehow explained how Kuo's methodology was supposed to be unspeakable in the first place. The methodology is not of drama per se, but that of the audience. The imagined audience speaks inside the actor narrating the voice-over.

Nevertheless, Kuo had a greater goal than merely directing Chinese dramas. He wished to appropriate Western art from a cultural subjective perspective. Kuo actually paralleled Bertolt Brecht (1898–1956), a German director who galvanized a particular style of performance called epic theater, wherein the audience is constantly reminded of the fictionality of the drama. While Kuo used the voice-over, Brecht created an "alienation effect" for his audience, which allowed them to retain a coolheaded, relaxed state of mind. Kuo knew exactly from whom Brecht developed such an idea: Mei Lanfang (1894–1961) (Bai 1998).[9] Brecht closely studied Mei's performance tour in America and Europe. Mei's artistic performance was psychologically distanced from the audience, which ensured that his audience would stay outside the narrative and the stage by enjoying his chanting and skillful body language. Brecht also saw the 打背躬 (i.e., one actor talking to the audience behind the back of another actor) in Mei's performance as a form of communication between the actor and the audience. Kuo determined that this alienation effect was Chinese in origin and consistently retained and applied such effect in his creative work.

Reading what sort of asides Kuo used in order to prepare his audience is instructive. In his well-known drama, *The Coffin is Too Big for the Hole*, an environmental official narrates his demand to cut the four corners off a coffin in order for it to fit into the incinerator. The voice-over reminds the audience of the Chinese tradition of "the dead being the greatest" (死者為大), which not only evokes the deep-rootedness of the long-held value of parental piety, but also the empowering Chinese subjectivity. In *Descendants of the Eunuch Admiral*, the voice-over provokes the audience by asking how a eunuch could ever have descendants, the implication being that Chineseness in Singapore has been culturally castrated before it came into being.

When the director or an actual third player offers such a reflection from a presumably culturally subjective position, the actor, who only focuses on the role, would seem unconcerned about how simultaneously to act as audience. On the one hand, the actor has no evaluative perspective when playing the dramaturgical role. On the other, the audience, immersed in the role, would be unable to empathize with the cultural messages designed by the director. The symbiosis of the dramaturgical actor (i.e., the body) and neutral actor (i.e., the culture) provides the audience with a relationship to the dramaturgical actor through the fusion of the audience and the neutral actor in the imagined resemblance in terms of Chinese cultural subjectivity. The unspeakable methodology implies an important methodological thought that reinforces and enlivens the cultural subjectivity expressed by the narrative through such a method. Kuo's turn to the Western artistic form for a solution to marketability was consequently able to proceed on the same track in searching for cultural subjectivity. This cultural subjectivity also reconnects the third-generation Chinese in Singapore with a legacy that is usually inaccessible through English sources. The possibility of retransforming China as outsider into China as same-group survives in Kuo's new drama.

Denny Yung and His Moving-Body Technique

Yung is mindful of a larger audience that includes the greater Asian sphere and Western countries. He engages in high-level politics by assuming Hong

Kong's cultural leadership, upon which he negotiates for exchanges worldwide. He is equally active in searching for liaisons among Chinese artists overseas, including Taipei and Singapore. His efforts raise Hong Kong culture to a transnational level, which compensates for the political inferiority of Hong Kong to China. Yung's duty as a cultural legislator partially explains why marketing was such an important element on his theatrical path. He is keen to involve the masses in the production of the narrative and in practical experimental theater. He especially enjoys designing and directing open-ended dramas with the effect of leaving the meanings of Chinese symbols, political or not, subject to constant reinterpretation and reappropriation by the audience as actor. His methodological preoccupation with apolitical technique and form is, accordingly, intrinsically political in nature.

Yung is very successful in convincing the Hong Kong authorities to support his art activities. Discovering the identity of Hong Kong has always been important to the intellectuals in Hong Kong since the date of the return was set as 1982. However, Yung's experimental theater and other performing art products are not about the restoration of Chinese identities. Hong Kong never lost its Chinese identity in the first place. The reconnection of Hong Kong with China in the process of returning to China nevertheless threatens to remove the distinctive in-betweenness of Hong Kong. Hong Kong has also notably accommodated generations of refugees from China. Reconnection by all means entails political discomfort in the populace that was historically anti-communist. The cross-cultural strategy for a distinctive Hong Kong would accordingly be one of in-between, vis-à-vis internal, Chineseness. The capacity to prescribe Chinese culture in ways that do not subsume Hong Kong identity is to reconstitute Chinese culture. Given the Chinese consciousness of its residents, the cross-cultural experimental theater, aimed at the identity of Hong Kong, is destined to rely more on creative forms than on substance. The preferable Chinese identity that contributes to a different Hong Kong identity points to the capacity for appropriating Chineseness for a much wider and even external (Western) audience by using techniques that are familiar and comfortable to the latter. Hong Kong can achieve an imagined sense of exoticness by disengaging from cultural fixation of any sort. To relate to outsider groups, Hong Kong enables them to own different kinds of exotic Chineseness. This occurs both in academia and the media. Churches, the intelligence sector, and think tanks were previously active (more in chapter 11). Hong Kong serves as a watcher of the various Western sectors that concern Chinese politics and policy. In academia, the traditions of the humanities, Confucian classics, and social science disciplines are present and use both Chinese and English.

The integration of these various perspectives into a Hong Kong identity to face its return to China is unnecessary and impossible. A disintegrated set of Chinese identities in Hong Kong could have made its return less drastic. Yung's naming of his performance group Zuni Icosahedron is a harbinger of what not to expect from the group; that is, an integrated symbol of the entirety of China (Enri 2012).

Any constructed image of China brought by anyone to Hong Kong is supposed to grow into something dissimilar or strange to its previous owner, once it is reflected through the Zuni Icosahedron. Therefore, avoiding a singular or monotonous treatment of China in Hong Kong becomes a more pertinent challenge to Yung than the preservation of Chinese subjectivities. Without an identity crisis of losing Chineseness, no urgent push exists regarding how methodologically to pave the way for a culturally minded actor to connect with the audience. In fact, a potential identity crisis is caused by the single-minded Chineseness implicitly held by the arriving motherland residents. Therefore, allowing the audience to remain divided and giving the divided audience a chance to participate in the making of the image of China substitutes for the mission of integrating and restoring cultural subjectivity.

Yung expects his dramas always to be subversive against 大雅, which is a Chinese classic expression of magnificence.[10] Therefore, he develops a unique style of moving bodies against specifically designed contexts. These moving bodies may appear similar across different stages, but each stage or context is distinctive. The stages symbolize something culturally, socially, or politically prior and given. Moving bodies arise from professional and citizen actors to indicate secularization and multisitedness. The seemingly aimless movements and body gestures suggest that no meaning stays in the long run despite the magnificence of the background. Only those who transcend prior relations can live their own lives. Their maximal relations exist in the imagined resemblance of the magnificent and yet distant background, which defines (practically irrelevant) Chineseness. Yung's dramas could liberate his audience by empowering his performing actors to determine the meanings of their own gestures. These actors are presumably citizens who are similar to the audience and who allow the audience to imagine how to read meanings that differ from those given to them in the larger context. No one is neutral, yet all are spontaneous and limited.

Instead of sympathetically embodying their roles, Yung's actors have a duty to create their roles spontaneously. However, these actors must improvise within the space provided by the director. The different designs of the background reflect Yung's talent in spatial art. His space is usually physically broad enough for actors to create different gestures. The unspecified meanings of the movement of the actors and the changeability of the context through the use of space, sound, and color techniques constitute Yung's image of a multiple, multisited China, albeit indirectly or metaphorically. These actors are Chinese, but their numerous agendas are hardly directed toward the restoration of Chinese subjectivity. The communication between the actors and audience through a neutral actor is neither good nor necessary.

Another noticeable contrast between Yung and Kuo is the former's echoing of the postmodern celebration of revisability, which attests to the impossibility of any ideology to claim monopoly. In one of his well-known films, *Romance of the Rock 97*, Yung arranges the moving bodies of the red guards from past documentary films against a fast-moving background that contains numerous Chinese cultural symbols and characters. While Hong Kong returns to China, the Chineseness of Yung's Hong Kong consists of the classic characters and the Red Guards, both of which communist China cleanses away. Therefore, Yung displays an opposing style to Kuo, who intends to prompt the audience to reconnect with something greater than their individuality. Yung painstakingly generates the legitimacy and capacity of individual Hong Kong residents to have faith in their own ways of transcending any version of the entirety of China.

Conclusion

China as insider and outsider is far from being the sole idea of China, given the presence of various notions of China in cross-cultural theaters elsewhere. Zhang Yimou, a director of numerous best-selling films, moves around and within geographical China and reappropriates local and cultural resources through the most advanced, and mostly Western, techniques. Zhang enjoys official support and an internationalized market equivalent to those of Yung. Therefore, Yung's style is not unique to Hong Kong, despite his consistently and purposely more nuanced and experimental topics compared with Zhang's obsession with scale and splendidness. Yung utilizes his location in Hong Kong to reconstruct China into exotic and individualized practices. Nevertheless, Zhang creates an imagined position, external to territorial and political China.

China can also serve as a broader perspective through which the distant world can be read with a creative interpretation. The twice Oscar winner

Ang Lee is a quintessential example of how Chinese cultural sensitivity has enabled the incorporation of distant cultural resources. Lee can establish cultural subjectivity through his unlimited capacity to appreciate differences instead of the self-interrogation for continuity because of the freedom from a potentially hostile racial and religious environment. Therefore, Lee is able to move beyond a Chinese perspective to a worldly site outside the Chinese cultural sphere. For example, Gao Xingjian treats China as neither insider nor outsider. China becomes inexpressible but, once expressed, China becomes a problem. An expressed notion of China will ironically impose pressure on its observers to reject China.

New Chinese immigrants continue to move to Singapore and Hong Kong, a situation that produces fresh challenges to the perception of China in the hosting communities (H. Liu 2005; Guo 1999). In Singapore, new immigrants arrive in response to the policy of the Singaporean authorities, who deliberately encourage the recruitment of professionals from China (Montsion 2012) to support the hiatus in human resources in Singapore and establish access to the expanding Chinese market. Kuo's legacy may not arouse the sympathy of those new migrants who are yet to doubt their insider position in Greater China, which used to alarm the anti-communist government. Local communities and Hong Kong professionals residing in Singapore, who migrated slightly earlier than the Chinese, may each appeal to some kind of post-Singaporeanness in face of the nascent Chinese immigrants. Chineseness is destined to serve conflicting relationalities in the years to come.

Chinese immigrants in Hong Kong seldom present an image of professionalism. These immigrants continue to provide new topics to interrogate the Chineseness of Singapore. Legally and culturally, Hong Kong remains China, but new Chinese immigrants reproduce the political need for Hong Kong to choose between imagining postcolonial resemblance of all Hong Kong people in collectivity and improvising the exoticness or hybridity of transient Chineseness individually to deconstruct simplicity. The social and political movements in 2014 and 2019 have bred both solidarity and division, neither of which are conducive to individualized improvisations for post-Chineseness. Contrary to Singapore, therefore, the discursive complication of the Chineseness of Hong Kong is in decline and Chineseness is increasingly reduced to a binary.

Chapter 10

Sticking My Head Out under the Sky

A Presbyterian for Taiwan Independence

Introduction

Chapter 10 presents a typical case of evolving civilizational Chineseness—China, conceived of as being outside Taiwan, constitutes Taiwan's identity by its civilizational otherness. According to chapters in part 2, civilizational Chineseness portrays China as an ideational force that can incur demonization, romanticism, and alienation, depending on the outsider group's purpose. This chapter tackles an unfamiliar string of Taiwanese independence that has received its cue from theology. This theology first inspired critical reflections on Japanese colonialism and, later, on the migrant Kuomintang regime in exile. Moreover, it is a testimony to the power of individual pursuit with a collective consequence. The chapter records how Shoki Coe almost single-handedly improvised such a Presbyterian relation that transcends demonization as well as nationalism. The Presbyterian Church perceives Taiwan's resemblance, or potential of it, to China in terms of religious solidarity, which blesses the political autonomy of all believers. In reality, impracticality of this imagined resemblance reinforces their mutual strangeness.

In the twenty-first century, Taiwan's increasing aversion to China is apparent (Hickey 2019; Jacobs and Kang 2018; Corcuff 2012b) because of China's rise and the overwhelming trend of mainlandization or re-Sinicization (Shih 2017b; S. Sun 2010; Yu and Kwan 2008; M. Chen 2004). Actors elsewhere likewise perceive China's threat and can understand intellectually the nature of such a threat in various ways, typically constituted by scientific/

policy Chineseness (table 5.1 and figure 7.1). The resulting international relations perspectives of power, interest, and identity point to China's tendency to become an expansionist, economic predator, or incorrectly attractive model (Pillsbury 2016; Nathan 2003; Yee and Storey 2002). Internal reasons exist for an active portrayal of the threat, too, especially in electoral systems where, sometimes, a campaign edge can be achieved, reminding people of China's threat (Ho et al. 2019; Sullivan and Lee 2018; Michael Yang 2017; David Chen 2010, A1). Taiwan is no exception. In the quest for independent statehood, Taiwan can easily detect China's territorial ambition, economic invasion, and violation of liberalism (Kuan-chen Lee et al. 2018; Wei and Lai, 2017).

Taiwan's nostalgia for colonial modernity adds a psychological dimension to its advantage (Lee and Chen 2014; Barclay 2016; Jacobs 2014), in which China appears inferior to Japan, which colonized Taiwan from 1895 to 1945. According to this point of view, which was already a practice of civilizational Chineseness, China's offer of reunification connotes a return to a backward regime. In addition, the leaders of Taiwan's past ruling party, the exiled Kuomintang, had almost passed away fifty years ago fleeing Taiwan in the aftermath of the Civil War. These past leaders believed in reunification. The historical development enables the connection with postcolonial sensibilities among subsequent generations of leaders who have consistently estranged China (Corcuff 2011).

All the similarities and differences between Taiwan's perceptions of China's threat appear to be familiar. However, a strand of the pro-independence force in Taiwan that does not particularly rely on the intellectual construction of the threat either to attain legitimacy for Taiwan's pursuit or to win support from international major powers exists. In other words, the intersubjective construction of China-Taiwan relations is neither contributive nor determinative of the evolution of a consciousness of independence. Rather, self-reflection on one's practical conditions, which was independent from any prior cultural resemblance to China, inspired the effort to reconstitute Taiwan's identity. Such process renders the threat of China a marginal issue, in which an antagonizing China is no longer essential to the legitimacy of Taiwan's independence.

Chapter 10 focuses on the perspective of contextual theology having evolved from Taiwan's Presbyterian tradition. Owing to its Western origin, the Presbyterian history in Taiwan has bred a completely different relational trajectory, that contrasts sharply with those prepared by the colonial and Civil War relations (C. Kuo 2008; C. L. Lin 1999). The latter relations come with moral competition, whereas the indigenous Presbyterian relies little on the view of China to drive the quest for independence. Although this tradition had worked within political relations during various periods, confrontation, othering, or demonization rarely characterize its strategic practices, as often seen elsewhere. Thus, the marginality of China's threat in the Presbyterian pursuit of Taiwan's independence is worth reviewing.

The chapter begins with a broader review of the different kinds of relations in which the pro-independence forces have embedded themselves to demonstrate the importance of their intellectual understanding of China to their pursuit. Then, we will demonstrate how the Presbyterian Church evolved differently. This process illustrates how individual prescription can be essential to the evolution of greater relations. These greater relations additionally suggest how a peculiar way of failing to understand China can practically add strength in the formation of approaches to China. The chapter argues that religion plays a significant role in this development.

Taiwan's Approach to China Embedded in Colonial Relations

The two earliest Presbyterian priests arrived in Taiwan in 1867 and 1872, prior to Japan's colonization in 1895. Japan would have a considerable influence with regard to determining Taiwan's fate in the next half century. In many aspects, colonial relations with Taiwan were the same as with other colonies (Aguiar 2011; Shin and Robinson 1999). Most importantly, Japan imposed colonial modernity, which, for the purpose of this book, refers to utility Chineseness (table 1.1), which was the process of modernization to facilitate the extraction of resources according to the need of colonial governance (T. Chen 2002; Komagome 2006; M. Lo 2002b). Despite Japan's resorting to suppressive control in general, the Presbyterian Church encountered little intrusion. In contrast, the indigenous population underwent colonization, with the most deeply rooted influences resulting from education and war. Education and war had reconstituted the political identities of Taiwan, especially in the higher strata of society.

Education was an effective mechanism of assimilation (Peng and Chu 2017). Young people acquired Japanese values, language, and identities, and learned to be loyal to the emperor. The social hierarchy was clear, but the colonized population had the opportunity to rise up from the past Chineseness qua inferiority. The colonial migrants equated Chineseness to slavery in nature, given the conquest of China by northern Manchurian barbarians. The colonized population was inferior not only because they were at the bottom of the colonized society but also because of their Chinese identity.[1] Such cultural configuration had a strong influence on the elite because of the need to demonstrate high culture to attain acknowledgment from the colonizing forces (Ching 2001; Henry 2016). An aversion to China was strategically spontaneous to establish self-respect (Chih-huei Huang 2003). With the colony and Japan joining forces to inflict war on China, this disposition was strengthened. On the other hand, the war tore the identities of those who perceived and maintained hybrid identities in Taiwan.[2] Nevertheless, the war expanded and deepened "Japanization."

Having planned to enforce the idea of the Greater East Asian Co-prosperity Sphere, the colonial government actively recruited Taiwanese youths. The Taiwanese draftees were initially military servants. As the war escalated, these draftees were able to serve officially as soldiers, which gave them an enhanced sense of pride. Many followed the Japanese army to Southeast Asia, Manchuria, Hainan, or other sites in China. This pride was an even stronger inspiration for becoming Japanese. By the end of the war, most of them had never experienced defeat. Some still recalled participating in impressive modernization projects in Southeast Asia. This inspiration explained how the soldiers' pride continued even in the war's aftermath. Except for soldiers who were sent to fight in the Chinese Civil War, returnees were unable to apprehend defeat (Louzon 2017). The arriving Kuomintang appeared similarly inferior to them in the same way as the Chinese troops appeared to the Japanese army during the war. Ironically, because Japan handed Taiwan over to China, the Taiwanese soldiers who unexpectedly belonged to the Allies were suddenly largely exempt from war trials. As a result, the Japanese identity remained superior in Taiwan's consciousness. Neither was decolonization seriously attempted in Taiwan.

China's takeover of Taiwan became dramatic yet bizarre after the Kuomintang lost the Civil War to the Communists. The Kuomintang became an exiled regime. The indigenous population had no effective access to governing positions and was deprived of entitlement to the property left by the former colonizing forces. The Kuomintang thus alienated the postcolonial population, especially the elite and the returnees who had adapted successfully to colonial rules. This alienation came about despite the Kuomintang's educational and economic policies, which provided equality as opposed to discrimination under colonialism. The Kuomintang's war on communist China further inflicted politics of suppression. Although suppression is aimed primarily at

Communist infiltration, such politics of moral Chineseness reinforced the alienation of the postcolonial population (Cook 2005). The same can be said of the education offered to the postcolonial society. The education was full of Chinese patriotism, which helped neither the decolonization necessary for the postcolonial population to reflect critically upon their assimilation into the Japanese system nor the connection between the colonial and Chinese conditions (B. Chang 2015; Morris, Shimazu, and Vickers 2013).

These historical events explain effectively the emergence of the aversion to China after the passing away of the Kuomintang migrant leadership. Liberalism has replaced the Japanese emperor to undergird Taiwan's civilizational superiority. Liberalism first appeared to legitimize political reforms that ended the Kuomintang regime. Subsequently, extensive electoral practices benchmarked the difference in sovereign scope between Taiwan and China (Lien 2014). Taiwan has also been active in establishing solidarity with the Alliance of Liberties to involve India and Australia, in addition to Japan, in containing China. Nevertheless, at the end of the day, their resemblance to one another in terms of liberalism continues to foreground the colonial modernity of the pro-independence identities while adding to it territory consciousness (S. Pan 2015; Shih 2007), which was embedded when defending Japan during World War II. In fact, the reenactment of Taiwan's defeat at the end of World War II in an ironically celebrative narrative has been a popular tactic of pro-independence politicians to avow their allegedly non-Chinese identities (Shih 2017b).

Note the Taiwan Statue, on which former President Lee Teng-hui (1923–2020) has inscribed his words, in the Okinawa Prefectural Peace Memorial Park. The statute indicates that Taiwan and Japan resemble to each other in terms of a shared destiny and nationhood that is doomed to estrange China. The statue was installed in 2018. The park displays prefectural statues from all over Japan to memorialize the dead, originating from their respective domains. Lee wrote in Chinese on the statue established by the then president-elect, Tsai Ing-wen, "Testimony to Nationhood" (為國作見證) (Morgan 2018). Several observations have been made. First, Taiwan is not a prefecture of Japan. Second, the president of Taiwan is, in every sense, higher than the level of prefectural governor of Japan. Third, the names of Taiwanese soldiers who died during the Invasion of Ryukyu, if any, have not been researched or inscribed in the statue as done by the Japanese prefectures. Finally, the term "nationhood" in Lee's inscription on the Taiwan statue summarizes his identification with Japanese nationhood. In fact, for a short time, Lee served in the Japanese military during World

War II. Briefly, none of these political sensibilities resonate with the two leaders' quest for independent statehood. That said, their inexpressible comfort with discursively becoming part of the Japanese nation insinuates their aversion to China.

Church Relations versus Colonial Relations

On the Taiwan Statute, Lee wrote "testimony." Implicitly, this wording reflects the Presbyterian influence on his discourse. Presbyterian indoctrination clearly had a very different trajectory to colonial relations. If the latter portrayed an inferior China to be excluded, the church was compulsorily inclusive. Lee's hybrid characteristics of Christianity and colonial modernity enabled him intellectually to sequence his career along bifurcating paths and place China in dramatically different images, simultaneously backward and worthy of appreciation (S. Tsai 2005, 91–109). Lee's adaptive style attests to a highly unstable religious practice. Lee's hybrid identity has been emblematic of Presbyterian followers in Taiwan, and, together, they implied the other distinctive approach to the politics of identity that is unavailable to colonial relations. In fact, the evolution of the "contextual theology" of the contemporary Presbyterian Church has not taken inferior China or China's threat as its premise. Eventually, it is this improvised notion of "context" that inspires the exclusionary sense of resemblance among residents of Taiwan and the strangeness of Chineseness.

A separate trajectory that paralleled colonial relations could not be Chinese, because this would have invited shaming. The European origin of the Presbyterian Church or, more precisely, the Scottish origin of its contemporary institution, bestowed a superior image on Japan, which once strove to adopt a UK-style of identity. For example, Thomas Barclay (1849–1935), a Glasgow-born Presbyterian missionary, was able to mediate between the colonial troops and the residents of Tainan in 1895 to achieve the Capitulation of Tainan peacefully (Y. Cheng 2005, 1–2). He received an award from the Japanese emperor for his services. In the same vein, the Japanese colonial government generally failed to restrict the spread of gospel that originated and was spread prior to the colonial period. James L. Maxwell (1836–1921) started preaching in Southern Taiwan in 1865 and George L. Mackay (1844–1901) in Northern Taiwan in 1872. The colonial government only began to expel Western missionaries from Taiwan when World War II broke out. By then, the Western missionaries had successfully trained over two generations of local priests who could continue the church's work (H. Wu 2003, 172–78).

Christian identity was a possible remedy for transcending colonial relations or explicit scorn toward the inferior. The Church's focus on medical sciences and humanities contrasts with the colonial modernity, which focused mainly on the infrastructure, weaponry, navigation, medicine, and extraction. Assimilation only began at a far later stage. As Presbyterian missionaries were from the Calvinist traditions and Protestant Reformation, the humanist and enlightening tendencies in their pedagogical orientation were assured. The bulk of the church's work in colonial Taiwan was Western-style schooling and medicine (Y. Cheng 2005, 201). Moreover, the missionaries executed their reform and religion, to a large extent, in local languages whereas the colonial government was eager to substitute the "progressive" Japanese for the allegedly backward Chinese.[3] Acquiring Japanese subjected the colonized more deeply to the colonial system, whereas acquiring English distanced them from the system. Thus, church modernity appeared to be heading in a direction that was categorically different from colonial modernity. Neither the Chinese identity of the Han residents nor the primitivity of the aboriginal communities created a barrier to accessing the revelation of Christ.

The important development that made the Presbyterian Church an indigenous religion was the adoption of the local conventions and language in teaching and training (Po-ho Huang 1999, 20–21). The church recruited local talents who were more effective in the improvisation of linguistic and racial resemblance to the local. Eventually, an indigenous consciousness could evolve after the Western missionaries had to leave because of pressure from the colonial authorities. An indigenous church served as the foundation for the indigenous theology. In comparison with postcolonial indigeneity, church indigeneity was hardly confrontational. Postcolonial indigeneity targeted the exiled Chinese regime by enlisting the identity of colonial modernity. On the contrary, church modernity that supported church indigeneity attended to the intrinsic value and solidarity that believers perceived in their service to God. In addition, such service would have to include liberating the Chinese people, even though they did not belong to the postcolonial society. Their exile qualified them for more, rather than less, attention.

The growth of the Presbyterian Church underwent a long cycle of political regimes. The literature has considered the political complexity that is unique and essential to the quest for the indigenization of the church (C. Lin 2009, 41–83; Y. Kang 1999, 156). Presbyterian missionaries arrived during the Manchurian period. The church encountered the colonial regime first, then the Chinese regime in exile. The last involved the Chinese Civil War and Cold War. The church and migrant Kuomintang jointly opposed communist China, despite their otherwise incongruent purposes.[4] In any case, each regime presented some difficulties regarding the quest for universal Christianity. Especially the colonial and the Civil War regimes were established after the Church already had its own network in Taiwan. The resulting lesson was that the church was compelled to develop an indigenous consciousness for the sake of resisting externally imposed restrictions. In face of the obstacles imposed by these regimes, a cognitive fault line emerged between inside and outside territorially.

Colonial relations inevitably set the most important parameters of Presbyterian identity in Taiwan in this realized territoriality. The simple practice that demarcated Taiwan as a distinctive site or category, independent of China and Japan, comprised the geographical scope of indigenous identity. Such scope not only enabled the colonizers to look down upon the population that could only resist in the name of Taiwan but also enabled the colonized population to acquire a perspective from within the predetermined boundary. Given that China fell outside this boundary, the exiled Kuomintang could not help but act upon an alien character, which made little sense to its leaders, who conceived of the party as a force for the liberation of the postcolonial society. In the same vein, the Cold War relations, informed by the practice of containment, reinforced the separation of Taiwan from China as a distinctive site of geostrategic significance. These territorially oriented parameters prepared the emergence of "context" in contextual theology. The colonial modernity and church identities as two externally bred civilizations have been able to support each other after World War II because of this resemblance of territoriality.

The Rise of Contextual Theology

Shoki Coe (or Huang Chang-hui, Huang Zhanghui; 1914–88), the founder of contextual theology, distinguished himself from contemporary pro-independence advocates due to his attitude toward colonial Japan. Instead of relying on colonial modernity to offset the migrant regime's obsession with Chinese patriotism and anti-communism, he derived his indigenous sensibilities from critical reflections of his own identity vis-à-vis colonial Japan. Coe's family background, academic training, and career development contrasted from other important pro-independence leaders since it was not embedded in the colonial system unlike Presbyterian political leaders, such as Lee Teng-hui, who was the first president of the ROC that supported Taiwan independence, Peng Ming-min (1923–) who led a pro-independence campaign in the United States, or Ng Yuzin Chiautong (1932–2011), the former leader of the world's Taiwan independence movement. These leaders grew up in the colonial system and took a strong view of China. Coe resembled Liao Wen Kwei (Joshua Liao, 1905–52), who was called the "father of Taiwan independence," in the sense that neither were trained in the colonial system and their pro-independence position did not rest upon loathing China.

Liao, likewise a Presbyterian follower, came from an established noble family, was educated in the United States, and returned to China to teach. Liao's approach and preaching were deeply embedded in liberalism, which was in line with his dissertation subject on liberal philosophy (J. Liao 1929, 1933). Liao was married to an American, which was already unusual at the time. His turn to Taiwan independence was the result of the suppression of the Kuomintang during the February 28, 1947, uprising and the loss of election due to the perceived fraud contrived by the Kuomintang (J. Liao 1950). The exiled regime from China was blamed for all its political manipulation. However, grievances were not held either against China or Liao's own Chinese cultural embedding. Liao drafted a declaration for Taiwan's independence. In his pursuit, the appeal to universal human rights reflected a religious conviction to bring the gospel to all. Nevertheless, his public activities reflect directly the Presbyterian string. In comparison, Coe's prescription was predominantly religious.

In the beginning, Coe's personal encounter was influential in his quest for an answer regarding his identity (Jonah Chang 2012, 74–75). He recalled the enlightening bitterness that he had suffered and reflected critically upon in his younger years. One was a fistfight with Japanese classmates while at school. He was called "the slave of the barbarian" (清國奴), referring to a social level lower than barbarian. This denotation was imposed by Japan on the colonized population, who were predominantly migrant Han previously ruled by the Manchu, a barbarian regime in the eyes of Japan. Coe was unsure what the terms meant to his people until his father reversely consented to his fighting upon hearing the insulting label. His father, a second-generation Presbyterian priest, usually insisted on the norms of peace. For Coe, this label created a strong impression that he was an inferior object in colonial relations.

More explicit was the second incident, when he unexpectedly ran into his brother on a cruise to Japan. Both felt elated and burst into their mother tongue. His brother was punished severely by his teacher for speaking the inferior language. Coe was compelled to dress in the most solemn Japanese style and explained to the teacher how the surprise reunion provoked his greeting in his childhood language intuitively. The local dialect and Taiwanese identity were rigorously connected in this experience.[5]

Unlike the quest for independence within the logic of colonial relations, Coe's indigenous sensibility arose from opposition to the colonial relations. His Presbyterian appeal to the universal human rights provided a discursive remedy to the sense of inferiority thus inflicted. For Coe's reflections to prevail, several events took place. First, Western priests were forced to leave during the war, urging more local priests to develop a practice informed by their indigenous identity. Coe actually served as the first Taiwanese head of the Tainan Academy of Theology. Second, the same appeal inspired his successors to face the anti-communist Kuomintang, as well as the People's Republic in the World Council of Churches. Coe was able to seek a plausible answer in his religious relations. As a third-generation Presbyterian priest, he was well acquainted with the Calvinist doctrine of universal enlightenment. However, he reflected upon this doctrine. He came to the conviction that God has a reason to place him in an indigenous context and, thus, he must delve into this context to relieve the indigenous population from their immediate predicament (Y. Huang 2014).

Despite the church being able to find a niche in different regimes in history, the anti-communist Kuomintang once again reminded the determined priest that an indigenous identity was essential for him to continue his work within this context. In the eyes of the indigenous population, the migrant Kuomintang's authoritarian rule treated the indigenous population as secondary citizens. The restriction on the use of the Fukinese dialect in school was particularly poignant and symbolic in this regard, reminding him of the alien character of the former authorities. The strong emotion that had accumulated since childhood reemerged powerfully. This emotion was a feeling of "unwillingness" (in Southern Fukanese that Coe spoke, 毋願 m̄-goān) (Coe 1993, 235). Such feeling accompanied each practical surrender to insult. This feeling prompted a desire eventually to enjoy "出頭天" (which means "sticking one's head out under the sky" or *chutoutian*) (Coe 1993, 235), an indigenous expression that consistently inspired pro-independence forces in subsequent generations.

Coe began to reassess the Western style and institution of preaching. He concluded that what was proper for Western colonies was no longer suited to the postcolonial independent nations (Coe 1963a, 60–62; 1963b, 1–14). Coe believed that the church must interact with its nuanced environment everywhere. The church reached remote mountains and small villages to appreciate the critical relevance of the context to the spread of the gospel. The land and faith purportedly constituted each other. The theory of contextual theology was the result (Coe 1993, 248). In 1972, Coe drafted the *Working Policy Statement—Third Mandate of the Theological Education Fund*. He suggested that the first step for local churches in the Third World was to decontextualize theology from the West and recontextualize it in the postcolonial societies (Pobee 1995, 61). As God creates various contexts in which man attains his image, according to Coe, priests cannot help but learn and gain inspiration from their contexts. All theological understandings are contextual in nature (Y. Cheng 2001, 30–33). Contextual theology frees up priests to use indigenous legends, folk stories, and songs to expound and exemplify the gospels. In the context of Taiwan, contextual theology led to "Chutoutian" theology (Po-ho Huang 1990). From there, three declarations emerged in the 1970s: *A Public Statement on Our National Fate* (1971), *Our Appeal Concerning the Bible, the Church, and the Nation* (1975), and *Human Rights Declaration* (1977). Together, these declarations culminated in the *Confession of Faith* (1985) (Po-ho Huang 1991).

Approaching China from the Perspective of Contextual Theology

None of the documents took on China directly as a subject or target. Indirectly, devotion to the land and faith in context has apparent implications regarding the question on China. In a nutshell, all of these religious movements increasingly marginalized China. For the Presbyterian Church, China's threat is perceived intellectually as being very thin. The threat began with the Kuomintang, who claimed leadership of all China, including Taiwan, and intervened in the church's relations accordingly. In the name of anti-communism, the Kuomintang strongly requested that the Presbyterian Church of Taiwan should become less involved in the World Council of Churches. The Kuomintang was anxious that the council kept in touch with the Communist areas and the presence of a Taiwanese member could compromise its anti-communist stance (Presbyterian Church in Taiwan 1967, 17; Presbyterian Church in Taiwan 1970, 167; Chin 2015). This request forced the church to face China, if only implicitly, by confronting the Kuomintang's Chinese identity, which justified its anti-communist policy.

Ironically, the Kuomintang reproduced the contextually oriented church through the binary of communism and anti-communism embedded in the politics of the Civil War and Cold War. The binary compelled the residents of Taiwan to take a mutually exclusive perspective on the Chinese mainland, which reproduced the same binary that has existed since the concession of Taiwan to Japan in 1895. The transition from the colonial to the exiled regime did not change the geographical border of the island of Taiwan, which encircled a self-sustaining population with its own regime. The two regimes have shown a superior self-image. The Presbyterian Church was, contrarily, not too embedded in the binary politics of the higher versus the lower. Instead, the church was preoccupied from the very beginning with how universal gospels could make better sense in the context of Taiwan. The lacuna of a civilizational or religious relationship vis-à-vis China negatively was apparent.

The lacuna revealed an unstated alienation from the subsequent colonial and Civil War/Cold War regimes, with each claiming a geographically greater role for Taiwan either as a bridge of colonial modernity for Japan to expand into Greater East Asia or as an unsinkable carrier to contain communist China. In fact, the Manchukuo established by Japan in China's Northeast was staffed by colonial officials from Taiwan. In contrast, the Presbyterian Church's inattention to China due to the introspective views of contextual theology presented a distinctive perspective, which was that China was outside Taiwan's context. China deserved no immediate attention as opposed to an alarming threat to a territorially broader self that these regimes represented. For these regimes, China, as it was perceived by them each according to their values, was an ideological or civilization threat.

This innocent perspective was insufficient to cope with the imminent participation of the Chinese church in the World Council. Even though the Chinese church had no intention of harming the Taiwanese church's religious activities, the Chinese church had been instructed by its government to request the Taiwanese church to adopt the Chinese nationality. For the Beijing authorities, the political premise of the Chinese church to join the World Council was the reassurance of the one-China Principle, according to which, the name of the Taiwan church must reflect its Chinese status. Direct interaction with the Chinese church, therefore, exerted pressure to ponder the China issue. Nevertheless, the reception of contextual theology among the members of the World Council engendered strong support for the Taiwan church to remain independent from a Chinese nomenclature.

A publication of the Tainan Academy of Theology recorded the position on the China issue in 1985:

> We believe that in Christ the Church is one, holy and catholic. It should transcend division of politics, culture and race. At this time when the church in China is beginning to make increasing contacts with churches in other countries, we affirm the self-hood of the Presbyterian Church in Taiwan and its role in international church organizations. Moreover, we continue to support its participation in the worldwide mission of the church.[6]

Accordingly, the Taiwanese church declared that it would not accept the placement under the "C" category in the country listing of the council. The Church must belong to the "T" category, or would have to withdraw from the council. In cooperation with the other thirteen churches[7] that arrived in Taiwan at the invitation of the church, another joint statement was issued in 1987 to welcome the Chinese churches upon the foundation of church autonomy in Taiwan:

> We deeply hope that the Taiwan Church, with its continuously renovating spirit and on the aforementioned premise of autonomy, along with all the Churches in the world, including the Chinese Church on the Mainland, shares God's love and benevolence in a mutually respectful attitude in our joint effort to establish God's kingdom. (Taiwanese Church Mission Association 1987, 1)

The church was becoming increasingly keen to emphasize the sovereign status of Taiwan as a nation-state. Accordingly, Taiwan has already entered the world of the church to be protected by state sovereignty and China is a potential object to be converted. The public statements maintained specifically that sovereignty was the access to universal human rights, for which all Churches work. The other side of the coin was the alert sent to the Chinese church that the Chinese authorities had violated human rights. The church demanded that the World Council should react to the Chinese church's failure to articulate these issues faithfully on behalf of the suppressed, in accordance with their belief. The church also urged that the World Council should refrain from assigning an important role to the Chinese church. However, the quest for sovereignty and attention to

Chinese human rights did not occur within the same colonial relations that pro-independence forces in Taiwan usually arise. In short, the issues do not accompany the aversion to Chinese believers or the Chinese church. The relationship between the two churches was situated painstakingly within religious relations (Lì 2013; World Council of Churches 2013).

Conclusion

Colonial relations necessarily bred a view of China for the colonized population in Taiwan that confirmed Japan's civilizational superiority. Taiwan was a hybrid of China and Japan under this circumstance. Decolonization did not take place after Japan was defeated and Taiwan was returned to China. The abortion of decolonization was due to multiple reasons. First, the regime in exile that took over failed to appreciate the fact that the postcolonial population lacked the same prior sense of Chinese ethnicity as the regime, though it could represent legitimately. The regime imposed Chinese patriotic education qua equal Chineseness (table 1.1), as it would have done in China had it not lost the Civil War. This education failed with its audience, who had already adapted to colonialism. The latter did not join the new leadership, because the Chinese officialdom was absolutely alien to them. In addition, the property left by the Japanese was confiscated by the Chinese regime in exile. As a result, the postcolonial elite was consistently disadvantaged politically, institutionally, and in terms of inheritance. To regain self-respect, the postcolonial elite could rely most conveniently on the colonial modernity brought by Japan. This perspective promoted the persistence of the image of an inferior China.

On top of the postcolonial politics that aborted decolonization, the postcolonial elite, as well as the returning soldiers loyal to the Japanese emperor, were exempt from war criminal trials because of their membership of the victorious Republican China. Hence, they were not under any pressure whatsoever to engage in critical self-reflection. In fact, many had never been defeated on the battlefront and could not accept the reality that superior Japan surrendered to inferior China. Their experiences ensured that the prior relations informed by colonial modernity would be the perpetual lens that undergirds the image of inferior China. Colonial relations constituted by an antagonistic kind of civilizational Chineseness have remained inspiring and vivid in the twenty-first century. They have provided a powerful morale for the Taiwan independence movement. This is the reason why alienation and aversion from China have been strong in the politically correct Taiwan independence. For Taiwan independence forces, China had posed a threat as an inferior civilization driven to engulf a more progressive Taiwanese civilization.

However, a particular string in the postcolonial relations did not assume Chinese inferiority, even though it had recognized the contemporary human rights problems in China that were unacceptable to the subscribers of this particular string. This string of thought is the Presbyterian Church, which entered Taiwan three decades ahead of the arrival of Japanese colonialism. The church had continued its preaching and operations during the colonial period and provided vibrant support for independence only after the Chinese migrant regime compelled it to withdraw from the world Christian network lest the Communist participants in the network should harm the legitimacy of the anti-communist regime. Thereafter, the Presbyterian Church was determined to overcome this ostensible representation of China by the regime in exile. Contextual theology resulted from the critical reflection and determination that emerged to guide the church's subsequent approach to China.

The new theological epistemology was initially an individual inspiration, but was upgraded to a prescription for the civilizational identity of politically independent Taiwan. It has its ironic origins in Coe's childhood encounters with the colonizing Japanese. The encounters reproduced a feeling of "being unwilling" to adapt to suppressive control. This feeling explained, partially, why colonial modernity estranged the Presbyterian tradition of Taiwan independence, which established its own rationale. Instead, the tradition engendered *"chutoutian"* as well as indigeneity in its pursuit of independent sovereignty for Taiwan. These concepts resonate easily with the universal value of liberty and human rights. For the independence advocacy informed by colonial relations, the issue of human rights immediately suggests the image of inferior China. However, for the church, the issue connotes a mission in China that the church should have cared about equally. This construction of a noninferior China is how religion has contributed to the civilizational (non-)Chineseness of Taiwan's independence.

Chapter 11

China Watch for No One

Relating Taiwan and China in Hong Kong

The Hong Kong Platform

While part 2 discusses post-Chinese possibilities under the assumption of stable collective identities of South and Southeast Asia, chapter 11 introduces individualized identity strategies in Hong Kong, where collective identities are neither integrative nor stable. The chapter pays more attention to Taiwanese migrant scholars in Hong Kong, whose in-between consciousness reinforces the in-between position of Hong Kong under the influence of China and international society. Chapter 11 additionally exemplifies the revision and the expansion of the 2x3 categorization in part 2 into a nuanced 3x3 table.

Taiwanese migrant intellectuals in Hong Kong form a significant and yet peculiar group of intellectuals in Hong Kong that does not easily fall into the category of China, the West, or Hong Kong. They are not merely undecisive between Hong Kong and China, but also between Hong Kong and Taiwan, as well as Taiwan and China. Consequently, the determination of their epistemological perspective does not tell how they want to improvise resemblance between China and their own groups, because their groups are unclear. Even so, the balance of relationship remains relevant, as their scholarship is a way to preempt China becoming a total stranger or a totalitarian and accordingly preserve some kind of Chineseness in their own identities. This means they still have to settle on a certain approach so that their scholarship and their China are co-constituted by a certain perspective. And yet, no one else in Hong Kong has a real stake in tracking or an interest in echoing their analysis.

With initially both the Chinese Civil War and later pro-independence politics in Taiwan poisoning relationships with China, the politically divided Taiwanese scholars enter a different environment in HK, which urges neither total confrontation nor complete loyalty in the face of China. The relational void of Taiwanese scholars in Hong Kong releases them from the puzzle of how to improvise their own national society's resemblance to China. Relational void can be embarrassing, though, to the extent that ideological and political alignment is essential to the career of other China watchers in Hong Kong or elsewhere. That said, they have the pressure to decide for themselves, albeit with much room, how they each want to act as an autonomous individual. This individualized conditions almost guarantees the attraction of liberalism to them and the flexibility as well as the instability in their relational strategizing. With Hong Kong at least their third home, their relational position vis-à-vis China falls easily in the category of sinological Chineseness. This is why a more nuanced categorization is necessary in this chapter.

Position and Purpose in Hong Kong's China Watching

The migrant experiences shake the certainty of identity to introduce fluidity in their epistemological proclivity. This is true for both intellectuals and laborers (Constable 2007). At the macro level, as a result, Hong Kong intellectuals adopt a variety of positions in terms of each's perceived relationship with China. They similarly possess different purposes in their presentation of China. The position and purpose are the two mechanisms, intermediated by travel, for understanding China watching in Hong Kong. Moreover, at the micro level, the position and purpose can apparently change as travel, physical as well as spiritual, crosses borders of all kinds continuously (Nedilsky 2014; Knowles and Harper 2009). The two mentions represent a moderate amendment to table 5.1, with the dimension of purpose denoting the functions of the scholarship on China, as opposed to the sources that are dichotomized into subjective and objective.

These two dimensions of the production of knowledge on China adopted in chapter 11 correspond to the internal determination regarding how a Hong Kong–based intellectual chooses her epistemological perspective. The first dimension—position—refers to *one's self-understanding as being inside or outside Chinese kinship, Chinese culture, or the Chinese nation, qua*

China. As in earlier chapters in part 2, the dimension can be qualitatively and yet deductively broken down into three positions—insider, outsider, and in-between watcher. These together make the top row of table 5.1, where Chineseness is treated as a temporal/subjective quality embedded in history, ideology, and civilization. Therefore, "insider" designates cultural Chineseness; "outsider," civilizational Chineseness; and "in-between," sinological Chineseness. The position dimension simply asks to which relational trajectories the intellectual believes that she belongs. Does the intellectual write on China as if she resembles just another Chinese, Westerner, or someone in between?

The other dimension—purpose—is related to the motivation of the intellectual inquiry. This refers to *the achieving of the normative, empirical, and practical functions that a particular narrative hopefully serves according to the circumstances and choices*. The purpose dimension further develops categorization in part 2 into nine possibilities according to inductive reading of interviews and writings of the Hong Kong–based China watchers.[1] The purpose dimension asks how the intellectual approaches her subject and, in view of that, explores (1) normatively how to evaluate China, (2) empirically what China is, or (3) practically what China is, or could be, doing.

To satisfy the purpose of each of these, an insider enlists Chinese cultural values to evaluate China subjectively, describe what China stands for objectively, or explore how the idea of China can contribute to people's choice practically. According to my induction, a self-regarded insider places priority on the question of how to be Chinese—how normatively to reconcile the apparent incompatibility between the traditional Chinese values and Western values, how empirically to discover whether or not China has changed in form or spirit, and how practically to prepare one's life by abiding by or rejecting the intervention of those acting in the name of modernity.

Inductively, an outsider uses a universal/Western standard to evaluate China subjectively, an intersubjective method to describe China objectively, or an idea of China to shape, inspire, and rationalize people's actions in life practically. Inductively, an outsider focuses on how to face China—how normatively to denounce or praise the difference of China, how empirically to accept and measure the difference of China, and how to uncover and describe the practices of Chinese lives.

Finally, an in-between watcher is, from my induction, concerned with how, in a balanced manner, to relate to the Chinese—how normatively to welcome or avoid Chinese nationalism, how empirically to translate China's reality to different audiences in terms of similarity and differences, and how practically to prescribe methods for achieving a goal for differing Chinese each in their context.

Table 11.1. Positioning China-Watch

Position \ Purpose	Norm (evaluative)	Representation (authentic)	Strategy (practical)
Inside[%] As Chinese ≅ Cultural	Tradition/ modernity to advocate New Asia College	Nationalism to sympathize Szeto Wah	Improvising to simulate Danny Yung
In-between[#] As HK/Taiwan ≅ Sinological	Nationalism/ Rights to explain Kuang-sheng Liao	Science to differentiate Peter NH Lee	Institution to acquire Byron SJ Weng
Outside[@] As Western ≅ Civilizational	Church/ communism to civilize CNA	Cross-cultural to compare Michael Bond	Internationalizing to exchange David Zweig

Source: author
[%] How to be Chinese (greater self) ≅ cultural Chineseness
[#] How to relate to the Chinese (no self) ≅ Sinological Chineseness
[@] How to understand the Chinese (self) ≅ civilizational Chineseness

However, no practical inquiry lacks normative implications (O'Neill 2009). The research prompted by the practical purpose should always have a sound empirical foundation, while an empirical research, contrarily, may have straightforward practical implications. Therefore, the chapter can further refine the categorization—the normative purpose, representative purpose, and strategic purpose.[2]

Being strategic, the China watching narratives portray how those under study consciously maneuver or surrender to an idea of China in order to achieve their goal in life at the moment. Temporally, this refers to short-term considerations as opposed to the normative purpose, which rests upon long-term considerations. In addition, a study of China that serves the function of representation reproduces the presumption of an authentic China via treating China as being unquestionably authentic and out there to be represented. An authentic China may appear in a passively and yet objectively delineable target. A comparative study of China easily falls into this assumption of ontological authenticity. An authentic China can likewise be subjective as long as a policy, cultural trait, and volition that exerts an influence on the world is attributed to calculation in the name of China. This refined distinction improves the division between the empirical and the practical, because the notion of authenticity avoids the pretention that the empirical research has no subjective purpose.

In short, regarding the second dimension, China is a source of norm, a way of representation or a choice of strategy. China, as a way of representation, relies on a discursive ontology, which presumably requires no further explanation. The major task is to indicate how China meaningfully exists in actuality. This ontological authenticity emanates from two sources. It can be a universal law that treats China as no more than a case. Alternatively, it can be a cultural memory that gives China a unique pattern that is so intuitively authentic that it requires no further justification. The strategic use of China differs from China as the source of cultural memory. The latter approach studies how China and its civilizational values, beliefs, and conventions can constrain intuitively (i.e., naturally) without any conscious effort. Cultural memory is less a choice than is strategy. Cultural memory is relatively easy to show on the societal level, while the strategy is largely at the individual level.

The qualitative 3x3 table yields nine combinations in total. In each combination, there could be creative narratives of all kinds. Chapter 11 will only illustrate each possibility with one example. Note that there is no presumption that an insider is necessarily an ethnic Chinese or an outsider, a Westerner. It is the perspective taken that is used as the primary standard to distinguish which category is appropriate for a particular intellectual and a narrative. However, empirically, Taiwanese intellectuals in Hong Kong appear more easily to fall into the category of in-between authors. The geographical distance to China of their teaching and living is far shorter than that of their hometown in Taiwan. The Taiwan Straits, traditionally known as the notoriously engulfing black gap, shows the psychological distance that has been generated due to the dangers of crossing in the premodern period. Needless to say, the political distance looms larger than Hong Kong after 1997.

Finally, the categorization is aimed at pedagogical as well as epistemological reflections. There is no intention to develop law-like propositions to explain or predict how intellectuals design their research. Rather, the categorization allows intellectuals to appreciate how their own narratives embody their positioning and how different combinations generate perspectives other than theirs. In other words, it is not any structural force embedded in the intellectuals' identity, ethnicity, and other innate quality that determine their entry in the table. The intellectual may transcend her category by simulating a different positioning or selecting a different narrative function to fulfill.

She may certainly stay where she feels comfortably belonging, too. In fact, shifting positions is a topic already discussed in chapter 7.

Between the Inside and the Outside

Liao Kuang-sheng

Liao Kuang-sheng (1941–2014) published on Chinese anti-foreignism in 1984 after graduating from the University of Michigan. He taught at the Chinese University of Hong Kong for twenty-two years and chaired the Department of Government and Public Administration before retiring to embark on an additional career in Taiwan in the early 1990s. During the transition to Taiwan, he began as Taiwan's overseas legislator serving in Hong Kong. Upon his return, he became President Lee Tenghui's national security councilman under Lee's tumultuous China policy in the quest for Taiwan's sovereign nationhood. After retiring from the government, he moved on to the University of Kaohsiung in Taiwan for a further two academic years. Kuang-shen inherited a liberal perspective from his older cousin, Wen-kwei. (See chapter 10 for more discussion.) His position in Hong Kong alerted him to nationalism. He was able to stick with liberalism to face China in contrast with the familiar nationalist perspective adopted by pro-Taiwan independence advocates. His position in Hong Kong urged him to study the Chinese unification policy closely. Apparently, aversion to nationalism should fare better in Hong Kong as well as internationally. His criticism that abides by liberalism demonstrates to Taiwan nationalism that an alternative international discourse on China is plausible (P. Yan 2012).

Liao came from a liberal tradition that has not been typical in Taiwan's political history. His far older cousin, "father of Taiwan-independence thought," Liao Wen-kwei, who had extensive academic experiences in China during Japan's colonial occupation of Taiwan, was an early liberal scholar who trained at the University of Chicago (J. Liao 1929, 1931). Most independent Taiwanese advocates came from the Japanese tradition, in which the lives of the Liaos had been deeply embedded, too. From the Japanese tradition, the ranking contrast between Taiwan and China is usually civilizational, with Taiwan representing the modern forces. Sharing a concern for Taiwan's entire alienation from China, the majority of other narratives of pro-independence have drawn on ethnic differences. However, Wen-kwei was able to remain an adherent of liberalism, which stresses individualistic values (J. Liao 1935, 1936). In fact, Wen-kwei's marriage to an Anglo-Saxon wife surprised the conservative Taiwan of the time. Liberalism was a string of thought that appeared equally salient in Kuang-sheng's subsequent reflections on Taiwan's future decades.

Wen-kwei's conversion has been a contemporary academic subject (R. Wu 1999, 47–100). He used to consider himself a posthumous heir to the Ming dynasty, indicating a strong Han identity, as opposed to the Manchurian Qing dynasty or the Japanese colonial rulers of his time. He had been a faithful follower of Sun Yatsen (J. Liao 1937). He published a textbook to assist young Taiwanese to breed a Chinese consciousness after Taiwan's return to China in 1945. However, the incoming Kuomintang was incompetent, especially in the contrasting memory of effective governance by colonial Japan. Wen-kwei came up with the idea of "Taiwan governed by Taiwanese" as a critique of the local regime. Experiencing a bloody confrontation between the anti-Japanese Kuomintang and those largely accustomed to the colonial Japan's value in Taiwan, Wen-kwei and his younger brother, Wen-yi, decided that the relationship with China had to be severed in order to cleanse the suppression by the Chinese regime entirely. However, they distinguished themselves from other pro-independence advocates, who were mostly pro-Japan, by a predilection toward a US-supported independence that embedded in anti-communism. Wen-kwei proceeded to publish a series of four articles, which were later collected in his *Formosa Speaks* to create the first systematic discourse on Taiwan independence (J. Liao 1950).

Compared with Wen-kwei's earlier adherence to Sun Yatsen's Chinese nationalism, his cousin, Kuang-sheng, found that nationalism was primarily a political instrument of the ruling regime in modern China in general and in communist China specifically. Nevertheless, Wen-kwei's interpretation of nationalism as a vehicle for justice via its service to anti-imperialism by all means carried the hope of freedom (J. Liao 1947). This explained how Wen-kwei could promote Taiwanese nationalism as a vehicle for promoting freedom for Taiwan from China. The Kuomintang acquired its image of an "alien regime" in Wen-kwei's conceptual turn, which proved the most powerful discourse that enabled pro-independence Lee Tenghui to indigenize the Kuomintang in the early 1990s. In fact, Kuang-sheng began his political career in Taiwan due to Lee's active recruitment. Kuang-sheng's suspicion of Chinese nationalism, first published in 1984 (K. Liao 1984), arose from its abortion for the sake of political control. Wen-kwei's later alienation from Chinese nationalism shared similar sensibilities to Kuang-sheng's lukewarm response to Lee's indigenizing campaign.

One of Wen-kwei's narratives fits badly with Kuang-sheng's; namely, the former's last item in the series on *Formosa Speaks*, in which Wen-kwei formulated a kinship-based argument for Taiwanese nationalism that includes indigenous as well as colonial inputs. Despite the fact that the kinship argument attracted pro-independence narrators for subsequent generations, Kuang-sheng found it incompatible with universal human rights. Kuang-sheng argued that nationalism after 1949 ceased to be an anti-imperialist movement. Rather, it became a political instrument for the political elite to maintain their legitimacy and justify their control. Not only did nationalism under the Communist Party system defy human rights, suppress freedom, manufacture propaganda and, consequently, harm economic development, but it also generated distrust of China within international society. At times, Kuang-sheng discovered that nationalism disrupted the political order by supporting the left's narrative to engage in a struggle with the alleged right. In short, he conceived of the post-1949 nationalism as more than just anti-foreignism.

The human rights argument, in comparison, appeared increasingly significant as the return of Hong Kong approached (K. Liao 1996a, 219–36). The negotiation between Beijing and London over the institutional arrangements for the return stirred enormous anxiety in Hong Kong to the effect of raising democratic concerns among all residents. The beginning of Kuang-sheng's career in Hong Kong coincided with this particular moment of transition. Facing the rise of nationalism in China in anticipation of the return, the more reliable discourse for those anxiously watching Hong Kong would be human rights. He examined how the idea of one country, two systems and the associated Hong Kong Basic Law might damage human rights in Hong Kong (K. Liao 1996b, 212–23). After he retired from the Chinese University, he served as advisor to the president in Taiwan. He applied the familiar human rights perspective as a substitution for the mounting support for independence in Taiwan. He believed that independence that could incur armed conflict was unwise, while the one-country, two-systems formula was ill-suited to human rights protection in Taiwan (K. Liao 2001, 2–3). He then supported the federal system that he believed protected Taiwan from the political chaos caused by China's unstable economy (K. Liao 1989, 50–57). After the Chinese economy took off, he expressed a firmer belief in democracy, which he thought would strengthen the people's emotional attachment to Taiwan and so serve as protection against China's intrusion (K. Liao 1996c).

Kuang-sheng exemplified a certain degree of sinological Chineseness (table 5.1 and figure 7.1) in his intellectual capacity to let the outside world appreciate the rise and practice of Chinese nationalism and the Chinese world to reflect upon the institutional recommendation based upon the human rights concerns of the outside world.

PETER NAN-HSIUNG LEE

As a parallel to Kuang-sheng, Nan-hsiung Lee (1940–) has taught at the Chinese University of Hong Kong since 1976. Like Kuang-sheng, he has been active as a writer, both academically and journalistically. However, his approach to China and Taiwan has been predominantly analytical rather than evaluative in nature. In fact, compared with Kuang-sheng, Nan-hsiung's career in Taiwan has been primarily academic rather than political. He served as the founding chair of political science of National Chiang Kai-shek University in Chiayi, Taiwan, in 1993, during a brief leave and returned to the NCKU for another term in 2003, after retiring from Hong Kong. His father, Wan-chu Lee (1901–66), was a leading Chinese nationalist and democrat, so Nan-hsiung likewise comes from a significant family tradition based in Chiayi, Taiwan. Wan-chu's childhood experience contrasted considerably with that of Wen-kui as the former witnessed the War of Resistance and the hardship suffered by the Chinese people before migrating to Taiwan.

Wan-chu's initial encounter with China was similar to Wen-kwei's. Both visited China and grew up with a Chinese nationalist attachment under the colonial rule in Taiwan. Wan-chu's turn to democratic thought matured during his seven years of study in France. It has been debated in the contemporary literature which of his nationalist and democratic identities was the stronger (Jinlin Yang 1993; Tai 2009; Hsieh and Lee 2001; W. Wang 1997). Wan-chu had never been converted into a pro-independence advocate, despite the fact that he physically suffered the threat of death during the 228 incident. His active participation in reforming the party politics of Taiwan under the early KMT authoritarianism also incurred suppression—his newspaper, *Public Forum News*, was confiscated; his properties were burned or dismantled; and his intended Chinese Democratic Party was banned before it began. While Wen-kwei sought help from Taiwan nationalism in order to resist the KMT's ruling that was justified by Chinese nationalism, Wan-chu had stuck with a Chinese identity in pushing for democratization. A noticeable difference in style that has existed between Kuang-sheng and Nan-hsiung's academic agenda may find a source in the older generation. In the case of Nan-hsiung, he has been readily shifting between being a detached scientist of Chinese politics and an involved public intellectual of China.

In fact, Nan-hsiung's career in Hong Kong arose from a specific sense of aversion toward Taiwan, where he vividly recalled the suffering of Wan-chu under the KMT's arbitrary ruling. Compared with the KMT, therefore, the communist China could not be a greater evil. On the other hand, Wan-chu's membership in the extreme anti-communist China Youth Party likewise has its legacy. Consequently, Hong Kong could appear to be an appropriate location for a career of China studies. In fact, Hong Kong has been the choice of many who felt unsatisfied with either the communist China or the KMT Taiwan. They should include the neo-Confucians hosted by the New Asia College of the Chinese University of Hong Kong as well as the Catholic *China News Analysis*. The latter two chose to migrate to Taiwan, nonetheless, in the 1980s due to the political changes in Hong Kong in general and in the hosting university specifically (K. Liao 2008).

Together with his bachelor's training in law and his encountering and submission to the Weberian methodology as well as the corporatist perspective, a focus on the institutional and informal politics of China emerged gradually in Nan-hsiung's theoretical predilection (Li 2011). Nan-hsiung's research reflects a curiosity regarding politics below the national level, where Kuang-sheng's interest in nationalism belonged. Nan-hsiung also displays expertise on institutional analysis, as opposed to normative analysis, embedded in human rights. In hindsight, Nan-hsiung has relied so heavily on the structural analysis and rationality in his research design and institutional critique that he has been able to remain aloof from the politics of identity, loyalty, and charisma. His respect for Deng Xiaoping, so apparent in his media commentaries and oral history, has not seemed to influence his scholarly thinking or the decision to migrate to the United States after retirement.

Nan-hsiung pays great attention to the distinctive features of Chinese politics, abiding by the Weberian sensitivity toward leadership and legitimacy. He has established his own agenda on the Chinese industrial sectors and managerial characteristics that incorporate Maoism and party politics (N. Lee 1981a, 35; 1979a, 71). He found the corporatist perspective more relevant than the Marxian analysis of class and preferred a top-down approach to the understanding of the state apparatus in China (N. Lee 1979b, 101). In his leadership study, though, he has not transcended the familiar and expedient division of the Chinese leaders into radicals and pragmatists (N. Lee 1977, 70–72), a division most appropriate for political briefing by those watchers serving the Western audience; hence, the naturalization of instability (74). However, he offers a critique on the Western theorists due to their inability to embed their explanation in the Chinese context (70).

His post-Weberian curiosity led to the urge for a certain institutional remedy to corruption caused by the routinization of charisma (N. Lee 1981b, 170). In his Chinese writing, he specifically points to the parallel between the Daoist and Weberian critiques on rationality.

In Nan-hsiung's Chinese writings, he is reversely used to adopting a comparative style in order to introduce the thought into English literature. He compares both institutionally and philosophically (N. Lee 1981c; 1983; 1984, 26–32), so, from a broader perspective, he searches for solutions to the problems of governance. He detects the plausible difference in policy lines in expounding Chinese factional politics, for example, to supplement the usual obsession with just power struggle among groups (N. Lee 1987, 23–26). The comfort of introducing comparative views to an unfamiliar audience testifies to a style of detached scholarship. Finding parallels between Chinese and non-Chinese sources is likewise difficult to embody by anyone else who is not registered with a Chinese consciousness as evident as is Nan-hsiung. His own wish to transcend Chinese politics and his familiarity with, and application of, Western social sciences reinforce each other and yet preserve a Chinese, though differing, identity that Kuang-sheng wished to avoid in his capacity as universal observer.

Nan-hsiung likewise exemplifies a certain degree of sinological Chineseness. On the one hand, he endeavors to adopt social science methods to communicate with his Western colleagues and yet Chinese op-ed comments to convince his Chinese audience of his appreciation of the problems and pragmatic attitude toward their solution.

Byron Song-jan Weng

Without a family tradition encountered by the suppression of the Kuomintang as in the cases of Kuang-sheng and Nan-hsiung, Byron Song-jan Weng (1934–) has never been cornered into having consciously to take sides. On the other hand, having been free from a family and political trajectory that constrain, as well as support, him, his traveling between different cultural and social environments requires higher sensitivity toward the encountered communities and personalities. If a wish for transcendence over a certain political root footnotes Kuang-sheng's human rights sensibility and Nan-hsiung's post-Weberian objectivity, Weng's scholarship appears distinct in two aspects. First, he demonstrates a readiness always to listen and adapt to the needs of his audience. His empathetic capacity allows him to provide useful advice to his host. Second, his all-round experiences and ongoing effective assimilation enable him easily to qualify an ostensibly unprejudiced request made by his current hosting audience so that he can broaden the latter's perspective. His academic investment in institutional and legal studies reinforces this approach of adapting and yet qualifying.

As a child, Weng first received a traditional Chinese education and then an official Japanese colonial education. His Chinese education returned to him after the KMT came to power in the aftermath of Worl War II. He has been able to enjoy both Chinese and Japanese culture at ease. His political enlightenment while at college developed through his reading of the *Free China Journal* until it was outlawed on the pretext of treason. The journal was launched by the determined anti–Chiang Kai-shek critics Lei Chen (1897–1979) and Yin Hai-kuang (1919–69), both of whom were Chinese migrants who fled to Taiwan after the Civil War. Weng was able circularly to acquire additional political information from Hong Kong magazines. Enlightened Weng then yearned for higher education in the Unites States in order to begin a process of adaptation both culturally and academically (B. Weng 2017).

As a harbinger of his scholarly breadth and flexibility, Weng began his career in the United States by practicing adaptation in accordance with the situation. For example, he switched his dissertation subject from New Guinea to China to avoid possible collusion with a UN official who was conducting similar research. He was compelled to teach a lot of courses that did not lie within his field of expertise. To prepare to teach, he formally entered China studies. He was able to exploit the advantages that he possessed regarding both language and history and introduced valuable information about China. Despite being at the very beginning of his career, he was able to see the limitation of those views that primarily reflected the local conditions. He was willing to present the Chinese situation to the anti-war audience while in Ohio, the reservations about China's investment in Tanzania to the patriotic audience while in Beijing, a defensive attitude toward the struggling democratization of Taiwan to a Chinese prodemocracy dissident while in Taipei, and so on.

What characterizes Weng's scholarship best is his institutionalist reply to his host's demand for pragmatic advice. His expertise in international law, together with his deep engagement with China studies (Weng 1972), strengthen an adaptive style of designing plausible solutions to local puzzles in Hong Kong, China, and Taiwan. For example, he joined a cohort study of the one country, two systems to discuss the institutional arrangements for the return of Hong Kong (Weng 1987). He assisted in drafting the

National Unification Guidelines as well as Hong Kong and Macau Relations Act for the ambivalent KMT government under the pro-independence President Lee Teng-hui. He offered advice to the constitutional proposal for a cofederal China to the overseas prodemocracy dissidents (H. Lin 2014). He has no clear personal purpose but generously and appreciatively shares perspectives elsewhere to improve the plausibility of the purpose in question. Embodying a transcendental scholarship, he is able to cope with invitations by different parties that stand in complete opposition to one another and make his knowledge useful to all of them and yet qualify potentially biased wishes behind each invitation in a friendly manner.

Establishing a career in Hong Kong was Weng's deliberate choice, upon considering Hong Kong's richer sources compared to the US and its less controlled environment compared to Taiwan. The idea of the Puerto Rico model distinctively demonstrates the breadth of his knowledge. According to this model, Hong Kong could retain the power of veto over the Chinese constitution (Weng 1983). Nevertheless, he was willing to support the CCP version of reunification with the qualification that the same model could not apply to Taiwan, which he believed was readily an independent state and thus required an entirely different reunification model (Weng 1984). He noted that Taiwan was far bigger. In addition, the KMT was earlier than the CCP in leading China's entry into the modern world. He then supported the principle of one country, two governments (as opposed to two systems) in the case of Taiwan. For both models, he maintained that "contradiction" in terms of value, identity, and institution should be the essential element of the model of unification. "Asymmetry" is another recognizable trait. Finally, he agreed that the element of "transience" was inevitable, given that unification was the aim of the model (Weng 1985a).

Since the Tiananmen incident in 1989, Weng remains alert to the suppressive, unstable nature of Chinese politics. Although his earlier research on Chinese constitutional development preserved a hope for constitutionalism, with the qualification that the rule of law was yet to materialize in the considerably improved version of the 1982 Constitution (Weng 1985b), he expressed disappointment after 1989. This reinforces his sympathy for Taiwanese identity (Weng 2001), to the extent that he praised Taiwan's quest for political subjectivity as a historical lift from a state of alienation resulting from the unremitting rule by migrant regimes over the past several hundred years (Weng 1995). He regarded concrete performance and political stability in China as two critical conditions in order to change the resistant attitude among the Taiwanese toward unification.

Weng has been consciously peripheral in his readiness to provide institutional coaching to his host anywhere, apart from possibly a short period. That was the period during the aftermath of a historical juncture, where the suppression of the prodemocracy movement in China and the rise of a pro-independence regime in Taiwan coincided. He was deeply disappointed at the one country, two systems in Hong Kong and hopeful regarding Taiwan's need for political change (Weng 2003). Throughout his career, however, he was able to cope with politics of difference more easily than either Kuang-sheng or Nan-hsiung. He empathizes quickly with, and yet remains alert to the limitation of, his host anywhere. His intensive involvement in Hong Kong and Taiwan's policy issues exempts him from suffering from an ontological fixation with any version of Chineseness, territorially, ideologically, or institutionally (Weng 1997). He could, therefore, intervene in politics without becoming trapped. Finally, the breadth of his many other engagements and lack of political ambition have allowed him to avoid either confrontation or submission. Weng's style is yet another illustration of sinological Chineseness.

A Comparison of Taiwanese Intellectuals in Hong Kong

The Insiders and Their Cultural Chineseness

New Asia Scholars and Normative China

A number of neo-Confucian scholars migrated to Hong Kong in 1949 to avoid Communist rule and established the New Asia College in Hong Kong. The college was initially led by neo-Confucian scholars, including Qian Mu, Tang Chun-i, Yu Ying-shih, and others. Neo-Confucian scholars considered the spirit of Chinese culture an essential component of modern Chinese life and thus promoted a return to the mind that could avert the danger of materialism caused by modernization. Their anti-communist outlook evolved from a narrative engrossed in the deep-seated Chinese identity. This narrative followed the rationalism that originated from the Confucian thought of the Song and Ming dynasties, having now proceeded to master modernity represented by science and democracy. The Communist motif of class struggle was, accordingly, an anathema to them. The New Asia scholarship embodied the attempt of Chinese humanism to evaluate Western civilization from a Chinese perspective, which could offer both criticism and adoption, a test that both the KMT and the CCP seemed to fail (Qian 1954; C. Tang; 1952; Y. Yu 1974; H. Ho 2001).

Szeto Wah and Authentic China

Having grown up during World War II, Szeto Wah never doubted the goal of a strong China. He was among the most active supporters of the return of Hong Kong to China. However, the tension between nationalism and democracy has been mounting since Chinese nationalism in Hong Kong could no longer target the colonial system that ended in 1997. In 1989, democracy and human rights have developed into real issues in Hong Kong, a site that not only anxiously watched the suppression of democracy but also offering a haven to dissidents fleeing the west. Szeto's nationalist performance most vividly showed in his leadership of the Chinese language movement as well as anti-Japanese campaign as regards the Rape of Nanjing and sovereignty over the Diaoyu Islands. His leadership in democracy successfully organized teachers' solidarity and campaigns for popular elections and civic rights. The notion of "patriotic democracy" that he coined resolved the contradiction via the conviction that the rich, strong democracy in China began in Hong Kong (Karl Ho et al. 2019). Szeto painstakingly enacted his identity, which was more Chinese than the Chinese (in the Mainland and Taiwan). Such authentic China undergirded his lifetime struggle against colonialism and rationalized his resistance to the Communist rule as an endeavor internal to Chineseness (W. Szeto 2011, 1987, 2003).

Danny Yung and Practical China

The name of Zuni Icosahedron already tells one something about Yung's purpose in preparing for Hong Kong's return. (See chapter 9 for more details.) This is his organization of experimental drama, presumably aimed at deconstructing any seeming canonical representation of China in the context of 1982, the year when he launched the organization. Yung was born in Shanghai in 1943, where his family connection has continued throughout his career. His Chinese sensibility is mediated by his career in Hong Kong in such a way that he is determined to ensure that China's taking over of Hong Kong should never be overwhelming. Zuni has been devoted to a methodology that encourages either a recombination of cultural symbols or the improvising of cultural meanings. The purpose is to subvert texts with jokes. For example, in one of his proud products—*Romance of the*

Rock 97—he uses four-character idioms against the Cultural Revolution background, thus signaling a Chinese culture that socialist China might find difficult to swallow. His work also often entails placing Chinese mountains and rivers on the backcloth of the stage. He invites the citizens' participation and coaches them on how to perform spontaneously on the stage to practice and multiply the possibilities of Chineseness and so deconstruct canonization, critically review the past, and create a progressive future (Yung 2012, 2009a, 2009b).

The Outsiders and Their Civilizational Chineseness

Chinese News Analysis (CNA) and Christian Sinology

Like the New Asia Confucian scholars, Laszlo Ladany (1914–90) migrated from China and launched this series in Hong Kong into an essential English anti-communist newsletter. He and his colleagues persevered before the second editorship crew, Wei-Xin, moved to Taiwan in order to avoid encountering Communists after 1997. The CNA combined the missionary purpose and secular China watching to achieve the publication of the worldwide consulting report. Based on the Jesuits' attention to Chinese civilization, CNA essentially examined Chinese foreign affairs from two perspectives. Given that the US changed its China policy from containment to engagement gradually after the 1970s, the first perspective of CNA argued that China would ensure that it achieved its goal of ideological Weltanschauung. To comprehend the peculiarities of Chinese civilization, the second perspective was to stand on the historical timeline before 1949 to analyze the distinctive nature of China's contemporary behavior and ponder how the Communist regime had influenced the Chinese values and way of life. According to these two distinct perspectives of the Jesuits' editorship, China researchers should speak in Chinese, study ancient history, and live in a Chinese-speaking environment; thus Chinese studies could be improved by reviving the relationship between historical legacies and contemporary China (Ladany 1987, 1988, 1992, 1970, 1994).

Michael Bond and Cross-cultural Chinese Psychology

A Canadian scholar who emerged from his cross-cultural encounter in Hong Kong, together with the initially aborted attempt to publish the non-indigenous research in the mainstream journals, Bond ran into Taiwanese psychologist Yang Kuo-shu to find inspiration in a reversed methodology that applies a comparative frame from Chinese cultural values to elsewhere instead of vice versa, as is more common. He has gained confidence in enlarging the range the cultural contrast based upon Chinese values, sensitive to the fact that in-cultural contrast is equally important. He combines personality and social psychology in order to explain why "a particular person from a particular cultural background behaves in a particular way." The *Psychology of the Chinese People* and the *Handbook of Chinese Psychology* are two of his publications of which he is proud. For Bond, it is important to bring out the sophisticated view that China is both universal at the individual level and distinctive at the cultural level; hence China's authentic difference. The same realization has led to his appreciation of Hong Kong as a particular cross-cultural site of pedagogy. According to him, the British educational system enables the training of bilingual psychologists in Hong Kong, enabling Bond to develop an ever-growing team of specialists on Chinese psychology (Chen 2013; Bond 2010, 1986; Leung and Bond 1984).

David Zweig and Internationalizing China

Conscious of his Jewish identity and the cultural memory therein,[3] Zweig studies China with a sense of disbelief and alienation regarding the government's allegedly successful reform. He finds internationalizing an exact concept to uncover the logic of Chinese reform. Via internationalization, the Chinese authorities defy the collectivist spirit, presumably cherished by a socialist party. Instead, internationalizing has been a means of control, in addition to a vehicle to windfall profits for those in the rent-seeking position. Zweig's diasporic sensibility, prepared by Jewish history and his own international travels, alerts him to the suffering of the lower echelons of society under the internationalization of the Chinese economy. For Zweig, the Jewish value of universal love contrasts with Chinese group culture. This contrast informs his research on the Chinese economy and his coping with the academic administration. He is critical of the Chinese group culture to the extent that it remains a nominal value and serves only a very few at the top. The same curiosity toward China's internationalizing leads to an expanded agenda regarding students returning from their overseas education. The practical difficulties facing the returning students further demonstrate the superficial aspect of the internationalizing image. China is practically reduced to a mechanism of control and profit-making, not to be shared by the majority of the population (Zweig 2002, 1999; Zweig and Chen 1995).

Conclusion

An epistemological position can constitute a deliberate choice as well as a realization that evolves gradually from a trajectory. An insider's position may be conducive to the breeding of a deliberate choice, because the encountering of the Western civilization by an insider is a historically imposed imperialism that insiders must consciously manage in order to preserve, or abandon, a meaningful Chinese identity. The emergence of the insider's position may also benefit from an abrupt change that compels the choice of a purpose to give direction at the civilizational crossroads. A change of this abrupt nature reminds one of the Chinese Civil War, the Cultural Revolution, the return of Hong Kong and the Tiananmen massacre, of which almost all self-perceived Chinese had to gain a certain impression.

The in-betweener's position can be so confusing, in comparison, that one encounters an innate hybridity that leads to the encountering of incongruent expectations that call for an intellectual solution. Usually, it takes an experienced scholar to be able to think and write in face of these role conflicts in a practiced manner. Finally, the position of an outsider is likely to be initially prepared by a mutually estranging atmosphere between the Western and the Chinese civilizations and then by a universalizing spirit to assimilate China's difference epistemologically. However, these hypotheses on the causes of positioning require more systematic research.

To embody a choice of position, one relies on a purpose to begin one's narrative. The choice of purpose may similarly be either deliberate or evolutionary. Any thinker can actually rely on more than one purpose in a life-long trajectory of her career, in sequence as well as simultaneously. Nevertheless, an evaluative purpose is more likely to be a deliberate choice, since it incurs a judgment of good and bad. The practical purpose can only be evolutionary, because it arises from the accumulation of cases and consideration of life situations. The practical purpose keeps any authentic claim from immediately interfering with the understanding of the actual process of life. The practical purpose thus emerges inductively. The representative purpose, in contrast, is probably a by-product of one's activities, which have the effect of reproducing a distinguishable China. This by-product is not unrelated to motivation, though, because the articulation of a Chinese cause, the scientific portrayal of China, and the contrast of Chinese culture would lack an ontological foundation without the belief in a certain kind of Chinese authenticity.

The nine cases illustrate possible (re)combinations of position(s) and purpose(s) in various different ways and the combination of the encountering and choice that ultimately breed each long and yet possibly unstable trajectory of the intellectual path. The in-between positions of the three scholars from Taiwan are reinforced by a family history and the individualized travel experiences that generated, or reduced, the degree of complication of their range of choices, depending on other factors. For Kuang-sheng and Nan-hsiung, their Western training enabled each to adopt a perspective that adopted a universal outlook: human rights for Kuang-sheng and social science for Nan-hsiung. However, while human rights helped Kuang-sheng to avoid appealing to Taiwan nationalism in order to maintain a position external to communist China, the scientific methodology contrarily allows Nan-hsiung willingly to engage in thinking about Chinese affairs without worrying about becoming politically engrossed. In comparison, Weng's training in the US alerts him to any perspective that exclusively serves the local purpose. He is inclined to seek a practical solution that institutionally both reflects the local purpose and prescribes for its usual problem of lacking sophistication. All three chose to leave Hong Kong after retiring, making China a further alienated object, thereby each to an extent mirroring the rising intellectual estrangement toward the scenario of Taiwan's reunification with China.

Chapter 12

Post-Western Politics and Mainlandization

Between Colonialism and Liberalism

Silenced by Nationalism and Liberalism

July 1, 2015, marked the eighteenth anniversary of Hong Kong's return to China. On its eve, a series of events took place that cast doubt on the handing over of Hong Kong as well as China's claimed sovereignty over Taiwan. The pro-independence front-runner in Taiwan's 2016 presidential campaign, Tsai Ing-wen of the Democratic Progressive Party, announced in Washington that she would build Taiwan into a base of new Asian values and would cooperate with Washington to maintain the status quo in the Taiwan Straits. Basically, her remarks constituted a rhetorical commitment to liberalism and reiteration of the strategic aversion to China; both indicate Taiwan's unreserved loyalty to Washington, politically as well as ideologically.

Tsai's return to Taiwan coincided with the veto by the Legislative Council of Hong Kong over a proposed electoral system approved by the National People's Congress in Beijing. The veto was grounded on the undemocratic stipulation that only indirectly nominated candidates would be eligible to stand. Subsequently, *Time* magazine featured Tsai on its cover and lauded her as the future president of "the only Chinese democracy."[1]

Certainly, these events cannot have been entirely unanticipated by Beijing. Aware of the continuous anti-China politics in Hong Kong as well as Taiwan, Beijing has not failed to repeat its warnings about such developments. The escalation has been more than apparent since 2014 in both places. Similarly, mutual reinforcement between Hong Kong and Taiwan was evident. Mass rallies erupted in 2014, known respectively as the Sunflower Movement (太陽花) in Taiwan and the Umbrella Revolution (or Occupy Central 雨傘革命or 佔中) in Hong Kong. Such rallies, which reoccurred in Hong Kong in 2019 on an even greater scale and with more violence, reflected the ironic evolution whereby, on the one hand, the all-round interaction between the Chinese mainland and the two claimed territorial sites had grown impressively, while the political alienation among the populace increased, on the other (Rowen 2015).

The intellectual and practical perspectives failed to provide an epistemological theme that could make sense of the simultaneous Sinicization and anti-Sinicization, the rise of trust and distrust toward the apparatus of the party-state, the China model and its liberal critique, and so on. Critical perspectives, which avoided the theoretical sanctioning of the universal propositions, declared the emergence of postmodern, postcolonial, and post-Western subjectivities everywhere, including Hong Kong and Taiwan. To a certain degree, however, the critical perspective reduced their varieties to a kind of universal mode of being "differently different" (Rowen 2015; Bilgin 2012). The nascent quest for post-Western international relations (IR) may as well use Hong Kong and Taiwan to rediscover approvingly their non-Western genealogy and reworld their distinctive geoculture under globalization.

From an alternative perspective, though, the phenomenon of mainlandization depicts the prevalence of the all-round influence of China on Hong Kong and Taiwan (Rowen 2015; Jones 2014). Both are pursuing a post-Chinese identity from China. Hong Kong and Taiwan, a former British colony for 155 years and a former Japanese colony for 51 years, respectively, have practiced liberal institutions and Chinese cultural lives at the same time. Intellectually, the postcolonial critics and their liberal rivals form an expedient alliance with regard to Hong Kong and Taiwan, in the sense that the subaltern rallies that oppose hegemonic China are similar to all those color and flower revolutions in terms of their practice of civil, allegedly liberal, disobedience, each peculiarly implemented in its local trajectory, against the authoritarian regimes (Roberts and Ash 2009; Polese and Ó Beacháin 2011; J. Wilson 2010; Abul-Magd 2012; Kennedy 2012).

China is assigned the double role of being a rising power and a noticeable target that represents the growing economic strength and political influence. Both roles represent an alternative (to liberal hegemony) to be attacked by the liberal West and its associates, and a hegemonic state to be averted by its postcolonial neighbors or internal subaltern groups. This explains why various tracks of the mainlandization of Hong Kong, Taiwan, and the Chinese diasporic communities everywhere proceed amid an atmosphere of contradiction, confrontation, and, to say the least, ambivalence. Re-Sinicization incurs shared cultural resources that threaten the indigenous citizenship as well as the identity of the Chinese populace outside the People's Republic.

The theoretical challenge of mainlandization is, therefore, how post-Chineseness—its promised multiple directions, undecidability, and, most importantly, a kind of indispensable Chineseness—can enable the networking, profitability, and rootedness that accompany unwanted embeddedness, corruptibility, and dependency. Mainlandization can expose the shared cultural resources, such as the linguistic aspect, religion, diet, and literature, which inspire the imagination of a common culture and ancestry. In the increasingly reconnected communities, mainlandization can also incur a certain common cultural memory resulting from colonization, ancestor worship, migration, anti-communism, and a Middle Kingdom mentality, any of which can trigger a ready sense of intimacy depending on the area of interaction, geocultural context, and improvisational leadership.

The incapacity of the rise of China to control the self-presentation of Hong Kong and Taiwan as a separate identity-entity alludes to a kind of post-Western as well as post-Chinese politics. The following discussion regards both as site. As opposed to location, place, or position, which privileges physical space, site refers to *the shifting domain where specific practices of specifically related players take place*. Sitedness conveys an interactive subjectivity as well as a self-sustaining trajectory. In the post-Western condition, subaltern sites assert their differences at the global level, despite the adoption of Western values and institutions at some point in their modern history. Post-Western politics aims to rediscover the silenced postcolonial sites. Taiwan and Hong Kong appear significant, as being double-silenced sites in face of both hegemonic liberalism and Chinese nationalism. The latter restrains the pro-independence forces of the two sites from seeking to adopt an international personality. Such international representation echoes the most lauded value of the post-Western IR—the reworlding of a site on its own terms.

Although both sites are Chinese and liberal at the same time, their struggle for reworlding and global representation encounters an embarrassing condition, in which resistance to one end (currently, Chinese nationalists) connotes submission to the other end (currently, Western liberals). This situation is caused by the alleged rise of China, which has made China a non- or anti-Western model. Such a condition speaks to the improbable alliance between postcolonial Taiwan and Hong Kong that seeks recognition in the hegemonic order, on the one hand, and post-Western IR that trivializes and provincializes the hegemonic order, on the other. Likewise, the condition insinuates the mutual alienation of the post-Western and Chinese IRs, despite their shared aversion to Western hegemony.

The following discussion reflects upon the discourse of resistance provided by the post-Western agenda (Vasilaki 2012; Shani 2008; McDonald 2014; Zhang and Buzan 2012; Liu and Vaughan-Williams 2014), its potential and yet improbable alliance with the Chinese IR, and the epistemological difficulty that such alliance encounters. From the aborted alliance in opposition to Western hegemony, the study traces the unlikely positioning among the Chinese, the post-Western, and the Western agenda in Hong Kong and Taiwan. Thus, the irony of mainlandization lies in its potential to reworld Hong Kong and Taiwan away from global liberalism, that might also silence their different levels of Chineseness. A call for the recognition of the emergence of the post-Chinese identity follows.

On the one hand, both former colonies share a grievance regarding the incapacity of the Chinese IR to appreciate the post-Western sitedness, thus suppressing the post-Western sensibilities. On the other hand, their peculiar appropriation of liberalism in the shared resistance to Chinese nationalism makes both quintessentially post-Western in actuality. Ultimately, mainlandization attests to a process of post-Chinese identification, through which all are ready to recollect a certain shared culture that would lead to the recognition of one another as the same, imagined Chinese, and yet they are actually aware of the peculiarities existing within their self- and mutual understanding.

The Irony of 2015, or Any Year

To demonstrate the irony of mainlandization, the discussion begins with an illustrative case of how anti-Chinese sentiment facilitates the representation of the seventieth anniversary of the end of World War II in Taiwan. While war and peace dominate the study of international relations, war is no longer a welcome tool under globalization. Even so, the topic of war continues to connect almost every current research agenda, directly or indirectly. The post-Western agenda attends to different meanings of war at a subaltern site, one that reappropriates the memory of, discourse on, and preparation for war.

World Word II has become a contested text in Taiwan, alongside the voice of pro-independence becoming increasingly articulate. This differs from the situation in Hong Kong, where the population generally consents to the orthodox view that China or the Allied Forces, or both, defeated Japan, the invader. In fact, the anti-Japanese sentiment has been intense among some of the prodemocracy campaigners in Hong Kong. They promote an anti-Japanese sentiment to the embarrassment of the Beijing authorities, who may not be interested in escalating tension with Japan.

In Taiwan, two contestations coincided in 2015. On the one hand, the Republic of China, led by the Kuomintang, the party that ruled Taiwan in 2015, won the War of Resistance, which has been the name given to the China-Japan war from 1937 to 1945. This position opposes the popular impression in China that the Communist Party led the fight. On the other hand, Taiwan should not celebrate the anniversary because it was part of the defeated colonial Japan during the war. An associated dispute is related to "comfort" women, which pro-independence historiography insists exerted some extent of voluntarism.

The two contestations are parallel at the same site on behalf of the same population but diverge politically. Their different positioning on the war reflects the different positioning on China as well as Taiwan. The celebrative voice reproduces the Chinese historiography of the Kuomintang and represents an aversion to Taiwan independence. In this view, comfort women were, by all means, the victims of forced slavery. By contrast, loser identification has determined that Taiwan deserts Chinese historiography; thus, it wants to memorialize the losers' experiences that are completely alien to Chinese historiography. However, it reads agency into the case of comfort women so that Taiwan would not appear as a sheer silenced victim under Japan. Rather, an imagined existential subjectivity, testified by the voluntarism of the comfort women, had already existed in Taiwan before Japan colonized it and therefore could justify the entitlement to independence status by a long-lasting autonomous past.

The capital city of Taipei inaugurated a pro-independence mayor in 2014, Ko Wen-je. He halted the contracted project of the seventieth anniversary of victory, signed by his predecessor, on the ground that Taiwan was on the losing side. Instead, the mayor proposed to recollect the mood of the loser and focus primarily on the Japanese who were born and were growing up in Taiwan at the time of the defeat. He rejected any celebration in the name of the Republic of China or its victory. The pro-independence party and intellectuals likewise launched a campaign to remove from the draft of the middle school textbook any wording that suggested that Japan was "colonial" during its fifty-one-year reign in Taiwan, that Taiwanese comfort women were conscripted participants, or that the end of the war marked a "defeat" for Japan (R. Lin 2015, 1). By contrast, a different campaign emerged to request compensation from the United States for its bombardment of the Japanese military in Taiwan during the war (*Taiwan People's News* 2015). This self-designated status is intended to reclaim Taiwan's image as an equal, willing participant, as opposed to a reluctant colony, during the war. Diplomatically, the continuation of the last move is deemed highly counterproductive, because the pro-independence movement typically treats Washington as its ally.

All of this maneuvering aimed to demonstrate that Taiwan was not pro-Chinese during World War II. Taking the Japanese side is a most emotionally provocative action in light of the Chinese being radically anti-Japan. Ko consciously relied on the Japan discourse to construct the People's Republic as the other Chinese since his inauguration. He was under tremendous pressure to read an ambiguous statement that "one China is not a problem," to ensure that the activities previously agreed upon by Taipei and the Chinese city of Shanghai remain effective (C. Lo 2015). Apparently, during the time of hard negotiations with his Shanghai counterpart, he stated in an interview with *Foreign Policy* magazine that "the longer the colonization, the more advanced a place is." He then moved to rank Taiwan higher than China (Wertime 2015).

However, with all his painstaking attempts to reconstruct Taiwan's Japaneseness (read: non-Chineseness), he was unable to appreciate the incapacity of the Japanese to deal with the defeat. Promoting the agenda to recollect the mood of the loser would be extremely embarrassing, if not shameful from the Japanese perspective. Ko was unable to detect the delicate sensibilities of Japan toward its loss. Not only did his self-revelation come from a position outside Japan, but it also indicated that his taking sides with Japan was inadvertently nothing more than a political consumption of Japan's image as a loser.

This lack of sensitivity toward the political taboo in Japan shares almost the same inconsiderate attitude of the Chinese populace toward Japan. In other words, Ko's simulation of Japaneseness through memorializing Japan's defeat partially mimics the Chinese self-image of being a winner. Given his purpose to be provocative to the Chinese, his Chinese style of using Japan's defeat was entirely ironic and even self-defeating. The rise of China, that has alerted the pro-independence sector to engage in anti-mainlandization, inadvertently reveals the postcolonial incapacity for articulating Taiwan's self in an affirmative tone.

Ko's provocation developed from his intellectual capacity to think Chinese, which a Japanese cannot do. This talent is not unique to Ko, because other pro-independence advocates have been capable of doing the same thing. A decade ago, the newly established Taiwan Solidarity Party (TSP), a radical pro-independence party led by the pro-independence former President Lee Teng-hui, sent a delegation to Japan on Chinese Ancestors' Day to pay respect to the Taiwanese ancestors worshiped at the Yasukuni Shrine, where Japanese war criminals were similarly worshiped by the Japanese people and officials. The past visits by the Japanese officials to the shrine have unfailingly provoked China to protest strongly. TSP delegations selected Chinese Ancestors' Day to worship at the shrine. The purpose was to declare that Taiwan's ancestors were Japanese, but the selection of the day of the visit was obviously aimed at the Chinese audience who are the only people to whom they could convey the significance of Chinese Ancestors' Day.

The underlying message of the ironic choice of being Japanese made by the pro-independence advocate was so provocative that the Chinese were probably the rare few in the world who could have understood the inflammatory implications. The intellectual capacity of the pro-independence Taiwanese to think Chinese enables them to be powerfully provocative. Probably implicit in this capacity is the unwanted cultural preparation that would enable them easily to appreciate many other shared cultural resources available to China. A situation in which pro-unification advocates could enlist these shared cultural resources on some future occasion and enable the pro-independent advocate to take an allegedly moral exit to becoming Chinese would be alarming.

Postcolonial conditions rarely deal with a site that simultaneously faces three external motherlands—Chinese, American, and British/Japanese. This kind of sited struggle requires the genealogical sensibility of the post-Western agenda to trace and decategorize. However, if the post-Western international relations laud the inevitable intertexts that allow fluid switches of position or the constant reconstructions of cultural and political identities, they may generate anxiety among the sited population. Conscious of the political correctness prevailing at the moment, the population could dread this uncertainty and regard shifting to a different possibility as dangerously incorrect. Resorting to confrontation to denounce such shifting could be violent. This explains why mainlandization usually invites a strong condemnation at the subaltern site, despite the vain efforts of the PRC authorities to avoid the image of forcing their way.

The Caveats of Post-Western Politics

Post-Western identification is applicable to postcolonial Hong Kong and Taiwan, in the sense that the nascent academic call intends to rediscover the subaltern subjectivities in the former colonies. The post-Western agenda adopts the self-other frame in analyzing the relationship between the hegemony and subaltern site, except for the conception of the post-Western self as a fluid, hybrid process without internal consistency or any fixed destiny. The post-Western agenda is non-Western to the extent that it presumes a site that usually, but not necessarily, lies geographically outside West Europe or North America; the site presumably owns a distinctive geocultural root of its own before the arrival of Western modernity.

The post-Western agenda discovers and records the agency of a sited self to combine and recombine values of all kinds creatively in accordance with the perceived need to survive, make sense, and succeed at its proclaimed site (Tickner and Blaney 2013; Shani 2008 Vasilaki 2012 Ling 2014b; Bilgin 2016a, 2020). Discursively, the post-Western self appropriates modernist discourses so that notions of sovereignty, progress, individuality, rationalism, liberation, and democracy, among others, acquire different and ever-changing meanings. Practically, the post-Western self improvises mechanisms and policies to reconcile conflicting needs and values in order to evade total control, suppression, or conversion, albeit in an institutional disguise that is ostensibly Western. Socially, the post-Western self simulates modern identities to win recognition in the world, avoid scrutiny or intervention by the hegemonic power, and confront other contending voices at its respective site or even discursively engage in self-silencing.

Ultimately, the post-Western agenda seeks to voice and reinterpret world politics, resist the synchronization of international regimes, and, as a result, provincialize the West as a local trajectory. The agenda fulfills all of these on behalf of an unlimited number of silenced or emerging subaltern sites. The post-Western agenda adopts a multi-forward moving historiography to provide each identified site with a history of its own. Methodologically, the post-Western agenda relies on genealogy to claim the legitimacy of the current sited practice by showing its root and celebrating the undecidable, coincidental quality of a cultural lineage in the process of evolution. The post-Western agenda, therefore, incorporates the spirit of empirical research, encourages the discovery of the silenced or emerging sites, and detects the ever-evolving meanings of practicing IR at the site.

Hong Kong and Taiwan are postcolonial and perfect for post-Western analysis. However, the request for unification from China engenders an immediate pressure. The request is overwhelming, such that China's liberal and hegemonic rivalry in the United States comes to the immediate rescue, discursively as well as politically. Discursively, the liberal economy of Hong Kong and electoral democracy of Taiwan provide the best illustrations of the successful transformation in front of a world where dependent countries have consistently failed to achieve either economic growth or political order. With Singapore and South Korea, Taiwan and Hong Kong comprise the four listed and celebrated newly industrialized countries in the 1980s that made an impressive rebuttal of the neo-Marxist critiques of the capitalist order. Turning consciously critical of the hegemonic system has been strategically senseless at both sites, because no alternative to reunification appears plausible apart from active participation, along with the associated recognition of the achievement unavailable in the sovereign order, in global liberalism.

The aborted post-Western potential in Hong Kong and Taiwan is being replicated in China, albeit in a different way. China resisted the Western values for thirty years before initiating the market economy in 1979. Regardless of the achievement of the Chinese economic reform, Chinese politics has not turned liberal. Even the Chinese economy still relies on state enterprises and party leadership, not to mention the continuation of the socialist ideology and the powerful return of Confucianism in the public discourse (Rudd 2015; Ford 2015), along with the peculiar combination of popular religions, such as Buddhism and Daoism (Madsen 2014; Laliberté 2015) and their profit-orientation. The rise of China further encourages the world to consider the China model as an alternative to that of the West (J. G. Smith 2010; Breslin 2011; Dickson 2011; Naughton 2010), rendering the West maximally a provincial practice.

Ostensibly, all of this makes China another perfect site for engaging in post-Western IR. However, no noteworthy interaction takes place between the Chinese and post-Western IRs. At best, Chinese IR is interested in being "non-Western" (Noesselt 2015; Zhang and Chang 2016). Across the entire Greater China area, the post-Western critiques of global liberalism and American hegemony echo weakly, if at all. Nevertheless, the post-Western discourse is instrumental to the quest for subjectivity in Hong Kong's and

Taiwan's mounting encounter with China. This can be done by using Chinese hegemony as a substitute for Western hegemony.

Note that the ability to adapt to the rise of China and appropriate Chinese cultural resources for their own benefit has apparently not contributed to any single direction of Hong Kong's or Taiwan's assimilation into the Greater China, either politically or culturally. The least success is registered in the field of psychology, as the aforementioned anti-China campaigns reached an unprecedented climax first in 2014 at both sites and in 2019 in Hong Kong. Therefore, the post-Western methodology of sited genealogy is pertinent to the understanding of the evolution of anti-China consciousness amid the fast-enhanced reliance on the Chinese economy.

To sum up, although both China and its two subaltern sites are post-Western in style, the discursive self-awareness of such is nonexistent. On the contrary, the two previous colonies are primarily concerned with the alternatives to any essential version of Chineseness. This preoccupation with the meaning of being differently Chinese distracts Greater China from their post-Western practices. Consequently, in their confrontation, China envisages an anti-Western option and yet the two sites remain as Western models. Neither is receptive to post-Western IR (Callaham 2008; Qin 2011a). Mainlandization and anti-mainlandization create a significant lacuna on the post-Western agenda.

To trace the post-Western process at the two subaltern sites, one should note the five potential dangers of the post-Western agenda. In other words, the post-Western pursuit can backfire.

1. The politicization of a site to the consequence that the site or the self loses fluidity and hybridity in privileging a particular fixed self-identity at the expense of other alternatives. For example, to cope with the return to China, Hong Kong is being transformed into a site that has its own integrated trajectory of self-identification, as opposed to disjoined yet coexistent parallels of cultural and generational cohorts in the unnamed "post-conditions" (G. Chou 2012), which inform post-Hong Kongness.

2. An invitation to hegemonic disciplining that would not have taken place without the post-Western celebration of being different, which alerts the hegemonic force to the potential subversion of the subaltern site engaging in reworlding. For example, both the pro-independence and the anti-independence forces in Taiwan articulate their respective China policy that can potentially defy the US strategic interests, each alarming enough in a different way to induce the intensive involvement of Washington in the island's politics (V. Wang 2015).[2]

3. Construction of an unwanted component of the self to split the entirety of an imagined greater self into mutually estranging others. For example, the increasing interaction between Taiwan and the Mainland incurs the charge of betrayal, on behalf of Taiwan's non-Chinese identity, against those Taiwanese engaging in interaction because of the potential obscuring effect of the interaction on the political distinction of Taiwan from China (F. Shih 2012).

4. Normalization of a genealogy of increased hybridity to the neglect of dialectical turns between nonsynthetic or even schizophrenic cultural components, some of which remain non-Western. For example, the coexistence of patriotism and prodemocracy in Hong Kong or anti-communism and anti-China in Taiwan makes the territorially oriented genealogy of a site misleading (M. Szeto 2009).

5. Overlooking the cyclical historiography that is not forward-moving but occasionally moves backward or in circle, which renders the post-Western agenda a stage of recycling. For example, the post-Western criticism of modernist rationalism parallels the ancient Chinese Daoist criticism of Confucian rationality, yet modernist discourses typically treat Confucianism as anti-rational; thus, the rational use of Confucianism by the Chinese Communist Party is overlooked (Shih and Yu 2015).

The postmodern and postcolonial critiques have encountered two caveats. Needless to say, they celebrate all of the fluidity and changeability in the process of mainlandization. They supply powerful discourses to deconstruct canonic interpretation of any kind, be it the end of history or the China dream. However, these discourses are inadequate to undergird the level of societal confidence in Hong Kong or Taiwan that is required to calm the population in the face of the seemingly overwhelming mainlandization. Thus, people strategically enlist liberal discourses to the effect of reproducing the other, which is far stronger than (Chinese) nationalist, hegemony. In reality, the postcolonial quest for sited subjectivity appropriates the liberal discourse of independence, equality, and freedom for anti-Chinese causes. The postcolonial anti-Chinese pursuit ironically joins forces with the hegemonic order to resist the Chinese influence. Liberalism is reduced to an anti-Chinese agenda. How ironically post-Western!

The second caveat is the same as that present in any quest for subjectivity—that the stress on sited subjectivity can become dangerously silencing regarding a presumably disunited repertoire of alternative identities. Social cleavages along the identity line not only divide political society but also split each personal self that contingently adopts different strategies toward her own Chineseness. This is how hybridity, a keynote of the postcolonial perspective, is misleading, at least in Hong Kong and Taiwan, if not elsewhere. The pressure to construct some degree of prevailing political correctness for the understanding of mainlandization is mounting. However, in the two postcolonial societies, the colonial, indigenous, and immigrant cultures have coexisted without any resultant synthesis, to which the notion of hybridity inadvertently alludes. Consequently, the counter-/anti-mainlandization that is embedded in political correctness provokes the internal rivalry and weakens the power to resist or prospect for a democratic politics.

Post-(Western-)Chineseness

The quest for post-Western IR, which has emerged since the beginning of the century, appears to be a promising perspective in making sense of the pluralization of Chinese identities worldwide. The post-Western agenda promotes a second-order identity in light of its search, primarily aimed at the deconstruction of the hegemonic order defined by the statist and liberal political economy at the international level. In a nutshell, post-Western IR acknowledges the multiple sources and varied practices of the statist and liberal rules that initially arose from the Western historical trajectories since Westphalia. The post-Western agenda incorporates the sited reappropriation of the hegemonic order that reflects both the sited geocultural trajectories and their adaptation to the encounter with the hegemonic order. In China, this could essentially mean the use of globalization to facilitate reunification with Taiwan (Tung 2003).

Methodologically, post-Western studies adopt a genealogy that can trace the evolutionary process whereby a hegemonic norm, value, and institution are recognized, imported, and practiced as well as how the process is revised differently at various sites. The ability of the local population to incorporate the hegemonic institution generates access to the global political economy, making the local actors relevant participants at the global level. Such site worlding presumably reconstructs the hegemonic order through the trivialization of the hegemonic institution. It also presents nuanced meanings to the hegemonic value, each of which is distinctively in accordance with the identity strategies of the sited population. For instance, the principle of state sovereignty has additional meaning in the Chinese context that conveys a determination to restore the national dignity that has been removed by historical imperialism during the earlier years (Callahan 2012).

Post-Western IR seems a plausible ally of Chinese IR, that seeks alternatives outside global liberalism. However, the post-Western agenda simultaneously deconstructs and reproduces the hegemonic order. The ubiquity of global governance based upon liberal governmentality testifies to the discursive tenacity and interventionary power of the hegemonic order. Nevertheless, the post-Western IR recognizes that the hegemonic norm and order cannot proceed with any consistent method and institution nor deliver the promised gate-keeping (Turton 2016). By engaging in the amelioration of the interventionary politics of globalization, the Chinese discourse consistently criticizes intervention as if China is more a counter or anti than a post-Western alternative (Weiwei Zhang 2011; D. Cohen 2011). Discursively, Chinese IR is generally lukewarm about being post-Western.

Chinese IR is preoccupied with how China stands in the world, which is a cliché (Kavalski 2013). This relational sensibility is noteworthy in the Chinese scholarship as well as the policy discourse (Feng Zhang 2009; T. Zhao 2009; Qin 2011b; Huang and Shih 2014), implying that China is generally uninterested in how others are being others in their own perspectives (Kavalski 2009). Mutual acceptance is the primary concern of China (Huang 2015). In comparison, China accordingly seeks acceptance from others, whereas post-Western IR is curious about differences. Methodologically, post-Western IR relies on genealogy to discover sites, whereas the Chinese literature is only interested in relationality. The former relies on curiosity, whereas the latter shuns it. Genealogy relies on curiosity about how each site differs, whereas Chinese relationality is concerned with how differences coexist in a mutually acceptable yet disinterested relationship.

The bottleneck for further dialogue between the post-Western agenda and the Chinese schools of IR can have several dimensions. From the perspective of the research design and the problematics of Chinese IR, the estrangement and aversion to the post-Western agenda are apparent. The theoretical problematics of Chinese IR is primarily concerned with order and stability. For instance, one significant strand of Chinese IR studies hierarchy as the typical structure of the international system (Cunningham-Cross 2012; X. Yan 2008). This is in line with Western realism to the extent that domestic characteristics are irrelevant. A consciously raised slogan of Chinese IR that attends to relationality and relationship is another example (Chiung-chiu Huang 2015; Paltiel 2009; Qin 2009). Along with the above-mentioned hierarchical studies, both schools stress the importance of order. Even the anti-hierarchy and anti-relationship approach of Chinese Daoist IR values are not the difference per se (T. Zhao 2006; Ling 2014). The Daoist disinterest in difference determines that the coexistence of different worlds is natural. Order exists in natural relationality that desensitizes difference.

The Chinese School's preoccupation with order differs dramatically from the post-Western quest for new possibilities outside the hegemonic designation of roles and functions. In the post-Western world, hegemony is impossible because readily available alternatives and further possibilities are abundant, such that hegemony can be no more than a pretense at a provincial identity, attempting to silence all of the rest. The mission of post-Western research is to demonstrate the impossibility of being just Western and to warn against all attempts to arrange the international order, given the inevitable deconstruction at subaltern sites that no hegemonic attempt could overcome. Post-Western IR could thus distrust the Chinese IR as a substituting hegemony. Reversely, the post-Western denial of the possibility of order affects the purpose of Chinese IR.

Chinese IR lacks the ontological sensibility toward subjectivity and emancipation. The individual identities of different societies or groups are unimportant; nevertheless, these may have some effect if not well tamed or disciplined (for further discussion, see K. Yang 1995, 1993; K. Hwang 2012). If order is the persistent concern, then it should be required of all, whether physically strong or weak, to exercise self-restraint to make room for others to live (Doupe 2003). In particular, how does a group with a specific geocultural trajectory stay within a relational network so that all of the peculiarities have a place of their own without worrying about intervention, conversion, or suppression while all resourceful groups enjoy freedom from invasion or revolution?

Chinese and the post-Western IRs agree that differences are no threat. Discovering differences is the purpose of the latter and differences are celebrated. For Chinese IR, differences are not problems to be dealt with, and hence do not cause disorder. If differences can be settled based on an orderly relationship, the further examination of the levels of difference between one another becomes no longer imperative. Differences should be examined because, for Chinese IR, a particular difference requires a particular treatment for the relationship to become truly reciprocal. However, this has nothing to do with curiosity. Curiosity is not an epistemological value in Chinese intellectual history, where empirical findings about the truth are less important than sociable relationships that bring forth order among groups. By contrast, the post-Western research is keen on curiosity. Accordingly, Chineseness is more about relationality than difference.

Consequently, for post-Western research, each site has its own genealogy and future trajectory; however, for Chinese IR, this genealogy or prospect for the future cannot interfere with the agreed relationship. The stress of such genealogy would only generate anxiety. Chinese IR is more comfortable with cycles instead of genealogy, because cycles predict the return of order after the occasional breakdown of reciprocal relationships. Cycles have no teleological end to pursue. This neglect of a future ideal reproduces indifference to cultural and value differences. Consequently, a thinking style behind the idea of the one country, two systems is created where the difference between socialism and capitalism has been dismissed to allow the more important issue of the Mainland–Hong Kong relationship to flourish.

Chinese praxis and post-Western praxis contrast sharply, because the former aims at the transcendence of the limited self to reach the higher ground of selflessness, whereas the latter aims at the emancipation of the self, resistance against hegemony, and the assertion of subjectivity that appropriates hegemony for its own use. Chinese praxis requires self-restraint, self-discipline, self-sacrifice, and, concomitantly, a determination to punish those who refuse to reciprocate. Chinese IR or center-periphery relationships are hence not always peaceful. Nevertheless, Chinese praxis and post-Western praxis coincide with regard to their shared aversion to universal rules whereby no reciprocal exemption is legitimate. The post-Western praxis further recognizes sited practices of an alleged universal rule that neither entirely negate nor entirely subscribe to the rule; however, the Chinese praxis discourages universal rule-making in favor of improvising relationality at each site (Yue 2015).

Up until 2022, the Chinese IR primarily relied on Chinese history and literature to inspire alternative world orders that could accommodate differences and shun universal rules. The post-Western IR, instead, embraces sited history and literature and painstakingly demonstrates how unlikely it is that a site will remain entirely untouched by the hegemony or entirely submit to its ruling. The official Chinese insistence on the beauty of Chinese culture reinforces the tendency to overlook how others differ in a distinctive way. The rise of China generates the self-expectation that China can substitute for the West. China on the rise does not need other subaltern sites to face the West. Filled with self-confidence in the twenty-first century, the Chinese agenda focuses on recollecting wisdom from China's own past (X. Yan 2011; M. Chou 2011). For the post-Western, such self-recollection is like a mechanism for the subaltern site to gain self-confidence and for them to support and appreciate their embedded differences. Chinese IR could find this kind of mutual appreciation unnecessary, because China alone can sufficiently face the West.

Implausible Chinese, Post-Western, or Western

The relational sensibility in Chinese IR's search for order adopts the one country, two systems approach to cope with the unification of the two former colonies of British and Japanese imperialism in the hope that its noninterference in the internal arrangement of Hong Kong or Taiwan can achieve a stable relationship between the Mainland and the recovered lands. The two former colonies have been intensively ingrained in the operation of global capitalism with a presumably typical post-Western make-up, which is neither Western nor Chinese. Both remain Chinese to a large extent in terms of diet, conventional festivals, languages, and even social and cultural values, and yet mimic the West's political institution and discourse, which primarily constitute their non-Chinese image under the global liberal circumstance in the twenty-first century.

The Chinese authorities' endeavor to provide Chinese identities for both sites estranges the liberal, and therefore global, identities of both sites. To accomplish their global representation, the identity strategy strives to ally with the West and strengthen their mimicry of the West. This use of global liberalism as a vehicle for transcending Chinese identities is a quintessential example of the post-Western phenomenon. Nevertheless, the sited effort to resist Chinese identities silences the post-Western potential that urges the use of genealogy to trace a non-Western geocultural trajectory. The goal of becoming global is a form of resistance to one's own Chineseness. Resistance to Chineseness alludes to the existence of Chineseness in one's self-understanding, as illustrated in the aforementioned practice of the Taipei City mayor. The post-Western agenda therefore alienates the sited population because their unwanted Chinese identities could reemerge as an important dimension of sited genealogy, which could defeat the purpose of becoming global qua anti-Chinese.

The dilemma of Hong Kong and Taiwan with regard to post-Western identities and Western identities repeats the familiar story of pre–World War II Japan as a country caught between European and Asian identities. Tokyo aborted the agenda of becoming European owing to the realization that European powers were reluctant to regard Japan as such. Once again, an

Asian country, Japan, needed to group all East Asians to obtain a credible competitor and overcome its own Western legacy (Goto-Jones 2010). This meant the dissolution of China into a more general East-Asian identity; hence, Tokyo had to overcome its Confucian legacy (Tanaka 1993), which undergirded the imagination of authentic Chineseness as not easily dissolvable. To convince Chinese people of Tokyo's capable leadership, Tokyo needed to demonstrate further, ironically, the achieved European modernity of Japan. This is what Hong Kong and Taiwan are striving to achieve in the twenty-first century—to demonstrate the non-Chineseness of their liberal constitution. Due to its adamant pre-modern identity, China, which pre–World War II Tokyo felt obliged to dissolve, is similar to Chineseness, which the pro-independent components of the two subaltern sites struggle to cleanse, in order to become Western.

The global liberalism of Hong Kong and Taiwan, together with the rise of China's economic power, ties them perfectly with the Mainland in terms of economy. Thus, choosing the identity strategy has become more complicated than that of pre–World War II Japan. Both sites rely on Chinese resources to compete at the global level in order to strengthen their liberal identities. The Chinese leaders, on the other hand, are thinking unknowingly post-Western in actuality. By adhering to the idea that supporting the two reluctant former colonies of the West to perform better under global liberalism, via making economic concessions to them, the Chinese leaders consider such action as relational rather than rational; that is, winning the hearts of the people in Hong Kong and Taiwan (Keng and Schubert 2010). These ironies are common-sensual, but together are undertheorized. They render all the effort to become post-Western, Chinese, or Western philosophically implausible. The post-Western characteristic, if celebrated, could destroy the anti-Western platforms of Chinese scholarship and policy. Similarly, it could discredit the anti-Chinese platforms of the two former colonies.

Taiwan and Hong Kong also display a dialectic characteristic that is unfamiliar to the post-Western agenda. Hybrid components of the two former colonies have yet to integrate into a ready site of synthetic hybridity. The Chinese, the postcolonial, and the Western components have not synthesized well into a sited identity. In Hong Kong, for example, generations of south-comers, whose migration started during the Qing dynasty, were anti-incumbent in their own historical trajectory; nevertheless, they shared a Chinese identity that belittled the colonized population of Hong Kong.

In contemporary politics, patriotism and anti-communism are equally apparent in Hong Kong. Likewise, in Taiwan, generational cohorts differ dramatically for being either pre- or postcolonization, being intra– or extra–Chinese Civil War, and being pro- or anti-communist. Taiwan, once considered a well-integrated place, has experienced the recycling of Chinese, colonial, and postcolonial identities in the past twenty years, with the result that no claim to a sited identity can do minimal justice to the entire population (Law 2009; Williams 2003).

Therefore, to be in line with post-Western acclaim, some people in Taiwan and Hong Kong are recollecting their Chineseness. In fact, many are recollecting Chineseness in their effort to reconnect China. Reconnection can initially serve as the instrumental reason through which some can utilize Chinese economic resources, concessions, and profit incentives. Reconnecting is also achieved by others for the sake of resisting the rising postcolonial identities that threaten their citizenship rights or desire to remain Chinese and for the practicality of peace-making with China as well as between different identity segments of their societies.

By contrast, to protect the non-Chineseness of their colonial and liberal constitution, some have been relying on global liberalism, qua the West. In other words, by composing a nonsynthetic and layered hybridity, these cultural and ideological identities have all once been politically incorrect in a period of history and yet are able to make their way back to the public discourse. The site is hybrid in the temporal sense, because all are potentially discursive resources to be triggered on a particular agenda, in a particular gathering, at a particular site, or in a particular relationship.

People may welcome Chinese interference of various kinds to enlist Chinese relationality. In instances where Taiwan confronts its neighbors, such as Japan, Vietnam, or the Philippines, the expectation that China will come and punish the other side may arise (Demick 2013). This would be truer on those occasions where the US steps in to control the confrontation to the advantage of the other side. For the US, confrontation between regional allies is always trivial, compared with the collective security needed to contain China. However, for Hong Kong or Taiwan, this would be depressing. Chinese relationality is, therefore, a mixed blessing for the two former colonies, connoting political incorrectness under liberalism but political correctness under the post-Western condition.

To understand these post-Western conditions, identifying the discursive mechanisms that enable the population to enact the liberal, postcolonial, and Chinese cultural resources is conceptually necessary. This conceptual perspective is post-Chineseness, and the post-Chinese world is emerging. Chinese groups in various places worldwide, each distinctive in terms of its cultural memory, continue to rely on similar cultural resources for self-presentation. They can communicate with each other easily, sometimes enthusiastically, yet anxiously, depressingly, or antagonistically at other times, probably because of the misunderstandings caused by the ostensible cultural sharing among them.

The post-Chinese world exhibits a variety of cultural combinations that cannot be simply reduced to the notion of hybridity. It celebrates cycles instead. Cycles are composed of Chinese cultural resources and local geocultural legacies, which parallel each other without actually combining into a synthetic subjectivity. The Chinese who diverge into unlike kinds, therefore, remain culturally prepared to reconnect to a past while being fully aware of the exits and being capable of passing through them. A past, shared culture, and cycles together testify to a relational identity that is far above the sophisticated as opposed to the sheer notion of hybridity.

Conclusion: Post-Chineseness and Mainlandization

Chineseness can be a misleading concept to the extent that it only attends to the difference among the Chinese populations anywhere. Chinese communities are indeed different from one another; nevertheless, they have yet to develop a curiosity about the differences. Post-Chineseness adapts to this nonexistent curiosity and shifts the focus of the research agenda to relationality. Relationality concerns the mechanism of reconnection among Chinese communities. They are all different; hence the designation of the undesignated "post." However, their potential and practice of reconnection arises from the incurring of shared, albeit imagined, cultural resources.

The "post" in post-Chineseness alludes to a temporal concept in which Chineseness is a layered characteristic, which is at least once active, ready for recollection, constantly revisable, strategically instrumental, and occasionally inspirational. To indicate Chineseness, practices and symbols are shared among Chinese groups. Chineseness, accordingly, involves processes of mutual recognition via shared cultural resources, in use as well as in memory. Mutual recognition may refer to any two groups sharing a certain Chinese culture or history. Any two Chinese groups may share a peculiar understanding of Chinese culture or history.

Continuous induction can build a cultural repertoire. The capacity and process for incurring resources in the evolving cultural repertoire, either currently in use or in oblivion, in order to improvise connections creatively and imaginatively, comprise the mechanism of Chinese relationality. Mainlandization, therefore, triggers the particular processes of Chinese relationality. By contrast, gathering the shared cultural resources that are being kept, developed, transformed, or silenced among different sites, however varied, is a matter of "post"-identification.

Mainlandization is the incurring of shared Chinese cultural resources in use or in memory to facilitate recovery (of lost territory), expansion (of the influence of the Communist Party), assimilation (of the formerly colonized population), reunification (of split regimes), integration (of an alienated ethnicity), submission (of a dissident group), networking (of a diasporic population), return (of a migrant cohort), and so on, to enhance the Chinese relationality of the targeted group, site, and sector anywhere, specifically those territorially proximate ones. The initiatives for mainlandization may come from all sources, hegemonic as well as subaltern, domestic as well as overseas, official as well as private, and political as well as psychological.

The caveat of mainlandization is the tendency to use a definite territorial reference, usually the sovereign state of PRC, to indicate China, at the expense of the multiple sources of Chineseness as well as the cyclical recollection of historical resources that enable those kinds of relationality and reciprocity that are external, transcendent, and partial to the Chinese borders. The rise of China generates the impression that enhanced Chineseness contributes to the strength of territorial/sovereign China or the ruling Communist Party and vice versa. The merit of post-Chineseness as a theme is precisely that, on the one hand, it acknowledges that the material strength of China accelerates the incurrence and invention of shared cultural resources and yet, on the other, demonstrates that the intensity and sophistication of the evolving relationality uncontrolled by the political center of territorial China reinforce the post-Chineseness rather than undermine it. Whether post-Chineseness is immediately supportive or resistant to the rise of territorial China, it favors the entire ecology of mainlandization, as cyclically interactive loops, in the long run, making even liberalism a part of it.

The key to the post-Chinese agenda is to identify the incurrence of the shared cultural resources. The rationale, process, and consequence of the incurrence and the embedded liberalism are practically mutually constituted in relevant societies and personalities. Chinese relationality and liberalism form "co-thesis," "para-thesis," or "nonsynthetic dialectics," capable of proceeding with a mixed, single, or cyclical thesis. To that extent, post-Chineseness also attains post-Western characteristics. Mainlandization that affects the operation of liberal institution in Taiwan and Hong Kong cannot help but accommodate liberalism, positively as well as negatively, in the Chinese discourse, institution, and the policy to facilitate the Chinese relationality of Hong Kong and Taiwan.

The rediscovery of shared Chinese resources has complicated, divergent implications for liberalism and vice versa; hence, post-Western sitedness.

1. Chinese relationality and liberalism can compete in the public forum similar to the case of Hong Kong, where pro-establishment and liberals vehemently confront each other with pro-liberal discourses easily in association with the anti-Chinese attitude. Even when liberalism has been silenced, as since 2021, pro-establishment forces can pick up liberal discourses to advance their political causes.

2. On different occasions, however, a liberal institution, for example, the legislature, the mass media, or religions, can provide a channel for the articulation of Chinese relationality similar to the case of Taiwan (and, e.g., Malaysia).

3. Contrary to the above point, liberal institutions can be a disguise for discrimination as well, to enable scapegoating that is sometimes required by anti-Chinese correctness.

4. The use of liberalism by the anti-independence narrator in Taiwan is a more sophisticated way to insinuate that Chinese identities, as opposed to the illiberal politics of the Communist Party, are where the real issue should not lie. As such, criticizing Chinese authoritarianism to enhance self-conscious Chineseness aims to shelve the issue of Taiwan's independence and its anti-Chinese orientation.

5. Liberalism and Chinese relationality can separately contribute to diplomacy, coping with different countries and by different people. For instance, liberalism always dominates Taiwan's US policy, whereas Taiwan's Chinese relationality primarily prevails among the targeted overseas Chinese or the Chinese Mainlanders.

6. As a political signal to those who use it, Chinese relationality is familiar to the anti-independence sectors in Taiwan. This is in contrast to liberalism, being the favored discourse of the pro-independence sectors.

7. Finally, Chinese relationality can curb liberalism either through active lobbying on behalf of a higher moral ground embedded in kinship, nationalism, and religious propriety, or through self-censorship out of a fear of being considered politically incorrect in China and socially culpable, as well as of being penalized.

In Lieu of a Conclusion

Noninternational Relations, Nonidentities

How can a book on post-identity conclude? Indeed, post-Chineseness can proceed to anywhere, forward as well as backward, but never conclusively. It can improvise relations, shamefully as well as shamelessly, but never autonomously. It can enact roles, constructively as well as destructively, but never consistently. No conclusion can stop post-identities. Post-Chineseness evolves cyclically, being both multiple and bilateral, either from the inside or outside, and at various levels (Shih, Tang, and He 2017). Conclusion is the last thing proper for such an intersectional agenda, which, if presented in a nutshell or in brief, misleads.

Oddly, with all the post-Western, postcolonial, genealogical, and re/worlding rhetoric and sensibilities, the critical literature is methodologically surprisingly disciplined and thus conniving to the extent that the presentation of case studies habitually conforms to the academic journals' stylistic request for consistency, clarity, and theoretical implications, as if a story that, narratively, connects an origin with an end could reflect the reality. This book is guilty of the same to some extent due to the limitation of its author's skill, but nevertheless he stays critical in the sense of consciously refusing to domesticate his narratives to fit the disciplinary discourses, be they international relations, ethnic studies, or China studies. Readers who seek international relations theorization end up in, from the literature point of view, a strange place, if indeed anywhere. Likewise, colleagues of China studies would probably not even bother giving it a glance.

On the one hand, being left alone, wondering and anxiously relating is a blessing, because this indicates the incapacity of the major disciplines to appropriate or ghettoize post-Chineseness in their multicultural windows for exhibition. On the other hand, though, a hiatus in the dialogue with imperialists and neighbors alike would fail the test of relational praxis badly and thus reduce the morale for the realignment of agents of post-identities of all sorts. This would be to repeat the sad story of Yadong, portrayed in chapter 3. Even so, the celebrative tone of the critical literature by all means romanticizes the emancipative agency of the subaltern population for transcendence. The allegedly demonstrated agency fares no better than the silenced post-Chineseness in terms of the perseverance to effectuate de- and reconstruction, as the late Arif Dirlik (1940–2017) derided it as merely a "postcolonial aura" that reinforces the attraction of imperialism (Dirlik 1994).

That said, post-Chineseness promises a coherent challenge in all of these fields; namely, all are bound to be related and the ways to remain related are contextual, agential, and geocultural in style. Equally important is its noticeable bilateral sensibilities that enable the ostensibly weak to assert a relational identity that can reconstitute the strong and neutralize the hegemonic rules. Therefore, the self-centric imposition of roles and identities by the strong inevitably evokes decentric cycles, regardless of how sophisticated or rooted these involved roles are claimed to be. In fact, the more culturally sophisticated a role is, the more unstable and incompatible the expectations of others it incurs, and the less consistent its adjustments. After all, to be related is, in the long run, a more apparent need than truth, value, or faith.

In lieu of a conclusion, three mini-agendas, whose theoretical implications tend to be undervalued, are worth mentioning. The first concerns the prospect of looking out from China, compared with that of looking in. The choice between looking out and looking in determines which of table 1.1 and table 5.1 to apply. As long as the actors intuitively feel that their prospects are typical and representative of Chinese in general, they are looking out. For others, who feel they lack the legitimacy to act or speak on behalf of China, their prospect is looking in. These prospects are unstable in nature. For example, Chinese Southeast Asians, especially Chinese-Singaporeans and Malaysians, may have experienced a shift since the end of World War II, from a prospect of looking out to one of looking in. The same shift occurred for the Taiwanese at the end of the Chinese Civil War. For another example, Taiwanese may still adopt a prospect of looking out when interacting with Chinese overseas. The same prospect is adopted by Chinese-Malaysians looking out on the indigenous population. They shift to a prospect of looking in when their targets are the Chinese mainlanders. These subtle changes in prospect over time and space are key to understanding a strategic pattern that is impatiently considered as vacillating, inconsistent, or irrational.

Secondly, when adopting an external prospect of looking in, sinological Chineseness and ethnic Chinesenesss are most unstable, compared with the other four shown in table 5.1. The issue for these in-between post-Chinese identities is which side of belonging to focus on at a particular time for a particular issue. Their major difference probably concerns mentality. Namely, ethnic Chineseness carries a degree of subalternity, so the people in the category mainly seek to conform to both sides, rather than preach them away from ignorance and self-centrism. However, once the double-sided conformity can evolve into an assertion of rights, ethnic Chineseness acquires the character of sinological Chineseness by presenting a different way of being Chinese. This is usually weak, though. Conversely, sinological Chineseness can yield to ethnic Chineseness if communicating with China or on behalf of China confronts a surge of politically anti-Chinese correctness. Under this circumstance, mutual knowledge would be regarded as threatening. China watching in Singapore during the Cold War illustrates such a change. Nevertheless, sinological Chineseness reflects a level of confidence that is socially far more tolerant and sustainable than other kinds of post-Chineseness.

The third potential agenda is the balance of relationships by those acting out of sinological Chineseness and ethnic Chineseness. In this context, the balance of relationships refers primarily to *preempting the estrangement of the Chinese target group and binding it to a mutual sense of resemblance*. Gift-giving to reproduce relationships for sinological Chineseness involves focusing on preaching the other side of the hybrid identity as an apologist for China. For ethnic Chineseness, it could be for the in-between group to adapt further to Chinese expectations at the expense of the other of its hybrid identity. The punishment for a perceived betrayal of relational obligation by China would be to tilt to the other side as a shaming technique to pressure China for some redress. Since these balance-of-relationships acts are mainly strategic, they are volatile in the long run and revealing of the improvisational as well as inescapable nature of relationality.

Prospects only affect the range of resources to be used to oblige each other, which are usually more skillful in arranging one type of resources than another. Ultimately, the key to strategizing role and identities concerns whose prior understandings of relations become the reference, upon which the interacting actors interrogate each other's prospect. Neither looking in nor looking out is necessarily privileged. However, conveniently improvised post-identities are inevitably premised upon a lingering sense of authentic but usually suppressing identities. Post-identities and identities thus create an endless cycle of changes.

Appendix

Post-Asia and IR Research: A Pervasive Agenda

How Universal Is Non-Western?

The rise of Asia and spread of nonstate actors are reconfiguring international relations. In the case of the Chinese people, Chinese civilization, and the Chinese state, re-Sinicization indicates a cyclical as opposed to linear and forward-moving historiography, a hybrid as opposed to homogeneous national identity, dislocation as opposed to territoriality, and reconnection as opposed to othering. In a nutshell, relationality instead of autonomy prevails. These processes do not simply represent the emergence of new players at various levels. Instead, the seemingly unfamiliar behavior that has emerged has challenged the purpose and meaning of foreign policy-making, its scope and boundary, and even the national as well as civilizational identities of policy-makers. To make sense of all this, one must either write them off as a transient deviance or develop alternative theories to enable the understanding of a plausible or emerging nonreality that has been ignored in the past as well as in the West.

Given the impossibility of defining Asia, as in the case of defining China, and the call for non-Western theorization, a future agenda can explore the extension of the study of post-Chineseness to the study of post-Asianness. It will suggest a few research agendas to enable the appreciation of the multiple and mutual constitutions of all identities, including Asian as well as Western identities, in IR. The main thrust is about particularism and universalism in this pursuit of non-Western IR.

The extension to post-Asianness alludes to universality as methodology regarding how one is always potentially capable of practicing or appreciating initially unfamiliar ways of life and thought. Universality, therefore, is processual, relational, and constantly in the making. One's becoming universal must involve socialization via role-taking or mimicry. Glocalization is one such example of relational universality. In short, anything can become more or less universal, given an additional relational trajectory on each occasion. This methodological agency for (usually collectively) learning and preaching something further implies a methodological agency for unlearning or purging it. Together, learning and unlearning Asia render ontologically determined or epistemologically prescribed universality neither un/necessary nor im/moral. Being irrelevant to ontology or epistemology, universality connotes a strategy of becoming Asian, informed by a relational choice that is both social (i.e., role-oriented) and volitionary.

Asia as Unfulfilled Epistemology

Let us consider the use of chopsticks as an art of eating. What kind of art is it, though? One could decide to make the use of chopsticks a "universal" art that is teachable to all for eating any food and yet brings forth alternative sequences, sociability, and joy that are unfelt or inaccessible without an appreciation of chopsticks. Conversely, from a modernization perspective, chopsticks are conceived of as "outdated" utensils to be extensively substituted and jettisoned. In between, the exotic practice of using chopsticks could be applied exclusively to the eating of Oriental food. Alternatively, practicing the use of chopsticks could involve a "collusive" epistemology, so that chopsticks, as well as any other Western utensils, are appropriate for all food but each only proper for a specific population to use. Among the universal, outdated, exotic, and collusive possibilities, the universal approach is the appropriate premise upon which a mutual understanding between the West and Asia is feasible. For anyone trying to know more about the West, no additional knowledge is worth learning from outdated, exotic, or collusive Asia.

Consider the rise of China and Chinese IR as an example of the field of IR being transformed by Asia. This raises the question, Do US hegemony and Chinese Tianxia (all-under-heaven) represent two distinctive modes of hierarchy that are embedded in the mutually irreconcilable perspectives of respective liberalism and Confucianism (Zhang and Chang 2016; Feng Zhang 2013; Shih 2010)? The popular answer from the Sinosphere is "yes" (Fenzhi Zhang 2015; Qin 2016; T. Zhao 2006, 2009). According to this view, making sense of and explaining Chinese IR requires at least an understanding of a completely separate epistemology. If so, then any further attempt at intellectual exchange and translation within the current epistemology of each side would prove redundant. An alternative view shows that allegedly differing Chinese IRs are similarly hegemonic (Feiling Wang 2017; Le 2016; Mingfu Liu 2015; Callahan 2008). This view argues that Chinese IR subscribes to the same patterns, or the lack of them, practiced elsewhere in IR. Nevertheless, Chinese IR is potentially valuable if it can generate new hypotheses to revise or substitute the ostensibly universal principles accepted in the West (Buzan 2010; Harding 1984). This last qualification provides the only epistemological legitimacy to engage in the theorizing of Chinese IR for an Anglophone audience. However, to date, the Chinese IR hypotheses that can lead to a different conceptualization of international politics have been unimpressive.

Being Critical also for the West

Specifically, Asian IR contributes to IR by providing lenses of understanding and ways of doing things unfamiliar to the "West" (or different Asians). In brief, the mission of Asian IR is for everyone to explain more clearly both Asian IR and Western IR through adopting each other's perspectives. Coexistence of multiple universalisms, or pluriversality, is not plausible until intersections that allow epistemological travel to each other's domain are available. Based on the ontological imagination showing that everyone's truth is accessible to everyone else, given the appropriate platforms, metaphors, or practices, the following discussion considers Asia in the theoretical terrains for a generalized audience. It selectively engages four closely related epistemological perspectives that are critical of Anglophone IR—post-Western IR, global IR, the national schools, and the relational turns. This end-of-book discussion aims to reconcile the mutually ghettoizing Anglophone IR and its rivals by proposing a research agenda that is undergirded by resources that are intellectually associated with Asianness or post-Asianness. Thus, the essay manifests an exit strategy to encourage "epistemological tourism" between any ontological arrangements in IR (Shih, Singh, and Marwah 2012).

First, in dissolving the false universality of Western IR, post-Western IR painstakingly records the manner in which the Anglophone IR discourses have arrived at a subaltern site, only to be practiced in a historical context with its own intellectual trajectory, revisability, reinterpretation, and even reappropriation (Shani 2008; Bilgin 2008; Ling 2014). The receiving site is "reworlded" through its participation in IR that necessarily reconstitutes IR as well as the West. Second, global IR moves beyond the revisability of the West, further retrieves and embraces non-Western patterns that predate the encountered West, and establishes among its practitioners a system of interaction that is unaffected by the West. A productive global-IR agenda presumably includes all of them (Acharya 2014b; Bilgin and Ling 2017). Third, each quest for a national brand of IR focuses on only one such pattern and yet incorporates historical and contemporary resources to show how a national or regional actor firmly owns some kind of non-Western IR (Aydinli and Biltekin 2017; Cho 2015; Shimizu 2015; Shimizu and Noro 2021; H. Wang 2013; Shih 2013b; C. Chen 2012). Finally, for students of the relational turn, all of the abovementioned claims occur each in their own habitus to make all, at best, parts of certain networks and network ingredients of their self-identities each to proceed in relational processes without any determining structures or a priori individualized subjectivity (Jackson and Nexon 1999; Bourdieu 1977).

Four Illustrative Agendas for Future Prospects

Cyclical Temporality and Post-Western International Relations

To begin with, Asia contributes to IR to the extent that it adds a temporal dimension to the almost exclusively spatial sensibilities registered in materiality, territoriality, and sovereignty. The Orientalized image of Asia as old could, in fact, prove an asset in this regard. Temporality appears significant in the pursuit of post-Western IR because the latter's preoccupation with sited genealogy reproduces a stylistically Western, forward-moving historiography and because ownership of a sited identity of its own, albeit fluid and hybrid, requires a sovereign-like, substantialist self-integrity to speak. By contrast, Asianness hosts a number of repetitive, cyclical, and dialectical modes of historiography embedded in Hinduism, Buddhism, Shamanism, Confucianism, and other beliefs. Asian civilizational resources are so rich that an encounter with Western IR easily diverges and makes a silenced Asian perspective appealing again to some people. The arriving West typically caused abrupt changes in institutions; therefore, the encounter created uncertainty for everyone in a locality and left the choice of the practical purposes and the recombination of identities constantly shifting in future generations. Re-incurring civilizational resources used to appeal to values that have ostensibly disappeared yet always remained strategically viable.

A particular IR agenda that may evolve from these temporal sensibilities leads to curiosity about patience—Why are some actors more patient than others during a conflict? Why is one more patient at one time, in one issue area, and with one particular actor than at another time, in another issue area, or with another actor? What is the emerging alternative for which one judges it is worth waiting? How does a politically silenced value persist and resurface many decades later? Such an agenda redirects the epistemological pressure of a sited identity, which enacts an imagined subjectivity among the subaltern population, toward an inquiry into temporal choice. Likewise, it can rescue Western IR from its epistemological negligence regarding the element of patience, so that every policy-making process can reflect on the dialectics between the layers of history, in the population targeted by the West, as well as in the West itself. For the disciples of post-Western IR, patience may as well engender the effective resistance that they desire, as silenced values are revived without anyone intending this at the moment of subjugation. For Western IR, cycles and patience are now accessible through this Asian epistemology. Consequently, nonsolution, noninvolvement, and nonintervention have become considered as rational and as goal-driven strategizing at any given time.

Worlding the West and Global IR

In the same vein, Asia contributes to global IR with its premodern IR practices that bred or reflected systemic cultures that were unheard of in the contemporary West. Global IR may have overstated the innocence of the West in light of the premodern Western travelers and the arrival of the modernizing West, since their initial contacts acquired intellectual perspectives and practices from Asia. Therefore, proposing the addition of non-Western IR to Western IR for the sake of global IR makes less sense than retrieving the early worlding experiences of Western IR. Reworlding the non-West composes an important stance of post-Western IR to reconstitute Western IR with sited identities. Provincializing the West creates a sister agenda. By contrast, worlding the West would allow global IR to achieve epistemological equality between the West and the non-West, as if they have already been mutually constituted in their genesis. The agenda of worlding the West would call for research on how Western IR has reconstructed and incorporated imagined Asian resources and practiced IR into an ostensibly Western hegemonic expansion.

Worlding or reworlding the West obliges nuanced analyses of the manner and reason regarding which various Western sites have appropriated certain Asian resources differently or similarly to one another. Unlike the non-West in post-Western IR, the West combines different kinds of sites, each owning an intellectual trajectory and a genealogy of acquiring Asian components in its self-understanding. The study of Orientalism, critical as it may be, is a model project of the manner in which the West has become Western. The use of Chinese civilizational resources, such as Confucianism, Buddhism, and Sun Tzu's *The Art of War*, in international management is a practical example of worlding the West (Palmer and Siegler 2017). Ultimately, global IR does not merely combine the West and the non-West. Instead, it is a study of the manner in which the West and non-West have mutually constituted each other intellectually, practically, historically, and presently, as well as multilaterally and bilaterally.

Ontological Escape and National Schools of IR

Whereas the quest for national schools of IR defeats the purpose of global IR because of its proclivity for national distinction over learning or exchange, national schools nevertheless serve as a foundation for global IR in their rediscovery of real or imagined indigenous roots. In addition, the construction of national schools takes advantage of historical conditions that have not been experienced by Western IR, which evidently include colonialism, socialism, and dependency. The quest for national schools of IR in China, India, Korea, Japan, the ASEAN, and even in the highly Westernized academic circle of Iran involves allies of both the global and post-Western IRs in their shared alienation from as well as resistance to Western IR. However, Asia is actually brimming with the spirit of escape. This statement is especially true as judged by (1) the impossibility of defining Asianness, (2) a long history of vast migration, and (3) the state as indistinguishable from society, with the consequence that, maximally, Asian nationalities indicate strategic essentialism that prepares the population for the cycles of entry and retreat in the long run, depending on the context, volition, and strategy. National schools demonstrate transient, if not pseudo, ontology at best. With the purpose of satisfying or aborting resistance, they will submerge. To that extent, ontology is essentially role-play. Role-altercasting is the style of national schools in Asia.

Asian ontology as a role points to a kind of anthropology of IR that collects ways in which IR is functional to the survival of a particular population so that its strategy of representation as well as nonrepresentation must adapt to the conditions. It shows the other side of the national schools in the sense that the quest for sitedness, once it becomes suppressive, engenders postnational populations that appropriate national identities into inexpressible opportunism. One likely agenda would be to examine the strength and persistence of the nations, under the influence of national IR, in requesting the performance of other actors, internally and externally, to comply with their scripts of national IR. A follow-up agenda would be the flexibility of these nations to shift to another ontological claim and commit to an entirely contradictive altercasting. An additional and perhaps more powerful agenda would be reflexive altercasting regarding the adaptation of particular Asian populations to the perceived expectations of different others and yet the exemption from the need for integral subjectivity. Their performance of self-denial would be simultaneously subversive to the national schools and deconstructive of Western IR.

Post-Asianness and the Relational Turns

Critical IR is most sensitive to difference, thus turning the universal West into something else, adding the non-West to complete the globe, or resisting the West entirely. Therefore, a difference always reveals itself when arguing that compared parties constitute each other's a priori worlds intersubjectively. The relational turn, accordingly, questions this "difference" approach by tracing the practices that, historically, open up the space where interactive actors necessarily constitute one another. Asia most significantly contributes to the relational turn in terms of the belief in and capacity for complex relationships. The relational turn denies that the West, or non-West, should adhere to a substantialist ontology. Instead, they are process-driven subjectivities that only make sense in a norm-sharing network. Hence, the relational turn requires one first to identify the relationships before studying their constituting parties. However, while remedying the obsession with difference and self-identity, the relational turn nonetheless exhibits several tendencies similar to the aforementioned ones. The relational turn continues to adopt a forward-moving historiography. Likewise, it attends to subjectivity, agency, and identity, albeit constituted by relationships. Moreover, it focuses on the constitution of the multilateral relationships of individual agencies or actors. By contrast, Asianness, or a kind of post-Asianness, indicates the strategic, transient acknowledgment of any two actors, imagining their shared Asianness. Sharing beyond the bilateral context would negatively affect the fluidity required by such relational role-playing.

First, a research agenda of post-Asian relationships may return to the bilateral relationship and interrogate the manner in which a multilaterally constituted identity can be flexibly revised in a dyadic context. Such revision relies on the capacity to incur accessible resources particularly to the two parties involved because of their past relationships. Cycles, reworlding, and altercasting would be most vivid in a bilateral relationship, either because the relationship is familiar to both sides or because it is easy to renegotiate. Bilateral relationality is transcendent in two other senses. First, it makes arrangements for unenforceable multilateral rules by relaxing them through a certain reciprocal concession. This relaxation facilitates the continuation of any ostensibly multilateral rule. Second, bilateral relationality enables nuanced studies of the process of reconnection whereby relationships rise and fall between any two agencies. Consequently, one can discern the ways in which a Western site and a non-Western site are always mutually constituted in a pluriversal world. This leads to the conclusion that all Western sites are potentially post-Asian sites, given properly incurred civilizational resources to establish such a reconnection successfully.

An Ethical Note

Whose responsibility is it that the West does not understand Asia, granted that both constructed role identities can be practiced differently? One answer points to Eurocentrism (Okano and Sugimoto 2017; Paramore 2016; B. Goh 2011). However, if people who promote national schools in Asia can understand the West, nonetheless, Eurocentrism must be a likewise minor issue. In other words, as long as the West possesses sufficient knowledge of Asia, even Orientalism cannot block understanding. The West cannot have such knowledge, though, unless Asian scholars provide it (Bilgin 2016b; Farid Alatas 2015; K. Chang 2003). The second answer regarding responsibility, therefore, points to Asian scholars who are slow to provide knowledge. Why so slow? The third possible answer regarding responsibility points to the academic culture—the debating style of the West might seem too uncomfortable for Asian scholars, embedded in the relational sensibilities; Eurocentrism might discourage equal or candid exchanges between the West and Asia; and Asian scholars might feel too inferior to reveal differences. When such notions are internalized in a certain way, some Asian scholars can even be more hostile to Asian IR than their Western colleagues. Perhaps, an imagined rise of Asia or China has a chance partially to ameliorate this irony.

Notes

Chapter 1

1. Chinese culture has its own prior resemblance, most noticeably registered in the amorphous notions of Dao (the Way, or acceptance of all), yi (oneness, or acceptance by all) or Qi (vapor, or the formation of all) (Ames and Hall, 2001; Hall and Ames 1995).

2. Alexander Wendt's (Wendt and Duvall 2008) analogy of being "contacted by an alien civilization" (Wendt 1992, 405) is applicable here.

Chapter 2

1. *BBC News*, "China Media: Li Keqiang's Pakistan Visit," May 24, 2013, http://www.bbc.com/news/world-asia-china-22650591.

2. Interview with Ambassador Shahid M. Amin, by Swaran Singh, March 10, 2012, http://www.china-studies.taipei/comm2/InterviewP01.pdf.

3. Interview with Tan Chung, May 18–19, 30, 2008, http://www.china-studies.taipei/act/india01.doc.

4. Interview with Ambassador Shahid M. Amin.

5. Interview with Ambassador Shahid M. Amin.

6. Interview with Ambassador Harun ur Rashid, by Reena Marwah and Swaran Singh, March 2, 2013, http://www.china-studies.taipei/comm2/InterviewB01.pdf.

7. Interview with Ambassador Humayun Kabir, by Swaran Singh, March 1, 2012, http://www.china-studies.taipei/comm2/InterviewB04.pdf.

8. Interview with Aman Memon, December 8, 2016, http://www.china-studies.taipei/comm2/InterviewPak%20Aman%20Memon_locked.pdf.

9. Interview with Aman Memon.

10. Mehtab Haider, Muhammad Saleh Zaafir, and Obaid Abrar Khan, "Pakistan Returns to World Trade," *The News*, August 30, 2016, https://www.thenews.com.pk/print/146372-Pakistan-returns-to-world-trade; Arif Anees, "Pakistan Has

Assumed New Identity Due to Economic Turnaround: Ahsan Iqbal," Associated Press of Pakistan, November 21, 2016, https://archive.pakistantoday.com.pk/2016/11/22/pakistan-has-assumed-new-identity-due-to-economic-turnaround-ahsan-iqbal/.

11. "Foreign Minister Wang Yi Meets the Press," Top Stories, March 8, 2017, Ministry of Foreign Affairs of the People's Republic of China, http://www.fmprc.gov.cn/mfa_eng/zxxx_662805/t1444204.shtml.

12. Two of his edited volumes are particularly keen on this multidirectional exchange (see Katzenstein 2012b, 2010; Kavalski 2016b; Bilgin and Ling 2017).

Chapter 3

1. See the introduction in Katan 2019.
2. The subtitle is a quote from Spivak 1988.
3. Sun Yatsen's speech on "pan-Asianism," on November 28, 1924, in Kobe, Japan, http://news.ifeng.com/history/special/sunzhongshan/200906/0627_7072_1222743.shtml.
4. All Sun Yatsen references are to Sun 1989, his complete works, by volume and page. The original dates of the individual writings are added in brackets.
5. Happiness in East Asia appears interchangeable with happiness in Yadong. This is perhaps the only useage of East Asia that likewise indicates solidarity as opposed to autonomy.

Chapter 4

1. This may result in longing for territory, though (Brophy 2016). Spatiality and temporality are derived from the objective and subjective standards of the previous chapters.
2. Cosmopolitan Christianity is named cultural Christianity in some of the literature (Zhuo 2015; Leung 2003) to highlight its cross-cultural characteristics.
3. This chapter will not explore whether Confucianism is ultimately a religion or not. It treats Confucianism as a faith in filial piety, practiced primarily through the ritual of ancestral as well as heavenly worship. Such rituals enable the imagination of the common ancestors of all Chinese.
4. This echoes S. Liu ([1939] 2011).
5. Barmé interestingly translates the English notion "new sinology" as "post-sinology" (後漢學) in Chinese.

Chapter 5

1. A sentiment revealed in the oral history of a good number of senior sinologists, to be discussed later.

2. Oral history of Phan Van Cac, http://www.china-studies.taipei/act/vietnam_04C.doc. The interview and all those following are accessible at the webpage of the Research and Educational Center for China Studies and Cross-Taiwan Strait Relations, which is affiliated at the Department of Political Science of National Taiwan University, http://www.china-studies.taipei.

3. Nguyen Huy Hoang enlightens me on this phenomenon.

4. Oral history of Nguyen Bang Tuong, http://www.china-studies.taipei/comm2/vietnam_06ch.pdf.

5. I benefit from an interview with Tran Thuy Anh on this particular reflection.

6. Oral history of Ly Viet Dung, http://www.china-studies.taipei/comm2/InterviewV%20Ly%20Viet%20Dung.pdf.

7. Oral history of Phan Van Cac.

8. Oral history of Le Huy Tieu, http://www.china-studies.taipei/comm2/InterviewV%20Le%20Huy%20Tieu%20Chinese.pdf.

9. Oral history of Le Huy Tieu.

10. I am indebted to Vu Duoan Luan for this observation.

11. I am indebted to Nguyen Tran Tien on this reflection.

12. I am indebted to Nguyen Huy Hoang on this observation.

13. I am likewise indebted to Nguyen Huy Hoang on this observation.

14. Oral history of Nguyen Huy Quy, http://www.china-studies.taipei/act/vietnam03anticopy.pdf.

15. Oral history of Phan Van Cac.

16. Nguyen Van Hong shared his own reflection with me in an interview.

17. Oral history of Nguyen Ton Nhan, http://www.china-studies.taipei/comm2/interview%20VN%20NGUYEN%20TON%20NHAN%20ch.pdf.

18. Oral history of Hồ Sĩ Hiệp, http://www.china-studies.taipei/comm2/InterviewV%20Ho%20Si%20Hiep.pdf.

19. Oral history of Pham Thi Hao, http://www.china-studies.taipei/comm2/interview%20VN%20PHAM%20THI%20HAO%20ch.pdf.

20. Oral history of Pham Tu Chau, http://www.china-studies.taipei/comm2/InterviewV%20Pham%20Tu%20Chau%20Chinese.pdf.

21. Pham Quang Minh shared this general impression with me in an interview.

22. Phung Thi Hue shared her experiences with me in an interview.

23. Nguyen Van Hong enlightened me on this particular reflection in an interview.

24. Oral history of Nguyen Van Hong.

25. Oral history of Ha Kien Hanh, http://www.china-studies.taipei/comm2/vietnam_13.pdf.

26. Pham Quang Minh enlightened me about the situation during this period.

27. My impression is indebted to Dao Thi Tam Khann's research experiences.

28. Oral history of Nguyen Van Khang, http://www.china-studies.taipei/comm2/InterviewV%20Nguyen%20Van%20Khang%20Chinese%201.pdf.

29. Oral history of Ha Kien Hanh.

30. Oral history of Ly Viet Dung.

31. Oral history of Nguyen Bang Tuong.

32. Oral history of Pham Thi Hao; as well as that of Tran Tuan Man, http://www.china-studies.taipei/comm2/InterviewV%20Tran%20Tuan%20Man.pdf.

33. Phung Thi Huy shares her son's learning experiences in China as positive, for example.

34. Oral history of Ly Viet Dung.

35. I am indebted to Pham Quang Minh on the effect of disloyalty and betrayal directed at Vietnam among Chinese.

36. Pham Quang Minh agrees that confrontations are by all means transient from the Vietnamese perspectives.

37. Oral history of Vu Khieu, http://www.china-studies.taipei/comm2/vietnam_07ch.pdf. Also, see the oral history of Nguyen Van Khang. In addition, one anonymous interviewee says that, having lived in the border area since childhood, she can see no distinction between the two peoples except with regard to the language they each use.

38. Oral history of Tran Le Bao, http://www.china-studies.taipei/comm2/InterviewV%20Tran%20Le%20Bao%20Chinese.pdf; as well as that of Nguyen Khue, http://www.china-studies.taipei/comm2/interview%20VN%20NGUYEN%20KHUE%20ch.pdf.

39. Oral history of Nguyen Huy Quy; as well as that of Phan Van Cac.

40. Oral history of Nguyen Ton Nhan.

41. Oral history of Tran Xuan De, http://www.china-studies.taipei/comm2/InterviewV%20Tran%20Xuan%20De.pdf.

42. I am indebted to both Tran Hoang Quan and Nguyen Tran Tien for this observation.

43. Oral history of Le Huy Thieu.

44. Hoang Thu Anh enlightened me regarding the impression that the Vietnamese easily distinguish the Chinese people from the Chinese government and understand that the desire to control Vietnam is primarily a government policy.

45. More than that between China and any other country, according to Ho Si Hiep. See his oral history.

46. Oral history of Vu Khieu.

47. Oral history of Nguyen Bang Tuong.

48. Sinology enables one to understand modern nationalism and the thought of Ho Chi Minh. See the oral history of Nguyen Van Hong.

49. Oral history of Buu Cam, http://www.china-studies.taipei/comm2/interview%20VN%20BUU%20CAM%20ch.pdf.

50. Oral history of Pham Tu Chau.

51. Oral history of Cao Tu Thanh, https://www.china-studies.taipei/comm2/interview%20VN%20CAO%20TU%20THANH%20ch.pdf.

52. So, China, assessed by democracy and peace, is a harbinger for Vietnam, assessed by the same criteria. See the oral history of Tran Le Bao.

53. Oral history of Nguyen Van Khan.

54. Strongly emphasized by many sinologists; for example, see the oral histories of Tran Le Bao, Nguyen Ton Nhan, and Pham Thi Hao.

55. Oral history of Phan Van Cac; as well as that of Vu Khieu.

56. Oral history of Tran Xuan De.

57. Oral history of Tran Tuan Man; as well as that of Nguyen Khue, who expresses pride and satisfaction in becoming a sinologist.

58. I am indebted to Nguyen Huy Hoang for this reflection.

59. I am indebted to Tran Viet Thai for this reflection.

60. I am indebted to Nguyen Tran Tien, who shared the brotherhood analogy stated by his father.

61. The anonymous interviewee uses "PGS TS Tran Le" as a pen name.

62. From the oral history of Tran Tuan Man.

Chapter 6

1. The following introduction is based entirely on the oral history of Hsu, interviewed by Li-chen Chiu on April 24, June 10, and July 13, 2009 at the Japan Research Institute in Taiwan, http://www.china-studies.taipei/act/tw-7.doc. The interviews in the chapter, with the exception of Che-hsiung Shih, come from the Research and Educational Center of China Studies and Cross-Taiwan Strait Relations, affiliated with the Department of Political Science, National Taiwan University.

2. The following introduction is based entirely on the oral history of Yeh, interviewed by Yuan-kui Chu on November 11, 18, and 23, and December 30, 2009, at Shih Hsin University, http://www.china-studies.taipei/comm2/InterviewTW17.pdf.

3. Shih (1918–2019) is better known in English as Su Beng, which is his name pronounced/spelled in Taiwanese/Hokkien. The following introduction is based entirely on the oral history, interviewed by Hong-lin Yeh at Shih's residence (with dates of interview not provided), http://www.china-studies.taipei/comm2/InterviewT31.pdf.

4. The following introduction is based entirely on the oral history of Chen, interviewed by Huan-lei Shao, Li-pen Wang, and Huang-ming Liu on May 29, 2010, February 4, March 20, April 22, and August 16, 2011, in his apartment, http://www.china-studies.taipei/comm2/InterviewT%20chen%20pon%20ren.pdf.

5. The following introduction is based entirely on the TV interview coordinated by Zen Master Hun Yuan in his Global WXTV Peace Forum, https://www.youtube.com/watch?v=HItzaXEsScM.

6. The following introduction is based entirely on the oral history of Chang, by Hong-lin Yeh on August 12 and 18, 2010, in Chang's office, http://china-studies.taipei/comm2/InterviewT%20A.pdf and http://china-studies.taipei/comm2/InterviewT%20B.pdf.

Chapter 8

1. Interview with Ambassador Humayun Kabir, by Swaran Singh, March 1, 2012, http://www.china-studies.taipei/comm2/InterviewB04.pdf.
2. Interview with Ambassador Humayun Kabir.
3. Numbers are collected separately for each selected country from *World Economic Outlook Database* of International Monetary Fund. The database that contains country reports by year is accessible at https://www.imf.org/en/Publications/SPROLLs/world-economic-outlook-databases#sort=%40imfdate%20descending.
4. This project, commissioned by the Research and Educational Center for China Studies and Cross–Taiwan Strait Relations of the Department of Political Science at National Taiwan University, has been executed by the Institute of China Studies at the University of Malay since 2012, For details of this project, see the item Malaysia on the list of the country projects at http://www.china-studies.taipei/act02.php.

Chapter 9

1. Regarding Kuo's own dilemma as he perceived it, the Kuo Pao Kun Foundation recommends that its readers should read P. Kuo 2001 (104–5); for further discussion on Chinese producers and film artists between the market and art or educational function, see Zhu and Rosen 2010.
2. Also see, for example, Tarn 1990.
3. For more discussion on Gao Xingjian's use of form of art to express his transcendental politics, see Quah 2004.
4. For Kuo Paokun's cultural consciousness, see Quah 2008.
5. One widely cited work is his *The Silly Little Girl and the Funny Old Tree*.
6. These works are *Hey, Wake Up!* (1968), *The Struggle* (1969), and *The Spark of Youth* (1970).
7. Some of Kuo's students actually attended Barba's workshops.
8. Also see, for example, Tarn 1990.
9. See also Tian 1997.
10. Regarding Yung's idea of hurting the magnificent (傷大雅), see Ju-chih Chang 2012.

Chapter 10

1. Interview with Chen Peng-jen, May 29, 2010, February 4, March 20, April 22, and August 16, 2011, http://www.china-studies.taipei/comm2/InterviewT%20chen%20pon%20ren.pdf.

2. One typical example is P. Tsai 1971; also see the comparable case of Korea in Fujitani 2011.
3. This has been the Presbyterian tradition (Sanneh 1993, 17).
4. Note, though, the first leader of the exiled Kuomintang—Chiang Kai-shek—was a faithful Christian, as were many of his associates, too.
5. Both incidents were recorded in Coe 1993 (235).
6. For a Chinese translation, see Lai 2009 (55). The joint public statement is "Statement from the Taiwan Inter-church Consultation," October 9, 1985, http://english.pct.org.tw/Article/enArticle_public_19851009.html.
7. Including the Council for World Mission, Basel Mission, Overseas Missionary Fellowship, Christian Church (Disciples of Christ) in the US and Canada, Presbyterian Church (USA), United Church of Christ in the USA, Taiwan Christian Church Council of North America, Taiwan Christian Church Council of North America, United Church of Christ in Japan, Jesus Christ Church in Japan, Taipei Korean Community Church of Presbyterian Church of Korea, and Presbyterian Church in Taiwan (Taiwanese Church Mission Association, 1987, 1).

Chapter 11

1. These are from those oral history files that are produced by the project on intellectual history of China studies available at the Research and Educational Center for China Studies and Cross-Taiwan Strait Relations. The center is affiliated with the Department of Political Science at National Taiwan University. To access the oral history files and other interviews of the same kind in different regions, use http://www.china-studies.taipei.
2. My categorization is, in principle, in line with Betti's distinction between recognitive, reproductive and normative hermeneutics (Betti 1987).
3. For more discussion, see Schwarcz 1998.

Chapter 12

1. The cover story—"She could lead the only Chinese democracy and that makes Beijing nervous" (Rauhala 2015)—of the East Asia edition of *Time* magazine, June 19, 2015.
2. Pro-independence politics risks overly escalating the cross–Taiwan Straits tension to request US direct and overinvolvement; anti-independence politics risks overly entrapping Taiwan into China's sphere of influence to ruin US strategic control over Taiwan.

References

Abbas, M. Ackbar. 1997. *Hong Kong: Culture and Politics of Disappearance.* Hong Kong: Hong Kong University Press.

Abul-Magd, Zeinab. 2012. "Occupying Tahrir Square: The Myths and the Realities of the Egyptian Revolution." *South Atlantic Quarterly* 111 (3): 565–72.

Acharya, Amitav. 2008. "The Spread of Security Communities: Communities of Practice, Self-Restraint, and NATO's Post–Cold War Transformation." *European Journal of International Relations* 14 (2): 195–230.

———. 2014a. *Rethinking Power, Institutions and Ideas in World Politics: Whose IR?* Abingdon, UK: Routledge.

———. 2014b. "Global International Relations (IR) and Regional Worlds: A New Agenda for International Studies." *International Studies Quarterly* 58 (4): 647–59.

Adler, Emanuel. 2005. *Communitarian International Relations: The Epistemic Foundation of International Relations.* London: Routledge.

Aguiar, Marian. 2011. *Tracking Modernity: India's Railway and the Culture of Mobility.* Minneapolis: University of Minnesota Press.

Ahmad, Anwar. 2015. "UAE an Exemplary Model of Multi-religion Cooperation." *The National* (United Arab Emirates), March 19. http://www.thenational.ae/uae/religious-leaders-uae-an-exemplary-model-of-multi-faith-cooperation.

Aljunied, Syed Muhd Khairudin. 2009. *Colonialism, Violence and Muslims in Southeast Asia: The Maria Hertogh Controversy and Its Aftermath.* London: Routledge.

Ambrosio, Thomas. 2012. "The Rise of the 'China Model' and 'Beijing Consensus': Evidence of Authoritarian Diffusion?" *Contemporary Politics* 18 (4): 381–99.

Amae, Yoshihisa. 2011. "Pro-colonial or Postcolonial? Appropriation of Japanese Colonial Heritage in Present-Day Taiwan." *Journal of Current Chinese Affairs* 40 (1): 19–62.

Ames, Roger, and David Hall. 2001. *Focusing the Familiar: A Translation and Philosophical Interpretation of the Zhongyong.* Honolulu: University of Hawaii Press, 2001.

Anees, Arif. 2016. "Pakistan Has Assumed New Identity Due to Economic Turnaround: Ahsan Iqbal." *Associated Press of Pakistan*, November 21. https://www.app.com.pk/pakistan-has-assumed-new-identity-due-to-economic-turnaround-ahsan-iqbal/.

Arase, David, ed. 2016. *China's Rise and Changing Order in East Asia*. New York: Palgrave Macmillan.

Aryodiguno, Harryanto. 2020. "Embedded Anti-Chinese Orientations: The Dutch Occupation and Its Legacies." In *Colonial Legacies and Contemporary Studies of China and Chineseness: Unlearning Boundaries, Strategizing Self*, ed. Chih-yu Shih, Mariko Tanigaki, Prapin Manomaivibool, and Swaran Singh, 121–46. Singapore: World Scientific.

Assmann, Aleida. 2006. "Memory, Individual and Collective." In *The Oxford Handbook of Contextual Political Analysis*, ed. Robert E. Goodin and Charles Tilly, 210–24. Oxford: Oxford University Press.

Au, Chi Kin. 2018. "The Academic Role of Hong Kong in the Development of Chinese Culture, 1950s–70s: From the Perspectives of Qian Mu and Luo Xianglin." *China Report* 54 (1): 66–80.

Auguste, Isabelle. 2010. Rethinking the Nation: Apology, Treaty, and Reconciliation in Australia. *National Identities* 12 (4): 425–36.

Auslin, Michael. 2020. "Trump's New Realism in China: Critics Aside, the Administration Does Have a Strategy, and It Is Based on Reciprocity." *Foreign Policy*, July 7. https://foreignpolicy.com/2020/07/07/trumps-new-realism-in-china.

Aydinli, Ersel, and Gonca Biltekin. 2017. "Time to Quantify Turkey's Foreign Affairs: Setting Quality Standards for a Maturing International Relations Discipline." *International Studies Perspectives* 18 (3): 267–87.

———, eds. 2018. *Widening the World of International Relations: Homegrown Theorizing*. Abingdon, UK: Routledge.

Babones, Salvatore J. 2017. *American Tianxia: Chinese Money, American Power, and the End of History*. Bristol, UK: Policy Press.

Bai, Ronnie. 1998. "Dances with Mei Lanfang: Brecht and the Alienation Effect." *Comparative Drama* 32 (3): 389–433.

Barbalet, Jack M. 2001. *Emotion, Social Theory, and Social Structure: A Macrosociological Approach*. Cambridge: Cambridge University Press.

———. 2014 "Greater Self, Lesser Self: Dimensions of Self-interest in Chinese Filial Piety." *Journal for the Theory of Social Behaviour* 44 (2): 186–205.

Barclay, George W. 2016. *Colonial Development and Population in Taiwan*. Princeton, NJ: Princeton University Press.

Barmé, Geremie R. 2005. "Towards a New Sinology." *Chinese Studies Association of Australia Newsletter*, no. 31. http://www.csaa.org.au/wp-content/uploads/2014/04/CSAA_Newsletter_31.pdf.

Baugus, Bruce P. 2014. *China's Reforming Churches*. Grand Rapids, MI: Reformation Heritage Books.

Beigel, Fernanda, ed. 2013. *The Politics of Academic Autonomy in Latin America*. Farnham, UK: Ashgate.

Bell, Macalester. 2013. *Hard Feelings: The Moral Psychology of Contempt.* Oxford: Oxford University Press.

Benn, James A. 2007. *Burning for the Buddha: Self-immolation in Chinese Buddhism.* Honolulu: University of Hawaii Press.

Berenskoetter, Felix. 2007. "Friends, There Are No Friends? An Intimate Reframing of the International." *Millennium* 3 (3): 647–76.

Bernard, Mitchell. 1996. "States, Social Forces, and Regions in Historical Time: Toward a Critical Political Economy of Eastern Asia." *Third World Quarterly* 17 (4): 649–65.

Betti, Emilio. 1987. "On a General Theory of Interpretation: The Raison d'Etre of Hermeneutics." *American Journal of Jurisprudence* 32 (1): 245–68.

Bilgin, Pinar. 2008. "Thinking Past 'Western' IR." *Third World Quarterly* 29 (1), 5–23.

———. 2012. "Security in the Arab World and Turkey: Differently Different." In *Thinking International Relations Differently*, ed. Arlene B. Tickner and David L. Blaney, 27–47. London: Routledge.

———. 2016a. *The International in Security, Security in the International.* Abingdon, UK: Routledge.

———. 2016b. "How to Remedy Eurocentrism in IR? A Complement and a Challenge for *The Global Transformation*." *International Theory* 8 (3): 492–501.

———. 2020. "Opening Up International Relations, or, How I Learned to Stop Worrying and Love Non-Western IR." In *Handbook of Critical International Relations*, ed. Steven C. Roach, 12–28. Cheltenham, UK: Edward Elgar Publishing.

Bilgin, Pinar, and L. H. M. Ling, eds. 2017. *Asia in International Relations: Unlearning Imperial Power Relations.* Abingdon, UK: Routledge.

Blaney, David L., and Arlene B. Tickner. 2017. "International Relations in the Prison of Colonial Modernity." *International Relations* 31 (1): 71–75.

Bond, Michael Harris, ed. 1986. *The Psychology of Chinese People.* Oxford: Oxford University Press.

———, ed. 2010. *Oxford Handbook of Chinese Psychology.* Oxford: Oxford University Press.

Bourdieu, Pierre. 1977. *Outline of a Theory of Practice.* Cambridge: Cambridge University Press.

Bovingdon, Gardner. 2010. *The Uyghurs: Strangers in Their Own Land.* New York: Columbia University Press.

Bradley, Mark Philip. 2004. "Becoming *Van Minh*: Civilizational Discourse and Visions of the Self in Twentieth-Century Vietnam." *Journal of World History* 15 (1): 65–83.

Brennan, Michael J. 1994. "Incentives, Rationality, and Society." *Journal of Applied Corporate Finance* 7 (2): 31–39.

Breslin, Shaun. 2011. "The 'China Model' and the Global Crisis: from Friedrich List to a Chinese Mode of Governance?" *International Affairs* 87 (6): 1323–43.

Brook, Timothy, and Gregory Blue, eds. 2002. *China and Historical Capitalism: Genealogies of Sinological Knowledge*. Cambridge: Cambridge University Press.
Brophy, David. 2016. *Uyghur Nation: Reform and Revolution on the Russia-China Frontier*. Cambridge, MA: Harvard University Press.
Brown, Kerry. 2019. *Contemporary China*. London: Red Globe.
Bukowski, William M., Clairneige Motzoi, and Felicia Meyer. 2009. "Friendship as Process, Function, and Outcome." In *Handbook of Peer Interactions, Relationships and Groups*, ed. Kenneth H. Rubin, William M. Bukowski, and Brett Laursen, 217–31. New York: Guilford Press.
Bunskoek, Raoul, and Chih-yu Shih. 2021. "'Community of Common Destiny' as Post-Western Regionalism: Rethinking China's Belt and Road Initiative from a Confucian Perspective." *Uluslararasi Iliskiler* 18 (70): 85–101.
Burke, Peter J. 1991. "Identity Processes and Social Stress." *American Sociological Review* 56 (6): 836–49.
Buzan, Barry. 2010. "Globalization and Identity: Is World Society Possible?" *Journal of Zhejiang University (Humanities and Social Sciences)* 40 (5): 5–14.
Cagle, Megan. 2016. "Faith and Community Leaders Launch National Refugees Welcome Initiative." Church World Service, May 21. http://cwsglobal.org/faith-and-community-leaders-launch-national-refugees-welcome-initiative/.
Calichman, Richard F. 2010. *Takeuchi Yoshimi: Displacing the West*. Ithaca, NY: Cornell University Press.
Callahan, William A. 2004. *A Contingent State: Greater China and Transnational Relations*. Minneapolis: University of Minnesota Press.
———. 2008. "Chinese Visions of World Order: Post-hegemonic or New Hegemony." *International Studies Review* 10 (4): 749–61.
———. 2012. *China: The Pessoptimist Nation*. Oxford: Oxford University Press.
Callero, Peter L. 1994. "From Role-Playing to Role-Using: Understanding Role as Resource." *Social Psychology Quarterly* 57 (3): 228–43.
Carlson, Allen. 2009. "A Flawed Perspective: The Limitations Inherent within the Study of Chinese Nationalism." *Nation and Nationalism* 15 (1): 20–35.
Chan, Hok Yin. 2018. "The Experiences and Participation of Immigrant Intellectuals in the Cultural Development of Hong Kong: A Study of Tang Junyi." *China Report* 54 (1): 48–65.
Chan, Joseph. 2001. "Territorial Boundaries and Confucianism." In *Boundaries and Justice: Diverse Ethical Perspectives*, ed. David Miller and Sohail H. Hashmi, 89–111. Princeton, NJ: Princeton University Press.
Chang, Bi-yu. 2015. *Place, Identity, and National Imagination in Post-war Taiwan*. London: Routledge.
Chang, Jonah. 2012. *Jonah Shoki Coe: An Ecumenical Life in Context*. Taipei: Wangchunfeng. Also reprinted in Geneva, by WCC Publications.
Chang, Ju-chih. 2012. "Denny Yung, the Founding Father of the Culture of Hong Kong" (香港文化之父：榮念曾). *Times Weekly* (時代週刊), August 30. https://cul.sohu.com/20120830/n351881159.shtml.

Chang, Kang-i Sun. 2003. "From Difference to Complementarity: The Interaction of Western and Chinese Studies." *Tamkang Review* 34 (1): 41–64.
Chang, Lung-chih, and Min-chin Kay Chiang. 2012. "From Colonial Site to Cultural Heritage." *Newsletter of International Institute for Asian Studies*, no. 59, 28–29.
Chang, Pi-chun. 2009. *An Examination on Chinese Alternative Discourses: Cross-cultural Perspectives on Chinese Nationalism, Postmodernism, and Neo-Confucianism*. Saarbrücken, Ger.: VDM Verlag.
Chau, Adam Yuet. 2008. *Miraculous Response: Doing Popular Religion in Contemporary China*. Stanford, CA: Stanford University Press.
Chellaney, Brahma. 2012. "Rising Powers, Rising Tensions: The Troubled China-India Relationship." *SAIS Review of International Affairs* 32 (2): 99–108.
Chen, Boyu. 2017. "Sovereignty or Identity? Significance of the Diaoyutai/Senkaku Islands Dispute for Taiwan." In *Asia in International Relations: Unlearning Imperial Power Relations*, ed. Pinar Bilgin and L. H. M Ling, 86–96. Abingdon, UK: Routledge.
Chen, Boyu, and Ching-chang Chen. 2021. "Rethinking China-Taiwan Relations as a Yin-yang Imbalance: Political Healing by Taiwanese Buddhist Organisations." *Third World Quarterly*. https://doi.org/10.1080/01436597.2021.1960158.
Chen, Ching-chang. 2011. "The Absence of Non-Western IR Theory in Asia Reconsidered." *International Relations of the Asia-Pacific* 11 (1): 1–23.
———. 2012. "The Impossibility of Building Indigenous Theories in a Hegemonic Discipline: The Case of Japanese International Relations." *Asian Perspective* 36 (3): 463–92.
———. 2015. "The Weakest Link? Explaining Taiwan's Response to the U.S. Rebalancing Strategy." In *United States Engagement in the Asia Pacific: Perspectives from Asia*, ed. Yoichiro Sato and See Seng Tan, 89–114. New York: Cambria Press.
Chen, Ching-chang, and Kosuke Shimizu. 2019. "International Relations from the Margins: The Westphalian Meta-narratives and Counter-narratives in Okinawa-Taiwan relations." *Cambridge Review of International Affairs* 32 (4): 521–40.
Chen, David W. 2010. "China Emerges as a Scapegoat in Campaign Ads." *New York Times*, October 9.
Chen, Julie Yu-wen. 2016. Review of *On the Fringes of the Harmonious Society: Tibetans and Uyghurs in Socialist China*, by Trine Brox and Ildikó Bellér-Hann. *Asian Ethnicity* 17 (2): 318–20.
Chen, Kuan-hsing. 1998. "Introduction: The Decolonization Question." In *Trajectories: Inter-Asia Cultural Studies*, ed. Kuan-hsing Chen, 1–55. London: Routledge.
———. 2010. *Asia as Method: Toward Deimperialization*. Durham, NC: Duke University Press.
Chen, Ming-chi. 2004. "Sinicization and Its Discontents: Cross-Strait Economic Integration and Taiwan's 2004 Presidential Election." *Issues and Studies* 40 (3–4): 334–41.
Chen, Shangsheng. 2015. "The Tributary System and Traditional International Order in East Asian Region: Focusing on Ming and Qing Dynasties of

the 16th Century." *China's Borderland History and Geography Studies*, no. 2, 4–20.

Chen, Tsui-lien. 2002. "Decolonization vs. Recolonization: The Debate over 'T'ai-jen nu-hua' of 1946 in Taiwan." *Taiwan Historical Research* 9 (2): 145–201.

Cheng, Tun-jen. 1989. "Democratizing the Quasi-Leninist Regime in Taiwan." *World Politics* 41 (4): 471–99.

Cheng, Yang-en. 2001. "The Taiwanese Indigenous Theologian Who Devoted to Ecumenism: The Short Biography of Minister C. H. Huang" (獻身普世運動的台灣本土神學家：黃彰輝牧師小傳). *New Messenger* (新使者), no. 64, 30–33.

———. 2005. *Taiwanese Churches with Indigenous Roots: Collected Works on the History of Taiwanese Christian Church* (定根本土的台灣基督教：台灣基督教史研究論集). Tainan: Renguang.

Cheng, Yongqi. 2016. *Tracing the History of Yadong Bookstore* (亞東圖書館歷史追蹤). Hefei: Anhui Education Press.

Cheng, Yu-shek Joseph. 2017. *Mainlandization of Hong Kong*. Hong Kong: City University of Hong Kong Press.

Chin, Ching, and Tsui-wei Li. *The Catalogue of Photographs of Yadong Print and Paint in National Library's Collection* (國家圖書館藏亞東印畫及照片目錄). http://www.nlc.cn/newhxjy/wjsy/yj/gjyj/201112/P020111213341987085270.pdf.

Chin, Chun Wah. 2020. "Development of Japanese Studies in Hong Kong from the Perspectives of Chineseness and Hong Kong's Subjectivity." In *Colonial Legacies and Contemporary Studies of China and Chineseness: Unlearning Boundaries, Strategizing Self*, ed. Chih-yu Shih, Mariko Tanigaki, Prapin Manomaivibool, and Swaran Singh, 193–230. Singapore: World Scientific.

Chin, Ken Pa. 2015. "Joseph and His Brothers 2: Forced to Separate from World Council—Ecumenism Accused of a Move of Pro-Communist or Alliance with Communists" (約瑟和他的弟兄們 2: 被迫與普世教會分離—教會合一運動被指控為親共與容共行為). *Taiwan Church News* (台灣教會公報), no. 3284. http://www.pct.org.tw/article_church.aspx?strBlockID=B00007&strContentID=C2015022500022&strDesc=Y.

Ching Hai. 2011. *I have Come to Take You Home*. Taipei: Supreme Master Ching Hai International Association Publishing.

Ching, Leo T. S. 2000. "'Give Me Japan and Nothing Else!': Postcoloniality, Identity, and the Traces of Colonialism." *South Atlantic Quarterly* 99 (4): 763–88.

———. 2001. *Becoming "Japanese": Colonial Taiwan and the Politics of Identity Formation*. Berkeley: University of California Press.

Cho, Il Hyun, and Seo-Hyun Park. 2011. "Anti-Chinese and Anti-Japanese Sentiments in East Asia: The Politics of Opinion, Distrust, and Prejudice." *Chinese Journal of International Politics* 4 (3): 265–90.

Cho, Young Chul. 2015. "Colonialism and Imperialism in the Quest for a Universalist Korean-Style *International Relations* Theory." *Cambridge Review of International Affairs* 28 (4): 680–700.

Cho, Young Chul, and Yih-Jye Hwang. 2020. "Mainstream IR Theoretical Perspectives and Rising China vis-à-vis the West: The Logic of Conquest, Conversion and Socialisation." *Journal of Chinese Political Science* 25 (2): 175–98.

Choiruzzad, Shofwan Al Banna. 2020. "To Build the World Anew: Decolonisation and Cold War in Indonesia." *Asian Perspective* 44 (2): 209–31.

Chong, Alan. 2020. "Indigenizing the Cold War in Malaysia and Singapore: Interethnic Decolonization, Developmental Syntheses and the Quest for Sovereignty." *Asian Perspective* 44 (2): 179–208.

Chou, Grace Ai-ling. 2012. *Confucianism, Colonialism, and the Cold War: Chinese Cultural Education at Hong Kong's New Asia College, 1949–63*. Leiden: Brill.

Chou, Mark. 2011. "Theorizing China's International Relations." *Australian Review of Public Affairs—Digest*, September. http://www.australianreview.net/digest/2011/09/chou.html.

Chou, Wan-yao. 1991. "The Kominka Movement." PhD diss., Yale University.

Chow, Rey. 1993. *Writing Diaspora: Tactics of Intervention in Contemporary Cultural Studies*. Bloomington: Indiana University Press.

———. 1998. "King Kong in Hong Kong: Watching the Handover from the U.S.A." *Social Text* 55 (16): 93–108.

———. 2014. *Not Like a Native Speaker: On Languaging as a Postcolonial Experience*. New York: Columbia University Press.

Chowdhury, Mahfuzul H. 2013. "Asymmetry in Indo-Bangladesh Relations." *Asian Affairs* 40 (2): 83–103.

Chu, Feng-yi. 2016. "Diverse Facets in Identities and Party Affiliations of Native Taiwanese Elders." *Issues and Studies* 52 (3): 1–24.

Chu, S. 2020. "Whither Chinese IR? The Sinocentric Subject and the Paradox of Tianxia-ism." *International Theory*. https://dx.doi.org/10.1017/S1752971920000214.

Chua, Beng Huat. 2009. "Being Chinese under Official Multiculturalism in Singapore." *Asian Ethnicity* 9 (3): 239–50.

Chuang, Ya-chung. 2016. "Taiwanese Identity in a Global/Local Context: The Use of Abuse of National Consciousness in Taiwan." In *Understanding Modern Taiwan: Essays in Economics, Politics and Social Policy*, ed. Christian Aspalter, 53–65. Abingdon, UK: Routledge.

Chung, Yih-hui. 2002. *China as Creativity: Danny Yung and Politics of Arts in Hong Kong* (創意中國：榮念曾與香港的藝術政治). Taipei: Research and Educational Center for China Studies and Cross-Taiwan Strait Relations, Department of Political Science, National Taiwan University.

Cismas, Ioana. 2014. *Religious Actors and International Law*. New York: Oxford University Press.

Claremont, Yasuko, ed. 2018. *Civil Society and Postwar Pacific Basin Reconciliation: Wounds, Scars, and Healing*. London: Routledge.

Clayton, Cathryn H. 2010. *Sovereignty at the Edge: Macau and the Question of Chineseness*. Cambridge: Harvard University Asia Center.

Clemente, Tina S., and Chih-yu Shih. 2019. *China Studies in the Philippines: Intellectual Paths and the Formation of a Field*. Abingdon, UK: Routledge.

Coe, Shoki (C. H. Huang). 1963a. "Reassessing the Theological Education Required for Today's Late-Coming Holy Church Workers, Part I" (今日教會後進聖工所需的神學教育之再檢討, 上). *Theology and the Church* 3 (2): 60–62.

———. 1963b. "Reassessing the Theological Education Required for Today's Late-Coming Holy Church Workers, Part 2" (今日教會後進聖工所需的神學教育之再檢討, 下). *Theology and the Church* 3 (4): 1–14.

———. 1980. "Contextualization as the Way toward Reform." In *Asian Christian Theology: Emerging Themes*, ed. Douglas J. Elwood, 48–55. Philadelphia: Westminster Press.

———. 1993. *Recollections and Reflections*. Ed. Boris Anderson. Washington, DC: Formosan Christians for Self-Determination.

Cohen, David. 2011. "China and Non-intervention." *Diplomat*, December 3. http://thediplomat.com/2011/12/china-and-non-intervention/.

Cohen, Paul A. 2010. *Discovering History in China: American Historical Writing on the Recent Chinese Past*. New York: Columbia University Press.

Constable, Nicole. 2007. *Maid to Order in Hong Kong: Stories of Migrant Workers*. Ithaca, NY: Cornell University Press.

Cook, Malcolm. 2005. "Taiwan's Identity Challenge." *SAIS Review of International Affairs* 25 (2): 83–92.

Corcuff, Stéphane. 2011. "*Liminality and Taiwan Tropism in a Postcolonial Context—Schemes of National Identification among Taiwan's Mainlanders on the Eve of Kuomintang's Return to Power.*" In *Politics of Difference in Taiwan*, ed. Tak-Wing Ngo and Hong-zen Wang, 34–62. London: Routledge.

———. 2012a. "The Liminality of Taiwan: A Case-Study in Geopolitics." *Taiwan in Comparative Perspective* 4:34–64.

———. 2012b. "Ma Ying-jeou's China-Leaning Policy and the 1683 Fall of the Zheng in Taiwan: A Cross-centuries Geopolitical Comparison." In *National Identity and Economic Interest: Taiwan's Competing Options and Their Implications for Regional Stability*, ed. Peter C. Y. Chow, 93–132. New York: Palgrave Macmillan.

Craib, Ian. 1994. *The Importance of Disappointment*. London: Routledge.

Crook, John H. 2012. *World Crisis and Buddhist Humanism*. Wayne, NJ: New Age. Kindle Edition.

Crossley, Nick. 2010. *Towards Relational Sociology*. London: Routledge.

Culp, Robert, Eddy U, and Wen-hsin Yeh, eds. 2016. *Knowledge Acts in Modern China: Ideas, Institutions, and Identities*. Berkeley: Institute of East Asian Studies, University of California, Berkeley.

Cumings, Bruce. 2004. "Colonial Formations and Deformations: Korea, Taiwan and Vietnam." In *Decolonization: Perspectives from Now and Then*, ed. Prasenjit Duara, 278–98. London: Routledge.

Cunha, Guilherme Lopes. 2017. "The China-Brazil Global Strategic Partnership: Identity and Perspectives." Presented at the International Studies Association Annual Meeting, Baltimore, February.

Cunningham-Cross, Linsay. 2012. "Using the Past to (Re)write the Future: Yan Xuetong, Pre-Qin Thought and China's Rise to Power." *China Information* 26 (2): 219–33.

Demick, Barbara. 2013. "China, Taiwan Protest Fatal Shooting of Fisherman by Philippines." *Los Angeles Times*, May 10. https://www.latimes.com/world/la-xpm-2013-may-10-la-fg-wn-china-taiwan-philippines-fisherman-shot-20130510-story.html.

Dépelteau, Françsois. 2015. "Relational Sociology, Pragmatism, Transactions and Social Fields." *International Review of Sociology* 25 (1): 45–64.

Dessein, Bart. 2016. "Historical Narrative, Remembrance, and the Ordering of the World: A Historical Assessment of China's International Relations." In *China's International Roles: Challenging or Supporting International Order*, ed. Sebastian Harnisch, Sebastian Bersick, and Jörn-Carsten Gottwald, 22–37. Abingdon, UK: Routledge.

Dhavan, Purnima. 2019. "Marking Boundaries and Building Bridges: Persian Scholarly Networks in Mughal Punjab." In *The Persianate World: The Frontiers of a Eurasian Lingua Franca*, ed. Nile Green, 159–74. Berkeley: University of California Press.

Dickson, Bruce. J. 2011. "Updating the China Model." *Washington Quarterly* 34 (4): 39–58.

Dimen, P. Muriel. 2001. "Perversion Is Us? Eight Notes." Psychoanalytic Dialogues 11 (6): 825–60.

Dinh, Cong Tuan. 2019. "Sourcing Contemporary Vietnam's Intellectual History in Russia: Sciences, Arts, and Sinology." In *China Studies in South and Southeast Asia: Between Pro China and Objectivism*, ed. Chih-yu Shih, Prapin Manomaiviboool, and Reena Marwah, 105–26. Singapore: World Scientific.

Dirlik, Arif. 1994. "The Postcolonial Aura: Third World Criticism." *Critical Inquiry* 20 (2): 328–56.

———. 2002. "Rethinking Colonialism: Globalization, Postcolonialism, and the Nation." *Interventions* 4 (3): 428–48.

Domes, Jürgen. 1990. "The China Watch: Fr. Ladanyi and His Friends." *CNA*, special commemorative issue, November.

Donati, Pierpaolo, and Margaret S. Archer. 2015. *The Relational Subject*. Cambridge: Cambridge University Press.

Doupe, Aaron. 2003. "Virtue and the Individual: Confucius' Conception of International Society." *Glendon Journal of International Studies* 3:2–8.

Duara, Prasenjit. 2004. *Sovereignty and Authenticity: Manchukuo and East Asian Modern*. Lanham, MD: Rowman and Littlefield.

Duffy, Mary, and Geoffrey Evans. 1996. "Building Bridges? The Political Implications of Electoral Integration for Northern Ireland." *British Journal of Political Science* 26 (1): 123–40.

Economy, Elizabeth C. 2018. *The Third Revolution: Xi Jinping and the New Chinese State*. Oxford: Oxford University Press.

Elias, Norbert. 2000. *The Civilizing Process: Sociogenetic and Psychogenetic Investigations*. Rev. ed. Oxford: Blackwell.

Embassy of the People's Republic of China in Islamic Republic of Pakistan. 2008. "China Overwhelmed by Pakistan's Generous Help During Earthquake." June 20. http://pk.chineseembassy.org/eng/sgxx2/t467294.htm.

Emirbayer, Mustafa. 1997. "Manifesto for a Relational Sociology." *American Journal of Sociology* 103 (2): 281–317.

Enri, John Nguyet. 2012. "Who Needs Strangers? Un-imagining Hong Kong Chineseness." *Chinese Journal of Communication* 5 (1): 78–87.

Entwistle, Phil. 2016. "Faith in China: Religious Belief and National Narratives amongst Young, Urban Chinese Protestants." *Nations and Nationalism* 22 (2): 347–70.

Epstein, Charlotte. 2012. "Stop Telling Us How to Behave: Socialization or Infantilization." *International Studies Perspectives* 13 (2): 135–45.

Erll, Astrid. 2011. *Memory in Culture*. London: Palgrave Macmillan.

Fan, Lilianne. 2013. "Disaster as Opportunity? Building back Better in Aceh, Myanmar and Haiti." HPG Working Paper, Humanitarian Policy Group, Overseas Development Institute, London, November.

Farid Alatas, Sayed. 2015. *Applying Ibn Khaldūn: The Recovery of a Lost Tradition in Sociology*. London: Routledge.

Faries, Nathan. 2010. *The "Inscrutably Chinese" Church: How Narratives and Nationalism Continue to Divide Christianity*. Plymouth, UK: Lexington Books.

Fei, Xiaotong. 1989. *The Structure of Multiple Oneness of the Chinese Nation*. Beijing: Central Nationalities College Press.

Fewsmith, Joseph, ed. 2010. *China Today, China Tomorrow: Domestic Politics, Economy, and Society*. Lanham, MD: Rowman and Littlefield.

Fierke, K. M. 2013. *Political Self-sacrifice: Agency, Body and Emotion in International Relations*. New York: Cambridge University Press.

Fingar, Thomas. 2012. "China's Vision of World Order." In *Strategic Asia 2012–13: China's Military Challenge*, ed. Ashley J. Tellis and Travis Tanner, 343–73. Seattle: National Bureau of Asian Research.

Fogarty, Patricia. 2013. "Riding Three Horses: Moldova's Enduring Identity as a Strategy for Survival." In *Russia and Europe: Building Bridges, Digging Trenches*, ed. Kjell Engelbrekt and Bertil Nygren, 230–48. Abidingdon, UK: Routledge.

Ford, Christopher A. 2015. "The Party and the Sage: Communist China's Use of Quasi-Confucian Rationalizations for One-Party Dictatorship and Imperial Ambition." *Journal of Contemporary China* 24 (96): 1032–47.

Formicola, Jo Renee, and Hubert Morken, eds. 2001. *Religious Leaders and Faith-Based Politics: Ten Profiles*. Lanham, MD: Rowman and Littlefield.

Fujitani, Takashi. 2011. *Race for Empire: Koreans as Japanese and Japanese as Americans during World War II*. Berkeley: University of California Press.

Fukuyama, Francis. 1993. *The End of History and the Last Man*. New York: Harper Perennial.

Fulton, Brent. 2015. *China's Urban Christians: A Light That Cannot Be Hidden*. Eugene, OR: Pickwick.

Gamer, Robert E., and Stanley W. Toops. 2017. *Understanding Contemporary China*. 5th ed. Boulder, CO: Lynne Rienner.

Gao, Xingjian. 1998. "Late-Arrived Modernism and Literature in Contemporary China" (遲到的現代主義與當今中國文學). *Review of Literature* 3 (June): 108–19.

Gertz, Geoffrey. 2017. "What Will Trump's Embrace of Bilateralism Mean for America's Trade Partners." Brookings Institution, February 8. https://www.brookings.edu/blog/future-development/2017/02/08/what-will-trumps-embrace-of-bilateralism-mean-for-americas-trade-partners/.

Gewirtz, Julian. 2020. "China Thinks America Is Losing: Washington Must Show Beijing It's Wrong." *Foreign Affairs* 99 (6): 62–72.

Glendon, A. Ian, and Sharon Clarke. 2016. *Human Safety and Risk Management: A Psychological Perspective*. Boca Raton, FL: CRC Press.

Goh, Beng-lan, ed. 2011. *Decentering and Diversifying Southeast Asian Studies: Perspectives from the Region*. Singapore: Institute of Southeast Asian Studies Publishing.

Goh, Evelyn. 2008. "Hierarchy and the Role of the United States in the East Asian Security Order." *International Relations of the Asia-Pacific* 8 (3): 353–77.

Goldman, Merle, and Elizabeth J. Perry, eds. 2002. *Changing Meanings of Citizenship in Modern China*. Cambridge, MA: Harvard University Press.

Goldstein, Melvyn C., and Matthew T. Kapstein. 1998. *Buddhism in Contemporary Tibet: Religious Revival and Cultural Identity*. Berkeley: University of California Press.

Golovachev, Valentin. 2018. "Soviet and Italian Sinologists in China during the Cultural Revolution: Elder Brothers, Revisionists and Spies or Colleagues, Friends and Cultural Mediators?" Supplement, *Rivista degli studi orientali*, n.s., 90 (S2): 117–32.

Goodman, David S. G., and Beverley Hooper. 1994. *China's Quiet Revolution: New Interactions Between State and Society*. Boston: Addison-Wesley Longman.

Goto-Jones, Christopher. 2010. *Political Philosophy in Japan: Nishida, the Kyoto School and Co-prosperity*. London: Routledge.

Graham, Michael C. 2014. *Facts of Life: Ten Issues of Contentment*. Denver: Outskirts.

Granoff, Phyllis, and Koichi Shinohara, eds. 2005. *Images in Asian Religions: Texts and Contexts*. Vancouver: University of British Columbia Press.

Gu, Jiegang. (1939) 2011. *The Chinese Nation Is One*. Baoshu Garden Literature. Beijing: Zhonghua Bookstore.

Guo, Huifen. 1999. *South Bound Chinese Authors and New Chinese Literature in Malaysia, 1919–1949* (中國南來作者與新馬華文文學, 1919–1949). Xiamen: Xiamen University Press.

Guruge, Ananda. 2005. *Buddhist Answers to Current Issues: Studies in Socially Engaged Humanistic Buddhism.* Bloomington, IN: Author House.

Hafner-Burton, Emilie M., Miles Kahler, and Alexander H. Montgomery. 2009. "Network Analysis for International Relations." *International Organization* 63 (3): 559–92.

Hagström, Linus. 2005. "Relational Power for Foreign Policy Analysis: Issues in Japan's China Policy." *European Journal of International Relations* 11 (3): 395–430.

Hall, David, and Roger Ames. 1995. *Anticipating China: Thinking Through the Narratives of Chinese and Western Culture.* Albany: State University of New York Press.

Hamashita, Takeshi. 2008. *China, East Asia and the Global Economy: Regional and Historical Perspectives.* Abingdon, UK: Routledge.

Hammond, Andrew, ed. 2004. *The Balkans and the West: Constructing the European Other, 1945–2003.* London: Routledge.

Han, Christina Hee Yeon. 2011. "Territory of the Sages: Neo-Confucian Discourse of Wuyi Nine Bends Jingjie." PhD diss., University of Toronto.

Harding, Harry. 1984. "The Study of Chinese Politics: Toward a Third Generation of Scholarship." *World Politics* 36 (2): 284–307.

Harnisch, Sebastian. 2011. "Role Theory, Organizational Actors and Regime Stability." Paper prepared for the Annual Meeting of the International Studies Association, Montreal, March.

———. 2012. "Conceptualizing in the Minefield: Role Theory and Foreign Policy Learning." *Foreign Policy Analysis* 8 (1): 47–69.

Harris, Ian. 2013. *Buddhism in a Dark Age: Cambodian Monks under Pol Pot.* Honolulu: University of Hawaii Press.

Hartig, Falk. 2012. "Cultural Diplomacy with Chinese Characteristics: The Case of Confucius Institutes in Australia." *Communication, Politics and Culture* 45 (2): 256–76.

———. 2015. "Communicating China to the World: Confucius Institutes and China's Strategic Narratives Politics." *Journal of Asian and African Studies* 35 (3–4): 245–58.

Harvey, Sean P. 2015. *Native Tongues: Colonialism and Race from Encounter to the Reservation.* Cambridge, MA: Harvard University Press.

Hashim, Che Noraini, and Hasan Langgulung. 2007. "The Muslim World and the West: The Potential of Educational Institutions in Building Bridges in the Context of Malaysia." *Bulletin of Education and Research* 9 (2): 1–17.

Hass, Ryan. 2021. *Stronger: Adapting America's China Strategy in an Age of Competitive Interdependence.* New Haven, CT: Yale University Press.

Hau, Caroline S. 2014. *The Chinese Question: Ethnicity, Nation and Region in and beyond the Philippines*. Kyoto: Kyoto University Press.

He, Kai, and Huiyun Feng. 2015. "Transcending Rationalism and Constructivism: Chinese Leaders' Operational Codes, Socialization Processes, and Multilateralism after the Cold War." *European Political Science Review* 7 (3): 401–26.

Heller, Monica, and Bonnie McElhinny. 2017. *Language, Capitalism, Colonialism: Toward a Critical History*. Toronto: University of Toronto Press.

Heng, Terence. 2012. "Understanding Diasporic Chineseness in Weddings: A Visual Sociology Approach." Lecture given at Asia Research Institute, National University of Singapore, February 2. https://www.youtube.com/watch?v=_guMkIfVkjg.

Henry, Todd A. 2016. *Assimilating Seoul: Japanese Rule and the Politics of Public Space in Colonial Korea, 1910–1945*. Berkeley: University of California Press.

Heylen, Ann. 2004. "The Modernity of Japanese Colonial Education in Taiwan: Moving beyond Formal Schooling and Literacy Campaigns." *Taiwan Journal of East Asian Studies* 1 (2): 1–36.

Heylen, Ann, and Scott Sommers, eds. 2010. *Becoming Taiwan: From Colonialism to Democracy*. Wiesbaden, Ger.: Harrassowitz Verlag.

Heyndrickx, Jeroom. 2005. "From China-Watchers to Partners in China Mission." *Tripod* 25 (138): 49–60.

Hickey, Dennis V. 2019. "What the Latest Opinion Polls Say about Taiwan." *National Interest*, March 5. https://nationalinterest.org/feature/what-latest-opinion-polls-say-about-taiwan-46187.

Higgins, E. Tory. 1987. "Self-discrepancy: A Theory Relating Self and Affect." *Psychological Review* 94 (3): 319–40.

Hillemann, Ulrike. 2009. *Asian Empire and British Knowledge: China and the Networks of British Imperial Expansion*. London: Palgrave Macmillan.

Hinde, Robert A. 1997. *Relationships: A Dialectical Perspective*. Hove, UK: Psychology Press.

Hirono, Miwa. 2008. *Civilizing Missions: International Religious Agencies in China*. New York: Palgrave Macmillan.

Ho, David Y. F. 1998. "Interpersonal Relationships and Relational Dominance: An analysis Based on Methodological Relationalism." *Asian Journal of Social Psychology* 1 (1): 1–16.

Ho, David Y. F., and Chi-yue Chiu. 1998. "Collective Representations as a Metaconstruct: An Analysis Based on Methodological Relationalism." *Culture and Psychology* 4 (3): 349–69.

Ho, Hsin-chuan. 2001. "Tang Chun-yi on the Spirit of Liberty in Confucianism" (唐君毅論儒學中的自由精神). In *Confucianism and Modern Democracy* (儒學與現代民主), ed. Hsin-chuan Ho, 86–112. Beijing: Chinese Social Science Press.

Ho, Karl, Stan Hok-wui Wong, Harold D. Clarke, and Kuan-chen Lee. 2019. "A Comparative Study of the China Factor in Taiwan and Hong Kong Elections."

In *Taiwan's Political Re-alignment and Diplomatic Challenges*, ed. Wei-chin Lee, 119–44. Singapore: Springer.

Hong, Zhao. 2007. "India and China: Rivals or Partners in Southeast Asia?" *Contemporary Southeast Asia* 29 (1): 121–42.

Hou, Guanghao. 2018. "A Mighty River Flowing Eastward: The Formation and Transformation of the Ethnic and National Identities of Situ Hua." *China Report* 54 (1): 81–98.

Hsieh, Kun-chuan, and Nan-hsiung Lee. 2001. *Memorial Collection of the 100th Anniversary of Late Mister Lee Wanju* (李萬居百歲冥誕追思紀念冊). Taipei: Memorial Committee on the 100th Anniversary of Late Mister Lee Wanju.

Hsu, Cho-yun. 1991. "Applying Confucian Ethics to International Relations." *Ethics and International Affairs* 5 (1):15–31.

Hsu, Francis L. K. 1971. "Psychosocial Homeostasis and Jen: Conceptual Tools for Advancing Psychological Anthropology." *American Anthropologist* 73 (1): 23–44.

Hsu, Jing. 1985. "The Chinese Family: Relations, Problems and Therapy." In *Chinese Culture and Mental Health*, ed. W. W. Tseng and D. Y. H. Wu, 95–112. Orlando, FL: Academic Press.

Hsu, Victor Wan Chi. 2016. "A Sobering Retrospective of the Canberra Assembly 25 Years Ago." World Council of Churches, February 15. https://blog.oikoumene.org/posts/a-sobering-retrospective-of-the-canberra-assembly-25-years-ago.

Huang, Chih-huei. 2003. "The Transformation of Taiwanese Attitudes toward Japan in the Post-colonial Period." In *Imperial Japan and National Identities in Asia, 1895–1945*, ed. Narangoa Li and Robert Cribb, 296–314. London: Routledge.

Huang, Chiung-chiu. 2015 "Balance of Relationship: The Essence of Myanmar's China Policy." *Pacific Review* 28 (2): 189–210.

———. 2020a. "Studying China from the Communist Comrade's Eyes: The Diverse Tracks of Vietnam's Sinological Development." *China Review* 20 (4): 245–72.

———. 2020b. "Interpreting Vietnam's China Policy from the Perspective of Role Theory: Independent Role vs. Interactive Role." *International Relations* 34 (4): 524–43.

Huang, Chiung-chiu, and Chih-yu Shih. 2014. *Harmonious Intervention: China's Quest for Relational Security*. Farnham, UK: Ashgate.

Huang, Chun-chieh. 2015. *East Asian Confucianism*. Taipei: National Taiwan University Press.

Huang, Philip C. C. 1991. "The Paradigmatic Crisis in Chinese Studies: Paradoxes in Social and Economic History." *Modern China* 17 (3): 299–341.

———. 2016. "Our Sense of Problem: Rethinking China Studies in the United States." *Modern China* 42 (2): 115–61.

Huang, Po-ho. 1990. *Religion and Self-determination: An Initial Attempt at Taiwan's Indigenous Mission* (宗教與自決: 台灣本土宣教初探). Taipei: Dao Hsiang Publishing.

———. 1991. *Faith Indigenously Rooted: A Brief Interpretation Taiwan Presbyterian Church's Confession of the Faith* (定根本土ê信仰：台灣基督長老教會信仰告白淺釋). Tainan: Renguang.

———. 1999. *Indigenous Theology Speaking* (本土神學講話). Tainan: Taiwan Church News.

Huang, Qingming. 2021. "The Pandemic and the Transformation of Liberal International Order." *Journal of Chinese Political Science* 26 (1): 1–26.

Huang, Ray. 1999. *Broadening the Horizons of Chinese History: Discourses, Syntheses, and Comparisons*. London: Routledge.

Huang, Yi-le. 2014. "100th Anniversary of Shoki Coe: The Prophet for the Taiwanese" (台灣人的先覺黃彰輝一百歲誕辰紀念). *Taiwan Church News* (台灣教會公報), March. https://tcnn.org.tw/archives/15817.

Huei, Peh Shing. 2016. "Commentary: The New Normal of Singapore's Relations with China." *Channel NewsAsia*, October 6. http://www.channelnewsasia.com/news/asiapacific/commentary-the-new-normal-of-singapore-s-relations-with-china/3184106.html.

Hui, D. Lai Hang. 2019. "Geopolitics of Toponymic Inscription in Taiwan." *Geopolitics* 24 (4): 916–43.

Huntington, Samuel. 1998. *The Clash of Civilizations and the Remaking of World Order*. New York: Simon and Schuster.

Hutcherson, Cendri A., and James J. Gross. 2011. "The Moral Emotions: A Social–Functionalist Account of Anger, Disgust, and Contempt." *Journal of Personality and Social Psychology* 100 (4): 719–37.

Hutchings, Kimberly. 2019. "Decolonizing Global Ethics: Thinking with the Pluriverse." *Ethics and International Affairs* 33 (2): 115–25.

Hwang, Alvin, Ann Marie Francesco, and Eric Kessler. 2003. "The Relationship between Individualism-Collectivism, Face, and Feedback and Learning Processes in Hong Kong, Singapore, and the United States." *Journal of Cross-cultural Psychology* 34 (1): 72–91.

Hwang, Kwang-kuo. 2001. "Confucian Theory of Relationality and Its Methodological Foundation." *Formosan Education and Society* 2 (1): 34.

———. 2009. *Confucian Relationality: Philosophical Reflection, Theoretical Construction and Empirical Research*. Taipei: Psychology Press.

———. 2012. *Foundations of Chinese Psychology: Confucian Social Relations*. New York: Springer.

Hwang, Kwang-kuo, and Jeffrey Chang. 2009. "Self-Cultivation: Culturally Sensitive Psychotherapies in Confucian Societies." *Counseling Psychologist* 37 (7): 1010–32.

Hwang, Yih-jye. 2010. "Japan as 'Self' or 'the Other'? The Turmoil over Yoshinori Kobayashi's *On Taiwan*." *China Information* 24 (1): 75–98.

———. 2014. "The 2004 Hand-in-Hand Rally in Taiwan: 'Traumatic' Memory, Commemoration, and Identity Formation." *Nationalism and Ethnic Politics* 20 (3): 287–308.

———. 2021. "The Births of International Studies in China." *Review of International Studies.* https://doi.org/10.1017/S0260210520000340.

Hwang, Yih-jye, Raoul Bunskoek, and Chih-yu Shih. 2021. "Re-worlding the 'West' in Post-Western IR: The 'Theory Migrant' of Tianxia in the Anglosphere." In *China's Rise and Rethinking International Relations Theory*, ed. Chengxin Pan and Emilian Kavalski, ch. 3. Bristol, UK: Bristol University Press.

Ikenberry, G. John. 2004. "American Hegemony and East Asian Order." *Australian Journal of International Affairs* 58 (3): 353–67.

Israeli, Raphael. 2007. *Islam in China: Religion, Ethnicity, Culture, and Politics.* Plymouth, UK: Lexington Books.

Ivanhoe, Philip J. 2016. *Three Streams: Confucian Reflections on Learning and the Moral Heart-Mind in China, Korea and Japan.* Oxford: Oxford University Press.

Jackson, Patrick Thaddeus, and Daniel H. Nexon. 1999. "Relations before States: Substance, Process and the Study of World Politics." *European Journal of International Relations* 5 (3): 291–332.

———. 2019. "Reclaiming the Social: Relaitonalism in Anglophone International Studies." *Cambridge Review of International Affairs* 32 (5): 582–600.

Jacobs, J. Bruce. 2013. "Whither Taiwanization? The Colonization, Democratization and Taiwanization of Taiwan." *Japanese Journal of Political Science* 14 (4): 567–86.

———. 2014. "Taiwan's Colonial Experiences and the Development of Ethnic Identities: Some Hypotheses." *Taiwan in Comparative Perspective* 5:47–59.

Jacobs, J. Bruce, and Peter Kang. 2018. *Changing Taiwanese Identities.* London: Routledge.

Jacques, Martin. 2009. *When China Ruled the World: The Rise of the Middle Kingdom and the End of the Western World.* London: Penguin.

Jaggar, Alison M. 1995. "Caring as a Feminist Practice of Moral Reason." In *Justice and Care: Essential Readings in Feminist Ethics*, ed. Virginia Held, 179–202. Boulder, CO: Westview.

Jain, Girilal. 1959. *India Meets China in Nepal.* Bombay: Asia Publishing House.

Jiang, Lingnan. 2015. "Acceptance of Concept of Autocracy and Initial Construction of Historical Genealogy of Autocracy in Late Qing P" (晚清專制概念的接受與專制歷史譜系的初構). *Journal of Historical Theory and Historiography* (史學理論與史學史學刊), 13:166–91.

Joffe, Hélène, and Christian Staerklé. 2007. "The Centrality of the Self-control Ethos in Western Aspersions Regarding Outgroups: A Social Representational Approach to Stereotype Content." *Culture and Psychology* 13 (4): 395–418.

Johnson, Ian. 2017. *The Souls of China: The Return of Religion after Mao.* New York: Patheon.

Johnson, Nicole V. 2012. "Turkish Reactions to the Arab Spring: Implications for United States Foreign Policy." *Global Security Studies* 3 (4): 1–10.

Johnston, Alastair Iain. 2008. *Social States: China in International Institutions, 1980–2000.* Princeton, NJ: Princeton University Press.

Jones, Carol. 2014. "Lost in China? Mainlandisation and Resistance in Post-1997 Hong Kong." *Taiwan in Comparative Perspective* 5:21–46.

Kam, Yip Lo Lucetta. 2010. "Hong Kong as a Taken Position" (香港作為一種立場). In *Local Discourses of 2010: New Class Struggles in Hong Kong* (本土論述 2010:香港新階級鬥爭), ed. Local Discourse Committee Synergy Net, 201–8. Hong Kong: Azoth.

Kang, Jie. 2016. *House Church Christianity in China: From Rural Preachers to City Pastors*. New York: Palgrave Macmillan.

Kang, Yuh-yng. 1999. "Retrospect and Prospect of the Trend of Research of Doctoral and Master's Theses on Taiwan Presbyterian Church" (台灣基督教長老教會博碩士論文研究趨勢之回顧). *Thoughts and Words* (思與言) 37 (2): 155–72.

Kanu, Yatta, ed. 2006. *Curriculum as Cultural Practice: Postcolonial Imaginations*. Toronto: University of Toronto Press.

Kashinath, Prarthana. 2016. "To Fend Off China, India Must Galvanize Ties with Bangladesh." *Diplomat*, October 29. http://thediplomat.com/2016/10/to-fend-off-china-india-must-galvanize-ties-with-bangladesh/.

Katan, David. 2019. "In Defence of the Cultural Other: Foreignisation or Mindful Essentialism?" In *Contacts and Contrasts in Educational Contexts and Translation*, ed. Barbara Lewandowska-Tomaszczyk, 119–42. Berlin: Springer.

Katz, Paul. 2014. *Religion in China and Its Modern Fate*. Waltham, MA: Brandeis University Press.

Katz, Paul, and Murray Rubinstein, eds. 2003. *Religion and the Formation of Taiwanese Identities*. New York: Palgrave Macmillan.

Katzenstein, Peter J. 2010. *Civilizations in World Politics: Plural and Pluralist Perspectives*. Abingdon, UK: Routledge.

———, ed. 2012a. *Sinicization and the Rise of China: Civilizational Processes beyond East and West*. Abingdon, UK: Routledge.

———, ed. 2012b. *Anglo-America and Its Discontents: Civilizational Identities beyond West and East*. Abingdon, UK: Routledge.

Kavalski, Emilian. 2009. "Do as I Do: The Global Politics of China's Regionalization." In *China and the Global Politics of Regionalization*, ed. Emilian Kavalski, 1–17. Farnham, UK: Ashgate.

———. 2013. "The Struggle for Recognition of Normative Powers: Normative Power Europe and Normative Power China in Context." *Cooperation and Conflict* 48 (2): 247–67.

———. 2015. "Complexifying IR: Disturbing the 'Deep Newtonian Slumber' of the Mainstream." In *World Politics at the Edge of Chaos*, ed. Emilian Kavalski, 253–71. Albany: State University of New York Press.

———. 2016a. "Relationality and Its Chinese Characteristics." *China Quarterly* 226:551–59.

———, ed. 2016b. *World Politics at the Edge of Chaos: Reflections on Complexity and Global Life*. Albany: State University of New York Press.

———. 2017a. *The Guanxi of Relational International Theory*. Abingdon, UK: Routledge.

———. 2017b. *Encounters with Eastphalia: Post-Western World Affairs in Asia*. Abingdon, UK: Routledge.

———. 2018. "Guanxi or What Is the Chinese for Relational Theory of World Politics." *International Relations of the Asia-Pacific* 18 (3): 397–420.

Kaya, Ayhan, and Ferhat Kentel. 2005. "Euro-Turks: A Bridge or a Breach between Turkey and the European Union? A Comparative Study of French-Turks and German-Turks." CEPS EU-Turkey Working Papers 14, CEPS, Brussels, January.

Keay, John. 1997. *Empires End: A History of the Far East from High Colonialism to Hong Kong*. New York: Scribner.

Keenan, Barry C. 2011. *Neo-Confucian Self-Cultivation*. Honolulu: University of Hawaii Press.

Keng, Shu, and Gunter Schubert. 2010. "Agents of Taiwan-China Unification? The Political Roles of Taiwanese Business People in the Process of Cross-Strait Integration." *Asian Survey* 50 (2): 287–310.

Kennedy, John James. 2012. "What Is the Color of a Non-revolution: Why the Jasmine Revolution and Arab Spring Did Not Spread to China." *Whitehead Journal of Diplomacy and International Relations* 13 (1): 63–74.

Khong, Yuen Foong. 2013. "The American Tributary System." *Chinese Journal of International Politics* 6 (1): 1–47.

King, Ambrose Y. C. 1985. "The Individual and Group in Confucianism: A Relational perspective." In *Individualism and Holism: Studies in Confucian and Taoist Values*, ed. Donald J. Munro, 57–70. Ann Arbor: Center for Chinese Studies, University of Michigan.

Kingston, Jeff. 2018. "Shadow Boxing: Japan's Para-diplomacy with Taiwan." In *Japan's Foreign Relations in Asia*, ed. James D. J. Brown and Jeff Kingston, 201–17. Abingdon, UK: Routledge.

Kluver, Randolf. 2014. "The Sage as Strategy: Nodes, Networks, and the Quest for Geopolitical Power in the Confucius Institute." *Communication, Culture and Critique* 7 (2): 192–209.

Knowles, Caroline, and Douglas Harper. 2009. *Hong Kong: Migrant Lives, Landscapes, and Journeys*. Chicago: University of Chicago Press.

Kohn, Margaret, and Keally McBride. 2011. *Decolonization: Postcolonialism and the Problem of Foundations*. Oxford: Oxford University Press.

Komagome, Takeshi. 2006. Colonial Modernity for an Elite Taiwanese, Lim Bo-Seng: The Labyrinth of Cosmopolitanism. In *Taiwan under Japanese Colonial Rule, 1895–1945: History, Culture, Memory*, ed. Liao Ping-hui and David Der-wei Wang, 141–59. New York: Columbia University Press.

König, Lion, and Bidisha Chaudhuri, eds. 2016. *Politics of the "Other" in India and China: Western Concepts in Non-Western Contexts*. Abingdon, UK: Routledge.

Kopra, Sanna. 2016. "Great Power Management and China's Responsibility in International Climate Politics." *Journal of China and International Relations* 4 (1): 20–44.

Koschut, Simon. 2018. "The Power of (Emotion) Words: On the Importance of Emotions for Social Constructivist Discourse Analysis in IR." *Journal of International Relations and Development* 21 (3): 495–522.

Kösebalaban, Hasan. 2008. "Torn Identities and Foreign Policy: The Case of Turkey and Japan." *Insight Turkey* 10 (1): 5–29.

Kovach, Margaret. 2010. *Indigenous Methodologies: Characteristics, Conversations, and Contexts*. Toronto: University of Toronto Press.

Kuehn, Julia, Kam Louie, and David M. Pomfret, eds. 2014. *Diasporic Chineseness after the Rise of China: Communities and Cultural Production*. Vancouver: University of British Columbia Press.

Kuik, Cheng-chwee. 2021. "The Twin Chessboards of US-China Rivalry: Impact on the Geostrategic Supply and Demand in Post-Pandemic Asia." *Asian Perspective* 45 (1): 157–76.

Kumar, Pranav. 2010. "Sino-Bhutanese Relations: Under the Shadow of India-Bhutan Friendship." *China Report* 46 (3): 243–52.

Kuo, Cheng-tian. 2008. *Religion and Democracy in Taiwan*. Albany: State University of New York Press.

Kuo, Pao Kun. 2001. "The Essence of My Dilemma: Protest, Provocation, Process." *Focas: Forum on Contemporary Art and Society* 2:104–5.

Kwong, Peter. 1996. *The New Chinatown*. New York: Hill and Wang.

Kyounghan, Bae. 2009. "Chiang Kai-shek and Christianity: Religious Life Reflected from His Diary." *Journal of Modern Chinese History* 3 (1): 1–10.

Ladany, Laszlo. 1970. "China: Period of Suspense." *Foreign Affairs*. 48 (4): 701–11.

———. 1987. *The Catholic Church in China*. NY: Freedom House.

———. 1988. *The Communist Party of China and Marxism, 1921–1985: A Self Portrait*. Stanford, CA: Hoover Institution Press, Stanford University.

———. 1992. *Law and Legality in China: The testament of a China-Watcher*. London: Hurst.

———. 1994. "Jesuit China Editor Was Always Objective" (letter to the editor). *Asian Wall Street Journal* 10 (25): 10.

Laliberté, André. 2015. "The Politicization of Religion by the CCP: A Selective Retrieval." *Asiatische Studien / Études asiatiques* 69 (1): 185–211.

Larramendi, Miguel Hernando. 2018. "Doomed Regionalism in a Redrawn Maghreb? The Changing Shape of the Rivalry between Algeria and Morocco in the Post-2011 Era." *Journal of North African Studies* 24 (3): 506–31.

Law, Wing Sang. 2009. *The Collaborative Colonial Power: The Making of the Hong Kong Chinese*. Hong Kong: Hong Kong University Press.

Lawrence, Bruce B. 2010. "Islam in Afro-Eurasia: A Bridge Civilization." In *Civilizations in World Politics: Plural and Pluralist Perspectives*, ed. Peter J. Katzenstein, 157–75. London: Routledge.

Lee, Chengpang. 2012. "Shadow of the Colonial Power: Kominka and the Failure of the Temple Reorganization Campaign." *Studies on Asia*, 4th ser., 2 (2): 120–44.

Lee, Chien-shing, J. A. Mangan, and Gwang Ok. 2018. "Taiwan under Japanese Colonial Control: Sport as a Component of Cultural Conditioning, Political Domination, and Militaristic Imperialism." In *Japanese Imperialism*, ed. J. A. Mangan, Peter Horton, Tianwei Ren, and Gwang Ok, 217–42. Berlin: Springer.

Lee, Ji-young. 2016. *China's Hegemony: Four Hundred Years of East Asian Domination*. New York: Columbia University Press.

Lee, Kuan-chen, Wei-feng Tzeng, Karl Ho, and Harold Clarke. 2018. "Against Everything Involving China? Two Types of Sinophobia in Taiwan." *Journal of Asian and African Studies* 53 (6): 830–51.

Lee, Nan-hsiung. 1977. "The Gang of Four: Radical Politics and Modernization in China." In *The Gang of Four: First Essays after the Fall*, ed. Steve S. K. Chin, 69–107. Hong Kong: Centre of Asian Studies, University of Hong Kong.

———. 1979a. "Modernization and Managerial Power in China, 1956–1966." In *Modernization in China*, ed. Steve S. K. Chin, 71–89. Hong Kong: Centre of Asian Studies, University of Hong Kong.

———. 1979b. "Industrial Development and Mass-Line Leadership in China, 1956–1966." In *China: Development and Challenge*, ed. Lee Ngok and Leung Chi-keung, 101–28. Hong Kong: Centre of Asian Studies, University of Hong Kong.

———. 1981a. "The Modernization Programmes in the Three Poisonous Weeds." In *Development and Change in China*, ed. Edward K. Y. Chan and Steve S. K Chin, 31–54. Hong Kong: Centre of Asian Studies, University of Hong Kong.

———. 1981b. "The Causes and Effects of Police Corruption: A Case in Political Modernization." In *Corruption and Its Control in Hong Kong*, ed. Rance P. L. Lee, 167–98. Hong Kong: Chinese University Press.

———. 1981c. "Historical Assessment and CCP's Policy: On the Issue of Mao Zedong's Historical Status" (歷史評價與中共政策：談毛澤東的歷史地位問題). *The Eighties* (八十年代), August, 61–63.

———. 1983. "The Ideal and the Reality of China's New Constitution" (中國新憲法的理想與實際). *Chung Pao Monthly* (中報月刊), February, 8–10.

———. 1984. "Crime and Penalty of Chinese Government Staff" (Zhong guo gongwu renyuan de zui yu fa). *Ming Pao Monthly*, August, 26–32.

———. 1987. "The Origin of the Issue of China's Democracy and Rule by Law as Revealed by the Fifth National Congress" (從五屆人大看中國民主法制問題的緣起). *Antarctic and the Arctic* (南北極), August, 23–26.

Lee, Raymond. 2016. "The Strategic Importance of Chinese-Pakistani Relations." Report, August 3. Doha: Aljazeera Centre for Studies.

Lee, Shin-yi, and Jui-sung Chen. 2014. "A Great Citizen Is Still 'Under-Construction': The Conflicting Self-identity in *Sayonara 1945*." *Journal of Literature and Art Studies* 4 (10): 840–47.
Leifer, Michael. 2013. *ASEAN and the Security of South-East Asia*. Abingdon, UK: Routledge.
Lesser, Ian O. 1994. *Bridge or Barrier? Turkey and the West After the Cold War*. Santa Monica, CA: Rand Arroyo Center. R-4204-AF/A.
Leung, Ka Lun. 2003. "Cultural Christians and Christianity in China." Trans. Stacy Mosher. *China Rights Forum* 4:28–31.
Leung, Kwok, and Michael Harris Bond. 1984. "The Impact of Cultural Collectivism on Reward Allocation." *Journal of Personality and Social Psychology* 47 (4): 793–804.
Lewis, Jeffrey. 2005. "The Janus Face of Brussels: Socialization and Everyday Decision Making in the European Union." *International Organization* 59 (4): 937–71.
Li, Chia-hui. 2011. *Self-awareness? Self-alienation? Intellectual Perspectives on China from The Father Li Wan-chu and the Son Li Nan-hsiung* (知己？異己？港台知識人：李萬居與李南雄父子的中國認識). Taipei: Research and Educational Center for China Studies and Cross-Strait Relations, Department of Political Science, National Taiwan University.
Li, Hsi Chang, Sam Mirmirani, Joseph A. Ilacqua. 2009. "Confucius Institutes: Distributed Leadership and Knowledge Sharing in a Worldwide Network." *Learning Organization* 16 (6): 469–82.
Lí, Sìn-jîn. 2013. "The Expectation and the Situation of the Presbyterian Church in Taiwan, PCT in the 10th WCC Assembly" (台灣基督長老教會參加第10屆WCC大會的期待與處境). *Madang*, no. 1 (October 30), 4. http://wcc2013.info/en/news-media/newspaper/Madang%20Newspaper%20-%20Issue%20I%20-%20October%2030-combined.pdf.
Lian, Xi. 2010. *Redeemed by Fire: The Rise of Popular Christianity in Modern China*. New Haven, CT: Yale University Press.
Liang, Qichao. (1905) 1989. "Observation on China as Nation in History" (歷史上中國民族之觀察). In *Collections of Yinbing Room* (飲冰室文集), vol. 8. Beijing: Zhonghua Bookstore.
Liao, Hsien-hao Sebastian, "Becoming Modernized or Simply 'Modern'?: Sex, Chineseness, Diasporic Consciousness in Lust, Caution." *Concentric* 36 (2): 181–211.
Liao, Joshua Wen-kwei. 1929. "Modern Idealism as Challenged by Its Rivals." MA thesis, University of Chicago.
———. 1931. "Morality versus Legality: Historical Analyses of the Motivating Factors of Social Conduct." PhD diss., University of Chicago.
———. 1933. *The Individual and the Community: A Historical Analysis of the Motivating Factors of Social Conduct*. London: Kegan Paul, Trench, Trubner.
———. 1935. *Comparative Civic Training* (比較公民訓練). Nanjing: Dacheng Press.

———. 1936. *A Philosophical Study of Human Life* (人生哲學之研究). Nanjing: Dacheng Press.

———. 1937. *Sun Yat-sen's Medical Science of Politics: A Comprehensive Thesis on the Words Left by the Late Party Premier* (孫中山之政治醫學：總理遺教綜論). Nanjing: Dacheng Press.

———. 1947. "Imperialism vs. Nationalism in Formosa." *China Weekly Review*, no. 104, 7.

———. 1950. *Formosa Speaks: The Memorandum Submitted to the United Nations in September, 1950, a Statement in Support of the Petition for Formosan Independence*. Hong Kong: Formosan League for Reemancipation.

Liao, Kuang-sheng. 1984. *Antiforeignism and Modernization in China*. New York: St. Martin's Press.

———. 1989. "Political Changes in Taiwan and the Legal Implications for China's Reunification Issue" (台灣政治變化與中國統一問題的法律探討). *Jurisprudence Review* (法學評論) 38 (6): 50–57.

———. 1996a. "Human Rights and Liberty of Hong Kong Residents in Face of Challenge" (香港居民人權與自由權利). In *The Return of Hong Kong and the Changes in the Chinese Mainland* (香港回歸與大陸變局), ed. Kuang-tai Hsu, 219–36. Taipei: Institute of International Relations, National Cheng-chi University.

———. 1996b. *The Difficult Situation of Democratization in Hong Kong: The Dispute between Return and Democratization* (香港民主化的困境：回歸與民主化之爭). Taipei: Asian Culture.

———. 1996c. "The Strategic Adjustment of Taiwan's Mainland Policy" (台灣大陸政策的策略調整). Presented at Conference on the Strategies for Another Breakthrough of Cross-Straits Relations, Taipei, April.

———. 2001. *CCP's Hong Kong Policy and Implications for Our Side* (中共對香港策略及其對我方之啟示). Taipei: Foundation of National Development Research.

Liao, Min-shu. 2012a. External Political Order of Qing China. In *Modern China: Culture and Diplomacy*, ed. Jinghe Ruan and Junyi Zhang, 101–53. Beijing: Social Science Literature Press.

———. 2012b. *Foreign Political Order of Qing China* (清代中國的外政秩序). Beijing: Encyclopedia of China Publishing House.

Liao, Ping-hui, and David Der-wei Wang, eds. 2006. *Taiwan under Japanese Colonial Rule, 1895–1945: History, Culture, Memory*. New York: Columbia University Press.

Lieberman, Matthew D. 2014. *Social: Why Our Brains Are Wired to Connect*. Oxford: Oxford University Press.

Lien, Pei-te. 2014. "Democratization and Citizenship Education Changing Identity Politics and Shifting Paradigms of Teaching and Learning in Taiwan." *Taiwan Journal of Democracy* 10 (2): 25–48.

Lilley, Rozanna. 1998. *Staging Hong Kong: Gender and Performance in Transition*. Honolulu: University of Hawaii Press.

Lim, Benjamin, and Ben Blanchard. 2013. "Xi Jinping Hopes Traditional Faiths Can Fill Moral Void in China: Sources." *Reuters*, September 29. http://www.reuters.com/article/us-china-politics-vacuum-idUSBRE98S0GS20130929.

Lim, Tai Wei. 2016. The Making of the East Asian Institute. In *The East Asian Institute: A Goh Keng Swee Legacy*, ed. East Asian Institute, 1–32. Singapore: World Scientific.

Lin, Chang-hua. 2009. "The Influence of Scottish Enlightenment on the Missionary in Taiwan During the 18th Century: The Case of Mackay" (十八世紀蘇格蘭啟蒙運動對來台宣教士的影響). In *A Sequel to the Collected Works of Young Cross-disciplinary Scholars on Taiwan History* (跨域青年學者台灣史研究續集), ed. Masahiro Wakabayashi, Masayoshi Matsunaga, and Hua-yuan Hsueh, 41–83. Taipei: Dao Hsiang Publishing.

Lin, Christine Louise. 1999. *The Presbyterian Church in Taiwan and the Advocacy of Local Autonomy*. Sino-Platonic Papers 92. Philadelphia: Department of East Asian Languages and Civilizations University of Pennsylvania.

Lin, Heng-kwang. 2014. The Second Interview of Weng Song-jan. In *Choosing the Institution to Cope with China: The Intellectual Evolution and Writings of Weng Song-jan, A Traveler between China, Hong Kong and Taiwan* (選擇面對中國的制度：翁松燃在中港臺之間的思學歷程與著述研究), ed. Heng-kwang Lin, 171–89. Taipei: Research and Educational Center for China Studies and Cross-Strait Relations, Department of Political Science, National Taiwan University.

Lin, Kaiti, and Chih-yu Shih. 2018. "Christianity, Anti-Communism, and Civilisational Sensibilities of the China News Analysis: Catholic Sinology vs. Catholic Sinologists." In *Oral History of China Studies in Italy*, ed. Luisa M. Paternicò and Chih-yu Shih. Rome: Fabrizio Serra Editore.

Lin, Man-houng. 2016. "The 'Greater East Asia Co-prosperity Sphere': A New Boundary for Taiwanese People and the Taiwanese Capital, 1940–1945." *Translocal Chinese: East Asian Perspectives* 10 (2):175–206.

Lin, Rachel. 2015. "Students Rally as Ministry Axes Reviews." *Taipei Times*, June 14.

Lin, Shaoyang. 2018. "Hong Kong in the Midst of Colonialism, Collaborative and Critical Nationalism from 1925 to 1930: The Perspective of Lu Xun and the Confucius Revering Movement." *China Report* 54 (1): 25–47.

Lin, Tsung-yi, Wen-shing Tseng, and Eng-Kung Yeh, eds. 1995. *Chinese Societies and Mental Health*. New York: Oxford University Press.

Ling, L. H. M. 1996. "Hegemony and the Internationalizing State: A Post-colonial Analysis of China's Integration into Asian Corporatism." *Review of International Political Economy* 3 (1): 1–26.

———. 2014a. *The Dao of World Politics: Towards a Post-Westephalian, Worldist International Relations*. London: Routledge.

———. 2014b. *Imagining World Politics: Sihar and Shenya, a Fable for Our Times*. Abingdon, UK: Routledge.

———. 2019. "Three-ness: Healing World Politics with Epistemic Compassion." *Politics* 39 (1): 35–49.

Ling, L. H. M., and Astrid H. M. Nordin. 2019. "On Relations and Relationality: A Conversation with Friends." *Cambridge Review of International Affairs* 32 (5): 654–68.

Liu, Hong. 2005. "New Migrants and the Revival of Overseas Chinese Nationalism." *Journal of Contemporary China* 14 (43): 291–316.

Liu, Hong, and Sin-kiong Wong. 2004. *Singapore Chinese Society in Transition: Business, Politics, and Socio-economic Change, 1945–1965*. New York: Peter Lang.

Liu, Joyce C. H., and Nick Vaughan-Williams, eds. 2014. *European-East Asian Borders in Transition*. Abingdon, UK: Routledge.

Liu, Mingfu. 2015. *The China Dream: Great Power Thinking and Strategic Posture in the Post-American Era*. New York: CN Time Books.

Liu, Shaoqi. (1939) 2011. *How to Be a Good Communist*. New York: Prism Key.

Liu, Yongtao. 2012. "Security Theorizing in China: Culture, Evolution and Social Practice." In *Thinking International Relations Differently*, ed. Arlene B. Tickner and David L. Blaney, 72–91. London: Routledge.

Liu, Yu. 2015. *Harmonious Disagreement: Matteo Ricci and His Closest Chinese Friends*. New York: Peter Lang.

Liu, Zhaojia, and Kuan Hsin-chi. 1988. *The Ethos of the Hong Kong Chinese*. Hong Kong: Chinese University Press of Hong Kong.

Lo, Chi-hao Jamese. 2015. "'One China' Comment Taken Out of Context: Ko." *China Post*, April 1. http://www.chinapost.com.tw/taiwan/china-taiwan-relations/2015/04/01/432554/One-China.htm.

Lo, Ming-cheng Miriam. 2002a. "Between Ethnicity and Modernity: Taiwanese Medical Students and Doctors under Japan's Kominka Campaign, 1937–1945." *Positions* 10 (2): 285–332.

———. 2002b. *Doctors within Borders: Profession, Ethnicity, and Modernity in Colonial Taiwan*. Berkeley: University of California Press.

Lomová, Olga, and Anna Zádrapová. 2016. "'The Song of Ancient China': The Myth of 'The Other' Appropriated by an Emerging Sinology." In *Sinology in Post-communist States*, ed. Chih-yu Shih, 189–211. Hong Kong: Chinese University Press.

Louie, Andrea. 2004. *Chineseness across Borders: Renegotiating Chinese Identities in China and the United States*. Durham, NC: Duke University Press.

Louis, W. Roger, and Ronald Robinson. 1994. "The Imperialism of Decolonization." *Journal of Imperial and Commonwealth History* 22 (3): 462–511.

Louzon, Victor. 2017. "From Japanese Soldiers to Chinese Rebels: Colonial Hegemony, War Experience, and Spontaneous Remobilization during the 1947 Taiwanese Rebellion." *Journal of Asian Studies* 77 (1): 161–79.

Lowe, John, and Eileen Yuk-ha Tsang. 2018. "Securing Hong Kong's Identity in the Colonial Past: Strategic Essentialism and the Umbrella Movement." *Critical Asian Studies* 50 (4): 556–71.

Lui, Tai-lok. 1997. "Evolution of the Hong Kong Consciousness in History in Hong Kong" (香港故事：香港意識的歷史發展). In *Continuation and Rupture of Civilization* (香港：文明的延續與斷裂), ed. Kao Cheng-shu and Chen Chieh-hsuan, 1–16. Taipei: Linking Publishing.

Lui, Tai-lok, Chun-hung Ng, and Eric Kit Wai Ma. 2010. *Hong Kong, Lives, Culture* (香港，生活，文化). Hong Kong: Oxford University Press.

Luoma-aho, Mika. 2009. "Political Theology, Anthropomorphism, and Person-hood of the State: The Religion of IR." *International Political Sociology* 3 (3): 293–309.

Lynch, Daniel C. 2004. "Taiwan's Self-conscious Nation-Building Project." *Asian Survey* 44 (4): 513–33.

Mackie, Diane M., Thierry Devos, and Eliot R. Smith. 2000. "Intergroup Emotions: Explaining Offensive Action Tendencies in an Intergroup Context." *Journal of Personality and Social Psychology* 79 (4): 602–16.

Madsen, Richard. 1998. *China's Catholics: Tragedy and Hope in an Emerging Civil Society*. Berkeley: University of California Press.

———. 2014. "From Socialist Ideology to Cultural Heritage: The Changing Basis of Legitimacy in the People's Republic of China." *Anthropology and Medicine* 21 (1): 58–70.

Majumdar, Munmun. 2015. "The ASEAN Way of Conflict Management in the South China Sea." *Strategic Analysis* 39 (1): 73–87.

Makeham, John. 2008. *Lost Soul: "Confucianism" in Contemporary Chinese Discourse*. Cambridge, MA: Harvard University Press.

Manomaivibool, Prapin, and Chih-yu Shih, eds. 2016. *Understanding 21st Century China in Buddhist Asia: History, Modernity, and International Relations*. Bangkok: Asia Research Center, Chulalongkorn University.

Maoz, Zeev. 2011. *Networks of Nations: The Evolution, Structure, and Impact of International Networks, 1816–2001*. New York: Cambridge University Press.

Marglin, Frédérique Apffel, and Stephen A. Marglin. 1990. *Dominating Knowledge: Development, Culture, and Resistance*. Oxford: Oxford University Press.

Marsh, Christopher. 2011. *Religion and the State in Russia and China: Suppression, Survival, and Revival*. New York: Bloomsbury Academics.

Mathou, Thierry. 2004. "Bhutan-China Relations: Towards a New Step in Himalayan Politics." In *The Spider and the Piglet: Proceedings of the First Seminar on Bhutan Studies*, ed. Centre for Bhutan Studies, 388–411. Thimphu: Centre for Bhutan Studies.

Matsumura, Toshio. 2018. "Indonesian Intellectuals' Experiences and China." In *China Studies in South and Southeast Asia: Between Pro-China and Objectivism*, ed. Chih-yu Shih, Prapin Manomaivibool, and Reena Marwah, 67–82. Singapore: World Scientific.

Mauss, Iris. B., Maya Tamir, Craig L. Anderson, and Nicole S. Savino. 2011. "Can Seeking Happiness Make People Unhappy? Paradoxical Effects of Valuing Happiness." *Emotion* 11 (4): 808–15.

Mayer, John E. 1957. "The Self-restraint of Friends: A Mechanism in Family Transition." *Social Forces* 35 (3): 230–38.

McCourt, David M. 2021. "Framing China's Rise in the United States, Australia and the United Kingdom." *International Affairs* 97 (3): 643–65.

McDonald, Terry. 2014. "Battered, but Unbroken: Epistemological and Theoretical Challenges to Western IR Theory." *European Scientific Journal* 10 (10): 449–54.

Meglino, Bruce M., and Audrey Korsgaard. 2004. "Considering Rational Self-interest as a Disposition: Organizational Implications of Other Orientation." *Journal of Applied Psychology* 89 (6): 946–59.

Michalski, Anna, and Zhongqi Pan. 2017. "Role Dynamics in a Structured Relationship: The EU-China Strategic Partnership." *Journal of Common Market Studies* 55 (3): 611–27.

Miskimmon, Alister, Ben O'Loughlin, and Laura Roselle, eds. 2017. *Forging the World: Strategic Narratives and International Relations*. Ann Arbor: University of Michigan Press.

Mitra, Debamitra. 2013. " 'Yam' between Two Boulders: Re-assessing India-Bhutan Relationship." *Jadavpur Journal of International Relations* 17 (2): 185–203.

Mizoguchi, Yuzo. 1989. *China as Method*. Tokyo: University of Tokyo Press.

Montsion, Jean Michel. 2012. "When Talent Meets Mobility: Un/desirability in Singapore's New Citizenship Project." *Citizenship Studies* 16 (3–4): 469–82.

Moore, Aaron S. 2017. "From 'Constructing' to 'Developing' Asia—Japanese Engineers and the Formation of the Postcolonial, Cold War Discourse of Development in Asia." In *Engineering Asia: Technology, Colonial Development, and the Cold War Order*, ed. Hiromi Mizuno, Aaron S. Moore, and John DiMoia, 85–111. New York: Bloomsbury Academic.

Morgan, Scott. 2018. "Japan-Taiwan Relations Should Be Deepened through Okinawa: Former President." *Taiwan News*, June 26. https://www.taiwannews.com.tw/en/news/3466245.

Morris, Andrew D., ed. 2017. *Japanese Taiwan: Colonial Rule and Its Contested Legacy*. London: Bloomsbury Academic.

Morris, Paul, Naoko Shimazu, and Edward Vickers, eds. 2013. *Imagining Japan in Post-war East Asia: Identity Politics, Schooling and Popular Culture*. Abingdon, UK: Routledge.

Morrissey, Thomas J. 2008. *Jesuits in Hong Kong, South China and beyond: Irish Jesuit Mission*. Hong Kong: Xavier.

Müller, Harald. 2004. "Arguing, Bargaining and All That: Communicative Action, Rationalist Theory and the Logic of Appropriateness in International Relations." *European Journal of International Relations* 10 (3): 395–435.

Muni, S. D., and Tan Tai Yong. 2012. *A Resurgent China: South Asian Perspectives*. New Delhi: Routledge.

Murray, Christopher. 2020. "Imperial Dialectics and Epistemic Mapping: From Decolonisation to Anti-Eurocentric IR." *European Journal of International Relations* 26 (2): 419–42.

Myers, David G. 1999. "Close Relationships and Quality of Life." In *Well-Being: The Foundations of Hedonic Psychology*, ed. Daniel Kahneman, Ed Diener, and Norbert Schwarz, 376–93. New York: Russell Sage Foundation.

Narváez, Benjamín N. 2017. "Subaltern Unity? Chinese and Afro-Cubans in Nineteenth-Century Cuba." *Journal of Social History* 51 (4): 869–98.

Nathan, Andrew J. 2003. "China's Changing of the Guard: Authoritarian Resilience." *Journal of Democracy* 14 (1): 6–17.

Naughton, Barry. 2010. "China's Distinctive System: Can It Be a Model for Others?" *Journal of Contemporary China* 19 (65): 437–60.

Nayak, Artatrana. 2007. "Rabindranath Tagore and Visva-Bharati Cheena Bhavan: A Centre Civilizational Dialogue." In *Review of China Studies in India: A Colloquium*, ed. Madhavi Thampi, 29–36. Occasional Studies 15. New Delhi: Institute of Chinese Studies.

Nedilsky, Lida V. 2014. *Converts to Civil Society: Christianity and Political Culture in Contemporary Hong Kong*. Waco, TX: Baylor University Press.

Neuman, W. Russell, George E. Marcus, Ann N. Crigler, and Michael MacKuen, eds. 2007. *The Affect Effect: Dynamics of Emotion in Political Thinking and Behavior*. Chicago: University of Chicago Press.

Neumann, Iver B. 2002. "Returning Practice to the Linguistic Turn: The Case of Diplomacy." *Journal of International Studies* 31 (3): 627–52

———. 2011. "Entry into International Society Reconceptualised: The Case of Russia." *Review of International Studies* 37 (2): 463–84.

Nexon, Daniel H., and Thomas Wright. 2007. "What's at Stake in the American Empire Debate." *American Political Science Review* 101 (2): 253–71.

Ngeow, Chow-Bing, ed. 2019a. *Researching China in Southeast Asia*. Abingdon, UK: Routledge.

———. 2019b. "Malaysia, Nanyang, and the 'Inner China' of Three Hong Kong Scholars: Huang Chih-Lien, Chang Chak Yan and Kueh Yik Yaw." In *China Studies in South and Southeast Asia: Between Pro-China and Objectivism*, ed. Chih-yu Shih, Prapin Manomaivibool, and Reena Marwah, 29–66. Singapore: World Scientific.

———. 2020. "Colonialism, Cold War and Nanyang University's Chineseness Dilemma." In *Colonial Legacies and Contemporary Studies of China and Chineseness: Unlearning Boundaries, Strategizing Self*, ed. Chih-yu Shih, Mariko Tanigaki, Prapin Manomaivibool, and Swaran Singh, 97–120. Singapore: World Scientific.

Ngeow, Chow-bing, Tek Soon Ling, and Pik Shy Fan. 2014. "Pursuing Chinese Studies amidst Identity Politics in Malaysia." *East Asia* 31 (2): 103–22.

Nguyen, Cong Tung. 2021. "Uneasy Embrace: Vietnam's Responses to the U.S. Free and Open Indo-Pacific Strategy amid U.S.-China Rivalry." *Pacific Review.* https://doi.org/10.1080/09512748.2021.1894223.

Nguyen, Nam. 2014. "A Local History of Vientamese Sinology in Early Twentieth Century Annam—the Case of the Bulletin Du học báo 遊學報." *East Asia* 31 (2): 139–56.

Noesselt, Nele. 2015. "Revisiting the Debate of Constructing a Theory of International Relations with Chinese Characteristics." *China Quarterly* 222:430–48.

Nordin, Astrid H. M., and Graham M. Smith. 2018. "Reintroducing Friendship to International Relations: Relational Ontologies from China to the West." *International Relations of the Asia-Pacific* 18 (3): 369–96.

———. 2019. "Relating Self and Other in Chinese and Western Thought." *Cambridge Journal of International Affairs* 32 (5): 636–53.

Nyanchoga, Samuel A. 2014. "Politics of Knowledge Production in Africa: A Critical Reflection on the Idea of an African University in Sustainable Development." *European Law and Politics Journal* 1 (1): 37–54.

Nyíri, Pál, and Danielle Tan, eds. 2016. *Chinese Encounters in Southeast Asia: How People, Money, and Ideas from China Are Changing a Region.* Seattle: University of Washington Press.

Oi, Jean C. 1989. *State and Peasant in Contemporary China.* Berkeley: University of California Press.

Okano, Kaori, and Yoshio Sugimoto. 2017. *Rethinking Japanese Studies: Eurocentrism and the Asia-Pacific Region.* London: Routledge.

Oldmeadow, Julian A., and Susan T. Fiske. 2010. "Social Status and the Pursuit of Positive Social Identity: Systematic Domains of Intergroup Differentiation and Discrimination for High- and Low-Status Groups." *Group Processes and Intergroup Relations* 13 (4): 425–44.

O'Neill, Onora. 2009. "Applied Ethics: Naturalism, Normativity and Public Policy." *Journal of Applied Philosophy.* 26 (3): 219–30.

Ooi, Kee Beng. 2015. *The Eurasian Core and Its Edges: Dialogues with Wang Gungwu on the History of the World.* Singapore: Institute of Southeast Asian Studies Publishing.

Palmer, David A., and Elijah Siegler. 2017. *Dream Trippers: Global Daoism and the Predicament of Modern Spirituality.* Chicago: University of Chicago Press.

Paltiel, Jeremy. 2009. "China's Regionalization Politics: Illiberal Internationalism or Neo-Mencian Benevolence." In *China and the Global Politics of Regionalization*, ed. Emilian Kavalski, 47–62. Farnham, UK: Ashgate.

Pan, Chengxin. 2020. "Enfolding Wholes in Parts: Quantum Holography and International Relations." *European Journal of International Relations* 26 (1): 14–38.

Pan, Chengxin, and Emilian Kavalski. 2018. "Theorizing China's Rise in and beyond International Relations." *International Relations of the Asia Pacific* 18 (3): 289–311.

Pan, Jiao. 2016. "Deconstructing Ethnic Minorities in China: Eliminating Orientalism or Re-Orientalizing." In *On China's Cultural Transformation*, ed. Keping Yu, 250–66. Leiden: Brill.
Pan, Shiyin Rung. 2015. "Changing Civil Society and National Identity after the Sunflower Movement." *Procedia* 202:456–61.
Pant, Harsh V. 2007. "India in the Asia-Pacific: Rising Ambitions with an Eye on China." *Asia Pacific Review* 14 (1): 54–71.
Paolini, Albert J. 1999. *Navigating Modernity: Postcolonialism, Identity and International Relations*. Boulder, CO: Lynne Rienner.
Paramore, Kiri, ed. 2016. *Religion and Orientalism in Asian Studies*. Sydney: Bloomsbury Academic.
Park, Hye Jeong. 2014. "East Asian Odyssey towards One Region: The Problem of East Asia as a Historiographical Category." *History Compass* 12 (12): 889–900.
Peng, Huan-sheng, and Jo-ying Chu. 2017. "Japan's Colonial Policies—from National Assimilation to the Kominka Movement: A Comparative Study of Primary Education in Taiwan and Korea, 1937–1945." *Paedagogica Historica* 53 (4): 441–59.
Penjore, Dorji. 2014. "Security of Bhutan: Walking Between the Giants." *Journal of Bhutan Studies* 10:108–31.
Perry, Elizabeth J., ed. 2007. *Patrolling the Revolution: Worker Militias, Citizenship, and the Modern Chinese State*. Lanham, MD: Rowman and Littlefield.
Pichamon, Yeopahntong, and Chih-yu Shih. 2021. "A Relational Reflection on Pandemic Nationalism." *Journal of Chinese Political Science*. https://doi.org/10.1007/s11366-021-09736-5.
Pillsbury, Michael. 2016. *The Hundred-Year Marathon: China's Secret Strategy to Replace America as the Global Superpower*. New York: St. Martin's Griffin.
Pittman, Don A. 2001. *Toward a Modern Chinese Buddhism: Taixu's Reforms*. Honolulu: University of Hawaii Press.
Pobee, John S. 1995. "Shoki Coe (C. H. Hwang)." In *Ecumenical Pilgrims: Profiles of Pioneers in Christian Reconciliation*, ed. Ion Bria and Dagmar Heller, 61. Geneva: WCC Publications.
Polese, Abel, and Donnacha Ó Beacháin. 2011. "The Color Revolution Virus and Authoritarian Antidotes: Political Protest and Regime Counterattacks in Post-communist Spaces." *Demokratizatsiya* 19 (2): 111–32.
Presbyterian Church in Taiwan. 1967. "The Minutes of the 14th Convention of the Presbyterian Church in Taiwan" (台灣基督長老教會總會第十四屆通常會議議事錄).
———. 1970. "The Manual of the 17th Convention of the Presbyterian Church in Taiwan" (台灣基督長老教會總會第十七屆通常會議手冊).
PTI (Press Trust of India). 2016. "Nepal Wants to Become Dynamic Bridge between India, China: Prachanda." *Indian Express*, October 17. http://indianexpress.

com/article/india/india-news-india/nepal-wants-to-become-dynamic-bridge-between-india-china-prachanda-3086434/.

Purushotam, Nirmala. 1998. *Negotiating Language, Constructing Race: Disciplining Difference in Singapore*. New York: Mouton de Gruyter.

Qi, Xiaoying. 2011. "Face: A Chinese Concept in a Global Sociology." *Journal of Sociology* 47 (3): 279–96.

Qian, Mu. 1954. "The Spirit of New Asia" (新亞精神). *New Asia College Journal*, February, 4.

Qin, Yaqing. 2009. "Relationality and Processual Construction: Bringing Chinese Ideas into International Relations Theory." *Social Sciences in China* 30 (4): 5–20.

———. 2011a. "Rule, Rules and Relations: Towards a Synthetic Approach to Governance." *Chinese Journal of International Politics* 4 (2): 117–45.

———. 2011b. "Development of International Relations Theory in China: Progress through Debates." *International Relations of the Asia-Pacific* 11 (2): 231–57.

———. 2016a. "Establishing Chinese School of IR." *Renmin Ribao*, February 15.

———. 2016b. "A Relational Theory of World Politics." *International Studies Review* 18 (1): 33–47.

———. 2018. *A Relational Theory of World Politics*. Cambridge: Cambridge University Press.

Qin, Yaqing, and Astrid H. M. Nordin. 2019. "Relationality and Rationality in Confucian and Western Traditions of Thought." *Cambridge Journal of International Affairs* 32 (5): 601–14.

Quah, Sy Ren. 1995. "Newly Rising Campaign of Nanyang Theater Movement in Penang: The Beginning of Left Tendency in Theater Movement in Singapore/Malaysia" (檳城的南洋戲劇運動新興：新馬戲劇運動左傾意識的開端). In *International Symposium on Chinese Culture, Society and Economics in Southeast Asia* (東南亞華人文化，社會，經濟國際研討會論文集), ed. Yeo Song Nian and Wong Hong Teng, 109–33. Singapore: Singapore Society of Asian Studies, Association of Nanyang University Graduates, and Singapore Federation of Chinese Clan Associations.

———. 2002. "Evolving Multilingual Theatre in Singapore: The Case of Kuo Pao Kun." In *Ethnic Chinese in Singapore and Malaysia: A Dialogue between Tradition and Modernity*, ed. Leo Suryadinata, 377–88. Singapore: Times Academic Press.

———. 2004. *Gao Xingjian and Transcultural Chinese Theater*. Honolulu: University of Hawaii Press.

———. 2008. *At the Borderline of Thought* (思維邊界). Singapore: Youth Bookstore.

———. 2009. "Performing Chineseness in Multicultural Singapore: A Discussion on Selected Literary and Cultural Texts." *Asian Ethnicity* 9 (3): 225–38.

Rauhala, Emily. 2015. "'Reunification Is a Decision to Be Made by the People Here': Breakfast with Taiwan's Tsai Ing-Wen." *Time*, June 18. https://time.com/magazine/south-pacific/3926185/june-29th-2015-vol-185-no-24-asia-south-pacific/.

Raychaudhuri, Anindya. 2018. *Homemaking: Radical Nostalgia and the Construction of a South Asian Diaspora*. Lanham, MD: Rowman and Littlefield.

Rehman, Iskander. 2009. "Keeping the Dragon at Bay: India's Counter-containment of China." *Asian Security* 5 (2): 114–143.

Reid, Anthony. 2009. "Escaping the Burdens of Chineseness." *Asian Ethnicity* 10 (3): 285–96.

Ren, Xiao. 2020. "Grown from Within: Building a Chinese School of International Relations." *Pacific Review* 33 (3–4): 386–412.

Renolds, Robert. 2007. "How Does Therapy Cure? The Relational Turn in Psychotherapy." *Counselling, Psychotherapy, and Health* 3 (2): 127–50.

Roberts, Adam, and Timothy Garton Ash, eds. 2009. *Civil Resistance and Power Politics: The Experience of Non-violent Action from Gandhi to the Present.* Oxford: Oxford University Press.

Roetz, Heiner. 1993. *Confucian Ethics of the Axial Age: A Reconstruction under the Aspect of the Breakthrough toward Postconventional Thinking.* Albany: State University of New York Press.

Rojas, Cristina. 2016. "Contesting the Colonial Logics of the International: Toward a Relational Politics for the Pluriverse." *International Political Sociology* 10 (4): 369–82.

Roseman, Ira J. 1984. "Cognitive Determinants of Emotion: A Structural Theory." *Review of Personality and Social Psychology* 5:11–36.

Rošker, Jana. 2016. *The Rebirth of the Moral Self: The Second Generation of Modern Confucians and Their Modernization Discourses.* Honolulu: University of Hawaii Press.

Rowen, Ian. 2015. "Inside Taiwan's Sunflower Movement: Twenty-Four Days in a Student-Occupied Parliament, and the Future of the Region." *Journal of Asian Studies* 74 (1): 5–21.

Roy, Denny. 2005. "Southeast Asia and China: Balancing or Bandwagoning?" *Contemporary Southeast Asia* 27 (2): 305–22.

Rozman, Gilbert, ed. 2013. *National Identities and Bilateral Relations: Widening Gaps in East Asia and Chinese Demonization of the United States.* Washington, D C: Woodrow Wilson Center Press.

Rudd, Kevin. 2015. "How Ancient Chinese Thought Applies Today." *New Perspectives Quarterly* 32 (2): 8–23.

Ruggie, John Gerard. 1982. "International Regimes, Transactions, and Change: Embedded Liberalism in the Postwar Economic Order." *International Organization* 36 (2): 379–415.

Saich, Tony. 2016. *State-Society Relations in the People's Republic of China Post-1949.* Leiden: Brill.

Sajed, Alina. 2018. "Interrogating the Postcolonial: On the Limits of Freedom, Subalternity, and Hegemonic Knowledge." *International Studies Review* 20 (1): 152–60.

Sanneh, Lamin. 1993. *Encountering the West: Christianity and the Global Cultural Process: The African Dimension.* World Christian Theology Series. Maryknoll, NY: Orbis.

Scheffler, Ted L. 1981. "The Ideology of Binary Opposition: Subject/Object Duality and Anthropology." *Dialectical Anthropology* 6 (2): 165–69.

Schiwy, Freya. 2007. "Decolonization and the Question of Subjectivity: Gender, Race, and Binary Thinking." *Cultural Studies* 21 (2–3): 271–94.

Schwarcz, Vera. 1998. *Bridge across Broken Time: Chinese and Jewish Cultural Memory*. New Haven, CT: Yale University Press.

Scobell, Andrew. 2020. "Constructing a U.S.-China Rivalry in the Indo-Pacific and Beyond." *Journal of Contemporary China* 30 (127): 69–84.

Sealey, Kris. 2018. "Resisting the Logic of Ambivalence: Bad Faith as Subversive, Anticolonial Practice." *Hypatia* 33 (2): 163–77.

Seeman, Melvin. 1983. "Alienation Motifs in Contemporary Theorizing: The Hidden Continuity of the Classic Themes." *Social Psychology Quarterly* 46 (3): 171–84.

Selg, Peeter. 2016. "Two Faces of the 'Relational Turn.'" *PS: Political Science and Politics* 49 (1): 27–31.

Sen, Tansen. 2003. *Buddhism, Diplomacy, and Trade*. Honolulu: University of Hawaii Press.

Seo, Jungmin. 2020. "Colonial and Post-colonial Legacies of the Intellectual History of China Studies in Korea: Discontinuity, Fragmentation and Forgetfulness." In *Colonial Legacies and Contemporary Studies of China and Chineseness: Unlearning Boundaries, Strategizing Self*, ed. Chih-yu Shih, Mariko Tanigaki, Prapin Manomaivibool, and Swaran Singh, 149–64. Singapore: World Scientific.

Shah, Ali. 2015. "The China-Pakistan Economic Corridor: Humanizing Geopolitics." In *Proceedings of International Conference on CPEC*, 24–28. Lahore: Government College University.

Shan, Mark C. 2012. *Beware of Patriotic Heresy in the Church in China: Drawing on the Historical Lessons of the Nazis' Volk Church to Analyze the Zhao Xiao Phenomenon*. Boston: CreateSpace Independent Publishing Platform.

Shani, Giorgio. 2008. "Towards a Post-Western IR: The Umma, Khalsa Panth and Critical International Relations Theory." *International Studies Review* 10 (4): 722–34.

Shepherd, Robert J. 2013. *Faith in Heritage: Displacement, Development, and Religious Tourism in Contemporary China*. Abingdon, UK: Routledge.

Shih, Chih-yu. 2007. *Democracy (Made in Taiwan): "Success State" as a Political Theory*. Lanham, MD: Lexington Books.

———. 2010. "The West That Is Not in the West: Identifying Self in Oriental Modernity." *Cambridge Review of International Affairs* 23 (4): 537–60.

———. 2012. *Civilization, Nation and Modernity in East Asia*. Abingdon, UK: Routledge.

———. 2013a. *Sinicizing International Relations: Self, Civilization and Intellectual Politics of Subaltern East Asia*. London: Palgrave Macmillan.

———. 2013b. "China Rise Syndromes? Drafting National Schools of International Relations in Asia." *Intercultural Communication Studies* 22 (1): 9–25.

---. 2014a. "Introduction: Humanity and Pragmatism Transcending Borders." *East Asia* 31 (2): 93–101.

---. 2014b. "China, China Scholarship, and China Scholars in Postcolonial Taiwan." *China: An International Journal* 12 (1): 1–21.

---, ed. 2015. *Re-producing Chineseness in Southeast Asia: Scholarship and Identity in Comparative Perspectives*. Abingdon, UK: Routledge.

---, ed. 2017a. *Producing China in Southeast Asia: Knowledge, Identity, and Migrant Chineseness*. Singapore: Springer Nature.

---. 2017b. "Can 'Post-Western' Be Chinese? A Note on Post-Chineseness of Hong Kong, Taiwan and Beyond." In *Mainlandization of Hong Kong: Pressures and Responses*, ed. Joseph Yu-shek Cheng, Jacky Chau-kiu Cheung, and Beatrice Kit-fun Leung, 27–60. Hong Kong: City University of Hong Kong Press.

---. 2018a. "Post-Chineseness as Epistemology: Identities and Scholarship on China in the Philippines." *Asian Ethnicity* 19 (3): 279–300.

---. 2018b. "Understanding China as Practicing Post-Chineseness: Selected Cases of Vietnamese Scholarship." *Inter-Asia Cultural Studies* 19 (1): 40–57.

---. 2018c. "Positioning China Watching: Is It Just Hong Kong?" *China Report* 54 (1): 118–36.

---. 2020. "Friendship in Chinese International Relations: the Confucian Theme of Distance in Practice." *Communist and Post-communist Studies* 53 (4): 177–99.

---. 2022. *Eros of International Relations: Self-feminizing and the Claiming of Postcolonial Chineseness*. Hong Kong: University of Hong Kong Press.

Shih, Chih-yu, and Chih-yun Chang. 2017. "The Rise of China between Cultural and Civilizational Rationalities: Lessons from Four Qing Cases." *International Journal of Asian Studies* 14 (1): 1–25.

Shih, Chih-yu, Chih-chieh Chou, Hoai Thu Nguyen. 2017. "Two Intellectual Paths that Cross the Borders: Nguyen Huy Quy, Phan van Coc, and Humanities in Vietnam's Chinese Studies." In *Producing China in Southeast Asia*, ed. Chih-yu Shih, 75–92. Singapore: Springer.

Shih, Chih-yu, Peizhong He, Lei Tang, eds. 2017. *From Sinology to Post-Chineseness: Intellectual Histories of China, Chinese People and Chinese Civilization*. Beijing: Chinese Social Science Press.

Shih, Chih-yu, and Chiung-chiu Huang. 2016. "The Balance of Relationship as Chinese School of IR: Being Simultaneously Confucian, Post-Western, and Post-hegemonic." In *Constructing a Chinese School of International Relations Ongoing Debate and Critical Assessment*, ed. Yongjin Zhang and Teng-chi Chang, 177–91. Abingdon, UK: Routledge.

Shih, Chih-yu, Chiung-chiu Huang, Pichamon Yeophantong, Raoul Bunskoek, Josuke Ikeda, Jay Yih-jye Hwang, Hung-jen Wang, Chih-yun Chang, Ching-chang Chen. 2019. *China and International Theory: The Balance of Relationships*. Abingdon, UK: Routledge.

Shih, Chih-yu, and Josuke Ikeda. 2016. "International Relations of Post-hybridity: Dangers and Potentials in Non-synthetic Cycles." *Globalizations* 13 (4): 454–68.
Shih, Chih-yu, Prapin Manomaivibool, Mariko Tanigaki, Swaran Singh, eds. 2020. *Colonial Legacies and Contemporary Studies of China and Chineseness: Unlearning Binaries, Strategizing Self.* Singapore: World Scientific.
Shih, Chih-yu, Swaran Singh, and Reena Marwah, eds. 2012. *On China by India: From Civilization to Nation State.* New York: Cambria.
Shih, Chih-yu, Lei Tang, and Peizhong He. 2017. Introduction to *From Sinology to Post-Chineseness: Intellectual Histories of China, Chinese People and Chinese Civilization,* ed. Chih-yu Shih, Lei Tang, and Peizhong He. Beijing: Chinese Social Science Press.
Shih, Chih-yu, and Po-tsan Yu. 2015. *Post-Western International Relations Reconsidered: The Pre-modern Politics of Gongsun Long.* London: Palgrave Macmillan.
Shih, Fang-Long. 2012. "Taiwan's Subjectivity and National Narrations: Towards a Comparative Perspective with Ireland." *Taiwan in Comparative Perspective* 4:6–33.
Shimizu, Kosuke. 2015. "Materializing the Non-Western." *Cambridge Review of International Affairs* 28 (1): 3–20.
Shimizu, Kosuke, and Sei Noro. 2021. "Political Healing and Mahāyāna Buddhist Medicine: A Critical Engagement with Contemporary International Relations." *Third World Quarterly.* https://doi.org/10.1080/01436597.2021.1891878.
Shin, Gi-wook, and Michael Robinson, eds. 1999. *Colonial Modernity in Korea.* Cambridge, MA: Harvard University Asia Center.
Shneiderman, Sara B. 2013. "Himalayan Border Citizens: Sovereignty and Mobility in the Nepal–Tibetan Autonomous Region (TAR) of China Border Zone." *Political Geography* 35:25–36.
Shue, Vivienne. 1988. *The Reach of the State: Sketches of the Chinese Body Politic.* Stanford, CA: Stanford University Press.
Silver, Rita Elaine. 2005. "The Discourse of Linguistic Capital: Language and Economic Policy Planning in Singapore." *Language Policy* 4:47–66.
Simon, Robin W. 1992. "Parental Role Strains, Salience of Parental Identity, and Gender Differences in Psychological Distress." *Journal of Health and Social Behavior* 33 (1): 25–35.
Singh, Sinderpal, and Syeda Sana Rahman. 2010. "India-Singapore Relations: Constructing a 'New' Bilateral Relationship." *Contemporary Southeast Asia* 32 (1):70–97.
Slaughter, Anne-Marie. 2009. "America's Edge: Power in the Networked Century." *Foreign Affairs* 88 (1): 94–113.
Slovic, Paul, Melissa L. Finucane, Ellen Peters, and Donald G. MacGregor. 2004. "Risk as Analysis and Risk as Feelings: Some Thoughts about Affect, Reason, Risk, and Rationality." *Risk Analysis* 24 (2): 311–22.
Smeyer Yü, Dan. 2014. *The Spread of Tibetan Buddhism in China: Charisma, Money, Enlightenment.* Abingdon, UK: Routledge.

Smith, James M., and Paul J. Bolt, eds. 2021. *China's Strategic Arsenal: Worldview, Doctrine, and Systems*. Washington, DC: Georgetown University Press.

Smith, Jennifer Grace. 2010. "The 'Beijing Consensus': China's Next Major Export?" *China Elections and Governance Review* 5:29–42.

Smith, Karen. 2017. "Reshaping International Relations: Theoretical Innovations from Africa." *All Azimuth* 7 (2): 1–12.

Smith, Linda Tuhiwai. 2012. *Decolonizing Methodologies*. London: Zed.

Snedden, Christopher. 2016. *Shifting Geo-politics in the Greater South Asia Region*. Honolulu: Daniel K. Inouye Asia-Pacific Center for Security Studies.

Solinger, Dorothy J. 1999. *Contesting Citizenship in Urban China: Peasant Migrants, the State, and the Logic of the Market*. Berkeley: University of California Press.

Southwell, Priscilla L. 2008. "The Effect of Political Alienation on Voter Turnout, 1964–2000." *Journal of Political and Military Sociology* 36 (1):131–45.

Spivak, Gayatri Chakravorty. 1988. "Can the Subaltern Speak?" In *Marxism and the Interpretation of Culture*, ed. Cary Nelson and Lawrence Grossberg, 271–315. London: Macmillan.

———. 1992. "Teaching for the Times." *Journal of the Midwest Modern Language Association* 25 (1): 3–22.

———. 2008. *Other Asias*. Malden, MA: Blackwell.

Stark, Rodney, and Xiuhua Wang. 2015. *A Star in the East: The Rise of Christianity in China*. West Conshohocken, PA.: Templeton Press.

Stephan, Walter G., and Cookie White Stephan. 1985. "Intergroup Anxiety." *Journal of Social Issues* 41 (3): 157–75.

Stolojan, Vladimir. 2017. "Curriculum Reform and the Teaching of History in High Schools during the Ma Ying-jeou Presidency." *Journal of Current Chinese Affairs* 46 (1): 101–30.

Strang, David. 1991. "Global Patterns of Decolonization, 1500–1987." *International Studies Quarterly* 35 (4): 429–54.

Sullivan, Jonathan, and Don S. Lee. 2018. "Soft Power Runs into Popular Geopolitics: Western Media Frames Democratic Taiwan." *International Journal of Taiwan Studies* 1 (2): 273–300.

Sun, Ge, Young-seo Baik, and Kuan-hsing Chen. 2006. "A Post-'East Asia' Viewpoint" (ポスト〈東アジア〉). In *A Post-"East Asia" Viewpoint* (ポスト〈東アジア〉), ed. Ge Sun, Young-seo Baik, and Kuan-hsing Chen, 1–4. Tokyo: Sakuhinsha.

Sun, Shun-chih. 2010. "'Taiwan's Sovereignty' as the Pre-requisite for the Synthesis of Taiwanization and Sinicization." *Taiwan International Studies Quarterly* 6 (3): 139–59.

Sun, Yatsen. 1989. *The Complete Works of Dr. Sun Yatsen* (國父全集). Taipei: Jindai zhongguo chubanshe, Academia Sinica.

Suryadinata, Leo, ed. 2002. *Ethnic Chinese in Singapore and Malaysia: A Dialogue between Tradition and Modernity*. Singapore: Times Academic Press.

———. 2007. *Understanding the Ethnic Chinese in Southeast Asia*. Singapore: Institute of Southeast Asian Studies.

———. 2017. *The Rise of China and the Chinese Overseas*. Singapore: ISEAS Publishing.
Susuki, Tadashi. 2002. "Culture Is the Body." *Blesok*, no. 29, 1–7.
Sutton, Donald S. 2003. *Steps of Perfection: Exorcistic Performers and Chinese Religion in Twentieth-Century Taiwan*. Cambridge, MA: Harvard University Asia Center.
Sylvester, Christine. 1999. "Development Studies and Postcolonial Studies: Disparate Tales of the 'Third World.'" *Third World Quarterly* 20 (4): 703–21.
Szeto, Mirana M. 2009. "Analyzing Chinese Nationalism through the Protect Diaoyutai Movement." *Concentric: Literary and Cultural Studies* 35 (2): 175–210.
Szeto, Wah. 1987. "Unleash the Deadlock, Stress the Mother Tone" (解開死結，重視母語). Presented at the Legislative Council of Hong Kong, March 25.
———. 2003. *The Blue Water* (滄浪之水). Hong Kong: Subculture.
———. 2011. *The Great Eastward River of No Return: The Memory of Szeto Wah* (大江東去：司徒華回憶錄). Hong Kong: Oxford University Press.
Szlachcicowa, Irena. 2017. "The Relational Turn in Sociology: Implications for the Study of Society, Culture, and Persons." *Stan Rzeczy* 1 (12): 191–214.
Tagliacozzo, Eric, and Wen-chin Chang, eds. 2011 *Chinese Circulations: Capital, Commodities, and Networks in Southeast Asia*. Durham, NC: Duke University Press.
Tai, Wan-chen. 2009. "A Study of Lee Wanju: Focusing on Running of Newspaper and Political Participation" (李萬居研究：以辦報與問政為中心). MA thesis, National Chung-hsing University.
Taiwanese Church Mission Association. 1987. "Joint Statement of the Taiwanese Church Mission Association, 1987" (1987 年台灣宣教協議會共同聲明). *Taiwan Church News* (台灣教會公報), no. 1858 (October 11), 1.
Taiwan People's News. 2015. "The Seventieth Anniversary of the Great Air Raid on Taipei and Its Historical Lessons for Taiwan" (台北大轟炸七十週年與台灣的歷史教訓). Editorial, May 30. http://www.peoplenews.tw/news/d9a0c5b2-8ba8-44d0-8d74-a95611bb9f76.
Taiwo, Olufemi. 1993. "Colonialism and Its Aftermath: The Crisis of Knowledge Production." *Callaloo* 16 (4): 891–908.
Takeshi, Komagome. 2006. "Colonial Modernity for an Elite Taiwanese, Lim Bo-seng." In *Taiwan Under Japanese Colonial Rule 1895–1945*, ed. Ping-hui Liao and David Der-wei Wang, 141–59. New York: Columbia University Press.
Tan, Chung. 2015. *Himalaya Calling: The Origins of China and India*. Hackensack. NJ: World Century.
Tanaka, Stefan. 1993. *Japan's Orient: Rendering Pasts into History*. Berkeley: University of California Press.
Tang, Chun-yi. 1952. "The Spirit of New Asia That I Have Understood" (Wo suo liaojie zhi xin ya jinshen). *New Asia College Journal*, June.
Tang, Siufu. 2016. *Self-realization through Confucian Learning: A Contemporary Reconstruction of Xunzi's Ethics*. Albany: State University of New York Press.

Tarn, Kwok-kan. 1990. "Drama of Dilemma: Waiting as Form and Motif in *The Bus Stop* and *Waiting for Godot*." In *Studies in Chinese-Western Comparative Drama*, ed. Yun-Tong Luk, 23–45. Hong Kong: Chinese University Press.

Taylor, Jay. 2011. *The Generalissimo: Chiang Kai-shek and the Struggle for Modern China*. Cambridge: Belknap Press of Harvard University Press.

Taylor, Rodney L. 1990. *The Religious Dimensions of Confucianism*. Albany: State University of New York Press.

Teets, Jessica C. 2016. *Civil Society under Authoritarianism: The China Model*. Cambridge: Cambridge University Press.

Terrill, Ross, ed. 2016. *Xi Jinping's China Renaissance: Historical Mission and Great Power Strategy*. New York: CN Times Books.

Thapliyal, Sangeeta. 1998. *Mutual Security: The case of India Nepal*. New Delhi: Spantech and Lancer.

Thayer, Carlyle A. 1992. "Comrade plus Brother: The New Sino-Vietnamese Relations." *Pacific Review* 5 (4): 402–6.

Thiele, Wolfgang Gerhard. 2017. "Decolonization and the Question of Exclusion in Taiwanese Nationalism since 1945." *Global Histories* 3 (1): 62–84.

Thies, Cameron G. 2010. "Role Theory and Foreign Policy." In *The International Studies Encyclopedia*, ed. Robert A. Denemark, 10:6335–56. Chichester, UK: Wiley-Blackwell.

———. 2012. "International Socialization Processes vs. Israeli National Role Conceptions: Can Role Theory Integrate IR Theory and Foreign Policy Analysis?" *Foreign Policy Analysis* 8 (1): 25–46.

———. 2015. "China's Rise and the Socialisation of Rising Powers." *Chinese Journal of International Politics* 8 (3): 281–300.

Thies, Cameron G., and Marijke Breuning. 2012. "Integrating Foreign Policy Analysis and International Relations through Role Theory." *Foreign Policy Analysis* 8 (1): 1–4.

Thomas, Peter D. 2018. "Refiguring the Subaltern." *Political Theory* 46 (6): 861–84.

Thrift, Eric. 2014. "'Pure Milk': Dairy Production and the Discourse of Purity in Mongolia." *Asian Ethnicity* 15 (4): 492–513.

Thurman, Robert A. F. 2011. *Why the Dalai Lama Matters: His Act of Truth as the Solution for China, Tibet and the World*. New York: Atria.

Tian, Min. 1997. "'Alienation-Effect' for Whom? Brecht's Misinterpretation of the Classical Chinese Theatre." *Asian Theatre Journal* 14 (2): 200–222.

Tibi, Bassam. 2012. *Islam in Global Politics: Conflict and Cross-civilizational Bridging*. London: Routledge.

Tickner, Arlene B., and David L. Blaney, eds. 2013. *Claiming the International*. Abingdon, UK: Routledge.

Tikhonov, Vladimir, and Torkel Brekke. 2013. *Buddhism and Violence: Militarism and Buddhism in Modern Asia*. Abingdon, UK: Routledge.

Tirole, Jean. 2002. "Rational Irrationality: Some Economics of Self-management." *European Economic Review* 46 (4–5): 633–55.

Tittle, Charles R., David A. Ward, and Harold G. Grasmick. 2004. "Capacity for Self-control and Individuals' Interest in Exercising Self-control." *Journal of Quantitative Criminology* 20:143–72.

Trevarthen, Colwyn. 2005. "Stepping Away from the Mirror: Pride and Shame in Adventures of Companionship: Reflections on the Nature and Emotional Needs of Infant Intersubjectivity." In *Attachment and Bonding: A New Synthesis*, ed. C. S. Carter, L. Ahnert, K. E. Grossmann, S. B. Hrdy, M. E. Lamb, S. W. Porges, and N. Sachser, 55–84. 92nd Dahlem Workshop Report. Cambridge, MA: MIT Press.

Trownsell, Tamara A., Arlene B. Tickner, Amaya Querejazu, Jarrad Reddekop, Giorgio Shani, Kosuke Shimizu, Navnita Chadha Behera, and Anahita Arian. 2021. "Differing about Difference: Relational IR from around the World." *International Studies Perspectives* 22 (1): 25–64.

Tsai, Hui-yu Caroline. 2009. *Taiwan in Japan's Empire-Building*. Abingdon, UK: Routledge.

Tsai, Pei-huo. 1971. *The History of National Movement in Taiwan* (台灣民族運動史). Taipei: Independence Evening News.

Tsai, Shih-shan Henry. 2005. *Lee Teng-hui and Taiwan's Quest for Identity*. New York: Palgrave Macmillan.

Tsoi, Grace. 2012. "Danny Yung." *HK Magazine*, November. https://www.scmp.com/magazines/hk-magazine/article/2034996/danny-yung.

Tuck, Eve, and K. Wayne Yang. 2012. "Decolonization Is Not a Metaphor." *Decolonization* 1 (1): 1–40.

Tung, Chen-yuan. 2003. "Cross-Strait Economic Relations: China's Leverage and Taiwan's Vulnerability." *Issues and Studies* 39 (3): 137–75.

Turner, Jonathan H., and Jan E. Stets. 2006. "Sociological Theories of Human Emotions." *Annual Review of Sociology* 32:25–52.

Turton, Helen Louise. 2016. *International Relations and American Dominance: A Diverse Discipline*. Abingdon, UK: Routledge.

Vaisey, Stephen, and Omar Lizardo. 2010. "Can Cultural Worldviews Influence Network Composition?" *Social Forces* 88 (4): 1595–1618.

Valenta, Marko. 2009. "Immigrants' Identity Negotiations and Coping with Stigma in Different Relational Frames." *Symbolic Interaction* 32 (4): 351–71.

Vasilaki, Rosa. 2012. "Provincialising IR? Deadlocks and Prospects in Post-Western IR Theory." *Millennium* 41 (1): 3–22.

Veer, Peter van der. 2013. *The Modern Spirit of Asia: The Spiritual and the Secular in China and India*. Princeton, NJ: Princeton University Press.

Vukovich, Daniel F. 2012. *China and Orientalism: Western Knowledge Production and the PRC*. Abingdon, UK: Routledge.

Walker, R. B. J. 1993. *Inside/Outside: International Relations as Political Theory*. Cambridge: Cambridge University Press.

Walker, Stephen G. 2014. "Thinking Small: Quantum Politics and the Miniaturization of Role Theory." Paper prepared for the 2014 Annual Meeting of the International Studies Association, Toronto, March.

Wallace, William, and Tim Oliver. 2005. "A Bridge Too Far: The United Kingdom and the Transatlantic Relationship." In *The Atlantic Alliance under Stress: US-European Relations After Iraq*, ed. David M. Andrews, 152–76. Cambridge: Cambridge University Press.

Walton, Matthew J., and Susan Hayward. 2014. *Contesting Buddhist Narratives: Democratization, Nationalism, and Communal Violence in Myanmar*. Honolulu: East-West Center.

Wan, Xiao. 2017. "The Name and the Substance of Tributary System and the East Asia That Is Outside of Tributary System: A Frame for Categorization, a Few Cases for Illustration, and Recommendations for Research." *Quarterly Journal of International Politics* 2 (3): 63–104.

Wang, Ban, ed. 2017. *Chinese Visions of World Order: Tianxia, Culture, and World Politics*. Durham, NC: Duke University Press.

Wang, Cheng-mian. 2014. "Chiang Kai-shek's Faith in Christianity: The Trial of the Stilwell Incident." *Journal of Modern Chinese History* 8 (2): 194–209.

Wang, Fei-ling. 2017. *The China Order: Centralia, World Empire and the Nature of Chinese Power*. Albany: State University of New York Press.

Wang, Gungwu. 1981. *Community and Nation: Essays on Southeast Asia and the Chinese*. Singapore: Heinemann Educational.

———. 2002. *The Chinese Overseas: From Earthbound China to the Quest for Autonomy*. Cambridge, MA: Harvard University Press.

———, ed. 2005. *National Building: Five Southeast Asian Histories*. Singapore: Institute of Southeast Asian Studies.

———. 2018. *Home Is Not Here*. Singapore: National University of Singapore Press.

Wang, Hung-jen. 2013. *The Rise of China and Chinese International Relations Scholarship*. Lanham, MD: Lexington Books.

Wang, Sumei. 2009. "Taiwanese Baseball: A Story of Entangled Colonialism, Class, Ethnicity, and Nationalism." *Journal of Sport and Social Issues* 33 (4): 355–72.

Wang, Vincent Wei-cheng. 2011. "'Chindia' or Rivalry? Rising China, Rising India, and Contending Perspectives on India-China Relations." *Asian Perspective* 35 (3):437–69.

———. 2015. "The U.S. Asia Rebalancing and the Taiwan Strait Rapprochement." *Orbis* 59 (3): 361–79.

Wang, Wen-yu. 1997. *Biography of Lee Wanju* (李萬居傳). Nantou: Taiwan Provincial Historical Commission.

Wang, Yiwei. 2009. "China: Between Copying and Constructing." In *International Relations Scholarship around the World*, ed. Arlene B. Tickner and Ole Waever, 103–19. Abingdon, UK: Routledge.

———. 2016. *The Belt and Road Initiative: What Will China Offer the World in Its Rise*. Beijing: New World Press.

Wasson, Leslie. 2015. "Identity Politics/Relational Politics." *The Wiley Blackwell Encyclopedia of Race, Ethnicity and Nationalism*, ed. A. D. Smith, X. Hou, J. Stone, R. Dennis, and P. Rizova. Wiley Online Library. https://doi.org/10.1002/9781118663202.wberen446.

Wehner, Leslie E. 2015. "Role Expectations as Foreign Policy: South American Secondary Powers' Expectations of Brazil as a Regional Power." *Foreign Policy Analysis* 11 (4): 435–55.

Wei, Chi-hung, and Christina J. Lai. 2017. "Identities, Rationality and Taiwan's China Policy: The Dynamics of Cross-Strait Exchanges." *Asian Studies Review* 41 (1): 136–54.

Wendt, Alexander. 1992. "Anarchy Is What States Make of It: The Social Construction of Power Politics." *International Organization* 46 (2): 391–425.

Wendt, Alexander, and Raymond Duvall. 2008. "Sovereignty and the UFO." *Political Theory* 36 (4): 607–33.

Weng, Byron Song-jen. 1972. *Peking's U.N. Policy: Continuity and Change*. New York: Praeger.

———. 1983. "The Future of Hong Kong: 'The Puerto Rico Model'" (香港前途：" 波多黎各模式"). *The Seventies* (七十年代), no. 167, 9–10.

———. 1984. "A Proposal about the Reunification Issue of China" (關於中國統一問題的建議). *The Nineties* (九十年代), no. 177, 49–51.

———. 1985a. "A Prospectus on One Country, Two Systems: The Concept, the Nature, the Contents, the Difficulty, and the Prospect" (一國兩制芻論：概念, 性質, 內容, 困難和前景). *The Nineties* (九十年代), no. 191, 30–40.

———. 1985b. *Collected Articles on the PRC Constitution* (中華人民共和國憲法論文集). Hong Kong: Chinese University of Hong Kong Press.

———. 1987. "Unification, Self-determination and One Country, Two Systems in the Perspective of HK Experiences" (從香港經驗看統一, 自決和一國兩制). *Ming Pao Monthly* (明報月刊), no. 263, 27–38.

———. 1995. "Taiwanese Culture Not Necessarily Sinicized" (台灣文化未必中國化). *Liberty Times*, April 16.

———. 1997. "Policies toward Hong Kong–Taiwan Relationship and Interaction of the Two Sides and the Three Sites" (兩岸三地的港台關係政策及其互動). *21st Century Bimonthly* (二十一世紀雙月刊), no. 41, 59–75.

———. 2001. "Sinification of Hong Kong and the Future of Taiwan-HK Relationship" (香港中國化與台港關係走向). *Teacher Chang for Taiwan Businessmen Monthly* (台商張老師月刊), no. 33. https://www.chinabiz.org.tw/News/GetJournalShow?pid=162&cat_id=174&gid=117&id=1582.

———. 2003. *A Pilot Discussion on the 2007 Review of Political Institution of the Hong Kong Special Administrative Region* (2007年香港特別行政區政制檢討初探). In *Hong Kong under One Country, Two Ssystems* (一國兩制下的香港), ed. Taiwan Advocates, 48–73. Taipei: Taiwan Advocates.

Wertime, David. 2015. "A Recording of FP's Interview with Taipei Mayor Ko Wen-je." *Foreign Policy*, February 2. http://foreignpolicy.com/2015/02/02/a-recording-of-fps-interview-with-taipei-mayor-ko-wen-je/.
Wheeler, Nicholas J. 2013. "Investigating Diplomatic Transformations." *International Affairs* 89 (2): 477–96.
Whyte, Jessica. 2017. "'Always on Top'? The 'Responsibility to Protect' and the Persistence of Colonialism." In *The Postcolonial World*, ed. Jyotsna G. Singh and David D. Kim, 308–24. Abingdon, UK: Routledge.
Williams, Jack F. 2003. "Who Are the Taiwanese? Taiwan in the Chinese Diaspora." In *The Chinese Diaspora: Space, Place, Mobility, and Identity*, ed. Laurence J. C. Ma and Carolyn Cartier, 163–92. Rowman and Littlefield.
Wilson, Jeanne L. 2010. "The Legacy of the Color Revolutions for Russian Politics and Foreign Policy." *Problems of Post-communism* 57 (2): 21–36.
Wilson, Shawn. 2009. *Research Is Ceremony: Indigenous Research Methods*. Black Point, NS: Fernwood.
Windsor, Duane. 2006. "Corporate Social Responsibility: Three Key Approaches." *Journal of Management Studies* 43 (1): 93–114.
Wittgenstein, Ludwig. 1986. *Philosophical Investigation*. Trans. G. E. M. Anscombe. Oxford: Blackwell.
Woeser, Tsering. 2016. *Tibet on Fire: Self-immolations against Chinese Rule*. Trans. Kevin Carrico. London: Verso.
Womack, Brantly. 2012. "Asymmetry and China's Tributary System." *Chinese Journal of International Politics* 5 (1): 37–54.
Wong, Heung Wah, and Hoi Yan Yau. 2013. "What Does It Mean by 'Being Colonized'? Reflections on the Japanese Colonial Policies in Taiwan." *Journal of Group Dynamics* 30:342–60.
Wong, John. 2012. "Goh Keng Swee and Chinese Studies in Singapore: From Confucianism to China Watching." In *Goh Keng Swee: A Legacy of Public Service*, ed. Emrys Chew and Chong Guan Kwa, 245–77. Singapore: World Scientific.
———. 2013. "Evolving Chinese Studies/China Studies in the 21st Century Southeast Asia." Paper presented at the conference "Retrieval or Revival: Intellectual History of Chinese Studies in Southeast Asia," Research and Educational Center of China Studies and Cross-Strait Relations, Department of Political Science, National University of Singapore.
Wong, Meiling. 2010. "Guanxi Management as Complex Adaptive Systems: A Case Study of Taiwanese ODI in China." *Journal of Business Ethics* 91 (3): 419–32.
Wong, Sin Kiong, Ruixin Wang, Zhuo Wang, and Shihlun Allen Chen. 2015. "Producing and Reconstructing Knowledge on China in Singapore: Perspectives from the Academics and Mass Media." *Asian Ethnicity* 16 (1): 8–27.

Wong, Timothy Ka-ying, and Shirley Po-san Wan. 2007. "The Research on Civic Identity in Hong Kong" (香港市民身分認同研究). *The 21st Century* (二十一世紀), no. 101 (June), 115–27.
World Council of Churches. 2013. "Work More Closely with the China Christian Council." *Madang* 7 (November 7): 4. http://wcc2013.info/en/news-media/newspaper/madang-nov-7/at_download/Madang%20Nov.%207.pdf?fbclid=IwAR04-xaoRwGTHsqYeIwFUCyYNispM-SJaMlGMxvHRI6T4tYKVXHxgnpucvg.
Wright, Teresa. 2010. *Accepting Authoritarianism: State-Society Relations in China's Reform Era.* Stanford, CA: Stanford University Press.
Wu, Hsueh-ming. 2003. *From Dependence to Self-sufficiency: A Study of the Southern Branch of Presbyterian Churches in Taiwan Before the End of War* (從依賴到自立：終戰前台灣南部基督教長老教會研究). Tainan: Renguang.
Wu, Rwei-ren. 1999. "The Dialectics of the Motherland: A Preliminary Analysis of Wen-Kwei Liao's (1905–1952) Taiwan Nationalism" (祖國的辯證：廖文奎（1905–1952）台灣民族主義初探). *Thought and Words* (思與言) 37 (3): 47–100.
Wulf, Claudia Mariéle. 2016. "Sacrifice—Action within a Relationship: A Phenomenology of Sacrifice." In *Sacrifice in Modernity: Community, Ritual, Identity*, ed. Joachim Duyndam, Anne-Marie Korte, and Marcel Poorthuis, 230–40. Leiden: Brill.
Wurmser, Leön. 1987. "Shame, the Veiled Companion of Narcissism. In *The Many Faces of Shame*, ed. Donald L. Nathanson, 64–92. New York: Guilford Press.
Yamaguchi, Mari. 2007. "Ex-Taiwan Leader Visits Japan War Shrine." Associated Press, June 7.
Yan, Haiping. 1992. "Modern Chinese Drama and Its Western Models: A Critical Reconstruction of Chinese Subjectivity." *Modern China* 35 (1): 54–64.
Yan, Pei-yu Yan. 2012. *Navigating Identity between the Indigenous and the Universal: The Views on China from Wen-kwei Liao to Guan-sheng Liao* (在本土認同與普世認同之間選擇：從廖文奎到廖光生的中國觀). Taipei: Research and Educational Center for China Studies and Cross-Strait Relations, Department of Political Science, National Taiwan University.
Yan, Xuetong. 2008. "Xun Zi's Thoughts on International Politics and Their Implications." *Chinese Journal of International Politics* 2 (1): 135–65.
———. 2011. *Ancient Chinese Thought, Modern Chinese Power.* Ed. Daniel A. Bell and Sun Zhe. Trans. Edmund Ryden. Princeton, NJ: Princeton University Press.
———. 2015. *Power Transition in the World: Political Leadership and Strategic Competition.* Beijing: Peking University Press.
Yang, Fenggang. 2011. *Religion in China: Survival and Revival under Communist Rule.* New York: Oxford University Press.
Yang, Jinlin. 1993. *Biographical Review of Lee Wanju* (李萬居評傳). Taipei: Renjian Press.

Yang, Kuo-shu. 1993. "Why Do We Establish Chinese Indigenous Psychology?" *Indigenous Psychology* 1:6–88.

———. 1995. "Chinese Social Orientation: An Integrative Analysis." In *Chinese Societies and Mental Health*, ed. Tsung-yi Lin, Wen-shing Tseng, and Eng-kung Yeh, 19–39. Hong Kong: Oxford University Press.

Yang, Mayfair Mei-hui. 1994. *Gifts, Favors, and Banquets: The Art of Social Relationship in China*. Ithaca, NY: Cornell University Press.

———. 2004. "Goddess across the Taiwan Strait: Matrifocal Ritual Space, Nation-State and Satellite Television Footprints." *Public Culture* 16 (2): 209–38.

———. 2008. "Goddess across the Taiwan Strait: Matrifocal Ritual Space, Nation-State, and Satellite Television Footprints." In *Chinese Religiosities: Afflictions of Modernity and State Formation*, ed. Mayfair Mei-hui Yang, 323–48. Berkeley: University of California Press.

Yang, Michael Murray. 2017. *American Political Discourse on China*. Abingdon, UK: Routledge.

Yao, Ming-li. 2018. "Creating and Re-creating the Nation of Taiwan: Representations of the History of the Japanese Colonial Era in History Textbooks and Teachers' Discourses." *National Identities* 21 (3): 305–20.

Yao, Xinzhong, and Yanxia Zhao. 2010. *Chinese Religion: A Contextual Approach*. New York: Bloomsbury Academics.

Ye, Wei. 2017. *Taking Chinese to the World: Culture and Identity in Confucius Institute Teachers*. Bristol, UK: Multilingual Matters.

Yee, Herbert, and Ian Storey, eds. 2002. *China Threat: Perceptions, Myths and Reality*. Abingdon, UK: RoutledgeCurzon.

Yeh, Wen-hsin, ed. 2000. *Cross-cultural Readings of Chineseness: Narratives, Images, and Interpretations of the 1990s*. Berkeley: Institute of East Asian Studies, University of California.

Yew, Chiew Ping. 2017. "The Evolution of Contemporary China Studies in Singapore: From the Regional Cold War to the Present." *Journal of Chinese Political Science* 22 (1): 135–58.

Yong, Cat. 2014. "English Online Radio Station DurianASEAN Launches for ASEAN." *Enterprise IT News*, March 10. http://www.enterpriseitnews.com.my/english-online-radio-station-durianasean-launches-targets-english-speaking-communities-in-asean/.

You, Ji. 2013. *China's Enterprise Reform: Changing State/Society After Mao*. Abingdon, UK: Routledge.

Yu, Fu-lai Tony, and Diana Sze Man Kwan. 2008. "Social Construction of National Identity: Taiwanese versus Chinese Consciousness." *Social Identities* 14 (1): 33–52.

Yu, Jimmy. 2012. *Sanctity and Self-inflicted Violence in Chinese Religions, 1500–1700*. New York: Oxford University Press.

Yu, Xue. 2011. *Buddhism, War, and Nationalism: Chinese Monks in the Struggle against Japanese Aggression, 1931–1945*. Abingdon, UK: Routledge.

Yu, Ying-shih. 1974. "For the Sake of a New Interpretation of 'the Spirit of New Asia'" (為「新亞精神」進一新解). *New Asia Life Biweekly* (新亞生活雙週刊), July 1. http://history.na.cuhk.edu.hk/en-us/%E7%B7%9A%E4%B8%8A%E8%A7%80%E8%B3%9E/%E6%96%B0%E4%BA%9E%E7%B2%BE%E7%A5%9E.aspx.

Yue, Ricky Wai-kay. 2015. "Beyond Dependency: The Promise of Confucianism in Post-Westphalia International Relations." *Bandung* 2 (4): 1–17.

Yung, Danny. 2009a. *China Is a Big Garden* (Zhongguo shi ge da huayuan). Hong Kong: E+Ezuni Icosahedron.

———. 2009b. *Creative Opinion* (創意意見). Chengdu: Siichuan Art Press.

———. 2012. *Learn Well and Strive for Better Every Day: Collective Work of Danny Yung + Conceptual Animation* (好好學習天天向上：榮念曾文集+概念漫畫). Guilin: Guangxi Normal University Press.

Zhang, Falin. 2021. "Power Contention and International Insecurity: A Thucydides Trap in China-US Financial Relations." *Journal of Contemporary China*. https://doi.org/10.1080/10670564.2021.1889229.

Zhang, Feng. 2009. "Rethinking the 'Tribute System': Broadening the Conceptual Horizon of Historical East Asian Politics." *Chinese Journal of International Politics* 2 (4): 545–74.

———. 2010. "Deconstruct the Tribute System" (解構朝貢體系). *Quarterly Journal of International Politics* (國際政治科學) 22 (2): 33–62.

———. 2013. "The Rise of Chinese Exceptionalism in International Relations." *European Journal of International Relations* 19 (2): 305–28.

———. 2015. *Chinese Hegemony: Grand Strategy and International Institutions in East Asian History*. Stanford, CA: Stanford University Press.

———. 2016. "Start of China's Coercive Diplomacy towards Singapore." *Straits Times*, October 6. http://www.straitstimes.com/opinion/start-of-chinas-coercive-diplomacy-towards-singapore.

Zhang, Fenzhi. 2015. *Xi Jinping: How to Read Confucius and Other Chinese Classical Thinkers*. New York: CN Times Books.

Zhang, Weiwei. 2011. *The China Wave: The Rise of a Civilizational State*. Hackensack, NJ: World Century.

Zhang, Yongjin. 2017. "Worlding China, 1500–1800." In *The Globalization of International Society*, ed. Tim Dunne and Chris Reus-Smit, 204–25. Oxford: Oxford University Press.

Zhang, Yongjin, and Barry Buzan. 2012. "The Tributary System as International Society in Theory and Practice." *International Political Science* 5 (1): 3–36.

Zhang, Yongjin, and Teng-chi Chang, eds. 2016. *Constructing a Chinese School of International Relations: Ongoing Debate and Critical Assessment*. Abingdon, UK: Routledge.

Zhang, Yongjin, Shogo Suzuki, and Joel Quirk. 2016. *International Orders in the Early Modern World: Before the Rise of the West*. London: Routledge.

Zhao, Suisheng. 2015. "Rethinking the Chinese World Order: The Imperial Cycle and the Rise of China." *Journal of Contemporary China* 24 (96): 961–82.

Zhao, Tingyang. 2004. *On the Possibilities of Lives: A Thesis on Happiness and Justice*. Beijing: Renmin University Press.

———. 2006. "Rethinking Empire from a Chinese Concept 'All-under-Heaven' (Tianxia)." *Social Identities* 12 (1): 29–41.

———. 2009. "A Political World Philosophy in Terms of All-under-Heaven (Tian-Xia)." *Diogenes* 56 (1): 5–18.

———. 2015. *A Possible World of the All-under-Heaven System: The World Order in the Past and for the Future*. Beijing: Zhongxin.

———. 2019. *Redefining a Philosophy for World Governance*. London: Macmillan Palgrave.

Zhao, Yukong. 2013. *The Chinese Secrets for Success*. New York: Morgan James.

Zheng, Victor, and Siu-lun Wong. 2002. "Identity of Chinese in Hong Kong: Changes before and after 1997" (香港華人的身分認同：九七前後的轉變). *The 21st Century* (二十一世紀), no. 73 (October), 71–80.

Zheng, Yongnian, and Liang Fook Lye. 2015. *Singapore-China Relations: 50 years*. Singapore: World Scientific.

Zhou, Fangyin. 2011. "Equilibrium Analysis of the Tributary System." *Chinese Journal of International Politics* 4 (2): 29–58.

Zhu, Ying, and Stanley Rosen. 2010. *Art, Politics and Commerce*. Hong Kong: Hong Kong University Press.

Zhuo, Xinping. 2015. "Discussion on 'Cultural Christians' in China." In *China and Christianity: Burdened Past, Hopeful Future*, ed. Stephen Uhalley, Jr., and Xiaoxin Wu, 283–300. Abingdon, UK: Routledge.

Zubrzycki, Geneviéve. 2006. *The Crosses of Auschwitz: Nationalism and Religion in Post-communist Poland*. Chicago: Chicago University Press.

Zuni Icosahedron. 2013. Annual report. https://www.zuni.org.hk/new/zuni/web/default.php?cmd=annualreport.

Zuo, Xiying. 2021. "The Trump Effect: China's New Thoughts on the United States." *Washington Quarterly* 44 (1): 107–27.

Zweig, David. 1999. *Distortions in the Opening: "Segmented Deregulation" and Weak Property as Explanations for China's "Zone Fever" of 1992–1993*. Hong Kong: Hong Kong Institute of Asia-Pacific Studies, Chinese University of Hong Kong.

———. 2002. *Internationalizing China: Domestic Interests and Global Linkages*. Ithaca, NY: Cornell University Press.

Zweig, David, and Changgui Chen. 1995. *China's Brain Drain to the United States: Views of Overseas Chinese Students and Scholars in the 1990s*. Berkeley: Institute of East Asian Studies, University of California.

Interviews

Amin, Shahid M. March 10, 2012. http://www.china-studies.taipei/comm2/InterviewP01.pdf.

Ang-See, Teresita. November 6, 2015. http://www.china-studies.taipei/comm2/Teresita%20Ang%20See.pdf.
Baculinao, Eric. June 23, 2016. http://www.china-studies.taipei/comm2/Eric%20Baculinao.pdf.
Baviera, Aileen. October 30, 2016. http://www.china-studies.taipei/comm2/Aileen%20Baviera.pdf.
Buu, Cam. n.d. http://www.china-studies.taipei/comm2/interview%20VN%20BUU%20CAM%20ch.pdf.
Cao, Tu Thanh. n.d. https://www.china-studies.taipei/comm2/interview%20VN%20CAO%20TU%20THANH%20ch.pdf.
Cariño, Theresa. June 24, 2016. http://www.china-studies.taipei/comm2/Interview%20with%20Theresa%20Carino%20by%20Dorcas%20Caraig-Ramos.v.2.pdf.
Chang, Parris Hsu-cheng. August 12 and 18, 2010. http://china-studies.taipei/comm2/InterviewT%20A.pdf. http://china-studies.taipei/comm2/InterviewT%20B.pdf.
Chen, Peng-jen. May 29, 2010, February 4, March 20, April 22, and August 16, 2011. http://www.china-studies.taipei/comm2/InterviewT%20chen%20pon%20ren.pdf.
Chu, Richard. June 13, 2016. http://www.china-studies.taipei/comm2/Richard%20Chu.pdf.
FlorCruz, Jaime. June 23, 2015. http://www.china-studies.taipei/comm2/Jaime%20FlorCruz.pdf.
Ghimire, Yubaraj. September 17, 2016. http://www.china-studies.taipei/comm2/Yubaraj%20Ghimire.pdf.
Go, Bon Juan. July 28, 2016. http://www.china-studies.taipei/comm2/Go%20Bon%20Juan.pdf.
Gwee, Yee Hean. April 6, 2010. http://www.china-studies.taipei/comm2/InterviewSingapore0.pdf.
Ha, Kien Hanh. n.d. http://www.china-studies.taipei/comm2/vietnam_13.pdf.
Haque, Ehsanul. March 24, 2016. http://www.china-studies.taipei/comm2/Ehsanul%20Haque.pdf.
Hau, Caroline S. September 13, 2015. http://www.china-studies.taipei/comm2/Carol%20Hau%20v.2.pdf.
Hồ, Sĩ Hiệp. n.d. http://www.china-studies.taipei/comm2/InterviewV%20Ho%20Si%20Hiep.pdf.
Hossein, Delwar. March 24, 2016. http://www.china-studies.taipei/comm2/Delwar%20Hossein.pdf.
Hsu, Chie-lin. April 24, June 10, and July 13 2009. http://www.china-studies.taipei/act/tw-7.doc.
Kabir, Humayun. March 1, 2012. http://www.china-studies.taipei/comm2/InterviewB04.pdf.
Karim, Iftikhar-ul. March 2, 2013. http://www.china-studies.taipei/comm2/InterviewB02.pdf.

Koirala, Bhaskar. September 16, 2016. http://www.china-studies.taipei/comm2/Bhaskar%20K.pdf.
Le, Huy Thieu. April 25, 2015. http://www.china-studies.taipei/comm2/InterviewV%20Le%20Huy%20Tieu%20Chinese.pdf.
Lee, Poh Ping. April 15, 2013. http://www.china-studies.taipei/comm2/interview/malaysia/InterviewM05.pdf.
Liao, Kuang-sheng. August 25 and October 7, 2008. http://www.china-studies.taipei/comm2/tw-5.pdf.
Lohani, Mohan. January 26, 2012. http://www.china-studies.taipei/comm2/InterviewN02.pdf.
Ly, Viet Dung. n.d. http://www.china-studies.taipei/comm2/InterviewV%20Ly%20Viet%20Dung.pdf.
Mallare, Florencio. November 29, 2016. http://www.china-studies.taipei/comm2/Florencio%20Mallare.pdf.
Memon, Aman. December 8, 2016. http://www.china-studies.taipei/comm2/InterviewPak%20Aman%20Memon_locked.pdf.
Nguyen, Bang Tuong. n.d. http://www.china-studies.taipei/comm2/vietnam_06ch.pdf.
Nguyen, Huy Quy. n.d. http://www.china-studies.taipei/act/vietnam03anticopy.pdf.
Nguyen, Khue. n.d. http://www.china-studies.taipei/comm2/interview%20VN%20NGUYEN%20KHUE%20ch.pdf.
Nguyen, Ton Nhan. n.d. http://www.china-studies.taipei/comm2/interview%20VN%20NGUYEN%20TON%20NHAN%20ch.pdf.
Nguyen, Van Khang. n.d. http://www.china-studies.taipei/comm2/InterviewV%20Nguyen%20Van%20Khang%20Chinese%201.pdf.
Ong, Charlson. October 4, 2016. http://www.china-studies.taipei/comm2/Charlson%20Ong2.pdf.
Pandey, Ramesh Nath. 2012. http://www.china-studies.taipei/comm2/InterviewN03.pdf.
Pham, Thi Hao. n.d. http://www.china-studies.taipei/comm2/interview%20VN%20PHAM%20THI%20HAO%20ch.pdf.
Pham, Tu Chau. April 28, 2015. http://www.china-studies.taipei/comm2/InterviewV%20Pham%20Tu%20Chau%20Chinese.pdf.
Phan, Van Cac. May 17, 2010. http://www.china-studies.taipei/act/vietnam_04C.doc.
Santa Romana, Chito. August 6, 2016. http://politics.ntu.edu.tw/RAEC/comm2/Chito%20Sta%20Romana1.pdf.
Tan, Chung. May 18–19, 30, 2008. http://www.china-studies.taipei/act/india01.doc.
Tran, Xuan De. October 22, 2013, and April 26, 2014. http://www.china-studies.taipei/comm2/InterviewV%20Tran%20Xuan%20De.pdf.
Tran, Le Bao. April 13, 2015. http://www.china-studies.taipei/comm2/InterviewV%20Tran%20Le%20Bao%20Chinese.pdf.
Tran, Tuan Man. n.d. http://www.china-studies.taipei/comm2/InterviewV%20Tran%20Tuan%20Man.pdf.

ur Rashid, Harun. March 2, 2013. http://www.china-studies.taipei/comm2/Interview B01.pdf.
Voon, Phin Keong. December 27, 2012. http://www.china-studies.taipei/comm2/interview/malaysia/InterviewM03.pdf.
Vu, Khieu. n.d. http://www.china-studies.taipei/comm2/vietnam_07ch.pdf.
Wang, Gungwu. September 25, October 1, October 5, January14, February 25, 2007, and March19, 2010. http://www.china-studies.taipei/comm2/Interview SGungwuW.pdf.
Weng, Byron S. J. February 20, 2017. http://www.china-studies.taipei/act/tw-8.doc.
Wong, John. November 5–9, 2016. http://www.china-studies.taipei/comm2/Interview SJohnWong.pdf.
Wong, Yoon Wah. March 26, 2012. http://politics.ntu.edu.tw/RAEC/comm2/Interview Singapore1.pdf.
Yasmin, Lailufar. March 25, 2016. http://www.china-studies.taipei/comm2/Lailufar%20 Yasmin.pdf.
Yeh, Chi-cheng. November 11, 18, 23, and December 30, 2009. http://www.china-studies.taipei/comm2/InterviewTW17.pdf.
Yen, Ching Hwang. 2012. http://www.china-studies.taipei/comm2/interview/malaysia/InterviewM02.pdf.

Index

Academy of Performing Arts, 195
African Union, 27
Alliance of Liberties, 215
Allied Forces (of WWII), 127, 251
Altercasting, 109–114, 116–122, 145, 147–154, 157, 166, 169, 278, 279, 280
America, 29, 32, 108, 166, 203, 205, 254
Ang-See, Teresita, 160, 161
Anti-Expedition Campaign, 200, 210
Art of War, 278
ASEAN (Association of Southeast Asian Nations), 27, 117, 174, 278
Association of Asia Scholars, 171
Australia, 68, 182, 195, 115
Australian National University, 182

Baik, Young-seo, 19
Baculinao, Eric, 161, 162
Balance of relationships (BoR) (*see also* Relation IR), 19–22, 23, 25–26, 28–30, 32, 33–34, 37–38, 58, 106, 227, 271
Bangladesh, 47, 60, 170–179, 181, 186, 188
Barclay, Thomas, 216
Barnett, Doak, 142
Baviera, Aileen, 157

Beijing, 138, 175, 238, 247
Beijing (as China's government), the, 1–2, 20, 27–38, 42–61, 77–81, 222, 234, 251
Beijing Olympics, 178
Beilun (River), 119
Belgrade, 178
Belt and Road Initiative (BRI), 27, 44, 52, 175
Bhattarai, Baburam, 176
Bhutan, 28, 170, 181
Bond, Michael, 230, 242, 243
Brecht, Bertolt, 205–206
BRICS, 170

Canada, 68, 289
Cariño, Theresa, 155
Central Asia, 43
Centrism
   China and, 17, 19, 20, 22, 29, 30, 103, 146
   Europe and, 19, 20, 22, 280
   the Self and, 18, 19, 29, 271
   the West and, 20
Chang, Parris Hsu-cheng, 142, 143, 144
Chen, Kuang-hsing, 19
Chen, Peng-jen, 139, 140, 144
Chen, Shui-bian, 131
Chen, Yi (Marshall), 179

340   INDEX

Chiang, Kai-sek, 83, 93, 94, 95, 140, 235, 238, 289
Chiang, Ching-kuo, 141
China (*see also* People's Republic of China), 23, 29, 52, 63, 71, 97, 100, 103, 129, 165, 170, 180, 193–194, 199–200, 203, 206, 253, 278
  anti-Communism, 201, 218, 222, 236, 257
  balance of relationships, 22, 28, 31, 33–38
  Bangladesh, 43 173–178, 188
  binary, 22, 26, 28, 38
  Bhutan, 181
  Brazil, 44
  Buddhism, 90–93, 173, 179, 188
  as category, 1, 3, 5, 6, 20, 51–54, 83, 227
  centrism, 1, 3, 17, 19, 21, 29, 30, 103, 114, 146
  Chineseness and, 4, 6, 14, 32, 52, 83, 103, 105, 110, 128, 144, 193, 264, 266
  Christianity, 94–96, 221–225, 236, 242
  Civil War, 148, 218–219
  as civilization, 51, 52, 55, 98, 115, 170, 174, 211, 214, 216, 222, 224, 252
  Confucianism, 28, 97–99, 124
  East Asia, 78, 80, 81, 263
  ethnicity of, 8, 120
  Global South, 170, 188
  greater China, 201–202, 210, 255–256
  Hong Kong, 95, 187, 194, 197–198, 200, 207–210, 227, 247–248
  as identity, 31, 32, 110, 167, 209–210, 263
  India, 41, 42, 44, 47, 171–178, 181, 188–189
  in IR theory, 6
  Islam (*see also* Muslim), 57, 172
  Japan, 73–75, 77, 79, 81, 82, 107, 128–129, 140, 144, 212, 214, 224, 251, 253
  Korea, 107
  Kuomintang, 78, 79, 80, 127–129, 137, 144, 214–215, 221
  Muslim (*see also* Islam), 57, 172
  as name, 1, 2, 8, 30
  nationalism, 83, 84, 100, 234, 235
  Nepal, 173–178, 181, 188
  Pakistan, 17, 39–51, 53–55, 56–61, 179
  the Philippines and, 157–162
  post-Chineseness of, 8–9, 30, 33–38, 52–53, 83, 104–105, 116–122, 128, 134–143, 153, 156, 273
  post-Pakistaniness, 55
  in post-Western IR, 7, 191, 255–256, 259
  Republic of China, 78, 83, 224, 251
  as relation, 7, 101, 268
  resemblance to, 20, 25, 27, 29, 38, 72, 87, 101, 124, 169, 173, 199, 212, 227–228
  reunification of, 3, 239, 245, 247, 255, 258
  the rise of, 5, 11, 28, 52, 100, 153, 164, 174, 184, 211, 249, 252, 261, 274, 281
  Singapore, 180–184, 187, 188, 195–196, 198, 200, 210
  in Southeast Asia, 151, 177
  strategic partnership of, 48
  studies of, 4, 5, 8, 9, 14, 104–105, 109, 115, 146–148, 155–156, 169, 180, 188, 244, 269–271
    by Chinese American, 8
    in Hong Kong, 8, 13, 15, 105, 142, 192, 193, 228–232, 240–243

in Indonesia, 8
in Malaysia, 184–185
in the Philippines, 13, 101–102, 105, 145, 149, 155–166
in Singapore, 12, 169, 171, 173, 180–187, 189
in South Asia, 101–102, 173–180, 187
in Taiwan, 8, 13, 15, 101–102, 105, 132–133, 182, 228, 232–240
in Vietnam, 101–102, 116–122, 147, 286
by Western scholars, 8
Taiwan, 73, 76, 77, 79, 81, 82, 84, 95, 132–135, 155, 181, 187, 211, 213, 218, 222, 227, 247–248, 257, 264
Taiwan independence, 130, 143, 191, 213, 215, 225, 232, 240
as territory, 1, 9, 36, 94, 209, 266
threat, 1, 211–213, 215–216, 221, 225
Vietnam, 107, 112–113, 115–118, 121–123
the West and, 6, 22, 28, 38, 95, 189, 255, 261–262
WWII, 151, 251
Xinjing, 59
Yadong, 64, 71, 72, 74, 78, 81
China News Analysis, 95, 230, 236, 242
China Pakistan Economic Corridor (CPEC), 40, 41, 43–45, 50, 51, 53, 56–61
China Youth Party, 236
Chinese Communist Party (CCP), 1, 2, 83, 96, 141, 170–171, 234, 239, 241, 251, 257, 266
Chinese Democratic Party, 235
Chinese Exclusion Act, 164
Chinese Filipino, 101, 102, 146, 147, 154, 155, 158, 163, 164, 165

Chinese IR (international relations), 5, 6, 12, 20, 21, 28, 48, 49, 250, 255, 259–262, 274, 275
Chinese-Malaysian, 107, 108, 109, 171, 182, 183, 184, 185, 270
Chinese-Singaporean, 181, 195, 197, 270
Chinse University of Hong Kong, 232 234, 235, 236
Chinese-Vietnamese, 107, 111, 119, 120
Chineseness (*see also* Post-Chineseness)
borderline Chineseness, 30, 32, 35, 54, 127
civilizational Chineseness, 112–117, 121, 124, 134, 138, 144, 149, 153, 157–158, 166, 169, 200, 211–212, 225, 229–230, 242
cosmopolitan Chineseness, 85, 88, 89, 90, 92, 94–99, 284
cultural Chineseness, 53, 91, 94, 97, 104, 112–113, 122–124, 133–136, 143–144, 148–149, 164–166, 188, 229, 230, 240
exotic Chineseness, 3, 32, 34, 89, 200, 207, 210
equal Chineseness, 30, 32, 35, 37, 76, 77, 200, 224
ethnic Chineseness, 112–114, 119, 124, 134, 140–141, 144, 149, 153, 156–157, 159, 160, 163–165, 169, 173–174, 188, 193, 196, 200, 271
experiential Chineseness, 41, 53, 54, 58–61, 72, 112–114, 120–124, 134, 139, 140, 143–144, 149, 153
hybrid Chineseness, 30, 32, 34, 37, 54, 57, 60, 82, 85, 90, 94, 97, 99, 110, 120, 155, 172, 210
moral Chineseness, 30, 32, 33, 37, 54–56, 60, 78, 104, 127–128, 200, 215

Chineseness *(continued)*
  objective Chineseness, 30, 36, 53, 54, 60, 134, 228, 230
  physical Chineseness, 54, 58, 59, 61
  policy Chineseness, 53, 54, 60, 80, 112, 134, 142, 169, 212
  political Chineseness, 85, 87, 90–92, 94–95, 97–98
  postmodern Chineseness, 93, 97–98, 101–102, 104–105, 107
  scientific Chineseness, 54, 112–113, 116–117, 121, 124, 134, 142–144, 149, 153, 155–156, 158–160, 166, 169, 211
  Sinological Chineseness, 112, 114, 117–118, 122, 124, 134, 136–137, 144, 149, 152–154, 157, 159–162, 169, 172, 174, 188, 199–200, 228–230, 234, 240, 271
  spatial Chineseness, 112, 113
  subjective Chineseness, 29, 53, 54, 62, 228, 229, 230
  utility Chineseness, 30, 32, 36, 54, 60, 182, 196, 200, 213
Chu, Richard, 160, 161
Chu, De (Marshall), 179
Civil War, 9, 30, 76–77, 127–130, 138, 143, 148, 151, 163, 181, 197, 212, 214, 218, 222, 224, 226, 238, 244, 264, 270
Coe, Shoki, 211, 218, 219, 220, 221, 225
Cold War, 11, 18, 46–48, 51, 53, 61, 64–66, 76–82, 90, 133, 161, 174, 181, 184, 186, 196, 218, 222, 271
Confession of Faith, 221
Confucius, 24, 86
Confucius Institute, 88, 97–99

Confucianism
  as institution, 23, 85
  as identity, 24, 28, 48, 89, 91, 98, 99, 106, 124
  as norm, 98, 255, 284
  as relationship, 57, 96
  as civilization, 25, 73, 86, 97, 99, 114, 122, 274, 276
  as cultural resource, 115, 116, 166, 172, 182, 257, 278
Contextual theology, 212, 216, 218, 221, 222, 225
Cuba, 55
Cultural nationalism, 17, 18, 83, 84, 85, 86, 95, 97, 100
Cultural Revolution, 42, 96, 98, 143, 179, 197, 201, 242, 244

Daoism, 24, 25, 114, 255
Democratic Progressive Party, 247
Deng, Xiaoping, 136, 196, 236
Dharamsara, 110
Diaoyu Islands, 241
Diaoyutai State Guesthouse, 180
Dirlik, Arif, 270

East Asia, 17, 19, 63, 64, 66, 70, 71, 73–75, 77–82, 107, 187, 222
East Asian Friendship Association, 81
East Asian Institute (EAI), 182–183, 185–188
East Asian Institute of Political Economy, 182–183
East Asian Relations Association, 81
East China Sea, 179
Europe, 28, 47, 71, 73, 88, 93, 129, 166, 203, 205, 254
European Union, 27, 28

Far East, 71
FlorCruz, Jaime, 156

France, 235

Global South, 68, 170, 188
Goh, Keng Swee, 186
Greater East Asian Co-prosperity Sphere, 74, 79, 80, 214
Guangxi, 107, 119, 123

Hainan, 214
Han Nom, 123, 124
Haque, Ehsanul, 177
Hau, Caroline, 156, 157
Hinduism, 276
Ho Chi Minh, 120
Hobbes, Thomas, 24, 137
Hong Kong, 1, 3, 35, 95, 106, 182, 185, 187
   China studies, 142, 227–245
   in comparison with, 8, 12–15, 37, 55, 132–133, 146, 152, 166
   identity of, 191–192, 193–201, 207–210
   post-Western IR, 247–251, 254–258, 261–266
Hossein, Delwar, 177, 179
Hsu, Chie-lin, 135, 136, 144
Hsu, Shih-hsian, 142
Huang, Chang-hui (*see* Coe, Shoki)
Huang, Zhanghui (*see* Coe, Shoki)
Huntington, Samuel, 51

India, 29, 35, 41, 42–44, 47, 51, 57–61, 68, 83, 129, 132–133, 148, 170–178, 181, 185–189, 203, 215, 278
Indonesia, 3, 8, 12, 107, 182, 187, 203
Institute of East Asian Philosophy, 182
Iran, 278
Islamabad (as Pakistan's government), 41–44, 47, 48, 52, 54–61

Japan, 19, 37, 56, 157, 166, 182, 203, 264
   Buddhism and, 92
   colonialism 2, 72–82, 106–107, 127–144, 172, 187, 212–233, 251–253, 278
   as international power, 28, 35, 117, 147, 151
   WWII, 47, 127, 196, 262–263
Jesus Christ, 84, 289
Juan, Go Bon, 163

Kabir, Humayun, 177, 179
Kaisa Para Sa Kaunlaran (Kaisa), 158, 161
Karim, Iftikhar-ul, 179, 180
Kashmir, 41, 42, 56, 57
Kathmandu, 175
Katzenstein, Peter, 51, 52
Kennedy, John F., 197
Kinh Chinese, 119, 120
Kitashirakawa, Yoshihisa (Prince), 135
Ko, Wen-je, 251, 252, 253, 262
Koirala, Bhaskar, 174
Kokang, 89
Kominka Campaign (Japanization), 129, 130, 131, 139, 140
Korea (*see* North Korea & South Korea)
Kuo, Pao-kun, 193–196, 201–206, 209, 210, 212
Kuo Pao Kun Foundation, 288
Kuomintang (KMT), 30, 76–81, 127–144, 151, 156, 211–214, 218–222, 233, 236, 238–241, 251, 289

Lasswell, Harold, 142
Lee, Ang, 210
Lee, Kwan Yew, 182
Lee, Peter Nan-Hsuing, 230, 235–237, 245

Lee, Teng-hui, 83, 131, 215, 216, 219, 232, 233, 239, 253
Lee, Wan-chu, 235–237
Lei, Chen, 238
Leninism, 30
Li, Keqiang, 41
Liao, Kuang-sheng, 230, 232–235, 245
Liao, Joshua Wen-kwei, 219, 232–235
Lohani, Mohan, 175, 176
Long, Ying-tai, 201, 202
Luo, Fu-ch'uan, 142

Ma, Shu-li, 140
Macau Relations Act, 239
Malaysia, 3, 169, 171, 172, 181–187, 267, 288
Mallare, Florencio, 164, 165
Manchukuo, 222
Manchuria, 135, 214
Mao, Tse-tung (see also Mao Zedong) 179
Mao, Zedong, 120, 179
Maoism, 158, 236
Marxism, 10, 27, 30, 48, 83, 115, 117, 138, 139
Mazu (Goddess), 87
Mei, Lanfang, 205, 206
Melbourne, 201
Middle Kingdom, 114, 249
Ming Dynasty, 45
Mizuguchi, Yuzo, 147
Mong Cai (Mangjie), 119
Mongolia, 3, 8, 28, 47, 56, 73, 87, 125
Monroe Doctrine, 164
Moscow (as Russia's government), 28, 47
Mujib, Sheikh, 178
Myanmar, 28, 89, 91, 92, 172, 174

Nanyang University, 182
Naoki, Kobayashi, 135

National Chengchi University, 141
National Chiang Kai-shek University, 235
National Institute of Dramatic Art, 195
National Kaohsiung University, 232
National People's Congress, 247
National Taiwan University, 135, 136, 142, 171
National Unification Guidelines, 239
National University of Singapore, 171, 182
NBC (National Broadcasting Company), 166
Nehru, Jawaharlal, 42
Nepal, 170–178, 181, 186, 188, 189
New Asia College, 230, 236, 240
New Delhi (as India's government), 28, 41, 42, 43, 57
Ng, Yuzin Chaiutong, 219
North Korea, 28, 47, 129
North Vietnam (see also Vietnam), 47, 120
Northeast Asia, 106

Occupy Central (see also Umbrella Movement), 248
Ohio, 238
Okinawa Prefectural Peace Memorial Park, 215
Ong, Charlson, 165
Orientalism, 147, 278, 280

Pakistan, 8, 13, 17, 28, 39–61, 85, 106, 175, 178, 179
Pandey, Ramesh Nath, 176, 179, 180
Peng, Ming-min, 219
People's Republic of China (PRC) (see also China)
  Chineseness of 53, 157, 194, 200
  diplomacy 27, 44, 80, 96, 161, 181, 201
  ethnicity of 5, 8, 110, 146, 183

religion and 83, 91, 93–94, 97, 220
as sovereign nation 9, 41, 42, 104, 147, 153, 155, 170, 249, 266
Taiwan and 78, 140, 254
Philippines, The, 3, 47, 55, 56, 80, 102, 105, 145, 147, 149, 154, 155, 157–167, 264
Philippine Association of Chinese Studies, 161
Philippine-China Development Resource Center, 161
Poland, 95
Post-Asianness, 19, 29, 273, 275, 279
Post-Chineseness (see also Chineseness)
altercasting and, 109, 113, 147, 148
balance of relationships and, 20, 26, 28, 32–38, 165, 271
as binary, 26, 144
Buddhism and, 90, 92
as category, 3, 56, 57, 58, 60, 104, 111–112, 144, 155
Chinese IR and, 20
Chineseness and, 17, 29, 38, 64, 128, 147, 149, 249, 265
Christianity and, 94
Confucianism and, 97–99
definition of, 4, 30, 51–53, 105–106, 108, 112
as epistemology, 29, 39
as essentialism, 70
ethnicity and, 7–8
in Europe, 88
in Hong Kong, 193, 201
IR theory and, 12
IR theory and, 6, 29
nationalism and, 84, 85, 100
in the Philippines, 145, 146, 167
post-Asianness and, 273
post-Pakistaniness and, 41, 49, 55–56
post-Vietnameseness, 107
as post-identity, 19, 66, 269, 270

as post-Western IR, 7, 10, 11, 264, 266
as relation, 5, 7, 13, 28, 49, 148, 265, 266
as resemblance, 29, 22–28, 148, 227
self-centrism of, 18, 19, 266
in Singapore, 193
in Sinology, 101, 103, 107, 109, 166, 169, 271
the West and, 14, 26
in Vietnam, 107
Yadong and, 64, 71, 85
Post-identity, 4, 5, 7, 11, 17, 19, 29, 33, 66, 82, 193, 269, 270, 271
Post-Western IR, 7, 10, 11, 13, 14, 191, 247–250, 253–267, 269, 277, 278
Presbyterian Church, Taiwan, 95, 211, 213, 216, 217, 221, 222, 223, 225, 289
Public Forum News, 235

Qian, Mu, 240
Qin, Yaqing, 20, 24, 33
Qing Dynasty, 88, 93, 137, 139, 219, 233, 263

Rashid, Harun ur, 179, 180
Relational IR (international relations) (see also Balance of relationships)
affect and 35, 37, 38
altercasting 118, 151
Balance of relationships 19–22, 26, 30, 32, 33, 37, 38, 227, 271
bilateralism of 13, 14, 17, 23, 25–28, 32, 41, 43, 57, 59, 60, 116, 177, 188, 280
Chinese school 6, 20, 38, 48, 49, 60, 259, 261–262
Chineseness 4, 5, 12, 15, 54, 85, 87, 148, 210, 264–268
civil war 76
Cold War 18, 61

Relational IR *(continued)*
  Communism 27, 195, 221
  Confucianism 24, 27, 94, 97, 106, 260
  Colonialism 13, 47, 63–69, 78, 82, 128, 132, 135, 139, 143–144, 170, 213–225
  as cultural identity, 90, 103–104, 107, 120, 124, 174, 186–189, 201, 233, 265
  ethnicity and, 13, 60, 101, 145, 154–155, 167, 195–196
  Imperialism, 47, 81
  multilateralism of, 13, 14, 17, 23, 24, 25, 83
  Nationalism, 88, 211
  as policy, 13, 27, 31, 34, 36, 39–45, 48, 74, 102, 109, 173, 178, 263
  Post-Western IR, 10, 101, 248, 253–254, 275
  Resemblance, 25, 112, 134, 194, 208
  rise of China, 3, 175, 212
  self and, 13, 14, 17, 26, 58, 84, 100, 117, 150, 176, 206, 228–229, 242
  as theory, 9, 37, 40, 46, 50, 51, 53, 56, 67–72, 86, 269–270, 274
  Western IR, 8, 11, 14, 22, 38, 46, 61, 250, 273, 275–276, 279, 280
Republic Revolution, 74, 94
Republic of China (ROC), 63, 74, 98, 131, 219, 251
Role
  Chineseness and, 12, 31, 104, 105, 112, 115, 127, 147, 200, 269
  consciousness of, 111, 121, 140, 164
  in drama, 103–108
  improvisation of, 60, 61
  of in-between actor, 55, 57, 117, 124, 152, 171–178, 180–184, 187–189, 222
  incongruence in, 125, 244, 248
  obligation of, 43, 48, 57, 102, 106, 109, 113, 118, 166, 278
  in relation, 26, 49, 59, 83, 110, 151, 193, 260, 271, 274, 279, 280
  resemblance of, 23, 30, 33
  self-expectation and, 130, 148, 149, 150, 156, 223, 270
  of stranger, 19, 213
Romana, Chito Santa, 158, 159
Ryukyu, 77, 80, 215

Sa, Meng-wu, 135
Saigon (as South Vietnam's government), 90, 120
Scalapino, Robert, 142
Shanghai, 138, 197, 241, 252
Shamanism, 89, 276
Shih, Che-hsiung, 140, 141, 142, 144
Shih, Ming, 138, 139, 144, 287
Shreshtha, Hiranya Lal, 176
Silk Road, 56
Singapore, 3, 12, 14, 15, 47, 102, 105, 132, 143, 155, 169–174, 178, 180–207, 210, 255, 270, 271
Singh, Mamohan, 176
Sinicization, 2, 3, 11, 34, 51, 52, 98, 137, 211, 248, 249, 272
Society of Jesus, 88
Song Dynasty, 27
South Africa, 170
South Asia, 13, 45, 47, 71, 88, 102, 169, 170, 177, 179, 227
South Asian Association for Regional Cooperation, 178
South China Sea, 157, 162, 164, 179
South Korea, 19, 47, 56, 80, 92, 107, 129, 133, 255, 278
South Vietnam (*see also* Vietnam), 47, 124

Southeast Asia, 7, 8, 45, 52, 97, 98, 102, 106, 147, 152, 166, 170, 177, 181, 182, 214, 227
Spivak, Gayatri Chakravorty, 64
Sri Lanka, 89, 91, 92, 172
Su, Beng (*see also* Shih Ming), 287
Sun, Ge, 19
Sun, Tzu, 278
Sun, Yatsen, 13, 64, 71, 73, 142, 233
Sunflower Movement, 248
Susuki, Tadashi, 205
Sydney, 201
Szeto, Wah, 230, 241

Tainan Academy of Theology, 220, 223
Taipei, 142, 207, 238, 251, 252, 262
Taipei (as Taiwan's government), 77, 79, 81
Taiwan, 8, 13, 19, 79, 80, 87, 132, 135–139, 181, 201, 222, 227, 231–236, 239, 245, 264
  Buddhism, 91, 92
  China and, 82, 132–144, 155, 211–212, 215, 222, 224, 228, 232–233, 247, 251–252, 256–258
  China studies in, 102, 115, 133, 137, 141, 147, 182, 187, 230, 238
  Chineseness of, 37, 55, 64, 78, 105–106, 108, 124, 127, 166, 191, 216, 225, 240–241
  Christianity, 83, 94, 95, 211, 213, 216–223, 225, 242
  Civil War, 9, 127, 195, 198, 212, 218, 222, 238
  Cold War and, 46–47, 218, 222
  colonialism and, 15, 63, 65, 76–82, 127, 136, 144, 212, 218–219, 222, 235, 251–253
  Confucianism, 86
  East Asia, 79
  Hong Kong compared, 133, 152, 187, 192, 240, 248–250, 254–255, 258, 262–267
  identity, 8, 14, 79, 80, 82, 85, 128, 131, 146, 211–214, 249, 257
  Japan and, 73, 78–81, 129–131, 136, 140, 214–215, 222, 224, 233, 251–253
  Kuomintang, 76, 129, 131, 139, 212–214, 235–236
  Mongolia and, 87
  nationalism, 92, 95, 131, 138, 232–233, 235, 245
  One-China policy, 56
  pro-independence, 3, 91, 95, 130–132, 137–138, 142–143, 202, 218, 224–225, 232–234, 240, 247, 267
  studies of, 8
  WWII and, 64, 77–78, 127, 139, 215, 250–252
Taiwan Solidarity Party, 253
Taiwan Straits, 231, 247, 289
Taiwan-Japan Relations Association, 89
Tang, Chun-i, 240
Tanzania, 238
Thailand, 74, 75, 91
Three Principles of the People, 140
Tiananmen, 52, 180, 239, 244
Tianxia, 6, 24, 25, 26, 31, 274
Tibet, 8, 19, 35, 56, 91, 92, 108, 109, 170, 175, 181
Tokyo (as Japan's government), 28, 77, 81, 262, 263
Trần Nhân Tông, 125
Tsai, Ing-wen, 131, 215
Tsai, Trong, 142
Turkey, 172

Umbrella Movement, 200, 210, 248
United Daily, 79, 81

United Kingdom, 37, 47, 68, 106, 133, 136, 184, 185, 187, 216
United States, 28, 35, 264
  China and, 27, 37, 42, 55, 171, 255
  Pakistan and, 57
  Taiwan and, 81, 82, 131, 132, 133, 135, 143, 219, 252
  Vietnam and, 117, 120
  Chinese American in, 8, 152, 157, 160, 185, 197, 236
  China watching, 161, 166, 238
  Singapore and, 171, 181
University of Chicago, 232
University of Malaya, 171
University of Michigan, 232
University of the Philippines, 160
University of Tokyo, 135

Vatican, 96
Vietnam, 3, 13, 19, 27, 28, 47, 55, 56, 72, 80, 90, 92, 101–125, 145, 147, 166, 174, 193, 264

Wang, Gungwu, 51, 52, 53, 183, 184, 185
War of Resistance, 251
Waseda University, 138
Washington (as the US government), 1, 2, 3, 24, 42, 46, 47, 57, 77, 147, 252, 256
Wen, Jiabao, 175, 178
Weng, Byron Song-Jan, 230, 237–240, 245
West, 6, 14, 81, 92, 188, 221, 227, 241, 273–280
  as civilization, 7, 10, 71, 93, 137, 172, 186, 189, 191
  as contrast to China, 20, 22, 26, 28, 38, 95, 146, 174, 262
  as imperialism, 2, 15, 72, 73, 80, 183
Wittgenstein, Ludwig, 85, 104
Wong, John, 182, 185, 187
World Bank, the, 44
World Council of Churches, 220–224
World War II, 46, 47, 64, 76–80, 127, 132, 139, 142, 151, 196, 215, 216, 218, 241, 250, 252, 263, 270

Xi, Jinping, 83, 87, 93, 97, 98
Xingjiang, 35, 41, 42, 43, 52, 56, 58, 59

Yadong, 13, 63–66, 70–82, 85, 270, 284
Yadong Industrial and Business Association, 81
Yang, Kuo-shu, 243
Yasmin, Lailufar, 180
Yasukuni Shrine, 79, 253
Yeh, Chi-cheng, 136, 137, 138, 144
Yen, Ching Hwang, 182, 185
Yew, Chiew Ping, 178, 182
Yin, Hai-kuang, 238
Yoshimi, Takeuchi, 19
Yu, Ying-shih, 240
Yung, Denny, 193, 194, 197, 200–209, 230, 241, 242, 288

Zen, 89, 92, 124, 125
Zhang, Yimou, 209
Zhao, Tingyang, 24, 25
Zheng, Chenggong (Koxinga), 139
Zheng, Ho, 45
Zhou Dynasty, 165
Zhuang Chinese, 119, 120
Zuni Icosahedron, 197, 198, 241
Zweig, David, 230, 243

www.ingramcontent.com/pod-product-compliance
Ingram Content Group UK Ltd.
Pitfield, Milton Keynes, MK11 3LW, UK
UKHW041915140426
5217IPUK00013B/166